In Performance

EDITED BY
CAROL MARTIN

In Performance is a book series devoted to national and global theater of the twenty-first century. Scholarly essays providing the theatrical, cultural, and political contexts for the plays and performance texts introduce each volume. The texts are written both by established and emerging writers, translated by accomplished translators and aimed at people who want to put new works on stage, read diverse dramatic and performance literature and study diverse theater practices, contexts, and histories in light of globalization.

In Performance has been supported by translation and editing grants from the following organizations:

The Book Institute, Kraków
TEDA Project, Istanbul
The Memorial Fund for Jewish Culture, New York
Polish Cultural Institute, New York
Zbigniew Raszewski Theatrical Institute, Warsaw

LOOSE SCREWS

NINE NEW PLAYS FROM POLAND

Edited and introduced by
Dominika Laster

Translated by
Bill Johnston
Benjamin Paloff
Philip Boehm
Margarita Nafpaktitis
Mira Rosenthal
and **Dominika Laster**

LONDON NEW YORK CALCUTTA

Seagull Books, 2015

Original text © Individual playwrights
Translation © Individual translators
Introduction © Dominika Laster, 2015
Photographs © Individual photographers

ISBN 978 0 8574 2 177 7

British Library Cataloging-in-Publication Data
A catalog record for this book is available from the British Library

Designed by Bishan Samaddar and Niharika and Vedika Jatia for
Seagull Books, Calcutta, India
Printed and bound by Hyam Enterprises, Calcutta, India

In Memoriam

Daniel Gerould
(1928–2012)

CONTENTS

ACKNOWLEDGMENTS

I am deeply grateful to Carol Martin for her initiative and incredible support of this project.

I gratefully acknowledge Adrianna Prodeus for her selection of the plays included in this volume and early contributions to the project. I am very grateful to Joanna Klass, Head of Theatre Programs at the Adam Mickiewicz Institute in Warsaw, for her help in facilitating my research.

I wish to thank Jerzy Onuch, the Director of the Polish Cultural Institute in New York for his support of this publication. I am grateful to David A. Goldfarb, the Institute's Literary Director, for his assistance in facilitating this project.

Dominika Laster

DOMINIKA LASTER

Theater and dramatic literature have long played a crucial role in the making and unmaking of Polish national identity. From Stanisław Wyspiański's 1901 drama *The Wedding*, written in the aftermath of two failed uprisings—which functions at once as the definitive "national drama" forging Polish identity while simultaneously confronting national myths and thereby pulling the strings of its own undoing—dramatic literature has been a site on which Polishness is rehearsed, enacted, contested, and revised. While the fatigued myth of Polish martyrdom—Poland as the martyr of nations—is perhaps the most exhausted within the Polish popular imaginary, the historical reality of Poland as a colonized nation is likely one of the features most overlooked by the exogenous gaze. Systematically partitioned since 1772, Poland's third partition went into effect on October 24, 1795, when the Polish-Lithuanian Commonwealth[1] was erased from the maps of Europe. From then until 1918, Poland existed as an imagined community—not a political fact. When Poland was re-established as an independent state in 1918, the country enjoyed a mere two decades of sovereignty before the joint invasion by Germany and the Soviet Union in 1939. After the end of World War II, Poland was dominated by the foreign

---

[1] The Polish-Lithuanian Commonwealth, also known as Pierwsza Rzeczpospolita (the First Polish Republic) or Rzeczpospolita Obojga Narodów (Commonwealth of Both Nations), was formed in 1569 through the consolidation of the Kingdom of Poland and the Grand Duchy of Lithuania. In the 16th and 17th centuries, it was the largest and most populated nation in Europe. The Commonwealth covered not only the former territories of Poland and Lithuania, but also included the entire region of Belarus and Latvia, large parts of the Ukraine and Estonia, as well as part of present-day Western Russia.

Soviet communist state. Exempting the two decades of Interbellum sovereignty, it was not until the Revolution of 1989 that Poland expunged foreign control and regained its independence. Throughout the two centuries of foreign governance, despite the varied attempts at the suppression of various facets of Polish culture, including intermittent prohibitions against the Polish language, Polish society constituted itself through the production of art and literature on and off the stage.

The century following the tripartite division of Polish lands between Prussia and the Austrian and Russian Empires (1795–1918), during which the country lost its sovereignty, had a profound and enduring influence on Polish culture. Poland's history as a colonized nation and its resistance to foreign occupation, which manifested itself not only in frequent military uprisings but also through art and literature—most notably in Polish Romanticism (1820–64) which emerged during this time—shaped the development of its theater and dramatic literature. Varied forms of resistance can be traced throughout the history of Polish theater. The comingling of dreams with brutal realistic satire—a feature that Czesław Miłosz argues to be one of the most significant contributions of Polish Romantic poet Adam Mickiewicz's (1798–1855) great national poetic drama *Forefathers' Eve* (1983[1969]: 224)—is a quality of Polish dramatic literature that will emerge again and again. Writers such as novelist and playwright Witold Gombrowicz (1904–69) deployed sharp allegorical satire even while critically interrogating Polish Romantic drama in his 1946 play *Ślub* (*The Marriage*).

The absurdist humor that marked much of the dramatic literature after World War II was soon supplanted by the obligatory political and aesthetic doctrine of Socialist Realism. This state-imposed style called for drama to be "national in form and socialist in content." Since it was not clear what "national in form" meant, and Socialist Realism was to be accessible to the masses, playwrights borrowed from popular dramatic forms of the 1850s (Kłossowicz 2007: 8). The years 1949–55 constituted the period of most severe state censorship. During this time many artists and intellectuals became adept at what Miłosz identifies in his 1953 book, *The Captive Mind*, as the practice of Ketman—the expression of false allegiance to authority while keeping one's internal opposition concealed. However, as Kłossowicz argues, it was more than a superficial compliance with the regime that Polish artists under communism mastered. It was a wide-ranging strategy involving the play of hidden meanings, an irregular warfare that playwrights, directors, and dramaturges waged against the censors of which the public was entirely conscious (ibid. 6). The poetics of absurdism that began to emerge during this period reflected the grotesque nature of the communist state, and was closely aligned with the techniques of documentary collage practiced by playwrights such as Tadeusz Różewicz. While the collapse of the communist regime in 1989 prompted the loosening of censorship, it also brought with it a substantial decline of state funding for the arts. Many theaters became commercialized as the nation teetered precariously toward a free-market economy. Post-1989 drama revolved around discourses of transition that exposed anxieties related to cultural commodification as well as the nation's rapidly changing identity and place within the larger structures and cultural policies of the European Union.[2] Post-communist Polish drama also became preoccupied with issues related to otherness and alterity.

Pre-partition Poland had prided itself in the ethnic, cultural, religious, and linguistic diversity of its inhabitants. Identifying itself

---

2 For a detailed discussion of the five dominant discourses that emerged in Polish drama immediately after the fall of communism, see Trojanowska (2005): 93–104.

as a nation embodying religious tolerance and social autonomy,[3] before the partitions Poland was the home of one of the most significant Jewish communities in the world. Between the 13th and 17th centuries, various groups of Muslim Tatars took refuge in Poland, where they were granted nobility status. The complicated history of religious minorities in Poland underwent a dramatic shift after the partitions and became inextricably linked to the drive to keep Poland on the map, which was often effectuated through a monolithic national unity requiring a symbolic and literal disappearance of religious and racial difference. In addition to what became the relative dearth of influx of racially and ethnically diverse peoples into partitioned Poland, Polish mentality began to be shaped by the cultivation of Polish nationalism, which excluded all internal cultural, racial, and linguistic difference. While undoubtedly part of a larger trend toward nationalism(s) within 19th-century Europe, the stakes for Polish nationalism—given Poland's lack of sovereignty—were high. It was precisely this threat to national identity and existence that precipitated the perceived need for the construction of a monolithic Polish identity premised on the systematic exclusion of minority groups such as Jews, Tatars, Lemkos, Kashubs (Kashubians), Rromani, and Armenians, among others. It is this rigidified construct that the new generation of Polish playwrights are beginning to unsettle after the collapse of the Soviet-controlled Polish communist state.

---

3 It is not my intention here to paint an idyllic picture of pre-partition Poland, as the relations between various religious and ethnic groups within Poland, since the founding of the Kingdom of Poland in 1025, were complex and by no means free of hostility. For instance, despite the determination of various reigning princes to protect Jewish populations within Poland, religious persecution, blood-libel accusations and pogroms were perpetrated against Jews throughout their centuries-long presence in Poland. However, I am gesturing to the nation's larger stances and policies vis-à-vis the influx of peoples, which might constitute the religious, ethnic, and linguistic Other in relation to the indigenous populations.

The present volume brings together nine contemporary plays that constitute individual and communal imaginings of contemporary Poland and revise, rehearse, and unmake found notions of individual and national identity. The collection opens with *The Files* (2007), a documentary play devised by Teatr Ósmego Dnia (Theatre of the Eighth Day). Originally founded in 1964 as a form of student poetry theater by Tomasz Szymański and his colleagues from the department of Polish Philology at the Adam Mickiewicz University in Poznań, Teatr Ósmego Dnia has since gained iconic status in Poland and become synonymous with politically engaged theater. Theater members' participation in the student demonstrations of March 1968 forged the link between Teatr Ósmego Dnia and political activism, which became constitutive of the theater's identity. The Theatre of the Eighth Day takes its name from Polish poet Konstanty Ildefons Gałczyński's (1905–53) famous quote: "On the seventh day God rested, and on the eighth He created theatre." Beyond making the allusion to the poet's Green Goose Theatre,[4] a collection of satirical dramatic sketches that premiered in 1946, the name gestures toward a utopian time-space outside of the oppressive system imposed by the regime, the dystopia of communist Poland. Positioned squarely within the counterculture movements of the 1960s—more specifically, a strand known within Poland as "alternative theater"—Theatre of the Eighth Day proposed just that: an alternative, an*other* day.

Premiering at the company's performance venue in Poznań, *The Files* look back to the historical moment of 1970s Poland—a time during which Teatr Ósmego Dnia began to be persecuted by

---

4 While the dramatic miniatures comprising the Green Goose Theater—also dubbed the "World's Smallest Theater"—have often been performed, the title of the work itself refers to a series of dramatic texts that Gałczyński published in Przekrój, a Polish weekly news magazine founded in 1945. In this instance, the terms theater and drama were used interchangeably.

the communist regime—through the prism of personal letters, memoirs, and newly declassified police files. The textual montage of the performance, created by actor Ewa Wójciak and Katarzyna Mandon-Mitzner, is in large part comprised of Ministry of Internal Affairs secret police files, which document the agency's surveillance, infiltration, and covert manipulation of the theater in the 1970s and 80s. The files of the former Polish communist security apparatus Służba Bezpieczeństwa (SB)[5] were made publically available in 1998 when by special legislation the Polish parliament established the Instytut Pamięci Narodowej, IPN (Institute of National Remembrance). IPN files contain the evidentiary data corroborating the painful collective memory of surveillance, detention, forcible disappearance, and torture perpetrated by the communist regime. In addition to housing the archival documents produced and accumulated by the state security authorities during the period from July 22, 1944 to July 31, 1990, the institute possesses lustration prerogatives and prosecution powers. The institute came under public scrutiny in 2005 when journalist Bronisław Wildstein leaked a partial list of names of former secret agents, informants, and victims copied from IPN files. The list—which named persons without indicating whether they were perpetrators or victims—eventually made its way onto the Internet. While what became known as the Wildstein List was published without IPN permission, the controversy surrounding the publicization of archival information was symptomatic of the nation's attempts to come to terms with the dark aspects of its past. The release of documents makes evident not only the criminal activity of SB secret agents but also the pervasiveness of civilian informants and thereby the ubiquitous nature of complicity with the oppressive regime.

---

5 Established in 1954, the Służba Bezpieczeństwa of the Ministry of Internal Affairs became the main government body responsible for political repression, particularly after 1968.

Theatre of the Eighth Day's use of the files in performance juxtaposes the official state archive with the living bodies of actors who are its subjects. The biographies of the actors are inextricably linked to the demise of the communist state and the theater's dissident activities are revealed in the course of the performance. The "intermingling of autobiography with history" in *The Files*, is one of the functions of documentary theater as outlined by Carol Martin (2006: 13) and tightly sutures the personal with the political—as do other plays in this volume. IPN files read during the performance disclose the clandestine and often theatrical operations by which the state surveilled its citizens. Using the *lingua franca* of the security service, secret agents unwittingly become theater critics quoting and commenting on passages from Theatre of the Eighth Day performances. The result is something akin to a theater review—encompassing pre- and post-performance events—articulated in Orwellian double-speak. The files disclose and document the scripted performances of its agents, replete with code names such as "Spider" or "Hygienist," along with instructions for enactment. The dramaturgy of deception played out by infiltrators approaches absurdist fiction, which it undoubtedly at times inspired, such as the absurdist dramas of playwright Sławomir Mrożek in the Polish context.

The Files contrasts the bureaucratic language of the IPN files with the personal letters and fragments of memoirs of the actors—the former operation targets—written during the same period. The actors' testimony paints a utopian vision of theater as a community, a space in which one could preserve the imagination by internally and externally resisting the censorship of the state. Performing both personal and state papers presents each archive in sharp relief and demonstrates analogies between the ways in which different kinds of meaning can be similarly constructed. The company's performance of IPN files turns the tables on authoritarian power by interrogating state action and its official narratives even as it uses similar methods. Martin's incisive critique is to the point here: "The hidden seams of documentary theatre raise questions about the continuum between documentation and simulation" (2006: 11). The critical efficacy of *The Files* lies in the simultaneously past and present sociopolitical perspective of the work. The text and its performance construct its own evidence and thereby frames the historical past in strategic ways for the present.

If the dichotomous line between perpetrator and victim—infiltrator and target—remains clear in *The Files*, Michał Bajer's *Eat the Heart of Your Enemy* (2005) confounds the disparateness of friend and foe. Set in 1849, Bajer's play delves into issues of cultural and artistic patrimony in the context of exilic experience. The action takes place in an apartment at 12 Place Vendôme, the Paris residence of Frédéric Chopin, on October 16, 1849, the historical eve of the pianist's death. Diverging from the actual time of death by several hours, the play commences at 4:59 p.m. with Chopin's already-deceased body laid out on an operating table onstage. The young and handsome Théodule Granvil infelicitously attempts to remove Chopin's heart from his body. Chopin had expressed the desire to have his heart removed before burial by writing the following sentence on a piece of paper shortly before his death: "Comme cette terre m'étouffera, je vous conjure de faire ouvrir mon corps pour [que] je ne sois pas enterré vif." ("As this earth will suffocate me, I implore you to have my body opened so that I will not be buried alive.") Chopin's heart was in reality removed from his body and returned to his homeland, according to his dying wish, where it was later immured in a pillar in Kościół świętokrzyski (Holy Cross Church), a baroque house of worship in the center of Warsaw. An epitaph inscribed on the pillar reads: "For where your treasure is, there will your heart be also" (Matthew 6:21). Chopin was forced into exile from Poland in 1831 and settled in France shortly after the November Uprising—an armed rebellion of partitioned Poland against the Russian Empire—had failed. He was part of the first wave of the Great Emigration (1831–70), which consisted primarily of political and artistic émigrés who, like Chopin, mostly settled in France.

Chopin's Romantic nostalgia for his homeland throughout his exile, evidenced through his music and the desire for his heart to be returned to his motherland if only in death, is syncopated in *Eat the Heart of Your Enemy*. By placing the task of surgically removing Chopin's heart in the hands of the young Granvil, an inexperienced proctologist, Bajer sets the scene for a dark comedy with a smattering of scatological humor. Drafting a hypothetical obituary, Chopin's private secretary Maurice Tansky asks, " '[. . .] Doctor Théodule Granvil, proctologist, removed Chopin's heart.' But we can't write that. You know, Monsieur, you know what the first question will be in people's minds? Which way! Which way did he take it out?" (43–4). In the scenes that follow, figures at various points of proximity to Chopin arrive to stake their claims on the patrimony to which they feel entitled. In addition to former friends and lovers—and in stark contrast to the artistic émigré elite—a certain Jean Jean appears who, apparently unaware of Chopin's death, harbors the dream of studying with the master to become a great piano virtuoso:

> I'm Jean. I don't actually have a last name. Just a first name: Jean. But, since everyone has to have a last name, the alderman registered me as Jean Jean. And if, for example, his holiness the parish priest screams at me "Jean!" then that's the last name, but if her honor the village elder screams at me "Jean!" then she means the first name. Jean Jean. You can call me whichever you prefer: Jean, or Jean, I'll know who you mean (56–7).

Chopin's identity and legacy is lightheartedly contested throughout the play by means of Bahktian carnivalesque subversion. Introducing narrative threads that allege Chopin's participation in a human smuggling ring, Bajer unsettles hegemonic notions of legacy. "High culture" mingles with the profane when opera singer and Chopin's former lover, Manon Delorme, dreams of starting a brothel: "A beautiful, warm brothel. Wallpapered in . . . musical notes . . . I know that Chopin would love it. And in the window a red sign: MARIOLA. [. . .] That's what I'd call the brothel. After my mom. My mom was Polish." (85) Over the course of the play, various identities are revealed and some are exposed as fraudulent. As the play progresses, more and more characters turn out to be of Eastern European descent. While most of them were either born in Poland or have Polish ancestry, the remainder are from the "Russkie shit-hole," separated from Poland by only a creek (50).

Bajer's comical anachronisms compress temporalities: he references Polaroid photography, Road Runner cartoons, and describes Chopin by referring to a 2002 biographical film:

GRANVIL. What sort of guy was he? Chopin.

MANON. Have you seen the movie, *Chopin: Desire for Love*?
He was just like that. So sweet (76).

A translator of French drama, Bajer intentionally borrows from *comédie-vaudeville* while shaping the formal aspects of his play. This minor form, whose popularity grew as it travelled the boulevard-theater circuit in mid-19th century France, was itself a reaction against the perceived self-indulgent ideology of the Romantic movement. Contrasting the Romantic cult of sensibility with a predilection for sensationalism—a feature characterizing the light-comedy genre of *comédie-vaudeville*—signals yet another collision between high and low. Bajer's use of *comédie-vaudeville* to interrogate the work, life, and legacy of the Romantic composer is in itself an excision performed on the formal level. These literary strategies expose the way in which Chopin's legacy has been continually reimagined by ensuing generations.

The quote "Chopin is more Polish than Poland," variously attributed to the pianist's lover George Sand and his friend Honoré de Balzac, and later cited by his biographer Louis Énault, encapsulates the notion of a quintessential Polishness which—in the case of Chopin in exile—exists as an island of Polish cultural and national sovereignty on foreign soil. If Chopin is a stand-in for a timeless Polish quality made foreign by virtue of the disappearance of Poland from the map of Europe, the plays that follow explore the reverse proposition: the disruption of any notion of a pure or monolithic Polish identity by attending to the internal Other. While Ingmar Villqist's *Helver's Night* (1999), which premiered at Teatr Kriket in Chorzów, closes the first section of the anthology, it further opens up themes touching on otherness that will continue to re-emerge in significant ways in other plays collected in this volume.

Villqist is the pseudonym of Jarosław Świerszcz, an art historian, critic, and curator who emerged as a playwright at the age of 38. While Świerszcz himself claims to have chosen the Norwegian pen name to distinguish his writing from the persona associated with his curatorial work, theater critics attribute greater meaning to this choice and point to the affiliation of his dramatic style with the Scandinavian masters such as Henrik Ibsen, August Strindberg, and Ingmar Berman. The influence of the tradition of psychological realism can certainly be felt in *Helver's Night*, as well as in his other plays, as he exposes the disquieting realities behind social facades in a manner reminiscent of Ibsen. Most of his dramas explore the lives of those who are in some way marked as the Other in the context within which they find themselves. Świerszcz's use of a foreign pseudonym—whether conscious or not—already signals alterity within the Polish context. In using a foreign pseudonym, he distances himself from his context, thereby accentuating difference or otherness in an act that precedes and informs his writing.

While in his other works Świerszcz explores themes of intimate homosexual relationships between both men (*The Anaerobes*, 2000) and women (*The Piece of Lard with Sweetmeats*, 1993), as well as death and disease, as in *Untitled* (2000)—which portrays a young man dying of AIDS—*Helver's Night* tells the story of Helver, a mentally disabled man in his 30s. The play depicts the deep and complex relationship between Helver and his caregiver, Karla. It is set against a fascistic takeover whose violent fervor seeps in through the windows and whose encroachment is tensely felt in the one-room apartment in which the two reside. Karla feverishly attempts to deny the militaristic upheaval that is fermenting in the streets by shutting the windows onto the outside world. Helver, swept up in the intensity of the fascist movement, dresses the part of agitator replete with black leather beret, silver badge, and folded flag, but his mental disorder prevents him from realizing that he is just a provisional pawn in the movement and that his mental illness marks him as an object of elimination by the fascists. Karla humors him and the two rehearse for war by enacting military drills and playing war—"just to pretend"—under the tent of their kitchen table (107). Karla's domesticity, represented by the potato soup she offers Helver, is both effectively interchangeable and ultimately supplanted by the pea soup from the field kitchens, which Helver consumes as part of his military training.

Helver's Night is a one-act play that abides by the Aristotelian unities. The classical form serves as casing for a thoroughly modernist sensibility and here it resounds strongly with Louis Ferdinand Céline's 1932 novel *Voyage au bout de la nuit* (*Journey to the End of Night*), which coincidentally was also published when its author was 38. Not only is *Helver's Night* intended to evoke the atmosphere of the mounting tension of pre–World War II Europe, like the novel, it is a nihilistic and antiheroic vision of human suffering set amid failing military and medical–industrial complexes. While Helver and Céline's antihero Barmadu occupy opposite positionalities within the psychiatric unit, the two authors similarly bind war and mental illness. Barmadu says: "I cannot refrain from doubting that there exist any genuine realizations of our deepest character except war and illness, those two infinities of nightmare."[6] Here the correspondence between personal and non-individual qualities— whether conceptualized as national or universal—is not unlike the relation between Chopin and the features of the Polish nation-state that he purportedly embodies, except that in this equation negative values are applied.

It is more than a pseudonym and soup that bind together *Helver's Night* and Amanita Muskaria's *Daily Soup* (2007). Denoting a poisonous and psychoactive mushroom commonly known as fly agaric, Amanita Muskaria is a pseudonym shared by a two-sister writing team: actor Gabriela Muskała and translator of German literature, Monika Muskała. Whereas Świerszcz's work privileges that which is often rendered socially and politically abject, *Daily Soup* serves the abject in its most fundamental form: food and the processes associated its consumption—defecation. The action of *Daily Soup* centers around domestic loci: the living-room television, the kitchen, and the bathroom (the relationship between the latter two is not unremarked by the father: "And the way to the kitchen should have been through the crapper!" (160)) The play revolves around three generations of women: grandmother, mother, and

---

6 "[J]e ne peux m'empêcher de mettre en doute qu'il existe d'autres véritables réalisations de nos profonds tempéraments que la guerre et la maladie, ces deux infinis du cauchemar" (Céline 1952: 370).

daughter, around whom the father orbits. The Muskała sisters beautifully craft the mundane interactions and conversations between the family, capturing with precision a relatable monotony of routine domesticity. The quotidian, is presented with a subtle sense of humor not bereft of a certain tenderness. While firmly grounded in the specificity of a Polish working-class family, the play sheds light on the effects of globalization, whose mediatized form penetrates the household directly through the portal of the television. The two older women's days revolve around a soap opera entitled "The Style of Success." It is presumably through this and other shows that the seeds of Western diet fads and other preoccupations and obsessions are sown. Members of the family have varied—albeit equally charged—relationships to food: the father overeats; the mother cooks (I cook, therefore I am); the daughter fasts and cleanses; grandma needs laxatives. Food becomes a signifier, which stands in a complex relationship to the needs and desires of the family: "Sweetie, look you didn't eat your soup . . . My blood pressure is rising. Can't you see how much we love you?" (170). The ingestion of soup is inextricably linked to the consumption of the soap operas that constitute the women's primary cultural consumption. It is also hard to overlook the allusions to the prayer for "our daily bread," once a staple of fundamental survival, and the shift to the social construction of desire that soap operas have, in part, engendered.

The interplay of desire and the social forms that create it is also a theme central to Michał Walczak's *First Time*. Premiering in 2005 at TR Warszawa, this tragicomedy stages a meeting between Magdalena and Charles, two young people who rehearse the social norms of a human encounter. The stage play grew out of Walczak's experiments with the genre of radio drama. The formal aspects of the piece are by-products of the author's conscious engagement with the ways in which the imagination can be mobilized solely through auditory means. Without the use of visual cues, Walczak resorts to the spoken word and dialogue to craft a narrative filled with the grotesque figures, sudden shifts in mood, and action that develops outside the laws of physics or biology.

Through numerous reiterations and trials to attain the perfect scenario, Magdalena and Charles attempt to find out how to be with each other for the first time. The paradoxical nature of their pursuit is compounded by the blurring of real life and performance. The assemblage process construed and enacted by the couple resembles Richard Schechner's notion of "restored behavior" or "twice-behaved behavior," which he designates as the main characteristic of performance: "performance means: never for the first time. It means: for the second to the *n*th time" (1985: 36). The theory of restored behavior sees behavior itself as separate from those behaving. This reflexive and critical distance created by the interstice between behavior and those behaving creates the possibility of storing, transmitting, manipulating, and transforming behavior. Conceptualizing restored behavior as strips of behavior that can be taken apart, rearranged, and reconstructed underscores the creative repetition and manipulation of behavior. This implies not only the processes of training, learning, revising, and repeating behavior in a conventional theatrical context but also extends to behavior in everyday life. Such is the quintessence of Walczak's dramaturgical work in the *First Time*. However, despite her efforts to script and enact the most detailed and "beautiful scene in the world," the "most self-aware first time ever," (206) the narrative takes an unpredictable turn, which even Magdalena herself cannot direct.

Krzysztof Bizio's *Let's Talk About Life and Death* (2001) is a dramatic text constructed primarily through a montage of phone conversations and short interactions between wife, husband, and son or Red, Blue, and White respectively. Perhaps it is not surprising that the elegantly crafted form of the play is authored by an architect who devotes himself to writing only in the afterhours of his primary occupation of architectural design. Bizio made his playwriting debut when he sent the play included in the present volume to *Dialog*, a leading Polish scholarly journal devoted to contemporary drama. When the editors decided to publish the text, however, they discovered that they had lost the envelope with the author's return address; the only remaining information about the writer was his name. Despite their best efforts, they could not locate Bizio. It was only after the editors decided to move forward and the text was published that Bizio was found.

Let's Talk About Life and Death demonstrates the author's attention to form. Bizio states, "In drama, I am interested in disenchanting form, and not a traditional narrative. I have always sought a new construction, into which the content will write itself automatically" (in Pawłowski 2003: 22, my translation). Bizio's attunement to the language of quotidian exchanges is beautifully crafted in his montage of phone conversations through which the characters of the play are revealed. It is precisely by means of the telephone that members of the household establish contact with the world in one-sided conversations that are lively, humorous, and full of unexpected turns.

The mother (Red) buys a lovely deep-red blouse to wear when meeting her best friend Ala's fiancé, Victor: "God, Ala, don't scream so loud. I'm not a slut. Ala, listen, let me tell you what happened. It's not my fault. Don't talk to me like that. I'm not a whore. What are you saying? It's all because of Victor, and you know how I start goofing around when I drink (237)." It is not only Red that strays; Blue—the husband—imagines himself as a tomcat, but it's a different kitten he's after. The son, Paweł (White), is a small-scale junkie, a rookie dealer who dreams big:

[W]e live in a fucked-up age. My grandpa made a fortune selling tomatoes, my father sells cars, and now I'm entering a whole new line of operations. Soon everything's gonna be one global fucking village. The only people left will be tycoons, and everyone else can go sweep the streets. Today, more than ever, individuality counts. You have to be someone, you know? You have to have your own big plan and deliver on it.

Shit, dude, in five years I'll be king of this city. I'll have the goods, the girls, and all the fucking icing on the cake. Clearly it's my calling.

Stick with me, and you'll get there eventually. See ya (238).

Paweł's induction into free-market capitalism through petty drug deals is as clichéd as the superficial social relations in which he and his parents are embroiled. The atmosphere of *laissez faire* permeates both social and economic exchanges between members of the family and the outside world. The characters struggle with their own sense of alienation as they confront criminal and social violence, pregnancies, abortions, and double mastectomies—the bloody side of life on which death encroaches.

While the preceding three plays create a space within which domesticity in the Polish context is rehearsed, the dramatic texts contained in the last section of this anthology radically contest and undo the established notions of Polishness enacted both in the private and public spheres. While the 1990s witnessed a relative dearth of drama produced and published by a young generation of Polish playwrights, that situation changed drastically around the turn of the century, coinciding with the formation of institutional support for new dramatic writing, most notably through the Radom Odważny, a competition and festival for contemporary drama; the Warsaw Laboratorium Dramatu (Drama Laboratory); Teatr

Narodowy (National Theater); and particularly through the Warsaw Rozmaitości Theater (TR Warszawa) TR/PL project under whose auspices the work of Wojcieszek, Bajer, and Masłowska—among others—was developed. The end of the 1990s also brought an influential wave of British Brutalism in Poland in the form of colloquial and often vulgar language, brutal violence, and pop-culture references. The influence of such "in-yer-face theater" exponents as Sarah Kane and Brad Fraser on the work of TR Warszawa and its directors Krzysztof Warlikowski and Grzegorz Jarzyna, cannot be overrated, and certainly had far-reaching repercussions not only on the work that was filtered through the TR/PL project but also on Polish dramatic writing more broadly.

British Brutalism is rooted in Brutalist architecture, which proliferated from the 1950s to the mid-70s in Europe and beyond. The term, coined in 1953, derives from the French phrase *béton brut* (raw concrete), used by Le Corbusier to describe the architectural style of many of his post–World War II buildings: rough, blocklike, concrete structures, which burgeoned in response to the need for low-income housing and government edifices. This architectural style is not unlike the products of urban design that emerged under Socialist Realism, the prevailing trend in the Soviet-dominated Eastern Bloc. Socialist Realism in architecture, whose guiding idea was to design an urban landscape that would help create a new social order, left an undeniable imprint on Polish cities and the psychological topography of its inhabitants. The psychogeography of the housing developments, which began to flourish in the 1950s within and on the outskirts of urban centers, is an integral part of the action in which the plays in this volume are set. While it is only the plays included in the first section of this anthology that explicitly interrogate history, the other plays—for the most part—refrain from drawing direct associations between the current sociopolitical moment and the historical past that formed them. Be that as it may, it is impossible to ignore the material remnants of the communist regime and the enduring imprint it left on Poland's landscape. The life portrayed in many of these dramatic texts takes place amidst the housing complexes erected by the communist regime. The poor quality of the materials and the regimentation implicit in the sameness of the cement-block building has produced a unique form of urban decay and decrepitude. *Daily Soup* is situated in an apartment in just such a building complex. Charles, in *First Time*, comments upon the housing complex in which his beloved resides: "It's just one apartment building after another out here, what the hell kind of urban planning is this? The same building over and over (187)." However, nowhere is the relationship between the totalitarian atmosphere of the Socialist Realism urban complex and the individuation it produces more prominent than in Przemysław Wojcieszek's *Made in Poland*.

The second sentence of *Made in Poland*, which premiered in 2004, calls for a revolution. When 19-year-old Boguś, with the words "Fuck Off!" in Gothic script freshly tattooed on his forehead, runs down the streets of the housing development, rod in hand, one can sense that an anarchic revolution is imminent. While the revolutionary path—beyond bashing the windshields of expensive cars— may not yet be clear to Boguś, his rejection of the status quo is as complete as his sudden transformation. Boguś, short for Bogusław, which in old Slavic means "He who praises God," is a former altar boy who returns his vestments to the church vestry amidst his violent rampage. Boguś is a product of the system into which he was born. Made in Poland, he is a high school dropout without job prospects who lives in one of the communist-era housing complexes with his single mother. His girlfriend, Anka, dumped him for being like all the rest of them. He's pissed.

VICTOR. Who do you hate so much, Boguś?

BOGUŚ. Everybody. Cell-phone assholes, tracksuiters, hipsters, gel boys from the music charts top ten, advertising asses, TV tramps, bastards from banks,
motherfucker priests, psychopaths from the army,
government, police, and corporations. I hate them. I
hate their wives, their husbands, their daughters,
their sons, sons-in-laws, brothers-in-law, fathers-in-
law. I hate the Russians, Germans, and Americans.
Americans in particular. Those motherfuckers want
to be everywhere, they want to govern everything,
those pricks with noseyitis have to pry into everything. I hate those shitty restaurants that are all over
the place now. I've never set foot in one and never
will. Like this McDonald's, for example. I'll never set
foot inside. I don't give a shit that the john is free.
I'll never even take a piss in a McDonald's, even if
I'm leaking. I'd rather piss in on the street. Because I
simply hate those sons of bitches (280–1).

His nihilistic condemnation of the world that surrounds him is
uncompromising. However, he lacks perspective—both about how
he could function within the system or rebel against it. Having
rejected his mentor Reverend Edmund, he turns to his former high-
school teacher Victor for guidance. Fired for his drinking, Victor
is a dejected alcoholic who slips in his own vomit—both literally
and metaphorically. Not the obvious role model, Victor does manage to slip Boguś a volume of poetry by Polish poet Władysław
Broniewski (1897–1962), which serves as an aperture for the young
man's imagination.

 In his search for true comrades-in-arms for the revolution,
Boguś meets two unlikely candidates: 16-year-old Emil whose

wheelchair does not prevent him from working nightly as security guard and his sister, Monika. Emil and Monika have a tracksuit for every occasion, which Boguś detests. And yet, "Monika is exquisite. She works at a butcher shop. Monika knows every kind of sausage. If they ever fire her—she will find work at any butcher shop. Everyone is looking for specialists these days (288)." Emil warms up to Boguś quickly and introduces him and his cause to Monika with enthusiasm:

> EMIL. He's a revolutionary. Boguś doesn't give a shit. Boguś has had enough and now he's fighting for justice—he's not waiting like the others!
>
> MONIKA. That's fascinating, tell me about it, Boguś.
>
> EMIL. Boguś has big plans. He is extraordinarily brave. He stood up to those horrible thugs—the ones who knocked over my wheelchair. Boguś won't give in to them, Boguś will fight till the end! (288–9)

Made in Poland is not Wojcieszek's first punk manifesto in dramatic form. His play *Kill Them All* (2000) was first released in 1999 as a film produced by Rebellion Films. The action of *Kill Them All* is set amid youth riots sparked by the police killing a young sports fan, but—as with most riots—the reactionary violence is symptomatic of larger social ills. The latter are also concretized in the communist-era housing complex in which the female protagonist, Ewa, lives: "And my city is just a fistful of concrete blocks surrounding a carpet factory. An ideal place to find a job, get married, have kids and raise them so that they don't lend a hand to the regime pigs" (Wojcieszek in Pawłowski 2003: 474, my translation). Ewa's aggressive stance vis-à-vis authority is much more violent that that of Boguś: "The boy's death is their fault. What we need is a generation that will wrangle them to the sea and drown them like pigs. And it's not going to be a generation of salesmen" (ibid.). Two years after the film came out, Wojcieszek himself called *Kill Them All* "naïve and pretentious" (ibid. 456). While *Made in Poland* loses some of the edge present in *Kill Them All*, it retains the same youthful viridity. Boguś possesses an endearing quality, which renders his anarchic revolt somewhat quaint and dampens the intended rebelliousness of his actions. Naivety and efficacy aside, Boguś' repudiation and rejection of the status quo are important acts of contestation.

A 2004 environmental staging of *Made in Poland*, directed by the author in Legnica, added another layer to the palimpsest of the haunting presence of communist-era architecture in contemporary Polish reality—on and off the stage. Inhabitants of a dilapidated housing complex in Legnica—much like the one in which *Made in Poland* is set—were astounded by the sight of a crowd gathering in front of a seedy and abandoned 1970s neighborhood supermarket where the play was performed (Pawłowski 2006: 400). One of them called the police when Eryk Lubos, the actor playing Boguś, began to demolish a car parked nearby as part of the performance (ibid.). This style of theatrical hyperrealism borrows not only from the historical avant-garde and more recent performance art practices; it is also reflective of the recent developments in Polish theater practice.

The theatrical experiments of a new generation of Polish directors such as Warlikowski and Jarzyna (TR Warszawa) are deeply conversant with adjacent artistic genres such as cinema. Wielding high-tech accruements, both directors engage in a cinematic mise-en-scène achieved through stage, sound, and lighting design as well as other special effects. Warlikowski and Jarzyna frame actors cinematically by projecting close-up shots through a live video feed onto a large screen above the actors. By staging multiple sequences simultaneously, they create a split-screen effect. Like Wojcieszek, Jarzyna reverses the more common adaptation sequence of stage to film, by staging films such as Danish director Thomas Vinterberg's 1998

Festen (*The Celebration*). Jarzyna's production of *Festen*, first staged in 2001, which is emblematic of the theater director's larger oeuvre, is the inverse of the Dogme 95 filmmaking manifesto of which Vinterberg's film was the first. While the avant-garde film movement initiated by Lars von Trier and Vinterberg rejects the use of elaborate technology and special effects, it is precisely these that the theater practice growing out of TR Warszawa embraces.

Another young playwright to have come out of the TR/PL project is Dorota Masłowska, whose 2006 drama *Couple of Poor, Polish-Speaking Romanians* is a fast-paced spree through the Polish countryside with Blighty and Gina. Masłowska's three-act drama opens with the nervous babblings of a middle-aged driver who has just encountered the Romanian couple. The speed, immediacy, and disjointed quality of this dramatic monologue—ostensibly the driver's report to the police—gives the play a stream of consciousness feel and adds to the sense of drug-induced altered perception experienced by the couple.

Contrary to what the title and the couple's cover story may suggest, the two in reality are neither a couple nor Romanian. Blighty is an actor from Warsaw who plays the decent "Father Ted" on a soap opera. Gina is a young, glue-sniffing, drunk, pregnant woman who cannot recall whether she picked up her kid from preschool. A mixture of partying and drugs prompts the two to impersonate Polish-speaking Romanians attempting to hitchhike across the country. While for Blighty, who dons a 1972 Salvation Army cardigan and blackens his teeth with a marker, the slumming escapade is intended as a blithe diversion, the antic goes disastrously awry:

> Since eight in the morning I'm pretending to be a Romanian who speaks Polish, and I'm talking about the detrimental effects of eating butcher's scraps all the time, only all of a sudden it turns out that I'm a Pole coming down, a fucking Pole coming down and speaking Polish (347).

Not a Romanian, but a Pole coming down: the equation drawn between the two implies a similarity between status and state respectively. "Romanian" is a misnomer often used in Poland to designate the Rromani ethnic group.[7] While the 2011 Polish National Census indicates no Romanians living in Poland, it lists 16,000 Rromani inhabitants. The Rromani people living in Poland arguably hold the lowest social status in the country. A poll conducted by Centrum Badania Opinii Społecznej, CBOS (Center for Public Opinion Research) investigating the relationship of Poles to other national and ethnic groups shows that, among 39 other groups, Romanians and Rromani peoples ranked among the three groups to elicit the most antipathy (2010).[8] The study confirms that which is clearly evident in the daily behavior toward Rromani people that can be observed in the streets. The Rromani peoples, almost exclusively referred to by Poles as Romanians, are the most despised group within Poland. Blighty effectively conflates "Romanians" with all abjected Others, thereby lumping them into one category designated as the "Romanian rubric":

> BLIGHTY. We're not students, we're Romanians who speak
> Polish. We're lesbians, fags, Jews, we work for an
> ad agency. Like I was saying, you know how it is,
> we're going to Israel to plant trees, the goddamn

---

7 The Romani people are an ethnic group originating from the Indian subcontinent and referred to most widely in the English-speaking world by the exonym "Gypsies." Rom and Romani are sometimes spelled with a double *r* to represent the phoneme /ʀ/. This spelling is most often deployed in Romania in order to distinguish the Rromani ethnic minority, which constitutes less than 4 percent of the country's population, from native Romanians who are considered a separate ethnic group.

8 The CBOS study shows that 19 percent of the people polled expressed antipathy toward Romanians, while an overwhelming 55 percent claimed antipathy toward Rromani peoples—the lowest ranking group included in the poll (2010).

people out here don't want to give us a ride, not one
centimeter (353–4).

Blighty and Gina's slippage into the Romanian rubric, and all that
this entails, is much more precarious than their beguiling capers
might at first imply. Masłowska's text both gestures toward the lack
of stability and permeability of these categories and denies the very
possibility of such imbrication. In the words of the driver into whose
car the "Romanians" have piled: "When I get back my 10-year-old
son asks me if there's such a thing as Polish-speaking Romanians. I
say of course there isn't, because he's an anxious kid, sort of talks
too much, kind of slow for his age, [. . .] (327)." Masłowska holds
in productive tension the preclusion of the possibility of a Polish-
speaking Romanian and its simultaneous enactment.

   Małgorzata Sikorska-Miszczuk's *Loose Screws* (2006), which
closes this collection, examines the ways in which various psychopathologies play themselves out in the private and public spheres
in the context of post-communist Poland. The play looks at the relationship between individual and social violence after 9/11. The
action of *Loose Screws* revolves around the bed of Victoria, "a most
unusual woman, unique 24-7." The play opens as Mr. Bleh, Victoria's itinerant lover and Prime Minister-for-Life, comes home:

VICTORIA. Mr. Bleh comes home from work. It's night.
       At work he has had to:
       Lie,
       Kill,
       Commit adultery,
       Bear false witness,
       Disrespect his parents,
       Have another God before the One,
       Etcetera.
       The list may be incomplete (371).

Mr. Bleh is utterly preoccupied with the question of recalculating his life-insurance premium. The seamless interweaving between the public and private that recurs throughout the play is already signaled by Mr. Bleh's instantaneous shift between the feeling of being had by the insurance companies and his desire to be had by Victoria: "That is why I am sitting here heavily at the edge of the bed with the feeling that no matter what I do, I'm screwed. That is why I have a question for you, actually, a request: Could you screw me as well?" (372). Sikorska-Miszczuk blurs more than the lines between the public and private, political, and personal. Dream and reality begin to impinge on one another when Victoria is visited by 99 Cent, a terrorist from Kuyavia.[9] Appearing initially as a dream, 99 Cent encroaches on Victoria's reality when he refuses to depart. The thread of the Kuyavian dream is further interwoven into reality when Mr. Bleh requests Kuyavian bran for breakfast, only to learn from Victoria that they are out because Kuyavia is in revolt. The immediacy of the connectedness between the political actions of a providence and the basic quotidian act of eating breakfast is drawn with satirical wit. Kuyavia represents the pristine and unspoiled region within Poland, which ironically revolts, resulting in a nation at war with itself.

A third voice is interjected into the couple's breakfast repartee; it is the voice of Poland, which is marked as female. The gendering of the nation is further evidenced by the ways in which Poland is mapped onto Victoria's body. Both need to be looked after. Speaking of her prime-minister lover, and husband but in secret only, Victoria states: "He recognized that he seldom took advantage of my anatomy, and that this might have historical consequences, for he is a creature of history, and an outstanding one at that" (375).

---

9 Kuyavia (Kujawy) is a region in north-central Poland, whose historical beginnings are connected with the tribal state of West Slavic Goplans.

While undoubtedly also an allusion to the terrorist activities of separatist ethnic minorities within the former Soviet bloc, such as those in Chechnya, 99 Cent's style of Kuyavian terrorism is deeply entrenched in the emergent globalized culture associated with terrorism. A connection to the traumatic events of 9/11 is established through tales told by ghosts, victims of Islamist terrorists, which haunt Victoria. Figured as bedtime stories, these narratives entangle a love story into the horrific accounts of death.

The intentional misuse of Arabic phrases such as "Insha'Allah" within the play, signal the misappropriation of the idiom often misguidedly associated with terrorism. In fact, 99 Cent's accessory Zachar discloses that he has just learned the term "Insha'Allah" and misuses it unabashedly—as does Osama bin Laden himself who at one point telephones Prime Minister Bleh. The misappropriation of the Islamist rhetoric of martyrdom is presented through a prism of dark satire punctuated by such grotesque proposals as 99 Cent's contest for the best suicide note. Sikorska-Miszczuk's conflation of categories and demarcations of Arab, Muslim, and Terrorist, are more than dark evocations of racist stereotypes. By positioning the terrorist as the Other within, Sikorska-Miszczuk points to the dubiousness of projecting the terrorist threat onto an Other positioned outside of individual and national borders.

Terror is no longer figured as the Other: it is within. The intimacy of politics and the politics of intimacy are not two extremes to be kept in opposition. As the dramatic texts included in this volume attest in a variety of ways, they are two poles to be held in productive tension with one another.

The diverse perspectives presented in the plays, which compose this anthology, produce a kaleidoscopic view of contemporary Polish reality. While the formal and thematic divergences may be vast, all of the texts expose ways in which individual and social violence impinge upon one another. Systemic oppression is inextricably bound to interpersonal brutality—the two bleed into one another. The overwhelming deluge of blood, urine, and vomit, which recurs throughout the plays, constitute the most material forms of abjection theorized by Julia Kristeva as both that which repulses and the experience of repulsion—a reaction to the threatened breakdown of meaning, the collapse between subject and object or self and other. Chopin's cadaver present onstage in *Eat the Heart of Your Enemy* brings us into our own materiality and *"shows me* what I permanently thrust aside in order to live" (Kristeva 1982: 3, emphasis in the original). The loathing of food in *Daily Soup* is an instance of the most elementary and archaic forms of abjection. Victoria's uncle in *Loose Screws* lives by the dictum *vomitum ergo sum*. His individuation emerges through the process—in this case, quite literally—of expelling that which he does not assimilate, that which he is not. In *Made in Poland*, Boguś' former mentor slips in his own vomit, the literalization of an abreaction to the structural and domestic violence of which he is both victim and perpetrator. Boguś' own slip is from revulsion to revolution. The abjection of the threatening Other, such as the "Romanians" or the mentally ill Helver, is exemplary of the same process by which individual and national identity is formed through abjection.

Kristeva's theory postulates that the cause of abjection is that which "disturbs identity, system, order" (ibid. 4). It is not an object in and of itself that is abject but its displacement. Abjection is matter out of place, which constitutes a perceived danger for someone. This understanding of abjection aligns itself with the idiomatic notion "to have a screw loose" from which Sikorska-Miszczuk's play and this anthology take its title. While in the popular imaginary having a loose screw connotes an eccentric, off-kilter individual who does not have everything in its proper place, the idiom appeared during the Industrial Revolution and originally indicated something wrong with a machine or mechanism. This etymological linkage and historical slippage reveals the interrelation between individual psychopathologies and the skewed structural mechanisms. The plays in this volume expose the ways in which the two mutually produce and perpetuate one another.

The abjection of difference finds another—albeit different—articulation in Masłowska's play *No Matter how Hard We Tried*, not included in this volume. Jarzyna's 2009 production of the play at TR Warszawa—without completely foregoing discursive meaning—emphasizes visuality and deploys a formal vocabulary reminiscent of Robert Wilson. The performance derides various modes in which consumerist desire is constructed and interrogates contemporary notions of Polishness by ridiculing stereotypes of nationhood. In a voiceover, a neutral male radio-announcer relates soothingly:

> In the olden days, when the world was still governed by divine law, all people on earth were Poles. Everyone was a Pole, a German was a Pole, a Swede was a Pole, a Spaniard was a Pole, everybody was a Pole everybody simply everybody everybody everybody. Poland was a beautiful country back then; we had beautiful seas, islands, oceans, a fleet to sail them and to discover ever new continents, which also belonged to Poland, there was among others the famous Polish explorer Krzysztof Kolumbus who predictably was later rechristened Christopher or Chris or Isaac or something. We were a great power, an oasis of tolerance and multiculturalism, all those not arriving here from another country, because back then as already mentioned there were none, were greeted here with bread . . . (Masłowska 2008: 70, my translation).

Alluding to the 16th and 17th centuries during which Poland was the largest and most populated nation in Europe, Masłowska mocks sentimental notions of grandeur and irrecoverable Polish greatness. She shows the underbelly of idealistic visions of multiculturalism existing beneath the benevolent protectorate of the Polish nation-state: the imperial impulse to seize, conquer, and dominate. The global projection of Polish identity obliterates difference and constitutes the inversion of the internal erasures of otherness effectuated over past centuries of Polish nationhood, which contemporary Polish dramatic literature is now only in the process of confronting. Masłowska's Polish title, the literal translation of which is *Between Us Things are Good*, emphasizes the "between us," or the relational aspect of human existence.

It is precisely through this relationality that the meanings and forms of the dramatic texts in the present volume emerge, whether through a confrontation with the past, quotidian interactions rooted in domesticity, or encounters with the external or internal Other in the private and public sphere. The attention to relationality is reminiscent of the first words of Gombrowicz's short introduction, entitled "The Idea of Drama," which prefaces his play, *Ślub*, cited earlier: "A human being is subjected to that which is created *between* people [. . .]" (Gombrowicz 1971[1946]: 63. my translation, emphasis in the original). Gombrowicz continues: "But all of this happens through Form: meaning, that people connecting with one another, mutually impose on the other a particular way of being, talking, acting . . . and everyone deforms others, and is at one and the same time deformed by them" (ibid.). Implicit in Gombrowicz's understanding of form, as that which emerges through relationality, is not only the new forms of dramatic literature that are beginning to appear in post-1989 Poland and are presented in this volume, but also the quotidian forms of human relationality that are actualized daily through our encounters with others. It is through the imaginative play with the creation of forms on both levels, that a body of cultural, national, and individual sovereignty that embraces internal and external difference can potentially emerge.

WORKS CITED

CENTRUM BADANIA OPINII SPOŁECZNEJ (CBOS). 2010. *Komunikat z badań: Stosunek Polaków do innych narodów*. Warszawa: Fundacja Centrum Badania Opinii Społecznej.

CÉLINE, Louis-Ferdinand. 1952. *Voyage au bout de la nuit*. Paris: Éditions Gallimard.

GOMBROWICZ, Witold. 1971[1946]. *Dzieła Zebrane. Tom V: Teatr*. Paris: Instytut Literacki.

KŁOSSOWICZ, Jan. 2007. *Antologia dramatu polskiego 1945–2005* (Tom 1). Warszawa: Prószyński i S-ka.

KRISTEVA, Julia. 1982. *Powers of Horror: An Essay on Abjection*. New York: Columbia University Press.

MARTIN, Carol. 2006. "Bodies of Evidence." *TDR* (T191) 50(3): 8–15.

MASŁOWSKA, Dorota. 2008. *Między nami dobrze jest*. Warszawa: Lampa i Iskra Boża.

MIŁOSZ, Czesław. 1983[1969]. *The History of Polish Literature*. Berkeley and Los Angeles: University of California Press.

PAWŁOWSKI, Roman. 2003. *Pokolenie Porno i inne niesmaczne utwory teatralne*. Kraków: Wydawnictwo Zielona Sowa.

———. 2006. *Made in Poland: dziewięć sztuk teatralnych z Polski*. Kraków: Korporacja Ha!art i Horyzont.

SCHECHNER, Richard. 1985. *Between Theater and Anthropology*. Philadelphia: University of Pennsylvania Press.

TROJANOWSKA, Tamara. 2005. "New Discourses in Drama." *Contemporary Theatre Review* 15(1): 93–104.

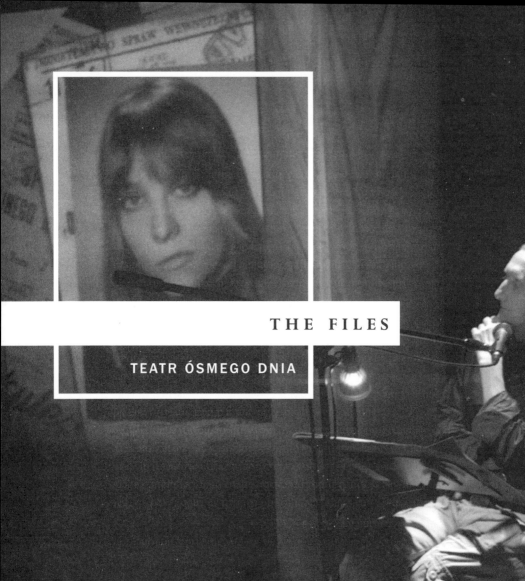

THE FILES

TEATR ÓSMEGO DNIA

IMAGE 1.1 Adam Borowski (left) and Ewa Wójciak (right) in Teatr Ósmego Dnia's production of *The Files*. Teatr Ósmego Dnia, Poznań, 2007. *Photograph by Przemysław Graf.*

THE FILES[1]

TRANSLATED BY BILL JOHNSTON

EWA. Letter written to Tadeusz when I was 19. Christmas 1970:

—"I'm sick of family holidays and all this stupid sentimentality. All I want is the few of you, who I can love and share my illusions with. (All this high-flown nonsense is going to make me puke.) I really believe in you, and in the Theatre, the

---

[1] For the New York presentation of *The Files* at 59E59 Theaters in October and November 2008, the following recorded text written by Bill Johnston was accompanied by black-and-white images of Poland under communism at the beginning of the performance:

> The Theatre of the Eighth Day—Teatr Ósmego Dnia—was founded in the 1960s in Poznań in western Poland as a student theater company associated with the Adam Mickiewicz University. Its heyday, in the mid-1970s, coincided with the beginnings of a protest movement that was to lead eventually to the birth of Solidarity. In this period the communist authorities, never willing to tolerate dissent, became even more suspicious of anything that smacked of alternative ways of thinking. The members of the Theatre of the Eighth Day were constantly harassed by the SB— the Służba Bezpieczeństwa or Security Service, the secret police of the Ministry of Internal Affairs—who also attempted to control or influence the activities of the company, often through a network of so-called secret associates—that is to say, informers, some of whom were close to the company members. Each 'secret associate' was given a pseudonym by their contact in the SB. Years later, after the fall of communism, the detailed files kept by the secret police were archived by the new Polish government. In 2005, the Theatre of the Eighth Day was presented with the files concerning the surveillance of their activities in the late 1970s and early 80s. In the files—maintained in great detail in stilted bureaucratic language laced with communist mumbo-jumbo—they discovered not only that the network of informers surrounding the company was much more extensive than they had realized; they also learned of attempts to infiltrate the company by secret police plants, and of numerous efforts to sabotage their work. The following play was written in response to the newly uncovered files.

brotherhood, and all that quixotic errantry; outside of that there's nothing for me. I'm incurably infected with the need for ideas and for the handful of people who have the same fixation."

ADAM. "It would never have occurred to me to become an actor. I'm discovering a captivating new world, half Theatre, half not, a world in which by learning everything from the beginning, you gain control over yourself. [. . .] It's like a drug. This Theatre [. . .] is quickly becoming the most important thing in my life, because working among people who have such an exceptional way of seeing friendship, love, creative work, it's a great adventure of discovery, of creating something extraordinary."

MARCIN. "A tiny rehearsal space with a pillar in the middle and a cramped little room by the men's john in the Od Nowa club. That's where we meet. The air's always thick with smoke, emotions, raised voices. On the table there's books and often a little vodka. Words appear: freedom, truth, mission—half-sacred words uttered straightforwardly, with a sense of conviction that they mean what they say. There's talk of Dostoevsky, Brzozowski, Camus. It's like a monastic order of the initiated, a handful of friends, conspirators sort of, who think the world can still be set right by way of the Theatre. For me this is the most important thing, this handful of people may be more important than the Theatre itself, because without them a Theatre like this could not even exist."

TADEUSZ. "I think there must be some overarching thing that connects a group of people who want to live their lives together. What's important is the idea of community, of building a different place, a different world, overcoming stereotypes. But what really connects us is the Theatre, our work. A Theatre that will serve its audience, not entertain, not shock. It ought to help them. Present them with new questions. And of course, we're connected by love. The love between us."

ADAM. Ministry of Internal Affairs

Case: Investigative operation codename "Hercules."

—Name of target: Marcin Kęszycki.

—Nature of case: Anti-state activity involving violation of civil and legal order.

—Reason for opening case: Target possesses hostile attitude to present reality.

—Threat (actual): Support of individuals engaged in hostile political activity.

—Affected area: Academic.

—Location: Adam Mickiewicz University and Theatre of the Eighth Day.

—Source: Secret Associate.

—Individual sources of information utilized in case: Secret Associate codename "Ojo," Secret Associate codename "Jacek," Secret Associate codename "Jan."

EWA. Excerpt from personal file

—Name of target: Adam Borowski.

—Codename: "Adam."

—Nature of case: Hostile activity as part of Theatre of the Eighth Day.

—Category of case: Appended to investigative operation codename "Scorpion."

—Basis for opening case: Field intelligence.

—Nature of crime or suspected crime: Illegal political propaganda.

—Location of commission of crime: Academic and artistic circles.

—Sector of economy negatively affected: Culture and the arts.

TADEUSZ. Ministry of Internal Affairs

Investigative operation: codename "Nana."

—Name of target: Ewa Wójciak.

—Nature of case: Deep involvement in hostile political activity in connection with the "Players" and work in support of the so-called Student Solidarity Committee; hostile activity as part of Theatre of the Eighth Day.

MARCIN. Extract from personal file

Name of target: Tadeusz Janiszewski.

Vetting operation codename "Judas."

—Nature of case: Anti-state activity in violation of civil and legal order; hostile activity as part of Theatre of the Eighth Day.

EWA. "I felt that I'd find kindred spirits and that with them I'd build a new order in which I'd be able to grow, think, trust, and live, and that otherwise I'd have no life at all. It wasn't a vision of a Theatre so much as a vision of a monastic brotherhood. We're together in order to do something, and so each of us needs to work and grow, if only so as to be able to offer the same to other people."

ADAM. Profile prepared by Regional Police Headquarters in Kraków. Marcin Kęszycki, son of Wojciech, graduated in Polish Literature 1977. Currently unemployed, actor of Theatre of the Eighth Day, Category D—unfit for military service in peacetime. [. . .] Initiator of Student Solidarity Committee in Poznań, participant in illegal gatherings, initiator and participant of many actions (petitions, leafleting, etc.), highly aggressive toward representatives of police and security services.

MARCIN. Ewa Wójciak, daughter of Juliusz, graduated in Polish from Adam Mickiewicz University 1974. [. . .] One of the more negative individuals, has instigated and carried out a series of actions of an anti-socialist nature, instigator of Student Solidarity Committee in Poznań. Close associate of Jerzy Nowacki, Stanisław Barańczak, and Marcin Kęszycki. Initiator of the most provocative performances.

EWA. Adam Borowski, son of Roman, first year student at State Academy for the Fine Arts, associate of the "Players," incited students in Poznań to take part in a mass said for Stanisław Pyjas.

ADAM. "My characters involved the exploration and exposure of various dark sides of my personality. In the Theatre I'm most passionate about 'vampiring' all that is squalid, dirty, petty, shamefully hidden—the darkest recesses of the soul. [. . .] Imagine a journey from Alyosha in *The Brothers Karamazov* to the ringmaster of a "Socrealistic Circus." Two extreme figures who have to fit in one person: naive decency and ruthless premeditation, honest faith and intoxication with power. I think I'm always oscillating between those two extremes. [. . .]"

EWA. Confidential

Marked: Important

Poznań, December 16, 1977

Introduction of SA codename "Wojciech" to be facilitated by fact that he works in local student film club, while SA "Spider" works in student club in Szczecin. Also by fact that SA "Spider" enjoys trust of main target of our operation.

Introduction to be carried out as follows:

SA "Wojciech" will be given task of traveling to Szczecin and meeting SA "Spider" as if by chance. During this meeting, among other things, he will start conversations about Polish opposition, censorship, etc. Among other things he will ask whether this kind of activity is going on in Szczecin student circles, indicating he knows little about what is going on in Poznań. He will mention he knows about Barańczak and the students in the literature departments, and that he's heard of Theatre of the Eighth Day and the Student Solidarity Committee. At the same time he will express doubts about whether their activities are as serious as rumors suggest. During conversation he will make it clear he is on side of the opposition. It will be explained to SA "Wojciech" that SA "Spider" is suspected of opposition activity in Szczecin, with support of contacts in the Poznań opposition. His task is to determine if this is in fact the case. In order for SA "Wojciech's" meeting with SA "Spider" to look accidental, SA "Wojciech" will be instructed to propose to his film club the idea of making a documentary film about student circles in Szczecin. [. . .] SA "Spider" in turn will be informed that a student arts activist, i.e.

SA "Wojciech" (SA "Spider" will be given his name), is coming to Szczecin to learn about student circles there. SA "Spider" will also be informed that SA "Wojciech" will probably be talking with student activists, including "Spider" himself, with the purpose of making a documentary film about Szczecin students. If the meeting comes about, "Spider" must engage "Wojciech" in conversation about political issues and make him understand he is on the side of the opposition. SA "Spider" will be told that SA "Wojciech" is suspected by Security Services in Poznań of working for the opposition and needs to be checked out thoroughly. For this reason SA "Spider" should first gain SA "Wojciech's" trust and then put him in touch with our target W. Fenrych. In this way, when SA "Wojciech" meets with Fenrych, he will simultaneously be able to monitor any activities he may be engaged in. SA "Spider" will also be able to monitor Fenrych indirectly. For Fenrych to agree, it will be necessary to suggest to him that among other things SA "Wojciech" has access to a photographic workshop. Carrying out the operation in such a way will prevent the two secret associates from revealing their identities to each other and furthermore will allow us to ensure the tasks assigned to them are carried out. Part of the present plan is the combined plans of action for SA "Wojciech" and SA "Spider."

Deputy Director, Division III

Regional Police Headquarters in Poznań

Major K. Górny

TADEUSZ. Profile

Secret Associate codename "Wojciech"

Registration number 19883

"Wojciech," age 21, Polish nationality and citizenship, class background: intelligentsia, bachelor, non party member, third-year student in Philosophy at Adam Mickiewicz University in Poznań, resident of Poznań.

Subject agreed voluntarily to cooperate. [. . .] SA was remunerated on numerous occasions. [. . .] Appears regularly for appointments. Carries out tasks assigned to him in a satisfactory manner. Despite lack of direct contact with opposition circles, SA attempts to indirectly acquire information of interest to us.

Inspector, Section III, Division III

Corporal J. Janów

ADAM. Secret Associate codename "Ojo"

Secret Associate codename "Jacek"

SA codename "Jan"

SA codename "Generał"

SA codename "Karolina"

SA codename "J-17"

SA codename "Kazimierz"

SA codename "Mietek"

SA codename "Scot"

SA codename "Janina"

SA codename "Janusz"

SA codename "Kuba"

TADEUSZ. SA codename "Mirek"

SA codename "Heniek"

SA codename "Piotr"

SA codename "Dalia"

SA codename "Washington Irving"

SA codename "Rafał"

SA codename "Ludwik"

SA codename "Chairman"

SA codename "Thunder"

SA codename "Andrzej"

SA codename "Papyrus"

SA codename "Zbrzozło"

EWA. SA codename "Marek"

SA codename "Paweł"

SA codename "Frenchman"

SA codename "Justyna"

SA codename "Robert"

SA codename "Mosquito"

SA codename "Krzysztof"

SA codename "Mietek"

SA codename "K"

SA codename "Cracovian"

MARCIN. SA codename "Vega"

SA codename "Home"

SA codename "Biologist"

SA codename "Detail"

SA codename "Leon"

SA codename "Stanisław Brzozowski"

SA codename "Ace"

SA codename "Hygienist"

SA codename "Józef"

SA codename "Z"

SA codename "Wojciech"

SA codename "Spider"

EWA. General assessment of Poznań circle

Active members of Poznań circle have low expectations of their own opportunities for action. There is a widely held belief that the entire opposition in Poznań consists of Stanisław Barańczak and a handful of young writers, plus 10 individuals from Theatre of the Eighth Day, plus about 20 students (mostly from the Department of Polish Literature).

Signed, Secret Associate codename "Return"

ADAM. Confidential. Marked: Important single copy

Official memo re: Theatre of the Eighth Day

On November 25 of the current year, at 9:00 p.m. in Od Nowa student club there was a performance by Theatre of the Eighth Day entitled *We Have To Confine Ourselves To What Has Been Called Paradise On Earth*. About 40 individuals aged 17 to 25 gathered in one of the rooms at the club. The play began punctually at 9 with the line:

"From generation to generation the information was passed down to us from the Paris Commune about the hour that would come . . ."

At a later point one of the actresses read the central idea of the play: ". . . freedom cannot be reconciled with earthly bread in plenty for everyone, because there is not and has never been anything so unbearable for human society as freedom . . ."

EWA. Alexander Solzhenitsyn:

"You have to enter there without aching for the life filled with warmth that has been left outside the gate. You have to tell yourself on the threshold: my life is over. A little too soon, but later it will be even harder. I no longer have anything of my own; my loved ones are dead to me and I am dead to them. From this moment on my body is something alien and useless to me; only my spirit and my conscience are still valuable and important."

MARCIN. Plan to make use of Secret Associate codename "Heniek" in operation to search premises of Theatre of the Eighth Day in Od Nowa club. Because of the position he occupies in Od Nowa student club, Secret Associate codename "Heniek" has natural access to all keys used on premises of said club. Therefore I propose arranging a meeting with SA in hotel room in the immediate future and giving him the task of obtaining keys of Od Nowa club and making copies of said keys. I propose presenting SA with this task in written form, accompanied with caution about maintaining full secrecy in these plans and actions.

Inspector, Section III, Division III

TADEUSZ. Source: Secret Associate codename "Heniek"

Report received by: Senior Staff Sergeant Michał Rychter

Information recorded on basis of oral relation by SA

During the meeting SA informed me that [. . .] the members and supporters of Theatre of the Eighth Day are a highly closed group of people. They do not discuss sensitive political issues with outsiders, but they behave in an arrogant way. [. . .]

Tasks:

—Pay attention to anything said about relationship of the Theatre to "Student Solidarity Committee" and about attempts to use this organization for their own purposes.

—Monitor all cultural events at Od Nowa club and immediately pass on information about any politically harmful activities.

—Provide list of persons associated with Theatre of the Eighth Day and identify those who are given free passes to the club.

Comments: SA is not liked by those in Theatre of the Eighth Day group because he is always scolding members of the Theatre for leaving a mess in the club. I advised SA to be very cautious in his contacts with the Theatre.

ADAM. Source: SA codename "Heniek"

Report received by: Senior Staff Sergeant Michał Rychter

Location: Outdoors

At the meeting SA delivered key to space used by Theatre of the Eighth Day in Od Nowa club.

Remarks: During delivery of key SA seemed highly nervous and frightened. Stated that key is absolutely essential for the purpose of installing listening device in theater space. Said that he is not convinced by other reassurances, and asks for extreme discretion, because by process of elimination the Theatre may figure out he was the one who provided key.

Repeated his requests several times.

SA also informed that from time to time the Theatre organizes alcoholic binges, but these are result of momentary decisions and it is hard to predict when company will arrange such an event.

EWA. Coded message no. 5927

Confidential

December 13, 1975, 4:00 p.m.

To: Director, Division III, Regional Police Headquarters in Poznań

Decoded at 5:40 p.m.

In period December 2–7, during 15th anniversary of "Kontrasty" Student Arts Center in Szczecin, there was a series of events including a performance by Theatre of the Eighth Day from Poznań of their play *We Have To Confine Ourselves To What Has Been Called Paradise On Earth*. The play presented a pessimistic and existential view of the restrictions on freedom of contemporary people and included the following quotes:

"Now we have absolute freedom, each person belongs to everyone and everyone to each . . ."

"Now and always, nine-tenths of people are people, while one-tenth are those who have lost any sort of individuality; they need to be killed."

"Every 30 years the powers that be have a falling out so that the masses should not get bored; boredom is a sentiment of the aristocracy . . ."

Over the course of the performance there were two instances of arson as a symbol of man being liberated from bonds that oppress him. The production ends with the line: "Everyone sharpens at his own throat the razor with which he will kill himself." We are sending this information for the sake of interest and possible exploitation. It is worth mentioning also that the above-mentioned performance was NOT reviewed by the Board of Censors in the Szczecin office of the Department for the Supervision of Press, Media, and Performances.

MARCIN. Cable

Confidential

To: Director, Division III, Regional Police Headquarters in Szczecin.

With reference to cable no. 5927 [. . .] it is informed that the performance by Theatre of the Eighth Day entitled *We Have To . . .* has been reviewed by the local Board of Censors and given permission to be presented to a student audience. According to instructions of Central Office of Department for the Supervision of Press, Media, and Performances, the regulations for student theater are less strict than for others; all quotations you quoted and setting on fire of denatured spirit were permitted by censor. The one exception is the line "they need to be killed," which does not refer to said nine-tenths of people and one-tenth of authorities, at least in the text passed by the censor.

TADEUSZ. Fyodor Dostoevsky:

"There never was freedom or equality without despotism, but in the herd there has to be equality. My conclusion is completely at odds with the initial idea that is my starting point. I begin with unlimited freedom and end with unlimited despotism. Yet I have to stress that there is not, nor can there be, any other solution to social questions. Humanity has to be divided into two unequal parts; one-tenth is given personal freedom and unrestricted power over the remaining nine-tenths. The latter lose their individuality, they become a herd, and boundless obedience leads them by way of transformations to primal innocence, a kind of prehistoric paradise in which, nevertheless, they will be obliged to labor."

EWA. "So if this nine-tenths exists and no one knows what to do with them, maybe it would be better to just blow them up?"

TADEUSZ. "Since the idea is practically unfeasible we have to confine ourselves to what has been called paradise on earth."

MARCIN. Confidential

Marked: Important

Single copy

Official memo concerning behavior and activities of Ewa Wójciak

While present at the Od Nowa student club on 10/11 of current year, Ewa Wójciak led a discussion about the group's theatrical activities. [. . .] Later in the evening there was consumption of large amounts of alcohol; only Adam Borowski did not drink. After several glasses of vodka Ewa Wójciak stated that she was bored by ideological-programmatic theorists, stated that she preferred to act, and act uncompromisingly. During subsequent conversation Ewa Wójciak stated that the present curriculum in elementary and secondary schools is inadequate, and therefore she has undertaken to write a new curriculum.

Following facts concerning Ewa Wójciak's behavior are worth underlining:

—She does not actually take part in any programmatic or ideological discussions, and does not express herself on these topics. She always takes an extreme position when discussing ideas for action.

—As concerns her comments about the system, she always takes a very hostile position toward any manifestations of the life of the state and the Communist Party.

—She employs an ironic and malicious tone on the subject of state and institutional holidays, councils, plenums.

—She tries to convince junior members of the Theatre of the foolishness of party members, party and state activists, and functionaries of the People's Police and the Security Services.

—She adds emphasis to all she says with extremely vulgar language. To be added to file.

Senior Staff Sergeant Michał Rychter.

EWA. From performance notes (1977):

"There was one young kid that wanted to pour gasoline over dogs and set them alight in public places, because, as he said: 'No one's ever set fire to dogs, and people love dogs, a dog is a man's best friend. Human torches have lost their interest.' [. . .] All rebellion and protest, all revolutions for centuries now have been defeated, and those defeats have also lost their interest. This is a time of universal tedium and stupefaction. Rebels and revolutionaries have also lost interest in their own revolutionary aspirations. [. . .] Because this is a time of boredom and ridicule. Until boredom and ridicule also lose their interest. Watch out, I beg you, watch out! Silence comes so imperceptibly, and downfalls are so gentle and so convincing. And appeasing the conscience is so very easy."

ADAM. Poznań, March 3, 1977

Confidential

Marked: Important

Single copy

Plan of operational actions in the matter of operation codename "Hercules."

On March 16, 1977, a search was conducted of Kęszycki's apartment with purpose of obtaining proof of illegally acquired earnings. Such proof was not obtained, but as a result of search the following items among others were confiscated:

—34 issues of *Kultura* journal published in Paris and books of poetry by Czesław Miłosz and Jacek Bierezin published by Instytut Literacki in Paris.

[. . .]

Action must be undertaken to:

—Expose and document his hostile activities. [. . .]

—Isolate him from the circle in which he works, amongst other things distancing him from other members of Theatre of the Eighth Day.

—Engage in harassment with the goal of changing his field of interests and discouraging him from further pursuing hostile activity.

—Monitor target permanently, closely, and systematically via personal sources of information, i.e., SA "Generał," SA "J-17," and SA "Karolina," and with the aid of technical operating equipment record his speech, behaviors, interests, and contacts at the university. [. . .]

Director, Section III, Division III

TADEUSZ. Poznań, March 17, 1977

Senior Staff Sergeant Władysław Kriger

Inspector, Section III, Division III

Confidential

Official memo

On March 16, 1977, we conducted a search of an apartment belonging to citizen Marcin Kęszycki [. . .]. Upon our entry into the apartment Marcin Kęszycki behaved rather aggressively toward us. Other members of the household were calm and collected. Search began in the room Marcin shares with his brother. Marcin Kęszycki kept asking what basis there was for the search. He questioned the legality of the warrant, asked which police station we were from, and then began to simulate mental illness. At one moment he attempted to snatch and destroy a handwritten document. When questioned about the appeal he wrote to peasants, explained that said document was a letter to his girlfriend of an intimate nature. The above-named had to be repeatedly called to order since he kept trying to impede us in carrying out our work. Was especially upset during search of his bookcase and desk.

MARCIN. "Whatever the family, whatever the love, the desire for ownership immediately arises. We will put an end to that desire. We will set in motion drunkenness, denunciation, slander. No distinctions. Absolute equality."

TADEUSZ. "[A]s of today, the motto of the entire globe will be: what is needed is that which is essential. Yet fear is needed, and that will be taken care of by us, the authorities. Complete obedience, complete annihilation of the individual, but every 30 years fear is unloosed, and then people start to jump at each other's throats, only to a certain point, so the crowd should not get bored."

EWA. That of course is also from Fyodor Dostoevsky's *The Possessed*.

MARCIN. Intelligence

June 7, 1977

Classified

Tadeusz Janiszewski was found guilty in 1975 of possession of a counterfeit student ID and of attempting to illegally obtain a train ticket at the student price. On May 19, 1977, he was given a suspended 18-month sentence, a 15,000 złoty fine, three years of supervision by the parole board, and was ordered to find permanent employment, for smuggling 350 US dollars out of the country. [. . .] In addition he was found to be in possession of 8 ounces of gold products (rings, bracelets) with receipts indicating he was trading in them.

TADEUSZ. "The parole officer was an agent of the secret police, of course. He harassed the people I was renting a room from, and forced them to ask me to leave. One time he came and asked: 'Is this the residence of Tadeusz Juda Janiszewski?' The lady whose place it was replied: 'There's no "Ju" living here!' He kept after me about not having a job, then when I did have work he'd arrange it so I'd get fired. I took whatever the Employment Office was offering. If I hadn't, they could have put me away for avoiding work. I was a waiter, a fire stoker . . . [. . .] One time I was working in a big cafe with a dance hall. I did whatever needed doing—took out the trash, stoked the heating stove, carried in tables, served the waiters' personal stash of vodka, tidied the yard. At that time there was a theater festival where we got an award. My friends from the Theatre came running to the cafe; they showed the waitresses my photo in the paper and asked if the guy in the picture was employed here, and the waitresses couldn't believe that someone from the front page of the newspaper was working down in the boiler room."

EWA. Intelligence

June 7, 1977

Classified

A characteristic of this theater group is that aside from the anti-socialist activities they are engaged in, the majority of the actors have committed a series of offences of a criminal or financial nature, allegedly with the goal of funding the theater. In reality some of them were not employed or lived off student grants, yet they led extravagant lifestyles. They held drunken orgies in their homes to the point where neighbors had to call the police. It can be stated unambiguously that if it were not for the involvement of actors of Theatre of the Eighth Day in anti-state activities, the poet Barańczak would be isolated and would have no support.

TADEUSZ. From notes on an improvisation session, 1978: "Scheming, getting by, everyday cunning, sticking to one's hiding places and one's own wretched possessions. It'll be worse and worse; they'll know less and less, and they'll be less and less willing, convinced of their own miserable temporariness [. . .]. Ever smaller, ever more claustrophobic storehouses of apartments, bigger and bigger crowds on the buses and streetcars, every-thing more and more sterile, socialism victorious, more and more well-fed overbearing cops, ever more imposing police stations, party buildings, and military barracks. More false-hood, more fake smiles, everyone falling asleep in front of their television sets, no one knowing how to talk with one another any more."

ADAM. Confidential Document #274

February 9, 1979, 3:00 p.m.

Cryptogram

To: Director, Division III, Regional Police Headquarters in Łódź

I respectfully inform you that Marcin Kęszycki, target of oper-ation codename "Hercules" currently being conducted by this office, an actor in Theatre of the Eighth Day, a group that is an ongoing object of our attention, has been offered the lead role in a film entitled *Knight*. The film is being directed by

Nyczak or Majewski, about whom nothing else is known, at the Łódź Film Studio. Marcin Kęszycki is one of the longest-serving actors in Theatre of the Eighth Day. [. . .] He has given the productions of this company a clear anti-socialist character. It is in our interest that Marcin Kęszycki should not be given this part. I respectfully request that the local Division III be informed and carry out the task in question.

Director, Division III, Regional Police Headquarters in Poznań

Captain J. Siejek, MA

encoded: Kaczmarek, 4:00 p.m.

decoded: Juszczak, 5:25 p.m.

EWA. Cryptogram #1456

Confidential

To: Director, Division III, Regional Police Headquarters in Poznań

In response to your cryptogram I am informing you that in connection with the "Marcin Kęszycki film role" case, we conducted a conversation with the head of the Profil Film Company which is to make the film. During the conversation it was agreed that Marcin Kęszycki would not be offered this part. The rejection would be conveyed without any explanation.

Director, Division III, Regional Police Headquarters in Łódź

Lt. Colonel Czesław Chojak, MA

encoded by: Bujała

decoded by: Kaczmarek

TADEUSZ. Official memo based on monitoring of correspondence: We possess information that target Marcin Kęszycki, along with Ewa Wójciak, target of operation "Nana," was recently asked by Michał Ratyński of Warsaw to act in a film to be made privately, without permission of authorities. A screenplay based on Witold Gombrowicz's book *The Possessed* (published Paris 1973) is being prepared by Jacek Zembrzuski. In all probability the film has been sold abroad even before production begins. All those involved in its making are to take a share of the profits . . .

Director, Division III, Regional Police Headquarters in Poznań.

EWA. The cast of this film, ladies and gentlemen, was also to include David Bowie.

MARCIN. Ruling issued by Student Affairs Disciplinary Committee of State Academy of Fine Arts in Poznań

The committee finds student Adam Borowski (First Year, Department of Painting, Graphic Art, and Sculpture) guilty of failing to complete compulsory work experience. Student Borowski completed part of the experience on the basis of a documented work contract. The remaining practical experience

IMAGE 1.2 (From left to right) Tadeusz Janiszewski, Marcin Kęszycki, Adam Borowski, and Ewa Wójciak in Teatr Ósmego Dnia's production of *The Files*. Teatr Ósmego Dnia, Poznań, 2007.
Photograph by Przemysław Graf.

was deemed community service. In view of the failure of the accused to follow the requirements of the Academy, Adam Borowski is hereby issued a reprimand and a warning. The Committee offers him the opportunity to complete the missing work experience in the course of the current academic year and in consultation with the institutional Party Cell appoints citizen Jan Gawron as his personal political guardian.

EWA. From: Adam Borowski

To: President, State Academy of Fine Arts in Poznań

With reference to your request for a written declaration of the reasons why I signed the petition to restore Dr. Stanisław Barańczak's faculty status, I wish to state that:

—Stanisław Barańczak is an outstanding poet. [. . .]

—He was one of the co-founders of Theatre of the Eighth Day. [. . .]

—He is a well-known literary critic and a valued scholar. [. . .]

—I know him to be an honest and upright man.

—I believe that signing the petition to have Dr. Stanisław Barańczak's status restored is in accord with the public interest and with the laws of the People's Republic of Poland.

—My signing the petition does not conflict with my obligations as a student and activist of the Socialist Union of Polish Students and above all it is required by fundamental ethical principles.

ADAM. The Poet Stanisław Brzozowski:

"I dreamed this, I dreamed that a whole crowd of us were rushing through the night, the night was darker than it ever is, copper-colored. The glint of weaponry could be seen, and above all, that rush: around us were horses; the entire space was rushing forward. Then all at once I saw Him. There He was, God's anointed one! He was riding on some kind of wagon and shouting, yet it was not words but something else. [. . .] It was not human. At the time, I understood that voice, I knew what it meant. It meant everything. When I woke up I forgot, I forgot everything. At the time I knew what people had lived for and that they would be no more, what people had lived for and that they would be no more . . . No, there is still life within me. That alone is there. To seek, to inquire why people exist, why they must exist."

MARCIN. Secretary of the Regional Committee of the United Polish Workers' Party in Poznań, Comrade Gawroński

Memorandum re: activities of Theatre of the Eighth Day and their association with Stanisław Barańczak.

Among the 15 members of Theatre of the Eighth Day, the following are actively engaged in anti-socialist activity:

—Lech Raczak, director of the Theatre

—Maciej Rusinek [. . .]

—Marcin Kęszycki [. . .]

—Jerzy Nowacki [. . .]

—Lech Dymarski [. . .]

—Tadeusz Janiszewski [. . .]

—Waldemar Modestowicz [. . .]

—Adam Borowski [. . .]

Ewa Wójciak [. . .] despite lack of direct contact with Barańczak, is pathologically active out of hostility toward the system. All nine actors have retyped and distributed statements from the Workers' Defense Committee KOR, false information about the internal situation, hostile lampoons, letters, and petitions. [. . .]

TADEUSZ. Kraków

Confidential

To: Director, Division III, Regional Police Headquarters in Poznań

In response to cryptogram #50 of January 13, 1978 we wish to inform you that Theatre of the Eighth Day has come to Kraków to perform their play *Sale for Everyone* [. . .] The overall idea of this play involves an attempt to juxtapose grotesque images of people thrust into a world of illusion, a state of antagonistic attitudes of decadence and contestation. The actors make use of highly specific means of expression, viz.: extremely vulgar curse words, extracts from high-flown speeches, allusions, and unambiguous political slogans that are negatively aligned with Communism. The censored version of the text differed from the text as it was performed since it omitted a crucial series of sentences that, along with the chore-ographic context, constituted a violent attack on the system, on socioeconomic relations, the actions of state agencies, and international relations with countries of the socialist bloc, and at the same time illuminated the central theme of the official text. To illustrate the storyline we offer the following quotations from the text as performed: "There will eventually come such a time, a splendid ball for many of us, at the happy destination where, in a crush in the main room, there will stand the builders of the Grand Hotel . . ." In the context this song must be understood as an anthem of hope for "all work-ing people" who are building the Grand Hotel-Poland (at present accessible only to the elite and the leaders) and who will eventually assume their rightful place in it. In one of the scenes, a young student is jostled past a line of standing per-sons who beat him with various objects, viz: ropes, knotted neckties, shouting:

"The man who believed."

"Maintain your dignity, don't despair . . ."

Then there appears a character who, according to the script, is a surgeon but who in reality is a man dressed in a torn tuxedo, symbolizing a representative of the security services, who orders the student to be put in a straitjacket, saying:

"Nice clean pajamas . . ."

". . . Diagnosis?—Hysteria, neurosis, delirium . . ."

The other actors act out scenes of beating and physical abuse, they are pushed down some stairs. On a raised platform two women dance, draped with placards bearing the slogans: "faith, hope, charity, liberty, equality, fraternity, independence."

There are innumerable examples of this kind with negative undertones. A particular moment that constitutes the climax of the play is a scene entitled "The Garden," which the script describes as a loose improvisation of shouted texts from classic literature, without offering any more details. In fact it is an image of Poland chained in its borders, which it is unable to cross to get to the outside, and within which it is impossible to live, think, and work freely.

FROM THE SCENE "NICE LITTLE GARDEN," IN *SALE FOR EVERYONE*

TADEUSZ. They've made a nice little garden for us. They've leveled it all. Tidied it.

ADAM. A nice little garden.

MARCIN. Come on everyone, I'll make chains of borders for you.

TADEUSZ. Let them say anything they want here. Just so long as nothing gets out. Lithuania, my homeland, you are as health to me . . .

ADAM. You left a great void here within my home, my dear Polish literature teacher . . .

MARCIN. Hurrah! (*All singing*) Only the horses, only the horses, only the horses will I regret . . .

ADAM. Veto!

MARCIN. Hurrah!

ADAM. Veto!

TADEUSZ. We have to kill off all the anarchists, the terrorists, all the perverts, the mentally ill, the oversensitive, the different. We have to prepare the way for our successors, our sons—blood of our blood, bone of our bone. Peace and health must once again reign.

ADAM. Pornography and prostitution NO PASARÀN! We say "NO!" to the dirty thoughts of political moles. Enough corruption and depravity. Our home will never be a whorehouse.

TADEUSZ. The nation, the magnificent nation. The nation shows its muscles:

Biceps.

Abs.

Pecs.

Sphincters ready for anything . . .

What do we have here? . . . A little idea has come along . . .

ADAM. The red phone! Connecting! The left-hand switch.

MARCIN. Connecting!

TADEUSZ. Totalitarianism.

ADAM. Had it already! Over.

TADEUSZ. Fascism.

ADAM. Had it already! Over.

TADEUSZ. Parliamentary democracy.

ADAM. Had it already! Over.

TADEUSZ. Pluralism.

ADAM. Ploo ploo!

(*All singing*)

All the fishes are sleeping in the lake . . .

The penguin has a great big bill, great big bill, great big bill . . .

TADEUSZ. Family, little holy family, it's snug and warm, mamma's at home, dadda's coming back soon.

ADAM. Hold me back, hold me back or I'll get the son of a bitch.

TADEUSZ. You bastard, you piece of crap, you four-eyed jerk, you.

ADAM. You're no Pole. You fucking student. C'mere and let me give it to you.

TADEUSZ. I'll give it to you, you Jew. You eternal student. Hold me back or I'll let him have it.

ADAM. You rat's dick. You're no Pole.

TADEUSZ. And now it would be best if we all held handsies together and made one big human family.

ADAM. Bring on the girls in their regional costumes!

TADEUSZ AND MARCIN. Have them bring the kołacz!

MARCIN. The more stupid something is, the closer it is to the heart of the matter. The more stupid it is, the clearer it is. Reason hides and dodges, reason is despicable, whereas stupidity is honest and straightforward . . .

EWA. Continuation of reply to cryptogram #50

The first performance was greeted with complete disapproval, as shown by expressions of criticism and disappointment on the part of the audience. There was a somewhat different reception for the second performance, which was attended by representatives of the Kraków Student Solidarity Committee, including Bogusław Sonik, Blumsztajn, Liliana Batko, and Kensy, led by Michnik and Kuroń. This group numbered about 30 persons who throughout the whole performance greeted every scene with a wave of laughter and cheering. Personal relations between members of the Student Solidarity Committee and members of the theater company were demonstrated by the following facts:

—Correspondence before the performance by means of cards delivered by special messengers, and direct congratulations and handshakes after the performance. An attempt to organize a discussion following the play was foiled by discreet operational action. [. . .]

Director, Division III, Regional Police Headquarters in Kraków

Lt. Col. Jan Bill

MARCIN. Declaration of the Committee for Social Self-Protection (the Workers' Defense Committee or KOR)

The KOR Committee for Social Self-Protection deems it necessary to inform public opinion of the particular victimization and police and administrative harassment to which the student company Theatre of the Eighth Day has been subject since Autumn 1976. Briefly, this consists of the following: continuous surveillance of the actors, searches of their apartments (in the course of which, in March 1977, typewriters that were the property of the company were confiscated [. . .]), preposterous accusations of alleged financial wrongdoings, the proliferation of false denunciations, the denial of paid employment to members and associates of the company, systematic restrictions on their creative activities. [. . .] On April 26, 1978, five members of the company traveling to Lublin to take part in the Festival of Youth Theaters did not have time to buy tickets for the bus taking them from one train station in Warsaw to another. Despite the fact that they were prepared to pay the requisite fine, the ticket inspector summoned the police, who severely beat two of the actors, and subjected all of them to vulgar abuse. [. . .] In the courtyard of the City of Warsaw Police Headquarters on Wilcza Street, all the actors were assaulted by plain-clothes police officers and were kicked, punched, and beaten with batons. All five were held for 30 hours. A few days later, the Central Warsaw public prosecutor's office charged them with hooliganism and assault and battery of police functionaries (Articles 234, 235, and 236 of the criminal code, with reference to Article 59). Such a charge could lead to prison sentences of up to 12 years, and the link to Article 59 makes a suspended sentence impossible. [. . .]

Warsaw, May 29, 1978

ADAM. Warsaw, September 5, 1978

Confidential

Marked: Important

Operational plan to secure the trial of five members of Theatre of the Eighth Day.

—The premises of the Central Warsaw District Courthouse will be secured by functionaries of Bureau B equipped with film and still cameras for the purpose of documenting possible hostile or provocational actions, demonstrations, etc.

—In the vicinity of the courthouse there will be two motorized patrols of uniformed officers for the purpose of interventional action in case of necessity.

—The police post inside the courthouse building will be reinforced with six additional officers.

—The participation of Polish journalists is being supervised by the Central Committee of the Polish United Workers Party and the Central Office of the Socialist Union of Polish Students.

—The participation of foreign (Western) journalists is being supervised by Division VII of Department II of the Ministry of Internal Affairs.

—During the process there will be 35 functionaries from the Warsaw Police and 10 persons from the Ministry of Internal Affairs present in the Courtroom.

Inspector [. . .], Department III, Ministry of Internal Affairs

Lt. K. Ziomek

TADEUSZ. Secret Associate codename "Jacek"

Meeting location: "Crossroads"

September 11, 1978

Confidential

Marked: Important

Information recorded on basis of oral account by SA—shorthand notes: A small crowd gathered in front of the doorway to the courtroom. [. . .] When the doors opened everyone began to push their way in. In the end, so many people entered the courtroom that members of the public were sitting in the dock. The judge cleared the room and ordered everyone to go and obtain passes. [. . .] A line formed at the door of the secretary's office, but the KOR people allowed their own leaders to go first. In this way, among others, Barańczak, Brandys, and Woroszylski were able to enter. [. . .] Nervousness among the

Theatre group started to make itself felt. The lads from KOR saved the situation by making jokes. At this point I had the "great undeniable honor" of exchanging a few words with Michnik, Kuroń, and Lityński. I also conversed, without knowing it, with Blumsztajn. The conversations were meaningless, just like the above-mentioned "words with the masters." Apparently, that day the proceedings were recorded by the actor Maciej Rejzacher. In addition, the proceedings were also recorded by the journalist Jankowska (I think that's her name), the radio patroness of Filipek, and his girlfriend, while Alina kept running to the bathroom to change the cassette tape. During the breaks, reports came about what was going on in the courtroom. It was mostly about the "tactics of the brilliant lawyers," who were the topic of the day and heroes of the cause: Lawyers Siła-Nowicki, Olszewski, Szczuka, and Grabiński. People were telling one another the stories of these people's lives, which one is which and how long each of them had been in prison. [. . .] People swapped conversational partners at frequent intervals. [. . .] Toward the end of the proceedings, before the verdicts were announced, a few people started to worry [. . .] that the secret police would round everyone up and throw them in jail. With this in mind, Leon from Lublin (he's finished his doctoral thesis but he has no money to publish it) ran off to visit all the floors and check out the "balance of forces." After the verdicts were announced, no one was upset. The verdicts were seen as strange—six months suspended for a period of four years. The ridiculous fine of 3,000 złoty to be paid to the Society for the Disabled was regarded as ambiguous.

EWA (*singing*). Who are broken-hearted,
who have yielded to despair,
who are frozen, petrified with fear,
who howl in powerlessness.
Who have gone blind,
who have long lost their sense of direction,

who are losing, losing strength.
Who have gone mad,
who drink,
who have fallen,
who if they knew about themselves .˙. .
who should try, you should try.
Who maybe still can be filled
with dense, bitter love.
Who are broken-hearted,
who yielded,
who are mad,
who howl,
who have weakened,
who have gone blind,
who will catch fire,
of whom there are. . .

MARCIN. Zbigniew Gluza

From review in *Politechnik* magazine, no. 35, 1978

Wrocław

We're gathering outside the Polski Theatre. Something momentous is about to happen. All we know is that several theater companies are to come out into the street. Theatre of the Eighth Day, the British company Triple Action Theatre, GIT from Spain, and perhaps some solo artists. There are several hundred people in the square; we're waiting. [. . .] Suddenly, from behind the Theatre there comes a soft song in multiple voices. A moment later a sizable group of people appears. The wordless song gathers in strength. There are banners. Placards. Torches light up the dark alleyway. Liberté d'expression! Liberté d'expression! Poles, Englishmen, Spaniards. And more. We join them. More and more people are singing. We chant. [. . .] In almost every window dark silhouettes appear; I have the impression I can hear shouts and cheers . . . [. . .] The torches reach us. The tension heightens, emotions intensify. Liberté d'expression! Liberté! The singing acquires an unexpected power, fusing into one all-embracing appeal . . . Someone runs alongside the procession, repeating in a strange, unnatural voice: "Let's try in Polish, in Polish now, surely we can, let's try. . ." But the word "wolność," freedom, dies away at the first attempts. Liberté! Liberté!

TADEUSZ. Central Office of the Socialist Union of Polish Students—after obtaining detailed intelligence from the Ministry of Internal Affairs, Warsaw, May 5, 1978.

Given the necessity of the continued existence of this theater company, the Arts Committee of the Central Office of the Socialist Union of Polish Students proposes among other things the following option:

[. . .] A gradual replacement of members of the company and the introduction of new persons. This will be difficult insofar as the company comprises a tight-knit informal group in the nature of a commune, within which infiltration and provocation are in practical terms extremely difficult. Individual new members will rapidly become corrupted under the influence of the existing group. [. . .] There is the possibility of further operational activity as an outcome of the court cases of individual company members. The successive suspension of members of the company, including the director, will make it possible to replace the director and lead effectively to a complete rotation of the company personnel.

MARCIN. Official memo

Confidential

To be carried out by Division III

Deadline: June 30, 1978

To involve leadership of Division III

In relation to all targets and their sympathizers, measures will be taken to obtain incriminating materials providing evidence of the commission of criminal offenses or violations of ethical and/or moral standards. Targets: Lech Raczak, Ewa Wójciak, and Adam Borowski, who regularly indulge in excesses of alcohol, will be directed by the police to a drying-out facility. [. . .]

Extract from improvisation entitled "Politburo"

(Oh, How We Lived In Dignity)

(*All singing*, *in Russian*)

"Ekh, zagulyal, zagulyal, paren' molodoy, molodoy . . ."

TADEUSZ. I like it here. This is a great bunch of people.

MARCIN. Should old acquaintance be forgotten.

TADEUSZ. We're the elite.

MARCIN. The crème de la crème.

TADEUSZ. I'm the elite of the elite.

MARCIN. Aha! This looks like some kind of dictatorship.

TADEUSZ. A dictatorship, that's right.

MARCIN. Give 'em an inch and they take a mile..

TADEUSZ. Next item: Alimentation.

ADAM. A potato, a potato of superhuman proportions. Let's plant the potato along the exit routes, the King's Trail, all our tiny little sections of motorway, in two neat rows, one on each side, a potato, a potato of superhuman proportions. . .

TADEUSZ. Lots of starchy ones, lots of fatty ones, like before the socialist working day commences.

MARCIN. Behold the alchemy of our agrarian revolution. The transformation of starch into divine human form.

TADEUSZ. A one-sided dialogue. We have to activate, mobilize grassroots social initiatives—make them look spontaneous—and provoke, provoke. I can't stand it any more, take this burden of responsibility from my shoulders. I don't understand these plans of yours. All these balance sheets, finances, agrotechnical operations . . .

MARCIN. Józu, Józu, why did you go there, those are not good people, they'll hurt you.

TADEUSZ. Taking advantage of every second of my weakness, knife in the back, I know you only too well, you revisionist fantasists, you gentlemen with short names starting with C. Cliques, coteries, corporations, oppositions . . .

MARCIN. I wish to lodge a complaint!

TADEUSZ. Who can you complain to here?

MARCIN. "*Habemus papam.*"

ADAM. The delegations are coming . . . Let's have our picture taken, come on.

TADEUSZ. At this point in time, I would like to offer the warmest welcome to the schoolchildren gathered here, to my dear little scouts, my dear combatants, my dear elderly.

—Leonid!

—Nicolae!

Several fanatical opponents have sought to assume power here. But we will never agree. Behind us stands the people, the entire godfearing nation, mineral resources, coal deposits, mines, steelworks, non-ferrous metals, superphosphates, superfertilizers, super super super. And the peasant doesn't invest in cattle for slaughter . . . and he doesn't get fed . . .

(*All singing*)

Trabajo si! Samba no!

EWA. "There exists a boundary of despair, beyond which one does nothing but howl for redress, beyond which one kills. Every night I think about ways to get rid of a few guys from over there. What kind of goddamn earth is this where young women waste their nights slitting throats. Yet those dreams enable me to live, enable me to accept each daily portion of hatred and despair."

MARCIN. Confidential

Single copy

Official Memo

This is to report that on May 16, in the course of a conversation with Personal Contact "MS," I obtained the following information: Theatre of the Eighth Day participated in the

Youth Theater Festival in Lublin on May 10–13, 1979, with a new play. [. . .] It is entitled *Oh How We Lived In Dignity*. Both the artistic value and the performance of the play were praised by the festival jury. [. . .] This is not a political play like *Sale* . . . or their other anti-system productions. The full script was passed by the censor. Thematically speaking, the play concerns existential problems. It takes place at the borderline of delirium being suffered by a person who is seeking higher values, [. . .] and who is unable to exist without "God." The questions that emerge from the play, questions about how to live, rather, concern new values, and their subtext does not constitute an attack on current reality. [. . .]

TADEUSZ. "Ladies and gentlemen, allow me to tell you our tragic story. We are disinherited sons. I think we understand ourselves here. After all, we come from a single father. We are oppressed by the same boot, yet we have the right to speak, and you have the right to listen. We all have the right not to consent."

EWA. Letter from me to Marek Erlich

Gorzyń, August 20, 1980

"We've been here since the beginning of August, working on a new play. [. . .] I don't know what it's going to be about; for sure it's emerging from optimistic beliefs about the independence of the human soul. [. . .] Dozens of years, landscapes, people are to appear in it . . . And there'll be the strangest meetings, perhaps between the hanged Decembrist Sergei Muravev-Apostol and a vocational school student who slit his wrists with a piece of razor in the john. [. . .] The epic of the strike is a big experience for us. I thought about going up to Gdańsk, then we found out that it's all shifting, or rather, catching on in more and more places. That awful TV news with the leader's speech! Luckily, it turns out that today's communists are complete morons and they're incapable of handling things discreetly and smoothly. Bydgoszcz, Świnoujście, Nowa Huta—this is the response to theirs machinations. Though I don't know why I'm telling you all this, you know it perfectly well already."

TADEUSZ. Description of threat (actual)

The difficult political and economic situation in the country has led to an increase in hostile activities by Marcin Kęszycki, target of operation code name "Hercules." On August 30, 1980, in the reading room of the International Press and Book Club (EMPIK), the above-mentioned individual, along with Adam Borowski (target of operation code name "Adam"), inserted leaflets containing information about the demands of the striking workers into certain magazines. Independent of this, during the strike by city transportation workers, both of them put flags in the national colors at streetcar stops.

Director, Division III, Regional Police Headquarters in Poznań

ADAM. "New Year's wishes for the streetcar driver"

I wish you great journeys, nightmares, and an afterworld.
And that you should dance in the Rio de Janeiro carnival.
I wish you tears, a knife, and blood.
And that you should tremble to see the eyes of Christ
on the ceiling of a Venetian temple.
And on, and on.
That you should sing and conspire.
That God should watch over you
and that you should not need Him.
That they should not hang you
before you've had time to pack your suitcase
my friend . . .

EWA. Article I wrote for *Odmowa* magazine, issue number 1, 1980:

A journalist for the *London Observer* once asked Vladimir Bukovsky how it was that he was never broken by the KGB. "It was inner freedom," responded Bukovsky. "When a person possesses inner freedom, the source of which is being true to oneself and one's friends, no one can take it away. It's easier to take one's own life. [. . .] In a political system whose success depends on the absolute terrorization of the citizens and in which all social relations are tainted with falsehood, being true to oneself, inner freedom, and human solidarity pose a terrible threat to the authorities." [. . .] Inner freedom is individual freedom; its scope is acquired as a person comes to know it. My years of work in the Theatre of the Eighth Day allowed me to understand that one can free oneself from police terror, from servitude, and from an awful passivity toward these things, only through the creation of values, through increasing one's own personal inner freedom, from the practice of spirituality. When fighting against falsehood, violence, and hatred, it is so easy to be poisoned by them. [. . .] All the more, then, it is a cardinal discovery to realize that one is a combination of that which is collective and shared, and that which is solitary and doubting. And also, that one can yield to collective elation with a clear conscience only when at the other side we feel the solid ground of a mind capable of learning and doubting. [. . .]

EWA (*singing* "Dance little girl"). Dance little girl
  Weep little girl
  Your closest friend is soon to die
  he will not answer your most important questions
  but the sun will arise once more and your friend
  will be a lark a green-colored leaf
  a silver lake.
  Dance little girl
  weep little girl
  those who murdered your freedom are here
  they will grope its sunlit flesh
  and overcome it, your eyes will fade
  but they will open once again
  and it will transpire that your freedom
  can never be tarnished.
  Dance, weep, and love
  love us in your purity
  you'll hear the inhuman voices of those who suffer
  you'll see the empty eyes of those living in poverty
  folly will begin to entice and entrap
  from great stages

you'll feel you are too weak
but your blood will grow thicker and darker
it will teach you anger.
Dance little girl
weep little girl
may your anger come of age.

EAT THE HEART OF YOUR ENEMY

MICHAŁ BAJER

CHARACTERS

MAURICE TANSKY

THÉODULE GRANVIL

MANON DELORME

JEAN JEAN

EMMA ZEIDLER

IVAN RUBINSTEIN

BLANCHE DE LA MOLE

ERNEST ZEIDLER

EAT THE HEART OF YOUR ENEMY

TRANSLATED BY BENJAMIN PALOFF

The action takes place in an apartment at 12 Place Vendôme on Tuesday, October 16, 1849, between 4:59 and approximately 6:30 in the evening.

A salon covered in vertical-striped wallpaper.

In the far wall, a window obscured by thick drapes. In the wall to the right, a door leading to the foyer.

In the foreground, on the left, an operating table on which lies the corpse of Frédéric Chopin. The body is covered by a white sheet; only the ribcage is exposed. There is a small case on the floor next to the table with surgical instruments, a basin, a water pitcher, and a towel. On the right, a modest writing desk piled with paper.

Additionally, the salon has a sofa, a few armchairs, chairs, and stools. There are also a few small tables: one short, beside the sofa; one round . . . Some candlesticks, a vase with withered flowers . . . Of course, there could be far less furniture, or it could be different. There is a broom leaning against one of the walls.

There are two figures on stage:

Théodule Granvil. 23 years old. Wearing a surgical gown. Pants and a simple shirt underneath. The picture of social mobility. As a child, an admirer of Napoleon.

Maurice Tansky. 44 years old. Wearing several sweaters. An old, threadbare suit underneath. An ugly, unkempt fellow. But there is something in his profile, or else in his face, that might suggest a trace of some beautiful, beautiful days long past (with an emphasis on "long past").

Granvil is on the left, scalpel in hand, standing at the operating table. Tansky is sitting on the right, next to the writing desk, leaning over a piece of paper.

Long pause. No action.

TANSKY (*writing*). On Tuesday, the sixteenth of October, in the year eighteen forty-nine, at four fifty-nine in the afternoon . . .

Somewhere in the distance we hear a clock chime five times. Tansky crumples the piece of paper into a ball and throws it on the floor.

Quiet. No one moves.

TANSKY (*a moment later, writing again*). On Tuesday, the sixteenth of October, in the year eighteen forty-nine, at five zero-zero . . . (*He crumples another piece of paper into a ball and throws it on the floor.*) . . . zero one . . .

GRANVIL (*fighting the need to faint*). I can't. I'm sorry. I cannot. (*He deserts his post.*) Do you have a light?

TANSKY. Calm yourself, monsieur. (*He lights his cigarette.*) Your hands are shaking.

GRANVIL. Thank you. It's the cold.

TANSKY. Would you like a sweater?

GRANVIL. The chill does me good. At least I'm not sweating. (*He doubles over to vomit.*)

TANSKY. That's from the cigarettes.

Granvil puts out his cigarette.

TANSKY. Monsieur, you smoke too much.

GRANVIL. It's nerves.

TANSKY. He smoked a lot as well, and you see for yourself . . . Smoking causes lung cancer and diseases of the heart.

GRANVIL. That has yet to be scientifically determined.

TANSKY. Science!

Granvil throws himself toward the window.

TANSKY. You have to take a deep breath. Through the nose. Deep. That's better. Well? Come now.

GRANVIL. It's the first time that's happened. Really, I've never had that before. I never . . . Please give me a few minutes . . .

TANSKY. You have all evening. The guys from the funeral parlor are coming for him in the morning.

GRANVIL. What funeral parlor?

TANSKY. What do you mean, "what funeral parlor?"

GRANVIL. What's the name of this funeral parlor?

TANSKY. I don't know. What difference does it make?

GRANVIL. None, it's nothing. (*He digs around in his pockets.*) But in the future . . . should you have the need, monsieur . . . in a similar situation . . . here is a calling card. And the address. "Cheap and conclusive," hee hee. And please do mention that it was I who recommended them. Granvil. G-R-A-N-V-I-L. (*He coughs.*) Might you have a handkerchief?

Tansky gives Granvil a handkerchief. Granvil dips it in the water and places it over his forehead.

TANSKY. Everything will be fine. One-two-three, and it's all done. You'll manage.

GRANVIL. I need a little time.

TANSKY. Like cutting out a chancre, it's rather like that.

GRANVIL. I feel better already.

TANSKY. Of course, it is hardly pleasant, removing a chancre, that moment when one dissects a cyst and pus pours out every-where . . . (*Granvil throws himself toward the window.*) Monsieur, I told you to breathe deeply.

GRANVIL. Did he really want this?

TANSKY. I'm sorry?

GRANVIL. Is this really what he wanted? For me to do this?

TANSKY. It is beyond doubt.

GRANVIL. He expressed himself quite clearly?

TANSKY. Quite.

GRANVIL. When? Did anyone hear him say it? Who? How can we be certain?

TANSKY. He went a step further. (*He digs around in his pockets and takes out a scrap of paper.*) Do you see?

GRANVIL. What is this?

TANSKY. Careful. (*He hands him the paper.*) He signed it with his own hand. A few hours before his death.

Granvil stares at the piece of paper.

TANSKY (*reciting from memory*). "When this cough extinguishes me, I beg that you order my body be opened, that I might not be buried alive . . ."

GRANVIL (*stammers*). ". . . And may my heart be cut from my breast, and may it be laid to rest in my Fatherland, among those flowery fields where birds soothe the soul with native songs."

TANSKY. That is, in the narrowest sense of the word, the last will of Chopin. If you please. (*He takes the paper back from Granvil.*) The matter has already been taken up by patriotic and cultural circles. Those who make opinions in society, people of high station; Princess Potocka, for instance: she is a friend of the wife of the president of your college, monsieur . . . Anyway, I do not wish to cause you stress . . . The heart is to be entombed in some church in Warsaw. The preparations are moving full steam ahead. Now everything rests in your hands.

GRANVIL. I think I would like that sweater.

TANSKY. As I suggested, monsieur.

He leaves and returns with a sweater and a bottle. He throws the sweater over Granvil's surgical coat and gives him the bottle.

TANSKY. Here. This will do you . . .

Granvil drinks.

GRANVIL. It's now or never.

He casts off the sweater and—in one leap—finds himself by the table. He takes the scalpel.

TANSKY. Just a moment!

He runs to the writing desk, takes a pen, and looks at his watch; very quickly:

On the sixteenth of October, in the year eighteen forty-nine, at five-o-four . . .

A moment of silence.

GRANVIL. It's too late. I was ready . . . Why did you interrupt me, monsieur . . .

TANSKY. Me?

GRANVIL. That half a second. I was ready! Then, not now! A split second before five-o-four.

TANSKY. Do you mean to say that it's my fault?

GRANVIL. Why did you interrupt me? No, certainly, it is not your fault . . .

TANSKY. You know, monsieur, that it would be a shame if you were to assign the blame to others for what you yourself . . .

GRANVIL. I really did not mean that you should take the blame.

TANSKY. I am merely doing my job!

GRANVIL (*yells*). I didn't say it was your fault! I'm sorry.

Silence.

TANSKY (*leans down and picks up the sweater that Granvil had thrown to the floor*). This is an expensive sweater. He brought it from Scotland. (*He brushes it off.*) Clearly, monsieur, you no longer feel cold. A moment ago, yes, but now, no. It is difficult to keep up with you.

Silence.

TANSKY. You know, monsieur, I am doing all I can to make this easy for you. Truly, everything I can. I am trying. So that we might have a pleasant . . . congenial atmosphere. For you to feel comfortable, for you to have everything you need. Do you think it's easy? That I have nothing better to do?

GRANVIL. I am sorry. I'm terribly cold. Might I have that sweater?

TANSKY. Please.

GRANVIL. Thank you.

TANSKY. And what am I to write? How should we announce it after the deed is done? "On Tuesday, the sixteenth of October, in the year eighteen forty-nine, at such-and-such an hour, Doctor Théodule Granvil, proctologist, removed Chopin's heart." But we can't write that. You know, monsieur, you know what the first question will be in people's minds? Which way! Which way did he take it out? Why did they send you here? It should have at least been a professor of cardiology.

GRANVIL. All the cardiologists have left. They're at a conference on Bora Bora.

TANSKY. And your superior?

GRANVIL. He went, too.

TANSKY. But you said it's a cardiology conference.

GRANVIL. It's a junket. None of the city's major doctors could take this case. Remember, monsieur, that he died of consumption, which is contagious. And incurable.

TANSKY. But do you even have a rough idea of where the heart is?

GRANVIL. It's just that I have little experience when it comes to the dissection of corpses. I typically treat the living.

TANSKY. Well, get to it, then! Get to it, Granvil! They got you into it, and there's no going back now. You cannot disappoint us. All it takes is one incision.

Granvil approaches the gurney. Tansky starts to laugh.

TANSKY. What a jackass! Is he fainting? He's fainting! . . . (*He laughs.*) Your parents were doctors, monsieur?

GRANVIL. I've always wanted to cure people.

TANSKY. Is that so?

GRANVIL. It is.

TANSKY. You were one of those children who set the broken paws of cats and such?

GRANVIL. Something like that.

TANSKY. Very well.

GRANVIL. You never wanted to do the same?

TANSKY. Never.

GRANVIL. I remember how, when I was 13, I first witnessed an oper-ation. It was nothing serious, some farmhand with a boil, something like that. I don't even remember whether it was performed by a doctor or a barber. It was then that I decided to study medicine.

TANSKY. How much did that barber take for the operation?

GRANVIL. Sorry?

TANSKY. I'm asking how much the barber took for performing the operation. Because he didn't do it for free.

GRANVIL. Certainly not. But I don't remember.

TANSKY. Interesting.

GRANVIL. What?

TANSKY. What you are saying, monsieur.

GRANVIL. Truly?

TANSKY. Quite . . . No one goes into medicine because he wants to cure people. Why don't you just say it, monsieur, that it is simply a matter of greasing one's palms, of getting posts in government ministries, of training sessions in Tenerife?
Am I right?

GRANVIL. We have nothing further to discuss.

TANSKY. No one feels the need to help other people. And even if they did—forgive me for saying, monsieur—no idealistic doctor would become a proctologist. Say what you please, but that is simply quite impossible. (*Silence.*) And you cannot say, monsieur, that I am mistaken.

Silence. Granvil sips from the bottle.

GRANVIL. Well, then, so what? What of it? What of it?

TANSKY. Take it easy.

GRANVIL. You're fucking right.

TANSKY. Calm yourself, monsieur.

GRANVIL. That's just how it is. I stick it in his ass . . . (*He bursts out laughing.*) . . . his ass! Fine. You understand, monsieur? I, into his! Fine. I stick it in the ass of that boar, de la Mole. And you know what? There's no holding me back. Nothing, no one, can hold me . . .

TANSKY. So long as your elder does not expose you.

GRANVIL. What are you talking about?

TANSKY. You know very well, monsieur.

GRANVIL. I do not.

TANSKY. Do you have any guarantee, monsieur, that he will not screw you over?

GRANVIL. I do.

TANSKY. What?

GRANVIL. That's my business. (*A moment later.*) I am engaged to his daughter.

TANSKY. Is she plain?

GRANVIL. It is not your affair, monsieur.

TANSKY. Surely it is her picture you keep in that locket, yes? May I see?

Granvil gives him the locket. Tansky opens it.

TANSKY. Taken by an eminent photographer?

GRANVIL. It's just a Polaroid.

TANSKY (*recognizing her*). Say no more! And how do you know, monsieur, whether she'll have you stick it in her rear as well?

GRANVIL. You would like to, huh? She loves me. Fine, then: she doesn't know a lot of guys. She was raised by nuns.

TANSKY (*returning the locket to Granvil*). At least you're a realist. Sacré-Coeur?

GRANVIL. What?

TANSKY. The school—was it Benedictine?

GRANVIL. Why?

TANSKY. Yes or no?

GRANVIL. She got back a month ago. How did you know?

TANSKY. People like Etienne always send their daughters to the Benedictines. Because it's not like they go to Sacred Heart. That's what I'm talking about. He . . . (*He motions with his head toward the operating table.*) . . . he understood it better than anyone. Do you know what the difference was between Chopin and, say, Liszt or Kalkbrenner? All three played the piano and were successful at it. But whereas Liszt and Kalkbrenner were let into the house by the servant's entrance, Chopin—and he alone—sprawled out like a lord in every one of those over-stuffed salons. When he gave a lesson, they didn't pay him like they paid everyone else. Oh no. They placed the money on his mantelpiece and left, so as not to make him uncomfortable. Because he grasped what those people were all about from the very start. That's why he was a genius. The point is to make it so that when they look into the mirror and then at you they can't see the difference. Only then will they pull down their trousers for you.

GRANVIL (*a moment later, sitting down next to Tansky*). Fine. So it's your opinion that . . .

Silence.

GRANVIL .Well? Go on, monsieur.

Silence.

GRANVIL (*standing*). OK. Don't, then. Go fuck yourself.

TANSKY. Sit down, monsieur. Do sit down! Perhaps you do not wish for this nitwit to look down on you for the rest of your life.

GRANVIL (*still standing*). I'm going to gut this ballet dancer or what-ever and get the hell out of here. (*He approaches the table, turns around immediately, and sits back down.*)

TANSKY. I can see it now, his bloated, piggish rictus, as he says: He may know how to remove hemorrhoids, but besides that this Granvil is a . . .

GRANVIL. How do you know he's bloated?

TANSKY. You said so yourself.

GRANVIL. No.

TANSKY. You said of him that he was a boar.

GRANVIL. But that does not necessarily mean that he has a fat mug.

TANSKY. Does he? Well then, monsieur, you see? It's just how I pictured him. (*He looks around. He makes sure that no one is eavesdropping under the door.*) I have a proposition for you. Please come closer. (*He reaches for the bottle.*) Damn, it's finished. Wait one moment.

He goes out and comes back with a bottle.

TANSKY. I knew there would be another one somewhere. Just between us: he used to get totally hammered. He didn't want it to get out, so that now you can chance upon a half-bottle in every corner. I found this one in the shoe cubby. (*He pours.*) Good. Now back to our affairs. The old man doesn't like you . . . I am certain that he simply cannot bear the sight of you. I don't know whether your parents had a haberdashery or a fish stall . . . It doesn't matter. The point is, I can help you. Please hear me out . . . I am certain that if you were but to take a few lessons with me—we'll call them lessons, but quite informal, to be sure—well, then, I am certain that in a very short time everything would be different.

GRANVIL. I don't think I understand.

TANSKY. Monsieur, do you know the story of Pygmalion? In three months' time I could turn you into the Chopin of the proctological arts!

GRANVIL. You?

TANSKY. I do not wish to boast, and I would especially wish that this not influence our mutual relations in any way whatsoever, but my family . . . I'll give you our roll of arms, you can inspect it at your leisure.

GRANVIL. Was it you, monsieur, who promoted this painter here?

TANSKY. Chopin? Well, monsieur . . . You could put it that way. Let's . . . let's just say that when I started working on him he was already a brand. But I was the one who made certain that his stock never fell. Did you know that from 1833 to 1849 Chopin gave 14 public concerts? Can you imagine? All of 14 operations in 16 years, and make several thousand a month? Wouldn't you like that? (*He hands Granvil the bottle.*) Another drop?

GRANVIL. Thank you.

Granvil drinks for courage.

TANSKY. Observation is the foundation of everything. It's the same in the natural sciences or in playing a musical instrument. It's a matter of the pupil observing his master's every move, and of the master watching over his pupil in turn. This is the only way it can work. And you understand, monsieur . . . (*He looks all around and wipes the sweat from his forehead.*) . . . that it is of the greatest import that we do not take a step backwards. To this purpose—you understand, monsieur, that it is on this that the rest depends—to this purpose it will be necessary for you to introduce me to academic society and . . . This wouldn't be so difficult for you, I suppose? How do you like the plan so far?

Silence.

TANSKY. Well, then? Another nip? To our project? There were glasses around here somewhere. Here they are. Well, then. (*He inspects the glass in the light.*) That cow was no good at washing dishes. To that, then . . . You know what I mean? (*He makes a vulgar gesture and bursts into loud laughter.*) The girl did outstanding work. (*He wipes his glass.*)

GRANVIL. I'm wondering about one thing.

TANSKY. Yes?

GRANVIL. How is it, monsieur, that you, given your qualifications . . .

Tansky knocks the bottle over.

TANSKY (*indifferently*). It's nothing. (*He kneels and wipes up the vodka with his handkerchief. He goes on suspiciously, in a somber tone.*) Please continue . . .

GRANVIL. It's not important.

TANSKY (*nervously*). No, please! Finish what you were saying, monsieur. Well? Go on. What was it you wanted to say?

GRANVIL. Nothing. Nothing at all.

TANSKY (*stands*). I know what you're thinking. How is it that I never had unbridled ambitions of my own? The station of Chopin's private secretary always provided me complete satisfaction. My collaboration with Frédéric was based on principles of mutual trust and respect.

Silence.

TANSKY. What are you looking at?

Silence.

TANSKY (*shouting.*) We're from the same Russkie shithole. The only thing separating his crappy land from mine was a stinking creek. No one gave a thought to cultivating it, so the place was overgrown with willows. He though he was the man, just because he went abroad.

Silence. Granvil looks very sick.

TANSKY. So what's it going to be? Do we have an agreement?

GRANVIL. I don't feel well. Perhaps . . .

He staggers.

TANSKY. Granvil? Do sit down.

GRANVIL. My head . . .

TANSKY. Take a deep breath.

GRANVIL. Leave me alone.

He sits in his chair. Tansky hands him the basin. Granvil hangs his head over it.

Manon enters the room. Granvil raises his head. Manon is 30 years old, a pretty, pampered woman. She is wearing a rather provocative dressing gown with a Chinese dragon on the back. She looks like she just got out of bed: the effect is intended, for in fact she has carefully planned her entrée. Her hair is in practiced disarray; she has even put on makeup.

MANON. Are there any cigarettes left?

Granvil stands. He stares at Manon.

MANON. Hi, Tansky.

GRANVIL. Please.

Manon looks at Tansky, then at Granvil. She smiles. She walks up to them. Granvil offers her a cigarette.

MANON. And might you have a . . .

Granvil lights her cigarette.

GRANVIL. Granvil.

TANSKY. Monsieur Théodule Granvil is a doctor.

MANON. Manon Delorme.

Manon offers Granvil her hand.

TANSKY. How was the opera?

MANON. So-so.

TANSKY. You didn't sing?

MANON. No.

TANSKY. They have you on less and less of late.

MANON. It's not my fault that Meyerbeer and Viardot have conspired against me. Viardot has become friendly with George Sand. It's to be expected that they should pull the rug out from under me.

GRANVIL. You are a singer, madame?

MANON. Do you attend the opera?

TANSKY. To be more precise, Manon is in the chorus.

MANON. A soprano.

TANSKY. Second soprano.

MANON. Were it not for the intrigue, they'd have moved me to first long ago. (*To Granvil*) I suppose you think, monsieur, that you can do nothing more for him?

GRANVIL (*looking at the operating table*). Him?

MANON. Poor guy. It's so cold in here.

TANSKY. We can't light a fire until after they take him away. Besides, the servants have left. And we're out of coal.

MANON. Why don't they just take him right now?

TANSKY. Everyone is waiting for Doctor Granvil . . .

MANON. Oh, monsieur! So you're the doctor who's to . . . I can't believe that this is really what he wanted.

GRANVIL. Exactly! From the very beginning I've . . .

TANSKY. There can be no doubt.

MANON. Strange. We never spoke of it.

TANSKY. But, you see, you didn't nurse him much.

MANON. Well, if that's what he wanted, then there's nothing else to say! My head hurts. We had some aspirin here. (*She opens a snuff box, looks at herself in a hand mirror, and then snorts something.*) Of course I nursed him. He adored my company. He said that with me he felt . . .

TANSKY. If that is so, then why did he hide his money from you?

MANON. He called me nurse. I even have a complete nurse's uniform back in my room.(*To Granvil*) How old are you, monsieur?

GRANVIL. 23.

TANSKY. Monsieur Granvil has just finished medical school.

MANON. In what field?

TANSKY. Proctology.

MANON. That must be very difficult, treating the brain. Do you feel alright, monsieur?

TANSKY. Everything will be fine.

MANON. Have a seat on the couch, monsieur. Please sit down. You must be excellent, monsieur, since they've put their faith in you. I'm sure there were many who wanted to do it—all of Paris is abuzz over this affair.

She pulls out a newspaper and several envelopes from her negligée.

MANON. It's all they're writing about.

She places the letters on the small table. Tansky takes the newspaper.

MANON. Look at the lithograph on the front page.

TANSKY (*reads*). "Chopin on His Deathbed."

MANON. If he were still alive, he'd take them to court. In life he ascribed great importance to his personal appearance. He was the world's second largest importer of gloves, after the United States. Compared to him, Imelda Marcos is some lady from Hoboken. (*To Granvil*) Did you see that, monsieur?

Tansky shows Granvil the lithograph.

MANON. If he were still alive, he'd take them to court.

Granvil looks at the lithograph and starts to cough.

MANON. Are you ill, monsieur? (*She touches his forehead.*) He may have a fever. Tansky! Where's the thermometer?

Manon whirrs around the room for a moment; in one drawer she finds a thermometer and some small bottles.

MANON. Here. I found some elixirs as well.

She gives Granvil the thermometer. In the meantime, Tansky keeps reading.

MANON (*examines the little flasks*). Just because it didn't help Chopin doesn't mean it's not good. (*She sips.*) Would you like some, monsieur? Do sit down. Please take the thermometer.

GRANVIL (*without moving*). I need to move around. To walk around a bit.

MANON. You're covered in sweat, monsieur.

GRANVIL. Am I really?

Manon takes out a handkerchief and wipes Granvil's brow.

GRANVIL. Thank you.

MANON. I'll get you a blanket.

Tansky looks over the top of the newspaper. He appears shaken. Manon pulls a blanket around Granvil.

MANON (*to Tansky*). Is everything alright?

Tansky hands her the newspaper.

MANON (*takes the newspaper and reads*). "Chopin's Correspondence Missing."

TANSKY. That's outrageous . . . but it . . . it can't be true . . . it's some kind of . . . oh God. Who . . . what . . . but who could have told them that?

Silence. Tansky approaches Manon.

TANSKY. I don't believe it. Say it's not true. Say it wasn't you, Manon.

MANON. I really don't know how they tricked me.

TANSKY. God.

MANON. I knew you'd get upset, but take it easy.

TANSKY. They'll kill me.

MANON. Who?

TANSKY. The Hotel Lambert. Princess Potocka. The Redemptorists.

MANON. It had to come to this sooner or later. A little fright, and it's over, and here you're getting all stressed out.

TANSKY. My God . . . And they've written here that I'm to blame.

MANON. But who else?

TANSKY. Well, you live here, too. You could have taken better care.

MANON. Yeah, but I wasn't his secretary.

TANSKY. And what were you, then?

MANON. His will was in there, too. I'm the one who's lost the most.

TANSKY. Manon, I'm begging you: try to remember. You must have seen that cardboard box.

MANON. I've already tried.

TANSKY. You're certain it wasn't in the bureau?

MANON. In what bureau?

TANSKY. On Monday you pawned the bureau. At the second-hand shop. You think I didn't know?

MANON. I was saving up for his treatment. I wanted to send him to Aspen.

TANSKY. Really? So where's the money?

MANON. There wasn't any cardboard box.

TANSKY. Did you check? I'm going there. Give me the address.

Silence.

TANSKY. You don't remember the address?

Manon says nothing. Tansky puts on his scarf and hat.

MANON. Where are you going?

TANSKY. I'm going out. I won't be back tonight, surely. I'll drag every antique dealer in the city out of bed. I am certain that his papers were in that bureau. This will be my second night in a row without sleep, but of course that's not your problem.

MANON. Maybe you could dig up a little coal while you're out. For we're all out of scores, aren't we? That third concerto didn't give much heat, anyway.

TANSKY. Put on a sweater.

MANON. I look awful in wool. (*She coughs.*) At this rate, I'm going to come down with consumption, too.

TANSKY. You've gotten quite demanding.

MANON. You mean to say I'm getting old?

TANSKY. I mean to say that a year ago you were less demanding.

MANON (*moving toward the sofa*). Fine. You'll surely die of hunger, monsieur. There were cookies here yesterday.

She looks around the room, then goes up to the couch and leans over Granvil.

MANON. Show me the thermometer. Perhaps he fell asleep. One hundred point four. A nice guy. You know him?

TANSKY. We talked for about a half hour.

MANON. I bet you tried to drag him into some shitstorm, huh?

TANSKY. Well, you know . . . you're exaggerating. You're just exaggerating.

MANON. But in the future, leave him alone. Just leave him alone.

TANSKY. Manon!

MANON. Peace and quiet. That's easy enough.

A bell rings.

TANSKY. Were you expecting someone?

MANON. No.

Maybe it's the guys from the funeral parlor?

TANSKY. They were supposed to come tomorrow morning. We'll have to wake Granvil.

Tansky leaves, comes back a moment later with Jean. Jean is dressed in a short Communion suit and an ugly striped shirt. In general, he looks like the firstborn son of a stove-fitter on his way to having his picture taken. He's holding a violin case.

JEAN. Hello. Monsieur Chopin, I presume?

TANSKY. Are you . . . Polish?

JEAN. Is that you, Maestro?

TANSKY. Well . . . that depends on who you mean . . .

JEAN. Is your name Chopin?

MANON. No.

JEAN. I would like to speak with Chopin.

MANON. Chopin has died. At two in the morning.

TANSKY. Monsieur, you are . . . (*he looks at his watch*) . . . fifteen-and-a-half hours late.

JEAN (*appears broken*). Well, then, I won't take any more of your time. Goodbye.

Could I just have a look at him?

TANSKY. Be my guest.

JEAN (*walks up to Granvil, asleep on the sofa*). He looks like he's asleep.

MANON. That's not him.

She points toward the operating table. Jean walks up to it and peeks under the sheet.

JEAN. Exactly as I pictured him. (*He cries.*)

TANSKY. Are you alright, monsieur?

Manon, have you a handkerchief?

JEAN. Thank you, I'm fine. It's just that I've been getting ready for this meeting for weeks, and now . . .

TANSKY. Getting ready, monsieur?

JEAN. That's right.

MANON. You had an appointment with Chopin?

JEAN. Yes.

TANSKY. And your name is . . .?

JEAN. I'm Jean. I don't actually have a last name. Just a first name: Jean. But, since everyone has to have a last name, the alderman registered me as Jean Jean. And if, for example, his holiness the parish priest screams at me "Jean!" then that's the last name, but if her honor the village elder screams at me "Jean!" then she means the first name. Jean Jean. You can call me whichever you prefer: Jean, or Jean, I'll know who you mean.

TANSKY. And you knew Chopin, monsieur?

JEAN. You cannot imagine the passion with which a poor country child with no last name can abandon himself to dreams of making music. Oh yes. I, Jean Jean of Hamlet—that's what my hamlet is called, just "Hamlet." A hamlet called Hamlet. You can call it Hamlet hamlet, if you like. I, Jean Jean of Hamlet, have always wanted to become a virtuoso.

As Jean Jean is telling his story, Tansky removes his scarf and hat.

MANON. And did you?

JEAN. I will not tell you of the hours spent in the forest, of my toils in the field of instrument manufacture as a cottage industry, using available materials . . . To which I would have to add false charges of burglary and my harsh rehabilitation—since then I've had a nervous tic.

TANSKY. I give my word, it's completely unnoticeable. Isn't that right, Manon, you can't see a thing? If you hadn't said so, monsieur, I would have never known.

JEAN. Thank you. I struggle with it as best I can.

TANSKY. Would you like a *petit four*?

JEAN. With pleasure.

TANSKY. Manon, where did those cookies go?

JEAN. I'm looking forward to them already. Truly, people don't realize the degree to which even the slightest pleasure can sweeten the life of an orphan.

Tansky and Manon look around the room.

TANSKY. Ayayay . . . I'm truly sorry . . . I don't know what's happened to them . . .

JEAN. It's not the first time I've been let down.

TANSKY. Perhaps a cigarette, then?

JEAN. Thank you, I don't smoke. But I don't mind if someone else does. (*He coughs.*)

TANSKY. Manon! Could you put that out? We have a guest . . .

JEAN. Please don't. The smell reminds me of my mother.

TANSKY. That poor woman who . . .

JEAN. . . . when I was three years old. Throat cancer. Everyone is entitled to a better tomorrow—just yesterday I still believed that. My luck was supposed to have changed the day I received Chopin's telegram.

TANSKY. Chopin? Chopin sent you a telegram?

JEAN. Yes.

TANSKY. When was that?

JEAN. Precisely one month ago.

TANSKY. So then why did you only arrive now?

JEAN. I walked.

TANSKY. But of course! Do you have this telegram with you, monsieur?

JEAN. It burned, along with the rest of Hamlet, during the last bandit raid.

TANSKY. What did this telegram concern?

JEAN. A scholarship from a foundation for gifted country youth. Monsieur Chopin was supposed to pay me a monthly stipend of 2,000 francs for four years, as well as to give me lessons.

TANSKY. It really is a shame that he died and can no longer keep his word. (*He presses Jean's hand.*) I'm quite moved. You're also quite moved, aren't you, Manon? She's also quite moved, she just doesn't show it. I'm sorry you have been let down, monsieur.

JEAN (*goes to the door*). Goodbye.

TANSKY (*runs after him with the case*). Your violin!

JEAN. Thank you.

MANON. You also play the violin, monsieur?

JEAN. I'm a violinist.

TANSKY. But Chopin was a pianist.

JEAN. A pianist? In that case I'm afraid that there must be some mistake. (*He digs around in his pocket and pulls out a crumpled piece of paper.*) Oh, my! It's clearly written here: Chaliapin! Chaliapin, not Chopin. And the address is wrong. How could I have gotten so muddled? To be honest, for some time my eyesight has been going rapidly downhill. It's a result of a diet bereft of vitamin B.

TANSKY. Manon! Might we have some vitamin B?

MANON. Here.

JEAN. Oh, no! Just one tablet.

TANSKY. Take the whole pack.

JEAN. I'd feel like a thief.

TANSKY. But what are you saying!

JEAN. It is really too much.

TANSKY. I'm happy that there is something we can do to help.

JEAN. But what about you?

TANSKY. What about us?

JEAN. Have you saved some for yourselves?

TANSKY. Sure. We have tons. Don't we, Manon?

MANON. Of course.

JEAN. Show me.

> *Silence.*

TANSKY. Alright, fine. We don't have any more. But tomorrow morning, first thing, we'll run out to the drug store. Word of honor.

JEAN. Why not today? Got you! Please, just have one each.

TANSKY. This really is unnecessary.

JEAN. I insist. It's very important to me.

> *Tansky and Manon each swallow a pill.*

JEAN. Well then, see you. (*He laughs.*) You get it? See you. Bye! Now that I have these pills I can say that. See you! (*He taps his eyelid.*) Get it?

TANSKY (*bursting into laughter*). Manon, did you hear that? She doesn't really have a sense of humor. Between us, she had a tough childhood, too.

JEAN. Oh. One more thing. Since we're already on such friendly terms . . . You understand . . . A symbolic gesture . . . for a taxi.

TANSKY. Manon, do you have any change? There we are . . . Take it. It's all I have.

JEAN. Thanks. Really, thank you. What's the way out? I'll find it! Bye now.

Jean Jean leaves.

TANSKY. People somehow get by!

MANON. You just gave him ten francs.

TANSKY. When I see something like that, it puts me in a good humor. You know: I have it bad. But he has it worse. That's why Mother Teresa was always smiling.

Silence.

TANSKY. Manon. What will become of us . . .

MANON. I don't know. If something comes up, I'll go to America. I've heard it's cool there. I'm going to get dressed.

Tansky sits without moving. He reaches for the bottle on the table and finds it empty. He walks slowly up to the sofa and stares for a moment at Granvil, asleep. Very slowly and very gently, he slips his hand underneath the cushion, feels around for something, and finally pulls out a bottle. Granvil sleeps. Tansky drinks. He realizes it's gotten dark, so he lights a few candles. In the apartment below, someone starts playing Chopin's Nocturne in E flat Major, Op. 9. Tansky takes a broom and knocks the handle against the floor. The music stops. Tansky looks around the room and picks up the bundle of letters that Manon threw on the table. He stares at the envelopes. He sits down at the writing desk.

TANSKY (*looking over the envelopes*). To Chopin. (*He holds a letter without reading it.*) To Chopin . . . To Chopin . . .

He takes a swig.

TANSKY (*to Granvil*). It's all gone to hell.

He drinks a little more and hides the bottle in a drawer. He stands and puts on his scarf and cap. The doorbell rings.

MANON (*from offstage*). Tansky! Are you going to get that?

Tansky exits and returns a moment later. He is accompanied by Emma Zeidler. She's in her 40s, but she's still trying. She was once beautiful. Now all she has are habits. She's dressed sexily in mourning c.1849 and in a black fur. A fur, and a hat with a veil. All quite tasteful.

EMMA. Atrocious weather. Where can I hang my fur?

TANSKY. If I were you, madame, I wouldn't take it off. It's terribly cold.

EMMA (*after a short pause, strolling through the room*). You know, monsieur, that according to Dante it is not flames that punish the most grievous sins. The greatest sinners dwell in eternal cold.

TANSKY (*bowing*). My name is . . .

EMMA. Emma Zeidler.

TANSKY. A pleasure.

I am . . .

Emma is not listening. She turns around and looks at the sofa.

TANSKY. Please pay no attention to him. He was feeling ill. An acquaintance.

EMMA (*inspects the empty bottle on the table*). I see that I'm late to the wake. How is it called where you come from? Octoberfest?

Manon enters in a red dress, carrying a cup of tea. Emma walks up to her and takes her cup.

EMMA. I'd like some preserves.

MANON (*taking the cup back from Emma*). The kitchen is on the left.

EMMA. I am familiar with the layout of the apartment.

MANON. A lovely fur. Is it fox?

EMMA. Thank you.

She measures up Manon with her eyes.

TANSKY. Madame Emma Zeidler. Mademoiselle Manon Delorme. A friend of Monsieur Chopin.

MANON. I'm a singer.

TANSKY. Would you like to sit down, madame?

EMMA. My coach is waiting downstairs. I've come for my letters. Frédéric and I corresponded. It is important to me that the letters should not fall into the wrong hands. Please return them to me. The letters, please.

TANSKY. That's not possible at the moment.

EMMA. I don't understand.

TANSKY. Have you not heard, madame? They've written about it in the *Courier*.

EMMA. I do not read newspapers.

Tansky hands Emma the newspaper. Emma falls back into the arm-chair.

EMMA. Who stole them?

MANON. The family. It could have been his family. There was a will in there. (*To Emma*) Chopin left me the apartment.

TANSKY. People get taken to court for slander, Manon.

EMMA. What are your intentions, monsieur?

TANSKY. Of course I am trying to . . .

EMMA. Have you informed the police?

TANSKY. This is perhaps not a police matter.

MANON. Are you married, madame?

EMMA. Quite right, monsieur. This is not a police matter.

MANON. Does your husband know about this? About your correspondence with Chopin?

TANSKY (*to Emma*). A cigarette, perhaps?

EMMA (*she reaches out and pulls her hand back*). I quit half a year ago.

TANSKY. Excellent. I always say that . . .

MANON. Some men are truly blind.

EMMA. Do you suspect anyone?

TANSKY. No one in particular.

MANON (*takes a book from the end table*). "Monsieur de Fayel looked threateningly at his unfaithful spouse. 'Did you enjoy the dinner you just feasted on?' 'Yes, monsieur.' 'Then know what it was you ate, poor woman: it was your lover's heart.' 'Raoul!' Gabriela whispered, and she fell unconscious to the floor."

EMMA. You must suspect someone.

MANON. Why don't you tell her? Go ahead, tell her, say it. Tell her whom you accuse. (*To Emma*) He takes it for a consequence of my foolishness: you know, madame, I am terribly, terribly foolish. I'm terribly stupid.

TANSKY. Manon!

MANON. Between us, it was I who wondered every day why Frédéric wasn't simply repulsed by the thought of touching me.

EMMA. What gives you the right to call him by his first name, mademoiselle?

She goes up to the operating table.

EMMA. This is he?

TANSKY. He passed away peacefully while listening to a psalm sung by Princess Potocka.

EMMA (*bursts into loud, vulgar laughter*). But her squawking would deafen a lumberjack.

TANSKY. If you are interested, madame, I will add your name to the orders for a unique death mask of Chopin. It's by subscription. A cast of the hands costs extra.

EMMA. His hands . . .

How much?

TANSKY. 500 francs.

Emma gives Tansky the money.

TANSKY. Please fill out this form.

MANON. "His hands . . ." His hands! What do you know of Chopin, madame? He once said to me, "Why is it that all these old ladies see only my hands? Why aren't they interested in my feet?" He loved to play footsie, he could play for hours. You spoke of my rights, madame. I am the woman who discovered Chopin's feet! Maybe that gives me some rights.

TANSKY. It will be delivered to your home. In discreet packaging.

EMMA. Will he have a nice funeral?

TANSKY. We were just about to set the budget.

Emma takes out her billfold.

TANSKY. We're also taking a collection for the musicians. They're going to play Mozart's "Requiem." Paulina Viardot is going to sing . . .

EMMA (*winces*). Viardot! Let me pay for the tomb.

TANSKY. We're sending out invitations.

EMMA. Oh, it's the least I can do. (*She stands.*) Do you have my address, monsieur? If anything comes up, do let me know. (*To Manon*) Might you loan me a small mirror, mademoiselle?

MANON (*gives her a compact*). Here you go.

EMMA. Thank you.

Emma opens the compact and starts making up her eyes.

TANSKY. It is true that we are not working under the best conditions here. If only we had the means . . . It would be good at least to have a nicer sheet . . .

Emma looks at herself in the compact. She licks her finger, tastes the powder, and snorts a little. She takes a few steps, staggers, and snorts some more. She casts her fur to the floor. Manon takes it into the anteroom.

EMMA. I saw his death. I was here this morning, did you know that? It was easy: all you had to do was find a place in the crowd. All of Paris gathered in this apartment. When I arrived it was quarter to seven. I squeezed past the people on the stairs and in the hall, and I stood right here. The door to the bedroom was open. I came closer and saw priests from every parish in Paris leaning over Chopin and telling him to kiss the relics. "Here! The hip of Saint Catherine. Kiss it! Come on! Kiss it!" There was even the Archbishop of Paris with the skull of Saint Geneviève, the city's patron saint: "Kiss it!" And nothing out of Chopin, just: "A bucket . . . quick, get me a bucket . . ." And so it went for six hours.

Emma falls back into the armchair.

EMMA. It appears that the responsibility of taking care of the keepsakes has fallen to you, monsieur. I wonder how Chopin's patriotically inclined countrymen will react to the news of their loss. But it is hot in here. I've gotten terribly hungry.

TANSKY. The cookies! There were cookies around here somewhere. Manon?

Tansky looks desperately around the room. He pulls out a tin from under a pile of papers on the writing desk.

TANSKY. Found them! Unbelievable. (*To Manon*) You see? They were here all along. Not 15 minutes ago I wanted to offer them to a poor, blind boy . . .

He offers Emma a cookie shaped like a heart.

EMMA (*chewing*). It's good.

TANSKY. Apropos a good heart . . . Have I told you, madame, that I am active in a foundation that helps adolescent cripples?

Is man—I mean the kind who has it good—is he grateful for his good fortune? No. But he should be.

It's me, Lord. I may not be the happiest person in the world, but I have healthy eyes. Thank you, Lord, for my healthy eyes. Eyes that see. For example, right this minute: I see the table—thank you, Lord—I walk up to it and see—I see!—this letter. I look at the postmark: it arrived with the evening mail, addressed to me. I open the envelope and . . . (*He screams.*)

MANON. You'll wake Granvil!

Granvil turns over on the couch, but doesn't wake up.

MANON. What is it?

TANSKY. "I have Chopin's papers. 300,000 by morning. Details to follow."

MANON. I told you it wasn't me. I told you it wasn't my fault.

Emma just now sees Granvil's face. She approaches the couch, and examines the sleeping man intently.

TANSKY. Is this some kind of joke?

MANON. You see? It wasn't my fault!

TANSKY. Whose, then? Who swiped them? And when?

MANON. Anyone could have. There were herds of people winding through here all night. You heard so yourself.

TANSKY. You think that's when they did it?

MANON. Maybe it was her.

TANSKY. Who?

MANON (*looks at Emma*). She was here yesterday.

TANSKY. Why? Why would she . . . That makes no sense.

MANON. I don't know, but she could have. Maybe she thinks we'll pay her. And besides, the criminal always returns.

TANSKY. Returns?

MANON. To the scene of the crime.

TANSKY. Manon. How can you . . . You know . . . it could just as well have been you who wrote this.

MANON. Me?

TANSKY. The first thing you said when I opened the envelope was, "See? It wasn't me." You lost or else destroyed the papers in your carelessness, and when you got your bearings you wrote this letter and threw it into the mailbox this morning. That might be what happened.

MANON. What for? Why would I do that?

TANSKY. To hide the truth.

MANON. From whom?

TANSKY. From me, for one.

MANON. You really think I'd care? You think there's anyone who's that afraid of you? Or that your opinion is that important to anyone? And now you're going to go down in history as the guy who lost Chopin's papers.

TANSKY. Watch it. I'm going to write his biography. I'll write who you were. How was the Opera? "So-so." So-so? They saw you in the Duke de Bouillon's carriage. You came home at ten in the morning. In a cab. Quite a step up. Just a year ago you could have worked in the rain.

MANON. I never walked the street!

Emma bursts into laughter.

Silence. Tansky sits down next to the sleeping Granvil.

TANSKY. If . . . If only you . . . If only you and I could come to an arrangement . . . If you weren't such a little brat, you'd appreciate this opportunity. The papers are lost . . . the paaaaapers . . . (*He laughs.*) What are they compared with what remains? The papers are gone, but Chopin is here. We still have the body. There are people in the world who are willing to pay the greatest sums for the slightest . . . teensy piece. It would require organization, effort, sure, but it would pay . . . I give you my word, it would pay . . . A little formalin and . . . Once, back in the old country . . . 8,000 cubic meters of Kochanowski's linden trees . . . Starting at a thousand bucks a stump . . . At the peak of business I employed four brigades of lumberjacks . . . It was beautiful . . . beautiful . . .

Granvil jumps up, screaming.

GRANVIL. I had some nightmare . . . I dreamt that I was supposed to cut out somebody's heart . . . Oh God.

EMMA (*walks up to Granvil*). Emma Zeidler.

MANON (*hands Granvil the tin of cookies*). Here, monsieur. These are for you. I baked them myself.

Granvil takes out a heart-shaped gingerbread cookie. He winces, but he eats it.

MANON. Do you feel better, monsieur?

GRANVIL. A little.

EMMA (*louder*). Emma Zeidler.

TANSKY (*to Granvil*). Madame Zeidler. Doctor Granvil, a friend of the house.

GRANVIL. A pleasure. (*He turns toward Manon.*)

MANON. Would you like another cookie?

GRANVIL. No, thank you.

MANON. Would you like some tea?

Emma realizes that no one is paying any attention to her. She steps into the middle of the room.

EMMA (*loudly*). Did somebody here need 300 Gs?

Silence.

EMMA. Could I have a piece of paper and something to write with?

Tansky hands her some paper and a quill. Emma sits down at the table.

TANSKY. What are you writing, madame?

EMMA. I'm writing to my husband.

TANSKY. Your husband . . .

EMMA. Yes. Acme International. The money will be here in half an hour.

GRANVIL. Money?

MANON (*transfixed by Emma; coming to, to Granvil*). Later.

TANSKY. And your husband, madame . . . Just like that . . .

EMMA. You were speaking, monsieur, of charitable activity. Will you arrange for the tax deduction?

TANSKY. I'm going to go find a courier. Or I'll take it myself. What address?

EMMA. Not necessary. My coachman is waiting downstairs.

GRANVIL. I need some fresh air. It will do me good.

EMMA. No need. (*She walks up to the window and opens it. To Granvil*) Come over here, monsieur. Please lean out this way. But don't fall! (*She grabs his ass.*) You see? My coach. Now, whistle. Do you know how to whistle, monsieur?

Granvil whistles.

EMMA (*screams*). Pierre! (*She casts herself across Granvil's back.*) Pardon me, I have vertigo. But it's so high! Hold me, monsieur. (*Granvil grabs Emma like Clarke Gable grabs Vivian Leigh on the poster for* Gone with the Wind.) Pierre is my coachman. (*Leaning her head out, Emma yells.*) Catch! (*She throws out the piece of paper.*) Oh!

We can hear the sounds of hooves on cobblestones.

EMMA (*Straightening up, to Granvil*).Thank you, monsieur.

Granvil closes the window. Emma fixes her hair.

EMMA. It's all taken care of.

The doorbell rings, followed by footsteps.

A man enters in a black leather overcoat and a hat pulled down to his eyes. Everyone moves back in terror.

MANON (*after a moment*). Are you?

RUBINSTEIN. Yes.

Ivan Rubinstein takes off his hat. He is a man of about 35 years. He does not look like a gangster. He doesn't even have a gold tooth. The only thing is that he speaks with a Russian accent. Rubinstein takes a few more steps, sticks his hand into the front of his coat, and pulls out a bottle of vodka; with the other hand he pulls out a jar of pickles from his coat pocket. He bursts out laughing and, his arms outstretched, approaches Tansky.

RUBINSTEIN. Chopin! You old hound!

Tansky frees himself from his embrace.

TANSKY. Please, monsieur . . .

RUBINSTEIN. You don't recognize me?

TANSKY. My name is . . .

RUBINSTEIN (*turns to Granvil*). Chopin! You old . . . you don't, at all . . .

Granvil does not react.

RUBINSTEIN (*a little consternated, examines Emma*). Oh, come now! You old perve! (*Pause.*) Fine. (*He puts away the vodka and pickles and becomes threatening again.*) What have you done with him?

GRANVIL (*steps into the middle of the room*). Who are you?

RUBINSTEIN. I'll ask the questions. (*He goes up to the operating table and lifts the sheet a little.*) Is that him?

Silence.

RUBINSTEIN (*howls*). Which of you? Who dared!

He throws himself on Tansky.

TANSKY. It wasn't me. (*Pause.*) It happened suddenly. Himself. He died himself.

Rubinstein grabs Tansky by the throat.

TANSKY (*chokes out*). Consumption.

Rubinstein lets Tansky go and returns to the operating table. He slips the vodka and pickles beneath the sheet.

RUBINSTEIN. Oh, brother! (*He cries.*) Ivan Rubinstein. Chopin and I did our military service together. (*He goes up to each of them individually. He kisses the women on the hand, yanking them by the arm so hard that they hiss with pain. When he's done, he turns toward the operating table.*) Remember the Battle of Olszynka Grochowska? 1831. (*He bursts out laughing.*) Bam! Bam! Charge! (*To the living*) We met in '28, at the military academy in Petersburg.

TANSKY. Chopin never went to Petersburg.

RUBINSTEIN. We met in '28! At the military academy!! In Petersburg!!!

TANSKY. Chopin never served in the army.

RUBINSTEIN. Are you saying he was a coward?

TANSKY. No, just that he was never in the army.

RUBINSTEIN. He wasn't in the army?

TANSKY. No.

RUBINSTEIN. Hold on . . . (*He ponders for a moment. Then he takes out a revolver.*) Down on the ground!

They all fall to the ground.

RUBINSTEIN. Fine. I wanted to do this the nice way, but it didn't work out. Where's the loot? (*Silence.*) Give me the loot.

MANON (*with her face to the ground*). Vi-va vee va va vah va va-vi.

RUBINSTEIN. What was that?

MANON. Vi-va vee va va vah va va-vi!

RUBINSTEIN. Could you lift your head up, mademoiselle?

MANON (*lifts her head up*). It will be here in half an hour.

Rubinstein looks deep into her eyes. Manon smiles and puts her head down.

RUBINSTEIN. I want it now.

EMMA (*lifts her head*). Perhaps you need not kill us, monsieur . . . (*She puts her head down.*)

RUBINSTEIN. Then give me the number.

TANSKY (*lifts up his head*). What number?

RUBINSTEIN. The box number.

EMMA. My husband's sending it.

RUBINSTEIN. The whole half million?

They all lift their heads.

TANSKY. Half million?

EMMA. Half a million?

TANSKY. It was supposed to be 300,000.

RUBINSTEIN. Cut the crap! (*He shoots into the air. He walks up to Granvil.*) You, there! Young man! (*Pause.*) I'm talking to you. (*Granvil cries.*) Talk! What gives?

GRANVIL. I don't know. I don't know anything.

MANON. I do.

RUBINSTEIN. Alright, *ma chérie.* 300 grand? What happened to the rest?

MANON. You wanted 300,000, monsieur. We have the letter. Tansky! Show him the letter.

TANSKY. It's there. On the table.

RUBINSTEIN (*takes the letter and reads it*). What's this?

MANON. That's not you?

RUBINSTEIN. No.

MANON. Christ.

Outrage. They all stand.

RUBINSTEIN. What's this all about?

TANSKY. That really isn't you? (*Pause.*) What did you come for then, monsieur?

RUBINSTEIN. I came for the money.

TANSKY. But what money?

RUBINSTEIN. Chopin owed me half a million. We worked together. Smuggling people in from the East. They arrived in France, and our group would get them jobs under the table: chambermaids, cleaning ladies, porters . . . The point was to get them into houses. Then they cleaned the place out, and Chopin fenced the goods. He took a hefty commission, but he still wanted to rip me off . . . Half a million clams.

EMMA. The money's in the bank, and you want to get to it?

RUBINSTEIN. *Si, bella* . . . Give me the number of the safety deposit box.

TANSKY. But we don't know it.

RUBINSTEIN. So look for it. Where are his papers?

TANSKY. They've been stolen.

RUBINSTEIN. By whom?

TANSKY. We don't know. That letter came by the evening post.

RUBINSTEIN. And you're going to pay it?

EMMA. The money will be here in half an hour.

RUBINSTEIN. Fine. (*He hands Tansky the letter.*) Give me that 300,000 and we'll call it even.

Consternation. To strengthen the effect, Rubinstein shows them the revolver.

TANSKY. But that . . . Aw, goddammit! We can't do that! (*He looks around.*) What are you all waiting for?! Goddammit.

RUBINSTEIN. Half-hour. I'll wait.

He takes a chair, sits in the middle of the room, takes out a newspaper, and lights a cigar.

EMMA (*coughs*). Could you smoke on the other side of the room, monsieur?

Rubinstein looks at Emma and drags his chair to the right side of the stage. Granvil crosses to stage-right.

GRANVIL (*takes out a cigarette*). Do you have a light?

Rubinstein lights his cigarette. A moment later, Manon also crosses to stage-right and lights a cigarette. Emma and Tansky remain stage-left. Emma looks furiously at Granvil and Manon and bites her tongue. She hesitates a moment, and finally she stands, resigned, next to Tansky.

EMMA. When I just think of all the misfortunes and cataclysms that have been brought on by smoking cigarettes, I mean, that sooner or later—and really sooner rather than later—what will befall the addicts of the species, when I just think about all of them, it simply makes me . . .

MANON. If you ask me, among all the characters in this play, I'd have to nominate Madame Zeidler. Yes, Emma. I'm sorry. Yes, you. And don't think it's anything personal. I mean, it obviously wasn't an easy decision, it was actually quite hard, because, after all, this sort of thing is always . . . unpleasant, even when it comes to Madame Zeidler. Even when it comes to you, Emma. But first, because it has to be somebody, second, it looks like you're not going anywhere, and third, because someone finally has to tell you the truth.

EMMA. . . . sad, just terribly sad. Wrinkles around your eyes, wrinkles around your mouth, wrinkles on your neck and wrinkles on your forehead. Bad breath, morning cough, evening nausea, rashes, wrinkles around your eyes, difficulty evacuating, heart murmur and sweating (like a pig), breathlessness, breathlessness, wrinkles around your eyes . . .

MANON. It was such a great play. It was such a great play until you showed up. I got a pretty dressing gown. With a dragon. Red. I could do my thing. There were cookies. A nice atmosphere. Cookies . . .

EMMA. Thank you, but at 39 I don't want people to take me for the older sister of Lady Ashton. On the other hand, this entire arsenal of ascetic practices, all these painful and degrading acts one has to square up against in order to expunge the habit from oneself completely and definitively, that one has to face to pull the habit up by its roots, that one must meet . . .

MANON. And it's not that you made a pass at Granvil. It has nothing to do with that. Though you did make a pass at him, and don't say you didn't.

EMMA. How many times have I later caught myself thinking, what's it to me to have no wrinkles around my eyes, no shortness of breath, or no wrinkles on my neck. What is not having shortness of breath or wrinkles around your eyes when you have acupuncture sessions, fitness trails, swimming in a cold pool, the smell of muesli in the morning . . .

MANON. Whenever I want to have something, even if it's a trifle, junk, some nasty pile of shit, I don't know: then some floozie always drags herself in and . . . Yes, Emma, you made a pass at him. Don't say you didn't, you slut!

EMMA. Suicide. The last time I tried to commit suicide was when I was about seven. I remember, I remember that day well. It's preserved in my memory. A beautiful summer day, a flawless day.

MANON. I remember, one year . . .

EMMA. I was at the seaside on vacation with my parents.

MANON. Must you always interrupt me?

EMMA. We went to the beach every morning.

MANON. It was summer. The sun was rippling the air.

EMMA. I will never forget the moment I opened the paper package.

MANON. Rays of sunlight became unhinged on the ends of waves.

EMMA. So great was my longing for that tube that I was out of breath. All the powers of my soul, strained to the point of my gag reflex, were concentrated in that one desire.

MANON. And seagulls . . . seagulls . . . well, seagulls . . .

EMMA. I longed for a red inner tube . . .

MANON. . . . were flying here and there, with a sonorous caw . . .

EMMA. . . . or purple. With polka dots. Or maybe they were stripes . . . with a fine frill . . .

MANON. . . . on their lips.

EMMA. . . . along the full length of its delightfully rounded edge . . .

MANON. The waves gently caressed their round backs . . .

EMMA. . . . delightfully rounded edge . . .

MANON. . . . gently, delightfully, caressed the round, seaside rocks . . .

EMMA. With quivering, quivering fingers I tore off the colorful crepe paper. And the stab of pain—as if my heart had been torn out—I felt as I lifted it in my hands, this flimsy, shriveled—When I put my lips to the blowhole and started blowing.

MANON. I have never been as happy as I was then.

EMMA. I blew and blew, filling the space with my soul, and when I stopped blowing . . .

MANON. That wave washed over me gradually, from the clear view, through the mounting fear, all the way to certainty . . .

EMMA. The inner tube was rectangular.

MANON. It was a square circle.

Tansky looks longingly at the writing desk situated stage-right. After a moment, he very carefully approaches the operating table and pulls the bottle of vodka and the jar of pickles out from under the sheet. A moment later, the bottle and the jar are making several rounds around the stage.

GRANVIL (*to Manon*). I must repulse you, mademoiselle. Even Tansky was braver than I.

MANON. Nonsense.

TANSKY (*to Emma*). It's you.

EMMA. When did you recognize me?

TANSKY. Almost right away. And you?

GRANVIL. I feel . . .

EMMA. When you stood up to Rubinstein. You made this sort of gesture . . .

GRANVIL. I feel like . . .

EMMA. Like a man.

MANON. Like, to me, you were great, monsieur.

TANSKY. You haven't changed so much.

EMMA. Don't lie.

MANON. Really, great.

TANSKY. Really.

GRANVIL. Really?

EMMA. Was it back in '23 or '24?

TANSKY. It was '22.

EMMA. The fastest skier in Grenoble.

GRANVIL. I know . . .

EMMA. And you always had lovely hands.

GRANVIL. I know that you can't really think that.

TANSKY. You can say that about anybody. Hands and eyes. Whenever someone is ugly, that's what they say, that . . .

EMMA. I like your hands.

TANSKY. Chopin's were lovelier.

GRANVIL. What sort of guy was he? Chopin.

MANON. Have you seen the movie, *Chopin: Desire for Love*? He was just like that. So sweet.

TANSKY. It really is hard, Emma. It's quite something . . . When you catch sight of your reflection in something and you have to say to yourself: That's me, my name is X. That's me.

MANON. You have something on your cheek, monsieur.

GRANVIL. Where? (*He rubs his cheek with his hand.*)

TANSKY. Your reflection.

GRANVIL. Still there?

MANON. Yes.

TANSKY. If only I could like myself a little. You know, just a bit. Me.

GRANVIL. Now?

MANON. More to the right.

TANSKY. It's so delicate. So. It's so frail. Delicate.

GRANVIL. How about now?

MANON (*laughs*). A little more.

> *Granvil laughs as well. Manon strokes his cheek.*

TANSKY. That moment in Road Runner cartoons when Wile E. Coyote realizes that he's failed yet again. Then he looks for a second into the camera, that is, at the cartoonist, and you understand that he's asking for some help.

MANON. Now it's gone.

GRANVIL. Thank you.

> *Rubinstein finishes his newspaper and cigar. He stands, pulls out a large plastic garbage bag from his coat pocket, and starts moving around the room, stuffing whatever he comes across into the bag: a candlestick here, a vase there, an ashtray. He pulls out the contents of the drawer of the writing desk, etc. He's quite absorbed.*

EMMA. Are you still writing plays?

TANSKY. Well, you know, there was Chopin . . .

EMMA. There was no Chopin back then.

GRANVIL. I'm 23.

TANSKY. That doesn't at all mean that I won't pull myself together.

GRANVIL. I've graduated.

EMMA. But then even if there had been. It wouldn't have meant anything.

GRANVIL. I want to be a doctor. I would like to be good. I would like to be an excellent doctor.

TANSKY. I really will make it. I'll fight for what's mine.

GRANVIL. I recently wrote an article.

TANSKY. I liked myself back then.

GRANVIL. They published it in the *Lancet*. Now, that's something. That's a kind of accomplishment. You write that on your CV, and it stays there.

EMMA. And me? Did you like me?

GRANVIL. My parents were glad, my mom . . . But I . . . I didn't . . . It wasn't my . . .

EMMA. Well?

GRANVIL. He gave me the subject, and I worked on it, I really did, but then it turned out that it was too hard.

TANSKY. I didn't know you lived in Paris.

EMMA. I left . . . Sort of to go after you.

GRANVIL. I really tried hard, and . . .

EMMA. I wanted to find you, to tell you . . .

GRANVIL. The experiments didn't work out, the results didn't match . . .

TANSKY. What? What did you want to tell me?

GRANVIL. I couldn't do it. It was too hard.

TANSKY. And you didn't look for me.

GRANVIL. Sometimes these great ideas suddenly pop into your head. When you least expect it, everything suddenly falls into place, like with Pasteur. You know, Pasteur . . .

MANON. The atom bomb guy?

EMMA. Zeidler and I have a daughter.

GRANVIL. Finally, I told him.

EMMA. She's 20.

GRANVIL. For me. He'd do the whole article for me.

EMMA. She didn't finish school. She took jobs here and there. She did infomercials for a while.

GRANVIL. From start to finish.

EMMA. She met him at some S&M club. She says she's happy with him.

GRANVIL. There wasn't a lot of it. I bought myself some diving equipment. I've always wanted to go diving.

EMMA. She showed me pictures.

GRANVIL. Once. With my future father-in-law. In August, on the Black Sea.

EMMA. . . . whether it hurts. I said: Honey, that must hurt terribly. She said she likes it.

Granvil kisses Manon, then they leave.

TANSKY (*to Rubinstein*). What are you doing?

RUBINSTEIN. Chopin owed me 500,000. You're giving me 300,000. Maybe I should be compensated for the remaining 200,000.

We hear a terrible noise by the window. Jean Jean, with his case, falls in from behind the curtain.

RUBINSTEIN. Get down, he could be armed.

Emma and Tansky fall to the ground. Rubinstein aims his revolver at Jean Jean. Jean Jean looks around, takes a few steps, and opens his case. Several kilograms of knick-knacks, some samovars, silverware, a candlestick, etc.

JEAN. I can explain everything!

TANSKY. You?

RUBINSTEIN. Who is that?

TANSKY. It's alright. I know him.

JEAN (*struggling to fasten the case*). They're souvenirs.

TANSKY. And to think that I gave you Vitamin B!

JEAN. I'm sorry.

RUBINSTEIN (*disgusted*). Amateur!

JEAN. Anyone can make a mistake. If I didn't get tangled up in the curtain, it would have worked out.

RUBINSTEIN. If I *hadn't* gotten tangled . . .

JEAN. Anyone can make a mistake!

TANSKY (*to Rubinstein*). I have to admit, he was doing really well up until then.

RUBINSTEIN. Linguistically, or factually?

TANSKY. Both.

RUBINSTEIN (*puts the barrel to Jean Jean's head*). Now what? Should we waste the bastard?

Jean falls to Rubinstein's feet and cries.

EMMA (*takes Jean Jean by the hand; to Rubinstein*). Please, monsieur! (*Pause.*) Would you like a cookie? (*She gives him the tin.*)

JEAN. Thank you.

EMMA. You're overacting a bit.

RUBINSTEIN (*goes up to Emma, points at her heart-shaped brooch*). That's pretty. Is it real? (*He puts out his hand.*)

EMMA (*taking off the brooch*). You don't seem to have a heart, monsieur.

RUBINSTEIN. I do now.

In the apartment beneath them, someone starts playing the Nocturne in E flat.

RUBINSTEIN. Of course. Because everyone else has feelings, but I don't. What? I'm the only one without a heart. (*Pause.*) I had a tough childhood, too. But I only started stealing when I was 18. I have feelings, too! (*Rubinstein goes up to Jean Jean's pile of would-be spoils and picks up a plastic recorder. He starts to play "El Condor Pasa."*) I always dreamt of playing music.

JEAN (*choking on a cookie*). You too?

TANSKY (*to Jean Jean*). Were you the one who stole Chopin's letters?

JEAN. Only the ones I saw.

TANSKY. And Anonymous, that wasn't you?

JEAN. Anonymous people disgust me.

TANSKY. Do you think he's telling the truth, monsieur?

Sound of shattering glass. Something crashes through the window and rolls across the carpet. The music breaks off.

RUBINSTEIN (*falling flat to the floor*). Get down!

Tansky, Emma, and Jean Jean look at him piteously.

EMMA. It's a rock.

RUBINSTEIN (*stands; he brushes himself off, sulking*). It is quite obvious that none of you has served at the front.

EMMA (*picking up the stone*). There's something tied to it. (*She pulls off a piece of paper.*) "300,000, tomorrow morning." There's an account number.

TANSKY (*looks out the window*). There's no one there.

RUBINSTEIN. In any case, it's out of date. The moolah's mine. (*He looks at his watch*). Another 15 minutes. (*He confiscates the case with its contents*). And this, as compensation for the rest. And I still won't break even.

TANSKY. You should sell it to the Chopin Fan Club, monsieur. They'll pay twice as much.

Manon enters with Granvil.

MANON. What happened?

TANSKY. Everything's under control.

MANON. Jean Jean?

TANSKY. Turned out to be a thief.

JEAN (*closing the tin*). I'm done. Can I go home now?

TANSKY. Someone will have to show him out.

RUBINSTEIN. I'll go with him. (*He puts the revolver to Jean Jean's back.*) Easy now. I'm familiar with troubled youth.

JEAN. Goodbye.

They leave.

MANON. What happened to the window? Jean Jean?

TANSKY. No. The guy who stole the letters. (*He shows her the rock with the letter.*) He gave us his account number.

MANON. Did you see him?

TANSKY. He ran off.

MANON (*looking at the window*). It'll have to be sealed up.

TANSKY. Don't bother. You're still not getting the apartment.

MANON. It'll still have to be sealed up.

Rubinstein returns.

MANON. I hope you didn't hurt him.

RUBINSTEIN. I am not a monster!

Blanche de la Mole enters the room. She is 19 years old, a pretty, delicate, golden-haired girl.

GRANVIL. Blanche!

BLANCHE. Good evening. The doorbell wasn't working.

GRANVIL. This is my fiancée.

MANON. Good evening, mademoiselle.

BLANCHE. My name is Blanche de la Mole. (*She catches sight of Tansky.*) Oh, Monsieur Tansky! Hello.

GRANVIL. Then you know each other?

BLANCHE. Monsieur Tansky is a patient of Papa's. Papa says it's a hopeless case . . .

GRANVIL. Everyone please excuse us for a moment. (*Pause.*) Blanche, you shouldn't be here. Does your father know where you are?

BLANCHE. Fooey, let me go. (*Pause.*) Where is he?

TANSKY. Who?

She goes up to the operating table and lifts the sheet.

GRANVIL. Blanche, what are you doing!

BLANCHE. Get away. You still haven't taken out his heart? (*Pause.*) I'll tear it out with my bare hands.

She stares at Chopin.

EMMA. Did you know him, mademoiselle?

BLANCHE. Did I know him? (*Pause.*) Why do you think that women crossed their legs whenever he played?

She sticks her head under the sheet and quite obviously kisses Chopin on the mouth. Everyone screams.

RUBINSTEIN. Oh, Jesus.

EMMA (*to Granvil*). Say something to her, monsieur.

TANSKY. Are you just going to stand there?

GRANVIL. Blanche . . . have you ever . . . have you ever heard of germs?

MANON. Atrocious.

Blanche falls back into the armchair. Granvil covers her with a sweater. Granvil and Tansky move off to the side.

TANSKY. Is everything alright?

GRANVIL. God.

TANSKY. What is it?

GRANVIL. I can't look her in the eye.

TANSKY. Who?

GRANVIL. Blanche!

TANSKY. Calm down, monsieur.

GRANVIL. Manon and I . . .

TANSKY. There's no reason to get upset.

GRANVIL. Yes, there is.

TANSKY. Perhaps you have fallen in love, monsieur?

Granvil does not answer.

TANSKY (*leans in and whispers something in Granvil's ear; after a moment*). Did you know that, monsieur? For real. There's no reason to get upset.

GRANVIL. She did these . . . things . . .

TANSKY. Really? A nice girl. Chopin was happy with her. George Sand gave him everything except for a decent fuck. So at the very end he needed Manon.

While Tansky is talking to Granvil, Manon takes out a flowerpot with a withered plant. She and Emma tear off a few leaves, roll them, and light them.

MANON (*to Emma*). That little Miss de la Mole's a piece of work.

EMMA. She has so-so teeth for her age.

MANON. Do you know Normandy?

EMMA. I was once in Rouen.

MANON. I was born a little bit farther. My aunt was a highly regarded Parisian courtesan. I never saw her. She died of consumption when I was seven. She left me her entire estate, stipulating one condition in her will: I was categorically forbidden from traveling to Paris.

EMMA. You're unlucky when it comes to wills.

MANON. You will be, too, when your husband finds out about you and Chopin.

EMMA. You really think I came here so that no one would find out? I want to retrieve those letters to have proof that I was Chopin's lover. To prove it, I need the letters: his letters to me.

MANON. You mean, you're not interested in your letters to him?

EMMA. Not even a little.

MANON. But . . . his letters to you . . . you don't have them?

EMMA (*takes out a bundle of papers bound with a red ribbon*). Only copies. (*She hands Manon the papers.*) It was his wish that I send the originals back to him. You understand, he was very sensitive about his image in the media. Even when he was alive he thought about the posthumous publication of his correspondence, and it was very important to him that nothing went missing.

Manon looks intently at Emma.

RUBINSTEIN (*to Blanche*). It's a pity that it's not me lying there, under that sheet.

BLANCHE. Who are you, monsieur?

RUBINSTEIN. Ivan Rubinstein. I had a bone to pick with Chopin, too. (*Pause.*) Him there, he's your fiancé?

BLANCHE. Yes.

RUBINSTEIN. Are you a natural blonde?

BLANCHE. Yes.

RUBINSTEIN. Have you read Tsvetaeva?

BLANCHE. No.

RUBINSTEIN *recites the text of the song "Nas ne dogoniut."*

EMMA. What would you do if you did get the apartment?

MANON. I'd start a brothel. A beautiful, warm brothel. Wallpapered in . . . musical notes . . . I know that Chopin would love it. And in the window a red neon sign: MARIOLA.

EMMA. MARIOLA?

MANON. That's what I'd call the brothel. After my mom. My mom was Polish.

EMMA. No kidding. Mine, too.

RUBINSTEIN (*to Blanche*). Her name was Marina. Do you speak Russian?

BLANCHE. No.

RUBINSTEIN. "Marina" is Russian for "Blanche."

Granvil goes up to Blanche.

GRANVIL. Blanche.

BLANCHE. What?

GRANVIL. Tell me. You and Chopin. Tell me what happened.

BLANCHE. I will not. I will never tell you.

GRANVIL. Why not?

BLANCHE. Or maybe I will. But some other time. (*Pause.*) Or maybe not. (*Pause.*) I'm talking to Monsieur Rubinstein.

RUBINSTEIN. Do you know Russia, mademoiselle?

BLANCHE. I've never been there. But my mother is Polish. That's sort of the same thing.

RUBINSTEIN. Mine was from near Szczyrek.

We hear knocking at the window. It's Ernest Zeidler. Monsieur Zeidler is about 50, stout, with a complexion that suggests high blood pressure. All of which is beside the point, since we do not see Ernest Zeidler at all. We only hear his voice.

ERNEST. Emma! Emma!

RUBINSTEIN. Who was that?

EMMA. My husband. (*She goes up to the window and opens it.*)

TANSKY. Where?

MANON. Monsieur Zeidler!

ERNEST. Please don't trouble yourselves. You can't see me. At all. Of course, this has gotten tiresome in the past. For example, when I was a child: they didn't let me take part in miming at school. But you cannot imagine how advantageous it can be in business. Emma!

Rubinstein signals for everyone to be quiet. He takes out the revolver and slides over to the window with his back against the wall. He motions for Emma to approach the window.

ERNEST. Emma! I'm talking to you.

EMMA. I'm coming.

ERNEST. Good evening, ladies and gentlemen. Emma, come here. (*To everyone else, in an explanatory tone*) The doorbell didn't work, and the door was locked.

EMMA. I thought you would send someone.

ERNEST. You're not pleased?

EMMA. What are you standing on?

ERNEST. On the ledge. There's a wide ledge out here.

EMMA. Come inside.

ERNEST. I can't. I'm caught on the lightning rod.

EMMA. Give me the check.

ERNEST. Help me.

EMMA. How?

ERNEST. Come here. Come on, come out to me.

EMMA. But I'm afraid of heights.

ERNEST. If you don't come out here, you're not getting the check.

> *Emma looks around at everyone else. Rubinstein motions for her to go out. Resigned, Emma climbs out the window. She is situated between the window sill and her invisible husband.*

ERNEST. I've got you.

EMMA. So now what?

ERNEST. Nothing.

EMMA (*drawing her head back and straightening her hair*). Ernest!

ERNEST. Let's see if you're still ticklish.

EMMA. Ernest! (*She writhes with laughter.*) Come on, Ernest!

ERNEST. We haven't been alone together for so long. I haven't had you near me for so long.

EMMA. I've had a hard day.

ERNEST. Is that all? You have nothing more to say to me?

EMMA. I wanted to read a little more.

ERNEST. What's the book about?

EMMA. You said you wanted to sleep.

ERNEST. No, I didn't.

EMMA. You said you were tired.

ERNEST. I'm not.

EMMA. Didn't you have a meeting?

ERNEST. I did. I don't want to talk about my meeting.

EMMA. You're getting up early tomorrow.

ERNEST. I can't sleep when it's light out.

EMMA. I only have three pages until the end of the chapter.

ERNEST. What's it about?

EMMA. Let me go!

ERNEST. You smell nice.

EMMA. Do you have the check?

ERNEST. You smell really nice.

The train of Emma's dress rises into the air.

EMMA. You'll tear my slip.

ERNEST. So fresh.

EMMA. God, and it's raining.

ERNEST. In sheets. Emma. Emma. Emma.

EMMA. Does anyone have an umbrella? Please. I just came back from the hairdresser's. (*Pause.*) Where are we going?

ERNEST. It's a surprise, Emma. Close your eyes, Emma. (*Pause.*) You can open them now.

EMMA. What's the occasion?

ERNEST. You really don't remember?

EMMA. I'm no good with dates.

ERNEST. Emma.

Tansky hands Granvil an umbrella.

TANSKY. You go. You're a doctor.

ERNEST. Emma.

Granvil walks up to the window and, turning his head away as far as possible, hands Emma the umbrella. Just then, Manon leaves the room. A moment later, Rubinstein also leaves the room.

EMMA. My stocking!

ERNEST. Emma, I love you. (*Pause.*) What did you say?

EMMA. Nothing.

ERNEST. What did you say?

EMMA. Nothing.

ERNEST. What did you say?

EMMA. Nothing.

ERNEST. What did you say? These potatoes are delicious. Have you seen my other slipper? Now that's what I call some tasty cauliflower. Did you pick the kid up from preschool? With cracklins. Emma.

EMMA. And who has been freed by their understanding of necessity? You could repeat that to yourself forever, you could even get it tattooed. And then who, after living for any decent time, can look around him without howling?

ERNEST. Emma. Emma. I love you, Emma.

EMMA. If only not to get into a cold bed every evening. If only to have someone you can fall to the ground with.

A moment of silence.

ERNEST. Here, your check.

With the others' help, Emma enters the room.

EMMA. Thank you so much. (*To Ernest, out the window.*) Aren't you coming in?

ERNEST. Forgive me, love, but I have to bounce. A meeting of the board of directors. Goodnight, ladies and gentlemen. I'm off!

Emma folds the umbrella and closes the window.
We hear noise backstage, followed by voices.

JEAN. I'm sorry!

MANON. Let me go.

JEAN. Are you alright?

MANON. Let go.

Rubinstein leaves and comes back a moment later with Manon and Jean Jean. Manon is holding a large satchel. She is also carrying Emma's fur coat.

TANSKY. You again?

JEAN. I came to return this.

He hands Emma a wallet.

JEAN. It fell out while you were doing push-ups on the ledge, madame.

EMMA. Thank you. (*She takes out a bank note and hands it to Jean Jean.*) For your honesty.

Manon forces the satchel on Jean Jean.

MANON. He's been stealing again! I caught him in the foyer.

JEAN. It wasn't me! It was her! (*He tosses the satchel back to Manon.*)

TANSKY. Don't you think that's taking it a bit far, monsieur?

JEAN. It wasn't me! Word of honor.

TANSKY. How did you even get in here?

JEAN. It really wasn't me. It was her. She was taking it to the door.

MANON. Stop lying!

JEAN. She was leaving with the bag!

MANON (*setting the satchel aside*). I found it in the foyer.

RUBINSTEIN. What were you doing in the foyer, mademoiselle?

EMMA. My fur . . .

RUBINSTEIN. Did you think you were going somewhere?

Silence.

MANON (*returning the fur coat to Emma*). God, how absent-minded I am! (*To Jean.*) I'm sorry that I misjudged you, monsieur. You have only yourself to blame. (*Pause.*) But now, madame and messieurs, please forgive me. I have a performance tonight; I'm almost late as it is . . . Adieu.

She walks toward the exit.

TANSKY (*looks at her reproachfully*). Manon!

Rubinstein intercepts Manon.

MANON. Well, fine. (*Pause.*) Might I have a cigarette? (*Granvil gives her a cigarette.*) Thank you. (*Pause.*) It was his idea. (*She points at Tansky.*) He's the one who came up with the blackmail scheme. I only went along with it to get the apartment back.

RUBINSTEIN. So it was about Madame Zeidler's money all along?

MANON. Not necessarily Madame Zeidler's. Chopin maintained relations with several loaded old broads. We knew that when news got out that his correspondence had disappeared, they'd get scared of a scandal and start sniffing around. It made sense that they'd first go to the place where the papers were lost, that is, here. Then all we had to do was to give them a good scare with a story about ransom: we wrote a note with letters cut out from the newspaper and paid the super's son to throw the rock with the message through the window.

RUBINSTEIN. Why didn't you send the letter directly to Chopin's lovers?

MANON. We didn't find their names. We only had a rough idea about these affairs. Chopin burned his love letters. Anyway, everything was going according to plan. Madame Zeidler read the article in the newspaper . . . (*She takes a crumpled newspaper clipping from the pocket of the fur coat.*) . . . and was ready to shower us in coin. And then Rubinstein showed up.

EMMA. So then you took my fur as a consolation prize?

MANON. No! 500,000 kept in the safety deposit box whose number is somewhere in Chopin's papers.

They all look at the satchel.

EMMA. If the papers were never lost, then why did you do it? After all, his will is in there, too.

MANON. Chopin did not write a new will. He promised me he would a few days before his death, but he didn't get around to it.

TANSKY. What a fool you are. The apartment didn't belong to him. He was only renting it.

MANON (*says nothing for a long time, takes a few steps, runs her fingers along the furniture, and finally says*). Does anyone know how much a ticket to America costs? They say that things are great there.

BLANCHE. Especially for sluts.

TANSKY. Leave her alone.

Silence.

Everyone stares at the satchel.

MANON (*to Emma*). Aren't you looking for the letters, madame?

Emma does not answer. She moves a few paces away and starts to put on her furs.

TANSKY (*loudly*). Any secretary can fake his employer's handwriting. I'll write him a life. Ten grand per fact.

Silence.

Granvil takes a moment to pull himself together. Finally, he approaches the operating table. He looks like a pianist at the keyboard. He takes the scalpel.

Darkness. Music: Fourth movement of the Sonata in B flat minor (in its entirety).

Lights.

Granvil is washing his hands. On the operating table there is a parcel bound with pink ribbon.

Granvil takes the parcel and tosses it to Tansky.

GRANVIL *(to Blanche)*. Get your things. We're going home.

Tansky stands, parcel in hand.

EMMA *(to Tansky)*. You're pathetic, monsieur.

She takes Jean Jean by the hand and moves close to him. Everyone is standing as if for a group photo.

EMMA. I will look after Jean Jean. Ultimately, there have to be a few good things about him. I'm going to die in 1870, during the Great Famine, in Paris, besieged by the Prussian army. I'm going to be strangled at the entrance to the zoo by a woman trying to get her hands on a giraffe neck.

RUBINSTEIN. I'm going to America with Manon. We'll never be married. We'll make a lasting contribution to the development of organized crime in Oklahoma.

BLANCHE. I'm going to become Granvil's wife. I'll give birth to three children. Our oldest son will drown while scuba-diving with his father in the Black Sea. I'll never get over it, and I will blame my husband to the end of my days. I will devote myself to collecting porcelain elephants with their trunks in the air.

Music: the last fado of Amália Rodriguez:

Maybe I'll die on the beach,
Caressed by the foam of the sea.
Maybe I'll die on the street,
On a dark and moonless night.
And maybe I'll die a natural death,

Quietly, in my sleep . . .

Everyone but Tansky moves around the stage, talking. The action is entirely voiceless. They speak only by moving their lips. Tansky is off to the side, holding the parcel.

MANON (*to Rubinstein.*) We'll have to look around for sales. There have to be some cheap flights.

EMMA. Fly Lufthansa. Their stewards are fucking awesome.

MANON. I don't like Nordic types.

EMMA. Then fly Alitalia. Oh, Naples!

BLANCHE. I want to go to Naples.

GRANVIL. Let's.

EMMA. Bellini was from Naples.

JEAN. From Calabria.

EMMA. I think it's nearby.

BLANCHE. Do you know any good hotels there?

EMMA. Give me your email. I'll send you addresses. I know a few good restaurants as well.

MANON. Oh, Ivan! Let's get pizza.

EMMA. Whenever I come back from Italy I can't get into my old clothes.

GRANVIL (*packing up his instruments, to Blanche*). Don't forget to give the sweater back.

EMMA (*to everyone*). Maybe we could all go out for dinner. Tour d'Argent? I'll reserve a table.

Manon and Rubinstein are a little concerned.

EMMA (*waves the check*). Monsieur Zeidler's paying.

GRANVIL (*to Rubinstein*). Showing up at the house of the dead and telling the bereaved about the shady dealings of the departed— is it lucrative?

RUBINSTEIN. It pays the bills.

GRANVIL. Did you hear that, Blanche? Maybe I'll retrain? (*Pause.*) She really doesn't have a sense of humor.

EMMA (*into her telephone*). For six. In 20 minutes. (*She laughs.*) All taken care of.

BLANCHE. What a lovely evening.

MANON. I love the moon.

> *Snow starts to fall onstage. Emma, Jean Jean, Granvil, Blanche, Manon, and Rubinstein start smiling, then laughing. They reach for the snowflakes.*

MANON: Let's get a taxi.

EMMA You're not coming with us?

MANON. We can't all fit. There's a cab stand just over there. (*Pause.*) See you.

> *She leaves with Rubinstein.*

EMMA (*to Jean Jean*). Is that a jacket?

JEAN: I'm an orphan.

EMMA. Tomorrow we'll buy you a new one.

JEAN. I'm not with you for the material comforts.

EMMA. Then you'll have a Ferrari. Give me a kiss.

> *Jean Jean kisses Emma.*

EMMA. You have lovely hands. (*Pause.*) Let's go.

BLANCHE (*to Granvil*). Come on.

GRANVIL. Go ahead. I'll catch up.

> *They leave.*

> *The music ends. Granvil goes up to Tansky.*

TANSKY. You're not going, monsieur?

GRANVIL. In a minute. I just wanted . . . I wanted to ask you something . . .

TANSKY. What is it?

GRANVIL. If it's like you said . . . If you really can copy Chopin's handwriting . . .

TANSKY. Yes?

GRANVIL. That piece of paper. The one on which he . . . where he asked . . . (*Pause.*) Did he write that, or not? (*Tansky bursts into laughter.*) Did he write it, or didn't he?

TANSKY. I'm not saying, monsieur.

Granvil makes for the exit. At the last moment he turns away from the door. He reaches into his pocket, takes out a scrap of paper, and writes something. He hands the paper to Tansky.

TANSKY. What's this?

GRANVIL. A prescription. De la Mole fucked up pretty bad, huh? Apply this twice a day. For a month.

He leaves.

Tansky looks around the room for a moment. Someone starts to play the Nocturne in E flat in the apartment below. Tansky grabs the broom and bangs it against the floor. It grows quiet. Next we hear a shot from a revolver, followed by an atonal bang on the piano. A few seconds later—all in the quarters one floor down—we hear a piercing female scream.

With a single sweep of his arm, Tansky pushes all the papers off the writing desk. He covers the desktop with a tablecloth and sets down a plate and silverware. He places the pink parcel on the plate, sits at the table, and pulls at the end of the ribbon.

Finis.

CHARACTERS

HE	30 years old, of medium build, a little on the heavy side
SHE	A little older than HE, brunette, somewhat tall

HELVER'S NIGHT

INGMAR VILLQIST

HELVER'S NIGHT

TRANSLATED BY PHILIP BOEHM

*A poor working-class kitchen with fairly high ceilings and a mix of fur-
niture that ranges in style from fin-de-siecle to the 1930s. A door on the
left opens out onto a stairwell; a man's coat, a woman's coat, a cap, and
a mesh shopping bag are hanging from three coat hooks fixed to the door
from the inside. To the right of the door is a large, double-sided casement
window with a broad sill: the window frame is painted red on the outside
and white on the inside. A potted flower, a few tin cans, and miscella-
neous small items are on the sill. Below the window is a wide wooden chest
covered with a white cloth. Directly opposite the audience is a wall with
a white door leading to the main room; at the top of the door we see a
small rectangular window with a curtain. Above the door is a reproduc-
tion of a hunting scene in a gilded frame. To the right of the door is a
white sideboard with a metal breadbox, some pots and pans, a large metal
alarm clock, a number of cans, a porcelain bowl, and a large radio from
the 1930s. The doors of the upper cabinets are glassed and draped with
curtains. Along the wall that forms the right side of the set we see a gas
stovetop with some pots containing dinner. Above the stovetop is a small
cupboard. A small table has been shoved against the wall between the
stovetop and a cast-iron sink; over the table is a calendar. Above the sink
is an oval mirror in a metal frame. There is a white table in the middle
of the kitchen, with an oilcloth cover on which we see newspapers, mugs,
and two places set for dinner. There are three white chairs and two small
stools. All the furniture has been painted with white oil paint. The play
takes place in the kitchen of a one-room apartment in the lower middle-
class district of a large industrial city in Europe.*

*The kitchen. Early evening. She is fiddling at the stovetop,
reheating supper, waiting for him. Now and then She crosses to the door
and listens. She opens one side of the window and looks out onto the street.
We hear the sounds of a demonstration growing louder and stronger. A
crowd of people is coming down the street. But not just this street: they*

*are marching throughout the district, and the din is growing louder and
louder—the rumble of shoes pounding the cobblestones and cement side-
walks, demonstrators shouting and chanting, glass shattering. As the
wave of people passes below, She closes the window and takes a step or two
back. She is worried and senses danger. The crowd outside is very loud.
She moves further away from the window and positions herself closer to
the door, where she listens expectantly and waits. We hear the gate to the
building clang open and close, and sounds of people running, shouting,
cursing, singing, chanting. A moment later we hear a person bounding
up the wooden stairs. She waits, eyes fixed on the door. We hear urgent
knocking, the door bursts wide open, and He steps into the kitchen, out of
breath and covered in sweat. He is wearing a pair of well-worn but carefully polished boots, brown breeches, a belt with a silver buckle, a white
short-sleeved shirt, buttoned at the neck, a leather black beret with a silver
badge, and is carrying a folded flag.*

*The kitchen. Evening. Outside is gray. Throughout, we hear the
noise of the demonstration rising and falling.*

*He stops just in front of the door and looks at her. He is excited,
worked up, animated. She looks at him calmly and expectantly. He slams
the door hard and flips the switch at the right door jamb to turn on the
light over the kitchen table—a bare bulb dangling from a tin lampshade.*

HE (*wild-eyed, with quick, nervous movements*). Do you know?

SHE (*controlling herself, although She is expecting to hear bad news*).
Hello, honey. It's good you're back.

HE. Do you know?! (*Gesturing toward the window with his flag.*) Do
you know what's going on?! Everybody! I mean everybody . . .

SHE. Put that away . . . (*Pointing to flag.*) And take off your beret.
I'm setting dinner on the table. Wash your hands please.
(*Crosses to the kitchen, picks up a pot of soup with a canvas mitt,
goes to the table and serves soup into the bowls.*) There, now, sit
down, please.

He doesn't budge. Tense and jittery, He follows her movements.

HE. Look out the window! The whole district! I'm telling you, the
whole district. And they say downtown as well . . .

SHE (*crosses to the window and shuts it firmly*). Let's sit down. (*Waits a moment and then sits down by herself.*) Are you going to eat anything?

HE (*provoking her*). No.

SHE (*starts to eat her soup*). It's your favorite—potato soup. Try it . . .

HE (*taking a step in her direction, holding out his flag*). Look what they gave me.

SHE. I put some bacon in it. A little marjoram . . .

HE (*another step*). Look! They gave me a flag. You see!? They didn't give one to everybody—

SHE (*tasting the soup*). Mmm. This is good. I think I'll have a little more . . .

HE (*crosses quickly to the window, opens it wide: we hear the din of the crowd*). Look! (*Leans far out the window.*) Hey yaaa!!! Hey yaaa!!! (*Shouts to the crowd and waves his flag.*) Hey!!! Hey!!!
She gets up very slowly from the table, goes to him and gently places her hand on his shoulder.

HE (*jumping away from the window at her touch, confused*). What!?

SHE (*calming him*). Don't lean out so far, it's the second story . . . Come on . . . (*Tries to put her arm around him.*) Let's eat. You must be pretty hungry by now.

HE (*stressing each syllable*). Don't you understand a thing? You don't, do you? (*Looking at the window the whole time.*) Everybody's out there! Look! (*Leans out the window and shouts.*) Heyyy! Heyyy! Hey-heyyy! Come on, shout something! Hey-heyyy! (*He waves his flag.*)

SHE. Come on, that's enough. (*Gently leading him away from the window.*) You're all flushed . . . Let's eat, then you can change.

HE (*tearing himself away*). I don't want to change. I don't want to eat anything . . . besides I just ate something.

SHE (*sits down and very slowly finishes her soup*). What did you eat?

HE (*as a challenge*). Pea soup.

SHE. Was it tasty?

HE. Um-hmm. (*Fast and close*) I'm telling you, the way we were all standing there, rank after rank lined up on the square in front of the post office . . . You know, I was standing in the first row, like this . . . (*Shows her.*) Then, all of a sudden, they handed out torches but Gilbert told us not to light them until we met up with the other units from the northern districts and then we'd all light them once it was dark and we'd all go at once and then the field kitchens arrived, you know the ones with the little chimneys, our garrison sent them out just for us, so we wouldn't go hungry and then each of us got a tin cup and a spoon and the cook gave me two ladles of pea soup, you know, two ladles, and there was a ton of bread as well, everybody could take as much as he wanted . . .

SHE. Did it taste good, this pea soup?

HE (*slowing down*). And then each man got a shot of liquor.

She eats in silence.

HE (*even more slowly*). I got one too . . . (*Speeding up*) They poured it out of these big green thermoses . . . (*Slowing down*) But just one shot . . . (*Speeding up again*) Because there were so many of us, standing one right next to the other, one right next to the other . . . And Gilbert says to me, "Down that schnaps!"

SHE (*gets up, goes to the stove*). Do you like Gilbert? (*Brings in two plates with the main course.*)

HE. Um-hmm. Gilbert is always telling me, "We'll make a soldier out of you yet, just you wait." And as we were standing there, Gilbert gave me this beret. (*Pulls off his beret and holds it right under her nose.*) You see? And then he pinned a badge on it himself. You see? He took it off some fat idiot who works in the laundry and pinned it on my beret himself. See?

SHE. That's a very nice beret. You look good in it.

HE. Um-hmm. He gave me the flag too. You see? He told me to carry it like this . . . (*He shows her.*) On my shoulder . . .

SHE. They didn't give you a torch?

HE (*uneasy*). No . . . (*To her*) Why do you ask?

SHE. I don't know. Did you ask Gilbert?

HE. No. Because he was talking with the officers. (*Quickly*) And they were standing straight as columns, you know. (*Shows her.*) They stood there holding their gloves in one hand and slapping them against the other, slapping them . . . and they lit cigars and Gilbert smoked one with them and they had helmets and sabers and one of them had a kind of glass in his eye with a little string . . . a little lens . . .

SHE. A monocle . . .

HE. Um-hmm. Why didn't they give me a torch?

SHE. I don't know. Maybe they only handed them out to the tall ones so everybody could see better.

HE. Exactly . . . And then Gilbert even smiled at me . . . And he praised the fact my boots were clean and said that an officer's boots have to shine like a dog's balls. (*More slowly*) That's what he said. He said that you could even shave with boots that shiny. I'm going to shave, I'll probably shave today, you know, because I'm going to start shaving.

SHE. Good. Tomorrow we'll go to the store and buy some shaving soap and a safety razor and a bowl and a big bottle of cologne.

HE. I'm going to use a straight-edge.

SHE. Fine, we'll buy you a straight-edge. I saw a really elegant one in the little shop by the tram stop, with an ebonite handle . . .

HE (*perking up*). That's exactly the kind Gilbert has, with a black handle, because he showed it and sharpened it on a belt.

SHE. We'll buy one tomorrow.

HE (*at a loss*). Not tomorrow.

SHE. Tomorrow. I'll do the shopping and buy a straight-edge. As soon as you've gotten up and eaten breakfast you can shave.

HE. Better not go to that little shop to buy a straight-edge.

SHE. Why?

HE. Because they don't have any.

SHE. I saw some there today on display.

HE. They don't have any straight-edges. Better buy it some place else. In the big store by the train station, where you always buy my soldiers.

SHE. Fine, but I still have to go to Hanssen's store to return the milk can.

HE. I'll get you a new one . . . Because . . . Because that shop isn't there any more. (*Quickly*) I mean, it's still there but it doesn't have any razor blades and it doesn't have your milk can because that little shop burned down and the whole place stinks and don't go there because it all stinks, the whole place stinks.

SHE. It burned down . . .

HE. To the ground . . .

She covers her face with her hands.

HE. But don't worry, don't worry, you can buy me a razor in the big store by the station. And will you buy me some more soldiers? But this time just the ones on the horses and buy some cannons and the musicians for the military band . . . Don't worry.

SHE. Were you near Hanssen's shop today?

HE. No. I stayed on the other side of the street. But I had the flag that Gilbert gave me and I was shouting.

SHE. What were you shouting?

HE. The same thing as everybody else.

SHE. And what were they shouting?

HE (*shrugs his shoulders, pinches his nose*). Pee-u. That's it. Pee-u. (*Speeds up*) Because as we were going down the street, everybody went "Aaaahhh" and ran over to that little shop, and then Gilbert took his billy club (*demonstrates*) like this and smashed in the window and then the old man comes running out with this knife I mean he had a kniiife and everybody with their torches . . . But I stayed on the other side of the street, on the sidewalk, right up against the wall, with that flag that Gilbert had given me . . .

SHE. And what happened to old man Hanssen?

HE. Nothing. (*Quickly*) But after everybody had run out of the shop Hanssen was on his knees in front of Gilbert and next, his shop was on fire and his daughter throws herself on Gilbert . . . (*Incredulously*) On Gilbert . . . and starts attacking him . . . (*Rabidly*) And Gilbert grabs her by her shaggy hair (*demonstrates*) and roars at her "You whoooooore!!!" (*with growing fury*) and then kicks and kicks that stupid shag-head . . .

SHE (*quietly*). You don't mean . . .

HE (*increasingly agitated, unfurls the flag, and plants himself in front of her, legs apart, shouting, and chanting*). Carc-ass!!! Carc-ass!!!

SHE (*watching him absentmindedly*). What are you saying?

HE (*sits at the table and moves the plate*). You can always tell who's a carc-ass . . . (*Speeds up*) Gilbert says he can spot one a mile away, from the smell (*Rabidly*) Carc-ass!!! (*Spits.*) Pee-u.

SHE. Don't spit on the floor.

HE (*slowly, alert*). And why not?

SHE. Because I spent all morning mopping . . . You've tracked it up enough as it is.

HE (*gets up suddenly and starts marching around the table, stomping loudly*). Trum-ta-da-dum, trum-ta-da-dum!!! That's how we marched, you see? Trum-ta-da-dum! And I was practically the first in the square. They came by foot, on bikes, in big cars. Trum-ta-da-dum! Because I can do it all now. (*Getting up*) Do you know? Gilbert ordered me to learn how. He gave me a book with pictures showing everything, everything. And I learned all of it. You don't believe me? Look. Atten-shun! (*He stands at attention.*) You have to stand straight, stomach in, your feet spread apart just a little, your hands at the seams of your pants, your head slightly raised. "At ease!" is like this (*demonstrates*). You move your left leg out. See how easy it is? I learned it all. Atten-shun! (*Stands.*) At ease! (*Assumes position.*) Atten-shun! (*Back to "attention"*) At ease! (*Back to "at ease"*) See how easy it is? You try it . . . It's easy . . . Atten-shun! At ease!

SHE (*smiling*). No . . . not me . . .

HE. But I'm telling you. It's easy as pie. Come on, try it.

SHE (*laughs*). Stop it.

HE (*fired up, excited, insistent*). Because it really isn't all that easy. Not at all. (*Slowly, alert*) It's not something any carc-ass can ever learn to do. (*Faster*) That's what Gilbert said . . . But I learned it all really quickly, you know? Very quickly. Gilbert said, "That's smart, that's smart." Do you know "Into two ranks fall in, dress right, dress?" Of course you don't. Because it's hard . . . Watch. Come on, look at me! They're moving and moving, all the ones that came to the square, and then you stand at attention and shout "Atten-shun!" And then they all stop and stand very quiet and you shout "Into two ranks fall in!!!" And they form two ranks just like that. You see? Can you do that? No. Because it's hard. And then, once they're all assembled, they have to break into ranks of four for marching. Then you have to shout . . . (*Thinks hard.*) "In four ranks, double-file, march!" And they march with torches and flags like the one Gilbert gave me, because Gilbert gave me a flag . . . Can you do that? Never. Not on your life. You'll never do that . . . because it's hard . . .

SHE (*taking the plates back to the stove; He watches her every move*). Want some dessert? There's strawberries and cream . . .

HE. You'd never be able to do that.

SHE (*cautiously, kindly*). Because only men can do that, not women.

HE. Carc-asses can't do it either. (*Quickly*) But you could do it. You could learn . . .

SHE (*shaking her head and smiling*). Me? No . . .

HE (*slowly*). You could learn if you wanted. (*Even slower*) You have to learn.

SHE (*very cautiously*). I have to? Why?

HE. Because Gilbert says that you—

SHE. Gilbert was talking about me?

HE (*thinking hard*). Gilbert says that you're a . . . (*Exploding*) That you could learn if you wanted to.

SHE. Gilbert says that.

HE. You have to learn. I'll teach you. Since I taught myself.

SHE. So what am I supposed to do?

HE. Everything . . . (*Very fast*) Because when they go on bivouac they sleep in tents and they keep watch and they drill and practice shooting and Gilbert even used a machine gun and they have duties and when they went to a real military training area with an airfield they even went inside a plane and Gilbert even flew in one and when some carc-ass ran tried to run off from his farm master they hunted him down and found him in a haystack and set it on fire and so he went running across the field and Gilbert gave the order to shoot him in the legs and when he fell Gilbert smoked one of his cigars, one of the carc-ass's, and the others smoked his cigarettes, because only Gilbert smokes cigars and one of the officers gave him one and (*very slowly*) Gilbert told me that someday I'll go on bivouac too.

She is silent.

HE. Gilbert said that the main thing is order. Wherever you are there has to be order, that's the most important thing.

SHE. Right, that's the most important thing . . . I think I'll go to bed, I'm very tired. And I have to get up again in the morning . . .

HE. You can't go to bed. You have to learn this . . . It's easy . . . I'll teach you everything. (*Goes to her and grabs her by the hand.*)

SHE. That hurts.

HE. I'll teach you everything.

SHE. That really hurts. Let me go. Please.

HE (*loudly, right in her face*). Atten-shun!!! What way to stand is that?

SHE. Please . . .

HE. Atten-shun!!! (*Adjusts her body.*) Legs together, hands by your side, feet apart. Head up. Now you're looking like a human being. OK one more time: Atten-shun!!! And now: At ease. Well: At ease! You think you're dancing? (*Quickly*) Atten-shun! At ease! Come on! Atten-shun! At ease! (*She clumsily executes all his commands.*) And now, hit the dirt!!!

SHE (*scared*). What do you mean?

HE. Ahh, you don't understand . . . I'll show you how it's done. Watch carefully . . . (*To himself*) Hit the dirt! (*Drops to the floor.*) Did you see? (*Gets up.*) Now your turn. Hit the dirt! (*She clumsily kneels on the floor.*) Not like that! Weren't you watching? Hit the dirt! (*Grabs her by the neck and throws her down.*) Do it! (*She gets up and drops down awkwardly.*) Again! Get up! Hit the dirt! Get up! Hit the dirt! Get up! (*She gets up, breathing heavily.*) What? Tired? That's good. You have to make yourself tired.

SHE (*gets up, laughs, pleading*). Whew. That's enough. I think I've got it now . . .

HE (*taken aback, angry*). No one gave the order to get up!

SHE. Let's take a break.

HE (*louder*). No one said to get up!

SHE. Just to catch my breath.

HE. Lie down!!! I told you to lie down!!! No one said to get up! Hit the dirt!!! (*Presses her to the ground.*) Hit the dirt and crawl!!! You have to learn! Come on, one-two, one-two . . . (*Grabs her.*)

SHE. (*tearing herself away, begging*). Stop it.

HE (*forcing her movements*). One-two, one-two.

SHE (*more insistent*). Stop it.

HE. You have to do it evenly. One-two, one-two . . .

SHE (*hysterically, struggling to break away*). Let go of me, you . . . imbecile!!!

He freezes and then gets up very slowly.

SHE (*getting to her knees, quietly, mostly to herself*). My God, I didn't mean to . . .

HE. I wanted to teach you, teach you . . . But you don't want to learn! Not in the least! (*She wants to get up, He grabs her and pushes her to the ground.*) So don't you go getting up! Don't you go getting up on me! (*He turns menacing, She senses that and freezes where she is on the floor.*) Je-sus!!! Je-sus!!! (*Grabs her.*) You don't understand a thing!!! And now, you, get up! Come on! (*Lifts her clumsily*) Get up! When I say "atten-shun" you get up. On "atten-shun!" (*Adjusts her body*) Well? Now what? (*Looks around the kitchen as if he's lost the thread*) What are you standing there for? Get to work! You have to work hard. Hard!

SHE (*quietly*). What do I have to do?

HE (*searches for a long time, then explodes*). Clean up! You have to keep this place clean!

SHE. I do clean.

HE (*vehemently*). But I see some disorder here! This is a mess! (*Circles her*) It doesn't . . . it smells in here. It smells. (*Solemnly*) Things can't go on like this. Not like this.

She expects the worst.

HE. You have to go to training. You have to learn everything. Don't you worry, you have to train.

SHE (*trying at all costs not to panic*). What are we going to do?

HE. OK. OK. Pack up . . . But you don't have a rucksack or anything . . . Do you?

SHE. No . . .

HE. Tough luck, but that's bad. Very bad. Take this (*Takes the shopping bag from the coat hook on the door and tosses it to her.*) This will be your rucksack . . . Well, put something in it . . . come on . . . And you have to have a belt . . . (*Ties a string around her waist.*) And a cap . . . (*Puts one on her—he's pleased.*) There, you see! And now we're going to march around a bit. (*He drags her around the stage.*) One-two one-two one-two one-two. Now you. One-two one-two one-two one-two. Lift those legs higher! (*She marches as He watches, conducting her marching with his hands.*) That's it! One-two one-two one-two one-two. Atten-shun! (*She stands at attention.*) Good, you see—you're in training. It's great, isn't it? (*Quickly*) And now you're going to sleep in a tent . . . Hmmm, under the table, just to pretend, under the table . . .

She tries to crawl under the table.

HE. Wait, wait . . . (*Tears off the tablecloth, spreads it out under the table, arranges some chairs around the table, places a few objects underneath including an alarm clock, mugs, dishrags, coats from the hooks on the door.*) There, you see? Your tent. Come on, get in . . .

She scoots under the table.

HE. Well, come on, lie down . . . Cover yourself up . . . You're comfortable, you see? Now go to sleep, go to sleep . . . (*Pushes her head against the floor.*) Go to sleep already, sleep . . . (*She stops moving.*) Are you asleep?

SHE (*very quietly*). Yes.

HE. That's good. Because it's already night . . . (*Stands and stares in front of him, glancing occasionally under the table.*) Enough!!! Enough!!! It's already morning. Time to get up! Stop sleeping! Wake-up time! (*Pretends to play the reveille on the bugle.*) Faster! Faster! (*Drags her out from under the table.*) You have to get up quickly. Quickly! Now it's time for gymnastics! Quickly! You have to run! Run! Well? (*She runs around the table.*) And now some squat-jumps. One-two one-two one-two. And now for the push-ups . . . Well, get down! Time for push-ups . . . (*She is very tired and out of breath, but tries to carry out his orders exactly.*) Well, you see? You see? And now you have to wash up, on the double. (*Drags her to the sink.*) Wash up, come on. (*She splashes herself with water, her hair and clothes are wet.*) Isn't it great? Isn't it great to wash up in the morning? Come on: One-two, one-two. (*Grabs her brutally.*) And now you have to strike the tent—make it snappy! (*Pushes her under the table.*) One-two, clean it up! (*Chaotically attempts to arrange the things under the table.*) Come on, snap to! (*Pulls her out from under the table, pushes her back, sticks his head inside.*) And who sleeps here?

She looks at him.

HE (*shouting*). Who sleeps here!!!

SHE. Me . . .

HE (*angrily, through his teeth*). You . . . you . . . (*Takes the objects under the table and throws them around the kitchen.*) Look at this filth, this dirt, this crud. Better clean it all up, and I mean fast. (*Grabs her and forces her to pick the things up.*) Clean that up! Clean that up . . . (*She tries to do so.*) Finished now? Come out. (*Pulls her out and sticks his head in.*) Who sleeps here?

SHE (*sobbing quietly*). Me.

HE (*muttering angrily, dives under the table, tosses things around the kitchen, upturns the table, knocks down a chair*). Pick it up! (*Grabs her.*) Pick it up!!! (*She picks up the scattered objects, rights the table, picks up the chair, and carefully places it under the table. He goes under the table and sticks his head out, looks at her, She is standing.*)

HE. Who sleeps here?

SHE (*crying*). Me.

HE (*scatters the things around the kitchen even more violently, making sure to turn over the table and chairs, then hits her hard in the shoulder with his fist*). What's-the-best-that-you-can-do. Study-dumbhead-till-you're-through. (*Grabs her head in his hands and shakes it hard.*) Dumbhead is right. Cause there's nothing upstairs! (*Hits her on the head with his fist.*) Boom-boom-boom. Boom-boom-boom.

She sobs with pain and terror.

HE (*arms akimbo*). What am I going to do with you? What? (*Different voice*) Poor boy, stuck with a dumbhead like that.

She tries to cozy up to him.

HE. Poor me all right. Saddled with the likes of you. With a noodle-head like you. A noodlehead, that's it. Poor little noodlehead . . . You know what they always say in Hanssen's shop? (*Different voice*) "Gone and ruined his life, He has, with a carc—I mean with an unfortunate girl like that. He has the patience of a saint that boy does." That's what they say. (*Quickly*) I always remember what I'm supposed to buy. You're the one who writes things down, so quickly you can't even read it . . . And you don't give me any change, always just a whole bill.

(*Imitates her.*) "Five crowns, I'm giving you five crowns." But now I've learned everything.

SHE. But I know . . .

HE. And you don't know how to do anything . . .

SHE. You have to teach me, please.

HE. I want to! (*Kicks a chair.*) But you can't remember anything! (*Kicks the chair.*) Not a thing!

SHE (*glances at the door and heads there*). I'm such a dumbhead . . . Teach me, I beg you.

HE (*standing by the window*). You have to try hard. Really try. And don't forget a thing . . . So you can say it all nice and proper when we go THERE again. (*She dashes for the door, opens it, He jumps onto her like lightning, they struggle and scuffle in the doorway. From the window we hear the roar of the crowd, in the panes of the open window we can see the reflection of the torches. He pulls her away from the door, throws her on the ground, locks the door, and hurls the key out the window. Then, very calmly*) You always have to tell them nice and proper whenever we go THERE. (*Using her voice*) So I don't have to be ashamed of you. We'll put you in some new clothes, a shirt and tie, part your hair to the side, part your hair and then we'll go back THERE and you'll have to say everything nicely and show what you know and figure out riddles and those funny rebuses, you know? And you have to listen to that man and think and think so that they don't take you for a ride and don't even think about mentioning (*wagging his finger*) you know what? You know what I'm talking about? You . . . (*goes to her and pulls her by the hair with all his strength, knocking her down, She struggles and breaks away, He straddles her and ineptly begins to strangle her.*)

SHE (*fighting him*). Stop it. Stop.

HE (*strangling her*). You have to. You have to learn.

SHE (*breaks away, catches her breath*). You are smart! You're very smart, you hear?!! Very smart!!! (*Sobs hysterically.*)

HE (*lets her go and slowly gets up, as if nothing has happened, slowly rights the table and chairs and picks up around the room, without looking at her, crosses to the sideboard, and turns on the radio: we hear what is clearly military march music*). I am smart. (*Looks at her.*) And I know that you will never learn anything. (*Goes to her.*)

SHE (*sitting on the floor, backing away*). I'll learn, you'll see.

HE. I have to ask you a question. One question. Because you have to know how to answer questions . . .

SHE. You ask and I'll answer.

HE. I'll ask . . . I'll ask the question . . . (*Standing in front of her.*)

SHE. May I get up?

HE (*quickly*). You have to sit . . . You have to sit right here.

She tries to smile expectantly.

HE. It's a difficult question. Real difficult.

SHE. I know. Very difficult.

HE (*a different voice*). Tell me boy, what do you see in that office?

SHE (*kindly*). You mean the kitchen?

HE (*throwing himself at her*). I know it's a kitchen!!! (*Calmly, slowly*) I was just talking. But I have a different question for you, a very hard one.

SHE. You ask very hard questions.

HE. There, you see . . . (*Different voice*) Tell me, boy, (*Very quickly*) what happens in winter?

SHE (*assuming the role*). In winter, when it starts to snow . . .

HE (*cutting her off, quickly*). No! Me! Me! (*Raises his finger like a schoolboy.*) I know. (*Very quickly, demonstrating*) In winter there's snow—white—and red hands and wet snowballs we throw like this (*demonstrates*) and coal to carry and a Christmas tree and colorful ornaments and it gets dark early and (*slowing down*) I'm all alone by myself because you're at your stupid work and I go downstairs by the gate and wait and wait for you because I don't want to be here alone and I wait and wait for you at the tram stop and it's snowing and I'm waiting and waiting and it's dark . . . (*lively*) You see? I know what happens in winter.

SHE. That's very good . . .

HE. Because that was a hard question, hard.

SHE. Very hard . . .

HE (*different voice*). And now tell me, my boy . . . Tell me, boy . . . (*Thinking, searching.*)

SHE (*helping out*). Yes? (*Wanting to prompt him*) Yes?

HE (*increasingly unsure of himself*). Tell me . . .

SHE (*quickly, trying to help*). What did you dream about last night?

HE (*a look of terror and fear flits across his face for a second, then he runs to her and holds her close, seeking protection, a reflex reaction, he wants to hide*). No, I don't want to . . . Not anymore . . . Please . . . No . . .

SHE (*holding him close*). Shhh, shhh . . . (*Caresses him, strokes his head.*) Shhh, now, shhh . . . (*He slowly calms down and catches his breath.*) Shhh . . . that's right.

HE (*moving away from her*). Why did you ask me a question like that?

SHE. (*caressing him*). What kind of question do you mean?

HE (*slowly, distantly*). You know that you're not allowed to ask questions like that. Never ever.

SHE. OK. OK.

HE (*knocking her down*). You asked me that question on purpose! So that I'd . . . so that once again I'd . . . (*Very seriously*) Don't you ever ask that question again. Never.

SHE (*nods her head*). Turn down the radio, would you please?

He goes to the radio and turns it up full volume, so that a march comes booming out. Then He looks at her and starts marching in place. He trumpets and stomps and takes two lids from the stove and clashes them together in a loud rhythm.

SHE. Stop it!!! Would you finally calm down?!! (*Runs to him, takes away the lids and turns off the radio. Outside we hear the tumult growing louder and more menacing.*) My God. You never let up, do you?

HE (*confused*). Now we'll . . . Now we are going to . . .

SHE. Just leave me alone for a minute would you please!!!

He keeps his eyes on her as He turns on the radio and looks for another station. We hear a lively, popular polka by Marlene Dietrich.

She is resigned, and shakes her head.

HE. Dance. You have to dance. (*Tries to get her to dance.*)

SHE (*brusquely*). Helver! Let go of me!

HE (*pulling her toward him, with force*). You like to dance. You always said you liked to dance.

SHE. I've had enough dancing.

HE. So let's dance. (*They start to dance, clumsily.*)

SHE. Don't jerk me like that, it's a polka after all . . . You have to feel the rhythm . . . There, right leg, left leg . . . No, no . . . (*Releases him and dances a polka by herself, flawlessly, becoming completely absorbed in the dance. He turns up the radio and squirms in place.*) I've had enough. I just can't dance another step.

HE. But weren't you dancing now?

SHE (*waves her hand, resigned. The next song comes over the radio, a slow waltz—"mood music"*). Turn that off.

HE. No.

SHE. Turn it off right this minute! (*Covers her ears.*)

HE (*slowly*). I know why you don't want to hear that.

SHE. What do you know about anything?

HE. Because you always start crying when that lady on the radio sings . . . I know why . . .

SHE. Leave me alone.

HE. I know . . .

SHE (*angry*). What do you know?

HE. Because when you found a present under the Christmas tree . . . when our pastor came to visit at Christmas—because our pastor came to visit at Christmas—he brought you a package from the Christmas angel and there was a record in the package with a picture of that lady (*points to radio*) the one who's singing now.

SHE. So what about it?

HE. Then the pastor told you that it was your favorite record and your favorite song and said you danced so well to that very same record at your . . . wedding.

She is very much on the alert.

HE. And I know what a wedding is.

SHE. How do you know what the pastor said?

HE. Because I hear everything . . . And when I shut my eyes very, very tight I can hear everything very, very far away . . . (*Slowly*) Because you took for wife a certain man . . .

SHE (*sharply*). Helver! Stop it! (*More gently*) And a woman doesn't take for wife: you say she married . . .

HE. Because you took for wife . . .

SHE. What are you talking about?

HE. And I know what that man looks like.

SHE. Helver . . .

HE. He has a beard like this and a moustache . . . (*Shows*) And a ribbon all tied right here . . . and a white flower in his lapel, a big white flower . . . and you have a white dress, a great big white dress, and a kind of scarf on your head that you can see your face through and flowers on your head and flowers in your hand . . . And you're standing together and your heads are touching. And you're looking at him like that and he's looking at you and you both are smiling.

SHE (*tears away and goes running into the room; we hear drawers and cabinet doors slamming shut; She bursts into the kitchen, furious*).

Where is my box?! I have a lot of important things in that box! Where is my box!!!

HE. I didn't take your box. I just took this box for keeping my tin soldiers . . .

SHE. How dare you rummage through my things!!! Give it back!!! You hear me you idiot!!! Give it back!!! (*Pounds on him with her fists.*) You ape-man! Give it back!!! Where is it!!!

HE (*slowly*). That's where I keep my tin soldiers . . . Because you buy me a lot of tin soldiers.

SHE (*screams*). Where is it!!!

HE. My soldiers.

SHE (*breaks away, searches through the kitchen, runs out to the room, and comes back*). Where are my things!!

HE (*afraid*). Hey, they're right here, under the table. (*Indicates a table by the wall.*)

SHE (*finds a big box that used to have chocolates, which she opens. Furiously, She dumps a collection of tin soldiers onto the table and tosses the box into the corner of the room*). Where are things that were inside!!! What did you do with them!!! (*Grabbing him.*) Well?! *He lowers his head.*

SHE. Did you throw them away!!!??? Did you!!!??? Well!!!??? You did, didn't you? You horrible ape-man! (*Imitates an ape-man, making fun of him, in a rage.*) I've had enough! You hear!!! Enough! My God, I must be dumber than you, spending so many years with a . . . pfui!!! Oh no, Helver . . . Oh no . . . (*Dashes to the sideboard, opens a small cupboard, pulls out an envelope with various seals and waves it in front of his nose.*) Do you know what this is!!!??? Well, do you!!!???

HE. No.

SHE (*sadistically*). This is a summons to the Clinical Certification Commission . . . Freshly printed . . . The postman just brought it today . . . For tomorrow morning, you hear!? Tomorrow morning we are going to the Clinic, to talk to the doctor inside his office . . . I'm packing up your shitty little soldiers and your toys and your berets and off you march!!! And the doctor will ask you: "Tell me, my boy . . . Tell me, my boy, what do you see in this office?" And you'll be so afraid you'll piss in your pants, because that big noggin of yours (*knocks his head*) is utterly and absolutely hollow! Hollow!!! And then the orderlies will come and take you and put you in a great big room with fifty others just as imbecilic as you and then you can all play with your shitty little soldiers . . . And at night . . .

HE (*balled up out of fear*). Don't talk like that. You weren't supposed to talk like that . . .

SHE (*she goes on*). And at night they turn off the lights . . . It's very, very dark, (*like a ghost*) ooo-ooo, ooo-ooo . . . And when you close your eyes . . . then . . . the worms start crawling out of your head . . .

HE (*sticks his fingers in his ears*). I can't hear you. I can't hear you.

SHE (*relentless*). And anyone who gets afraid, or pisses in his pants, they tie up and take a needle and give injections straight into their empty noggins . . . And the ones that can't figure out the rebuses they attach these wires to their heads and send a current through like this (*shakes herself*) just like that.

HE. And where will you be?

SHE. I'm just going to leave you there!

HE. But you're coming with me into the doctor's office when he asks me questions.

SHE (*curtly*). No.

HE. Where will you be?

SHE. Somewhere. Enough of this. You hear!? Enough! . . . Besides, they're going to take you right out of the Clinic anyway and then it's over. You hear? They'll take you away and then you're done for.

HE (*gets up and pulls out a packet of photographs from under the sideboard, letters wrapped with a ribbon, and slowly places it in front of her*). I didn't throw them away. I just took the box . . . and hid them there . . . (*Pointing under the sideboard.*) I hid those pictures and papers there so they wouldn't get lost . . .

She stares at the photographs and letters, petrified.

HE (*sits across from her and starts to place his tin soldiers on the table, points at a photograph*). That's that man you took for wife.

SHE (*wiping her eyes*). Yes, that's him.

HE. You were . . . In love?

SHE. Very much.

HE. And he said to you: "Will you take me for wife?"

SHE (*almost moved*). No, he asked me if I would do him the honor of accepting his proposal . . .

HE. He said it nicely.

She is holding back tears.

HE. And then what? You cried and laughed . . . That's called . . . that's when you're happy . . . and even more . . . when you are m-m-moved . . . right?

SHE. Yes, I was very happy.

HE. And in love . . .

SHE. Yes . . . Very much in love . . .

HE. In love . . . that means that you cried and laughed and laughed and cried and your eyes were happy and not sad . . . like they always are . . .

She is still holding back tears.

HE. So why are you here with Helver and not happy with that man? People with a wife live together, together. Are you and I man and wife?

She bursts into sobs.

HE. And they have children . . . Did you have . . . (*as if ashamed*) a child?

SHE (*dry, broken sobs, practically howling*). Yes . . . I had . . . I had . . . a child . . .

HE. Boy or girl?

SHE. A little girl . . . (*Cries*) A little girl . . .

HE. Is she pretty?

She cries, something breaks inside her.

HE. And where is she, where is she now, your little girl?

SHE (*sobs*). I . . . I . . . that man and I . . . My husband and I had a child . . . a little girl, so small . . . We loved each other very, very much, you know? We had a house, with a little garden . . . Then we had a little girl . . . and I . . . and I . . . when she was born (*sobs*) she . . . she . . . it happened that she was very very sick (*bawls*) she was a little monkey, you know? (*Cries*) A kind of monkey . . .

HE (*curious*). Like an animal?

SHE. No . . . she was very sick . . . and I . . . (*Breaks down.*) I didn't want her . . . (*Through her tears.*) I mean I wanted her . . . but I couldn't . . . everything had been so beautiful . . . our house and everything . . . and she was so . . . so . . . (*Cries*) That man, you know, my husband . . . everything changed when I gave birth to her . . . He stopped smiling, just sat on the threshold and looked at the garden and smoked his cigarettes, one after the other, you know? And I held her all day long in my arms, kissing her, I wanted to calm her down somehow because she was always screaming, day and night, day and night, howling away . . . For a whole month she screamed like that . . . and I said to my husband "Say something to her . . . (*Cries*) Hold her . . . (*Cries*) Smile at our child." And he got up and walked out of the house without even looking . . . Once when he fell asleep in the big chair after working, and she suddenly stopped crying, just like that, I covered her little mouth with a napkin, because she had a little bitty beak of a mouth you know . . . She was very sick . . . and I laid her very gently on my husband's knees . . . (*Quickly*) He jumped up and she fell down . . . "What are you doing?" I asked . . . and he ran out of the house screaming "That's not my child!" (*Cries*) I stayed up all night long waiting for him . . . And the next morning I took her to the Institution.

HE. The hospital?

SHE. Yes . . . no.. it's like a hospital but different. I took her there at
five in the morning, left her at the gate and ran away . . . Ran
away! (*Cries*) And when I came home, my husband was waiting for me . . . with flowers and a little wooden puppet, you
know, the kind you pull on the string and it moves its arms
and legs . . . And asked me to forgive him, that he thought
everything over and understood that a child, that everybody
has a right to live . . . he smiled and cried and hugged me . . .
He told me he'd spent all night with the pastor, and the pastor
had explained everything, that it was the most important conversation of his life and in our life . . . He said there were a lot
of families that had children that were . . . well, that were different, and that they loved them even more . . . He said that
now we were going to love our little monkey . . . (*Sobs and
howls.*) He hugged me and kissed me and cried so much . . .
and then he held me for a long time, so tight, and finally he
said: "And now let's go to our little monkey we love so much
. . ." (*Cries*) And he pulled me into the child's room . . . I stood
there paralyzed, I wanted to die, you know, die. I tore myself
away from his loving arms and ran to the Institution . . . I don't
even remember the way . . . just that it had this huge iron gate
. . . and it was closed, and our little daughter wasn't there any
more, our little monkey . . . I stood in front of that gate, a
crowd of workers from our foundry was coming off the night
shift and knocked me down . . . and I knew that was the end,
the end of everything . . . No one in the Institution wanted to
talk to me . . . They looked at me strangely and told me to get
out, get out! And I knew, I felt, that my little monkey was
there . . . I started to scream and hit those horrible doctors and
those nurses with their evil eyes and they called the police.
They took me to the office of the director of the Institution
and made me sign a paper that I . . . that I would never look
for her . . . When I told my husband what had happened . . .
(*Cries*) He wouldn't let me in the house . . . He hit me with
all his might and screamed that I was dead, that I was dead

for him forever . . . (*Explodes*) Oh how I looked for her later! I looked everywhere. For years and years . . . I knew that when I found her we would go to him together, to that man, to my husband and . . . and that he . . . (*Cries*) would hold us tight . . . so tight . . . (*Cries*).

HE. And did you find your little monkey?

SHE. No . . . I didn't. (*Firmly*) But God is my witness that I tried . . . I would have given everything just to look at that funny little beak of hers . . . Later . . . after I'd been everywhere . . . Finally I wound up at an enormous old Institution on the other side of the country . . . There this gray-haired doctor told me that it was pointless, that I should stop looking . . . Because she didn't exist anymore . . . not in this world . . . He said that no one needs or wants ones like that but only the good Lord holds them more tightly than others, than the normal ones . . . and then I really did die, you know?

HE. But you're alive . . .

SHE. I walked out of that place, down on a long cobbled avenue and every step seemed to be my last . . . and then . . . (*Smiles.*) I met you, Helver . . . You were sitting on an old iron bench under a tree, wearing funny pajamas with blue stripes . . . You were staring off into the distance, swinging your legs and you had this strange, delighted smile . . . Just staring off into the distance . . . We started to talk, remember?

HE. No . . .

SHE. You asked me if I was your mother.

HE. You're not my mother.

SHE. And I looked in your eyes and in your smile and saw hope, hope that everything will change . . . that at least in this way . . . (*Dry sob.*)

HE. And then you took me . . . You held my hand and we walked to the station . . . And there were so many people . . . And we rode in the train and rode . . . And you bought me some colored water to drink, and then, when we got out . . . In that shop near the station . . . You know, right here . . . You bought me some soldiers . . . but that was a long time ago, because I just had two soldiers (*takes them from the table*) this one and this one . . . And now I have all these (*points proudly at the pile on the table.*)

SHE. That old doctor agreed. He gave you to me. They called a commission together and a week later we were here. And we've been living like that ever since . . . Except we have to go to our Clinic once every three months and answer questions and riddles . . . so that they don't take you back away from me . . . But when we go tomorrow, because we're going together, it will all be fine . . .

HE. But you're going with me.

SHE. Of course I'm going with you and I'm going inside with you and I'll hold your hand like always . . . Remember? When I pinch you you say "No" and when I rub you you say "Yes." Remember?

HE. Um-hmm. Last time I had my whole hand all pinched up, but the doctor said "Not bad, my boy, not bad." But my whole hand was pinched up . . .

SHE. Now I'll make you supper, I'll make you some rolls, with sauce and cracklings . . .

HE. Um-hmm. But I'll make the dough balls.

SHE. Just don't eat the dough because you'll get a stomachache.

A burst of broken glass. A stone comes flying into the kitchen, then another, then a third, and finally a flaming torch. We hear the roar of a crowd outside the window, groups of people running up and down the stairs and breaking into apartments on various floors of the building, screams of people being dragged out of their homes. He and She stare at the shattered window. She stamps out the burning torch and pours water on it. Fierce knocking at the door. They freeze for a moment. Outside the door we hear shouts and screams and people being dragged out of their apartments, sobbing and the sounds of beating. She locks the door and barricades it with the table.

SHE. Helver . . . Now listen carefully . . . Look at me . . . (*Shakes him.*) Look me in the eye . . . You have to es—you have to go now. Right now.

HE. Go?

SHE. I'll explain later . . . Get dressed . . . Put on your shoes . . . Not those . . . The boots . . . Boy do they shine . . .

HE. Gilbert said that an officer's boots have to shine like a dog's balls . . . That's what Gilbert said . . .

SHE. Put on your pants . . . (*Helps him get dressed.*) Hurry, put them on. Now we'll fasten your belt . . . and now your shirt. Wait the button tore off . . . I'll sew it right back on . . . (*Retrieves needle and thread from the drawer in the table and starts sewing on the button as she speaks.*) Helver, you know what we're going to do now?

HE. We're going to . . . We're going to do . . .

SHE (*sewing*). You'll get dressed . . . (*Bites the thread with her teeth.*) Stay still would you . . . Put on your coat . . . There . . . Let's button the buttons . . . Now the belt . . . Now your beret . . . That's a really neat beret you have, you look like a real soldier . . . Now you sit down and I'll pack your rucksack. (*Brings a rucksack in from the main room.*)

HE. So you do have a rucksack.

SHE. I had forgotten . . . Remember, I'm packing a whole loaf of bread, sausage, three apples . . . socks—the warm ones—a shirt . . . (*Wipes her tears.*) And here . . . (*Holding out some money.*) you have some money. You understand? Many, many crowns . . . Put them in your boot. Here . . . (*Helps him take off his boot and stash the money.*)

HE. But now it's pinching me . . .

SHE. That doesn't matter, it will loosen up. That will be our secret and nobody else's.

HE. Good, our secret and nobody else.

SHE. Now put on your beret.

HE. I have the badge right here, the badge that Gilbert gave me . . .

SHE. Right . . . You have a nice badge . . . and now we'll put on your pack . . . There . . . (*Helps him with the rucksack.*) And now Helver is ready for a trip, right?

HE. I'm going to training. To training. Gilbert told me I'd go to training . . .

SHE. You're going on a big expedition.

HE. What's an "expedition"?

SHE. Something more than "training."

HE. Aha . . .

SHE. There . . . (*Hands him the flag.*) Take it and hold it high, that way nobody will . . . (*holding back tears.*)

HE. Gilbert gave me that flag, Gilbert gave it to me . . .

SHE. That's right . . . Now listen to me . . . Look me in the eye. Now you're going to go out and straight to the train station . . . You can get there, right?

HE. Of course. The station is near the shop with the soldiers.

SHE. Bravo. There will be many many people at that station. Because they're all running there now. They will be running and screaming and crying. But don't look at that, all right? Don't worry about that . . .

HE. OK.

SHE. There will be trucks there and soldiers and police and people with torches and dogs and flags . . .

HE. Like the one Gilbert gave me . . .

SHE. That's right. Now, when you get to the station you're going to raise your flag high and (*doesn't know what to say next.*) And . . .

HE. And I'm going to shout: "Carc-ass, carc-ass!!!" And do like this . . . (*Runs his finger across his throat.*) Right . . .

SHE. Excellent, Helver, bravo! You are very smart. You walk by them, and if someone stops you, you know, one of the ones with the torches or dogs, you say . . . you say . . . that Gilbert gave you that flag.

HE. Because Gilbert gave me the flag, Gilbert gave it to me.

SHE. And that Gilbert ordered you to go to the station and you have to go there because Gilbert ordered you to. Can you remember that?

HE. And Gilbert said . . .

SHE. Listen, Helver. Then you go to the ticket counter, you know where that is? That little window where a man or woman sells tickets. You understand?

HE. Um-hmm.

SHE. And you ask for one ticket to Ellmit. Can you remember? Ellmit, that's a little fishing village, right by the sea . . . That's where that Institution is, the big one . . .

HE. Where we came from . . .

SHE (*very pleased*). Yes! Yes! (*Hugs and kisses him.*) Here are seven crowns. The ticket costs seven crowns: five paper crowns— (*Hands him the bill.*)—and two coins. (*Hands him the coins.*) Hide them under your beret. When you get your ticket hide that under your beret as well. Don't take off your beret . . . You wait for the train on the platform . . . Don't walk around, just stand there and wait . . . When the train comes . . . There will be a huge crowd and everybody will be pushing and shoving and screaming . . . Helver, listen! As soon as the train pulls up to the platform, you run to the nearest open window— there's always one open—and climb inside, into the compartment through the window, understand? Will you climb inside?

HE. I'll climb inside.

SHE. And sit there and don't move. Don't move. You hear? And whatever you do, don't get up. And if you start to fall asleep, open your eyes very very wide and say to yourself: "I won't fall asleep, I can stand it. I can stand it because I am smart."

HE. You mean you don't sleep if you're smart?

SHE (*holding back tears*). Not tonight . . . Tonight smart people don't sleep . . . You'll ride on that train all night long. Then you'll get to Ellmit, remember, Ellmit, it will already be morning. It

IMAGE 2.2 (From left to right) Jolanta Dapkūnaitė and Arūnas Sakalauskas in Jonas Vaitkus' production of Helver's Night. Lithuanian National Drama Theatre, Vilnius, 2003.
Photograph by Dmitrij Matvejev.

will already be light, you know? That's the last station. The last one, and everybody will get out, you understand? You'll get out with them and walk straight out of the station, remember, straight out of the station down a long, long avenue, straight to the Institution.

HE. Where you went and found me and brought me here . . .

SHE. That's right . . . (*Hugs him.*) That's right . . .

HE (*wary, uncertain*). Home . . . you brought me home, right?

SHE (*tears are running down her face*). I brought you home . . . to our . . . to your real home . . .

HE (*quickly*). So why do I have to go now?

SHE. Helver! Listen to me for God's sake! When you get there you say that you have very important information for Doctor Gerdman. What will you say?

HE. For Doctor Gerdman.

SHE. Right. For Doctor Gerdman. He's an old man with a gray beard and funny glasses. He's a good man, very good. He will remember you . . . Now listen carefully . . . Tell him, tell Doctor Gerdman that Karla told you to come. Repeat that.

HE. That Karla told me to come.

SHE. Very good . . .

HE. But you're Karla . . .

SHE. That's right . . . And wait there for me. Be calm and wait. I'll be there very soon. Wait calmly. I'll be there in two or three days . . .

HE. And where will you be?

SHE. I just have one very important thing to take care of here and I'll join you right away, right away.

HE. For sure?

SHE. For sure.

HE. For sure?

SHE. For sure . . . Now go, please . . . (*Pushing him out the door.*) Come on, go . . . (*Goes to the window: outside the crowd is roaring.*) Please, go, I beg you . . .

HE (*reaching for the handle*). But you're coming for me?

SHE. Yes, I'm coming. Go, Helver, now . . . (*Urging him out.*) Please . . .

HE. I'd like . . . I'd like . . .

SHE (*she listens to what is going on in the stairwell and urges him out*). Helver, I beg you, go . . .

HE. I'd like . . . I'd like you to smile at me like you did at that man in the picture. At that husband . . . For you to take me by the hand, for us to hold hands . . . (*She is holding back sobs.*) That our heads would touch like with that man in the picture (*She hugs him and they stand there awkwardly like newlyweds at the photographer's.*) Because . . . Because if you had a little girl here now, a little monkey, like you told me, I wouldn't scream at her or at you . . . I would play with her . . . (*Faster*) And I'd teach her, I'd teach her . . . (*Slowing down*) And I'd give her soldiers . . . and put her on my knee . . . and stroke her face . . .

SHE (*unable to hold back the tears, she opens the door and tries to push him outside*). Go, quickly . . . (*Crying*) While you still can . . . Go . . .

HE. Because . . . You're not my mama. And you're not my . . . wife either . . . But you're a little like my mama and a little like a wife . . . Because I am laughing a little now and crying a little and that means that I l—. . . that you, that Helver very much lo— . . .

SHE (*spasms*). Go . . . (*Shoves him into the hall.*) Go . . . (*He disappears behind the door.*) Run away . . . My dearest dearest boy . . . (*We hear quick steps, the crowd outside the window is roaring, but the stairwell is quiet. She listens, very afraid.*)

Karla is alone in the kitchen. Outside the window the commotion continues: shouts, single muffled shots, dogs barking. On the stairs we hear people running in and out, shouts, isolated beatings, doorhandles being rattled and doors being kicked open. Karla starts packing in haste: she brings a suitcase in from the room, puts it on the table, runs back into the room, and returns with a pile of her things, puts them inside the suitcase, along with objects from the kitchen: the clock, a plate, the picture above the door—all very chaotically, the way a person does who must suddenly abandon his home.

Karla puts on her coat, a cap, carefully looks out the window. Then she slows down, resigned to the fact that escape is pointless, and sits on a chair . . . Suddenly we hear amplified shouting from the stairwell, the sound of someone being hit, and then running away. A loud noise at the door, fists pounding, a muffled cry . . . Karla stands still, more banging at the door . . .

Karla doesn't move; she has resigned herself to her fate. Then she slowly approaches the door and unlocks it . . . The door bursts open . . . At the same time the lights go out: someone has cut off power to the building. We can see the light of swaying lanterns outside the window . . . Sound of doors slamming shut. Darkness. A figure stands near the door, breathing heavily. Constant noises from the stairwell and outside: trucks driving up, shouts, dogs barking.

SHE (*in the dark*). Who is it? (*Lights a candle and holds it overhead.*)

It is Helver. He has been mauled and beaten; his coat is filthy with mud; he has one boot; his buttons have been torn off; he has lost his beret; his face and head are bloody; he has no belt; and he is holding his torn rucksack and the broken staff of his flag.

SHE. Helver!

HE. And they took my boot when I was on the stairs, as soon as I was on the stairs . . . and I don't have my flag . . . Because Gilbert took it away from me . . . He took it away here in our stairwell and broke it because I didn't want to give it to him, because Gilbert gave me that flag, Gilbert gave it to me . . .

SHE. Good God, Helver! What happened?

HE. Because when I went to the station where you told me to go, when I went out on the street, right here, just near our gate . . . And there were so many people, so many people . . . I ran down the sidewalk, along the wall, along the wall to that big square where there's that big statue with that man on a horse . . . (*Very quickly*) There were so many people there, so many people and cars with these black dogs and torches and flags like the one Gilbert gave me . . . And I held my flag up very high, very high and ran and ran to the station, didn't even look at anyone just ran to the station . . . and then this man with these scabs on his lip, you know, the one who always yelled at us on the street, don't you remember? He always yelled and called us bad words . . .

SHE. Helver, tell me what happened . . . Why didn't you run away—

HE. And the man with the scabs when he saw me he started to yell, you know: "Helver! Helver the retard! Catch Helver! Get the carc-ass!" And he jumped down from the truck and some others, I know them well, put their legs out to trip me and they kicked me and wanted to take my flag that Gilbert . . . But I didn't let them . . . I held the flag high, I held it tight and yelled: "Carc-ass! Carc-ass!" Just like you told me . . . They kicked me here . . . (*points to his head and face.*) But I yelled anyway . . . And they said bad things about you, very bad things.

SHE. Helver, my Helver.

HE. That you . . .

SHE. Don't say anything . . . Don't say it . . .

HE. That you and I . . . that you do things with a carc-ass . . . That's what they said, they said "We'll fuck you over and that woman of yours" and the words they used, the words . . .

SHE. My little Helver . . .

HE. And then they grabbed me and threw me into the truck. And when they carried me this one man with a big huge shaggy dog shouted to his dog: "Fetch the carc-ass, fetch!" And the dog was called Murcek. Because then the man said: "Good dog Murcek, good dog."

SHE. Show me . . . Don't move . . . I have to disinfect the wound . . . My God, he bit right through . . . Hold your finger here . . .

HE. And on that truck . . .

SHE. Helver, don't move, I have to put a bandage on . . .

HE. And in that truck where they threw me, they had all the idiots from our neighborhood. The man who works in the laundry, with a head like a cucumber, and the girl who always moves her head like this (*demonstrates*) and little Hainel who walks like an idiot and you know who else was there? That stupid Helmut who goes around with a cart to the paper collection and every one of them, you know . . . (*taps his head.*) The whole truck was full of them . . . and they laughed, those idiots laughed when they were being beaten, but some of them cried

. . . But I didn't cry . . . And one officer said "To the Clinic with them and finish them off!" So I jumped right out of the truck (*demonstrates*) like that, and they all fell over and I ran away and ran away . . . Because I'm not going to that Clinic because you told me you would always go with me, that's what you said, because that's what you said . . .

SHE. That's true, Helver, I'll go with you everywhere, everywhere . . .

HE. Even to the Clinic?

SHE. Even to the Clinic.

HE. When I ran away they grabbed my beret so I don't have that money for the ticket, you know . . .

SHE. That doesn't matter, it's not important . . .

HE. But I have the money in my boot, because they only pulled off that one boot here on the stairs and now this one really pinches . . . And when I ran away, to the entrance of a building, our pastor stopped me, you know? Our pastor was there. He was all dirty and tattered, he hands were all torn up . . . I told him you told me to run to the train station and that they caught me and I ran away . . . The pastor asked where you were, and I told him you were home and that you had to take care of some very, very important things and that in two or three days you would come join me in Ellmit, in Ellmit.

SHE. What else did our pastor tell you? What did he say?

HE. He said that I should run to you very fast, run home . . . I told him that you had told me to go to the station and take the train to Ellmit, to Ellmit. He said that now you would want me to run home quickly, so I ran. And they pulled off that boot here on the stairs, because they wanted to catch me, but I kicked them and ran upstairs . . . And they were still yelling at me, you know . . . When they pulled that old couple the Wildes from the second floor, the ones who have that little grandson Tadzio with the stupid laugh who only walks in a circle. They shouted after me: "Run home, run home, Helver, we'll catch up with you, we'll get you . . ." And they said those words, those bad words . . . And Gilbert shouted . . .

SHE. You mean Gilbert is here?

HE. Um-hmm. He's standing and guarding while they pull out the Wildes and others from their home and he took little Tadzio by the head and then against the wall against the wall and shouted "Holy shit! Holy shit!" Then Gilbert called after me: "You're done for, carc-ass! You're done for!" I'm not a carc-ass.

SHE. No you're not, Helver. You're not a carc-ass . . . What else did the pastor say? Try to remember . . .

HE. He said . . . he said . . . "Tell Karla . . ."

SHE. What? What were you supposed to tell me?

HE. Our pastor said: "Helver tell my dear Karla that the Lord knows what he is doing." That's what he said.

SHE. That's all?

HE. And then he said . . .

SHE. What else did he say?

HE. He said "Pray with Karla for you, for me, for everybody." And then he said he was going back to the church because the church was burning . . . You know? The church was burning and and he was also going to pray for us, for himself and for everybody . . . And the church is burning, it's glowing in the sky like our foundry when they open all the ovens, what a glow . . .

SHE (*carefully approaches the window*). Yes . . . Our church . . .

HE. Now we're going to . . . we're going to . . . I know! Now we're going to pray! I know how to pray! I know! Because you always taught me, always. You pray to the pictures above your bed and the ones you have in that little black book . . . I know how to pray . . . (*Kneels and pulls her down onto the floor, She kneels beside him, passively giving in.*) Like this . . . (*crosses himself.*) Right? You see, I learned . . . You lower your head . . . "Angel of God, my guardian dear . . ." What's wrong? Don't you remember? Say your prayers, say your prayers! "To whom his love entrusts me here." You see? I learned! Say your prayers, say them!

SHE (*breaking away*). Helver! You know what?

HE. What?

SHE. Let's play now, let's play puzzles!

HE. How do you play that?

SHE. Come on, I'll show you. Get up. Let's move the table and clean
up here . . . Come on and give me a hand . . . Take that suitcase
into the room . . . I took it out because I picked up a little . . .
Come on, hurry . . . That's good, a clean table . . . Now for
the chairs . . . Let's light some more candles, bring me that
candelabra from the sideboard and light all the candles . . .
That's right . . . And now let's make ourselves a big mug of tea
. . . Oh what am I thinking, we don't have power . . . So let's
pour some water in a big mug with a little cherry juice . . .
That's right . . . So sit down at the table, Helver, that's it . . .
I'll sit down in just a second, I just have to bring . . . (*Takes
three medicine bottles from a cupboard in the sideboard, fairly large
ones, of brown glass, and sets them on the table.*)

HE. Those are my pills.

SHE. That's right . . . But now we're going to pretend that they're
our puzzle pieces.

HE. But they're my pills that you always buy from Mrs. Kersten in
the pharmacy. There's a skeleton there . . . Mrs. Kersten always
says to me "Swallow your pills, Helver, or else the skeleton will
get you." Why does she say that? After all I swallow my pills
and swallow them.

SHE. You swallow your pills very nicely, Helver, just that sometimes
you make a face.

HE. Because they get stuck in my throat, like this (*demonstrates*).

SHE. You swallow them very, very nicely. And that skeleton in the
pharmacy is made of cardboard, you know? It's just a display,
just pretend, not for real.

HE. And that skeleton won't get me?

SHE. No . . . (*on the verge of sobbing.*) It won't get you . . . Helver,
pay attention. I have three bottles of pills here . . . I'm going

to pour them all out. (*Pours them onto the table.*) There, you
see? See all the colors? Look how many there are.

HE. I know. See, these. (*Shows her.*) Green ones, you always give me
two, so that the day will be clear and good and . . . (*Quickly*)
So I won't wave my arms. And these. (*Pointing to the table.*)
Red ones you always give me after dinner . . . so that . . . so
that I will learn and remember and have a smart head on my
shoulders . . . And these. (*Pointing to the table.*) White ones you
always give me at bedtime so that . . . so that I'll have good
dreams and so I'll sleep and sleep . . . Because when you sleep
. . . you sleep. (*Using her fingers, Karla moves the colored pills she
has sprinkled onto the tablecloth. Her face is tense, but she adroitly
hides her expression behind a warm smile as she attempts to draw
Helver into playing "puzzles." Only her eyes are empty and motionless. She isn't even crying, the tears simply glass over her eyes, and
occasionally during the game she muffles a sob.*)

SHE. Helver, let's use those pills to make a colorful house. How do
we make a house?

HE (*thinks, moves some pills on the table*). First . . . (*Starts to arrange
them.*) Comes a little square . . . there, and then the roof . . .
But I'll use the red pills to make that! Next is a chimney . . .
and a little tree . . . and then I'll make a window. I'll make a
window!

SHE. Helver, we forgot about your bedtime pills. Look how late it is.

HE. It's very late . . . (*Keeps arranging the pills.*)

SHE. So swallow those two white ones . . . (*Gives him the pills.*) And
drink them down with some water. It's very cold.

HE (*takes the pills, all the while concentrating on his puzzle, puts them
in his mouth and swallows them with some water*). And now I'll
make a little sun . . . there . . . what else?

SHE. What a nice picture you made . . . You know what? You still
have some here . . . (*Gives him the pills.*) Two green, two red,
and two white. Swallow them down and you won't have to
tomorrow, all right?

HE. Um-hmm. (*Still working at his puzzle, He swallows the pills and drinks some water.*) So now what should I make?

SHE. Make a . . . make a boat. With a mast and smokestacks and a sea with waves . . .

HE (*excited by the idea*). Good . . . (*He starts to make a new picture.*) But you make a puzzle too. Look how many tablets there are . . . What are you going to make?

SHE. Maybe a flower?

HE. Who is that flower for?

SHE. For you, Helver . . .

HE. For me? (*Shrugs his shoulders.*) No one ever gave me a flower. Not you, not anybody . . . Why give me a flower?

SHE. It will be a flower just for you . . . (*She makes it.*)

HE (*arranging*). And what will my boat be called?

SHE. Boats have different names . . .

HE. But what? What names?

SHE. Well, like a city, or a famous person, or they have their own names, different names . . .

HE. But what? (*Yawns, and slowly, very slowly starts to feel sleepy.*)

SHE. Helver, which color pill do you like best?

HE. All of them . . . But probably the green ones . . .

SHE (*holding back her sobs*). Hey, you probably couldn't swallow any more pills.

HE. Yes I could. But which ones?

SHE (*through her sobs, despair*). Four green, four red, four white . . . Could you swallow all that?

HE. Of course. (*He takes a handful of pills, puts them in his mouth, drinks them down with water, and yawns.*) I swallowed them. That's not hard. They're good. Because of the color on them, it's sweet, you see?

SHE. Do you like sweet things?

HE. Um-hmm. But most of all when you bake a cake or make fried dough . . . (*Yawns, his lids are slowly starting to close, his movements slower and slower.*) Or when you make those "cat eyes" with the marmalade in the middle. I like sweet things.

SHE (*through broken sobs*). So swallow just a couple more white ones, then some red ones and some green ones, but hold them longer in your mouth and tell me which taste the sweetest . . .

HE (*more and more slowly, sleepily, delayed, imprecise movements*). Now I'll make an airplane . . . (*Arranges pills and puts some more in his mouth, sucking on them like candy.*) They're sweet when you suck on them, you know . . . And what are you going to make now?

SHE. What would you like me to make?

HE (*working on his picture*). Make me something . . . something so I wouldn't be this way . . . you know . . . so I wouldn't be . . . Helver, so I wouldn't be . . .

SHE (*through muffled spasms*). Helver you are the most wonderful and kind and the most lovable . . .

HE (*very slowly, very truthfully*). But I am so . . . I'd like so much if . . . if I . . . But I can't . . . and if my head weren't this way . . . if it weren't this way . . .

SHE. Helver my dear beloved Helver . . .

HE. I swallowed a lot of pills today . . . And you always told me . . . you always said "just two, just two" . . . I think I'll stop making pictures . . . because there are only . . . one two three four five six pills left. You see? You probably won't make any more either . . . Should I swallow these pills as well?

SHE (*through her sobbing*). Yes, swallow them quickly Helver . . . Swallow them . . .

HE (*puts them in his hand and to his mouth, he wants to say something but he chokes, and coughs, spewing the pills onto the table and floor, he coughs and coughs. She jumps up, picks up the pills from the table and floor and pushes them into Helver's mouth. He pushes her away, still coughing. She breaks his weak resistance and places the pills in his mouth, and pours some water down his throat from the mug. He snorts out water, chokes, and slowly catches his breath).* Hey I swallowed them, I swallowed . . . (*Sinks onto a chair.*)

SHE. I know, I know, my dear . . .

HE. And my stomach hurts and my head and heart . . . Look how fast my heart is beating (*places her hand on his heart.*) Do you feel it? Like a machine gun: boom-boom-boom-boom-boom-boom . . .

SHE. Drink some more water . . .

HE. There are two more pills down there by the table leg . . . (*Squints*) Green, no, white . . . or golden probably . . .

She picks the pills up off the floor, holds them in her hand and throws them in the corner of the room. She hides her face in her hands and breaks out in sobs.

HE (*barely conscious*). Don't cry . . . don't cry . . . I'll swallow them too . . . I'll get them down right now except I'm feeling a little . . . (*Collapsing on the table.*)

SHE (*A shout of horror*). No!!! No!!!

HE. I think I'll sleep now . . . But hug me close face to face . . . and give me something to hold . . . a soldier . . . that one on the horse . . . and tell me something . . . Tell me . . . (*Collapses heavily onto the floor.*)

SHE (*kneeling by him, shaking him hard*). Helver!!! Helver!!! (*More quietly*) Helver . . . (*Sobbing.*)

HE (*curls up against her with the rest of his consciousness*). Hold me tight . . . Kiss me . . . (*She holds him, kisses him, her face covered with tears.*) And do this on my face (*takes her hand and caresses his face.*) On my face . . . (*Very quietly, almost inaudibly*) Because Gilbert gave it to me. (*Even more quietly*) Gilbert gave it to me . . . (*Still more quietly*) Karla . . . (*Shallow, last breaths.*) Mama . . . Ma . . . ma . . . Ma . . . ma . . . Ma . . .

SHE (*a scream, a yelp, madness*). Forgive me!!! Forgive me!!! Lord God forgive me!!! (*A break—breath—explosion—hysterical scream.*) Because You alone know what you are doing!!!???

(*She howls with pain.*) Do you know!!!??? What do you know!!!??? . . . What!!!??? (*Tries to lift Helver's body.*) Look!!! Look what you did!!! (*Hugging Helver's body.*) Why!!!??? (*Her scream turns into sobbing.*) He knew his prayers . . . (*Dry spasms.*) Better than anybody!!! (*Pulls Helver's body.*) Tell Him! Tell him! (*Swallowing sobs.*) "Angel of God, my guardian dear . . ." You hear!! You hear how beautifully he says his prayers . . . (*Sobs*) He's the only one you should hear now . . . The only one . . . (*Quietly*) The only one . . .

Violent banging on the door, sounds of kicking. Karla realizes the end has come. Shouts behind the door. A few stones come flying through the window into the kitchen, we hear truck horns, dogs yapping. Karla holds Helver's body and caresses it, carefully takes off his torn coat. She gets up slowly, looks at the door, which looks like it will come bursting out of its frame at any moment. She fixes her hair, straightens her dress, very slowly turns to the audience, and smiles. And in that smile, through all her terror and her tears, there is also some determination, the awareness of a chapter being closed, an attempt to justify herself, an expectation that she will be understood, but that smile must also protect her from sympathy, from even attempting to believe in hope.

Karla takes two steps toward the audience, smiles, and looks . . . The door bursts out of the frame with a bang. Karla stands motionless, looking at the audience. She is already outside the world of the stage. She is alone with the audience.

People break into the kitchen: we hear sounds that are evocative and fully illusionistic: the sounds of beating, a scream, kicking, panting, people running out of the kitchen. They run down the stairs dragging two bodies that bump against the steps. Karla stays standing throughout, smiling. The lights come up slowly, along with the music: the same waltz that Karla once danced to so beautifully. It grows louder and louder, and accompanies the audience out of the theater, into the lobby, the coatroom, and long after they have left the building, from speakers placed outside, onto the street.

CHARACTERS

DAUGHTER
MOTHER
FATHER
GRANDMA

AMANITA MUSKARIA

DAILY SOUP

DAILY SOUP

Translated by Margarita Nafpaktitis

A third-floor apartment in a tenement. The action takes place in a large room with an adjacent kitchen. The apartment building opposite can be seen from the window. Winter.

SCENE 1

Darkness. The voice of a child or perhaps a very old woman humming a song.

> To the city of Lwów, so I have heard tell
> Came a tightrope walker, the Human Fly
> From the third floor he fell
> And they say that he died . . .
> From the third floor he fell
> And they say he died . . .

There is a clatter and a crash in the darkness, as if something large has fallen and shattered.

MOTHER. Mama?! Mama, what are you doing in here?

GRANDMA. I'm looking for my own mama . . .

MOTHER. But Mama, your mama died a long time ago!

GRANDMA. No, she didn't die, she was here a moment ago . . . she wanted . . . she was calling me . . . for me to go with her . . . oh, she was here, she was standing right here . . .

Mother turns on the light. She and Grandma stand facing each other in their nightgowns. Grandma closes her eyes, because the light dazzles her.

GRANDMA. Mama . . .? Mama?

MOTHER. Stop it, Mama, there's no Mama here . . . Jesus, Mary, and Joseph . . .

Day. Grandma is standing near the window. Father is in an armchair reading the newspaper. Mother is in the kitchen.

MOTHER (*to herself*). I'll make something right now . . . I'll make soup . . . (*To Father*) Do you want any soup?

FATHER. Yes.

MOTHER (*to herself*). I bought soup vegetables at the kiosk, because the last time I bought them at the grocery store, they were moldy the next day . . . Uh oh, no potatoes, well never mind . . . they were probably already moldy when I bought them . . .

FATHER. Did you say something?

MOTHER (*to Father*). It's nothing, nothing, keep reading, I was just saying that there are no potatoes . . . (*To herself*) You buy them, they look fine on the outside, but inside . . .

FATHER. Should I go get potatoes?

MOTHER (*to herself*). . . . mold is a nasty poison . . .

FATHER. Did I buy something moldy?

MOTHER (*to Father*). No need to buy anything, just keep reading, don't get up . . . (*To herself*) . . . you could get cancer . . . Too bad, no potatoes today . . . I'll throw in some noodles to give it some substance . . . (*To Father*) Do you want macaroni in it?

FATHER. What?

MOTHER. I'm going to toss some macaroni into the soup.

FATHER. It's all the same to me.

MOTHER. Or maybe I won't add any . . .

Father doesn't say anything.

MOTHER. Would you rather have it without macaroni?

FATHER. Makes no difference to me.

MOTHER. There's still a little barley, I could add that, but I didn't soak it overnight, because I thought that there would be potatoes . . .

FATHER. I said I could get some . . .

MOTHER. Read, read . . . (*To herself*) I'll be done here in a minute . . . (*To Father*) What are they writing in the paper?

FATHER. Should I tell you?

MOTHER. No, I'm just asking.

FATHER. Should I read out loud?

MOTHER. What's gotten into you? If I want to read it, I'll read it myself, just read, read . . .

FATHER. What's going on?

MOTHER. Nothing, nothing's going on! You're the one who's upset, for some reason.

FATHER. I'm not upset, I'm reading!

MOTHER. Then read! Did I tell you not to read? I said that there aren't any potatoes, that's all. Maybe we can live without potatoes for once.

Father tosses the newspaper onto the table and disappears into the next room.

MOTHER. No, well honestly . . . with a man like that . . . there's no way . . . there's just no way . . . and that's life.

GRANDMA (*by the window, sighing heavily*). My God . . . my God . . . it's killing me . . . so much pain . . . oh, Jesus . . . I can't remember it ever hurting this much before . . .

MOTHER. Do you want one of your pills, Mama?

GRANDMA. I'm sick and tired of this . . . horrible . . . why am I here . . . I should be in my own home . . .

MOTHER. The weather is changing, and that's what's aching you, it's normal.

GRANDMA. Horrible . . . It gives me the distinct impression . . . that I am not looked upon here in the most kindly light.

MOTHER. Take your pill!

GRANDMA. . . . I'm only passing through . . . passing through . . .

MOTHER. Iwonka will be here any minute and we'll have supper. Go see if her light is on.

GRANDMA. I'd rather go home . . .

MOTHER. But Mama . . . you are at home. Iwonka lives at your place now. Have you forgotten?

Grandma doesn't respond.

MOTHER. I bought a delicious cake.

GRANDMA. Cake? Oh good. I have to have something sweet after supper. Even if it's just a bite. To go with my tea. Otherwise it would be like I hadn't eaten at all.

The doorbell rings. Daughter enters. She opened the door with her own key.

MOTHER. It's good that you're here! I'm about to go crazy!

DAUGHTER. What happened?

MOTHER. Nothing. What was supposed to happen?

Daughter goes into the bathroom. There is the audible sound of the door being locked from the inside. Father appears from the next room.

FATHER. Why did she lock herself in . . .? (*At the door*) Why did you lock it . . .? You're at home.

SCENE 3

Everyone is at the table. Mother ladles soup into bowls. Father takes his blood pressure. The blood pressure monitor sits between the bowls. Its characteristic sound is audible. Mother peeks at Father, then turns her eyes away.

GRANDMA. That's enough, thanks! Now that's too much!

MOTHER. I didn't give you any more, Mama.

GRANDMA (*uneasy*). It's enough for me—as long as it's hot.

MOTHER (*to Daughter*). I think that's a silly idea. How do you imagine that you'll be able to not eat meat at all?

FATHER. One hundred six over ninety-three. (*He sets aside the monitor and begins to eat his soup.*)

MOTHER. That's protein, child. You need protein to live. Or at least you need to replace it with something else. What do you want to replace protein with?

DAUGHTER. . . . there are things like . . .

MOTHER. Just eggs and cheese? . . . You think that you can survive on those? You've got a tough job, child. You sit in an office, all hunched over, pulling, drilling, getting all worked up. That's physical labor! I'm telling you you'll end up anemic.

GRANDMA (*has already eaten her soup and is sitting over the empty bowl*). It's enough for me as long as it's hot.

MOTHER (*to Grandma*). Wait a minute, Mama, I'm about to bring the main course. (*To Daughter*) You work a lot, you get up early, you go to bed late . . . Do you think that I don't see how late you keep the light on? Why do you keep the light on so much? With that and this diet I have no idea why you don't collapse from exhaustion.

DAUGHTER. . . . there are vegetables, grains . . .

MOTHER (*turns to Grandma with a platter of cutlets*). Here, Mama, have two of these breaded cutlets, and one without breading. Since you've been getting so bloated lately, you can eat this one without breading, can't you? (*To Daughter*) And in any case, do you think I'm going to cook two dinners?

DAUGHTER. . . . I do have my own kitchen. I can do it by myself . . .

Mother freezes with a cutlet on her fork. Father lifts his eyes up from the plate.

MOTHER. What do you mean *by myself*? Why do you want to eat by yourself . . .?

DAUGHTER. . . . no . . . well . . . only sometimes . . .

MOTHER (*energetically putting cutlets on everyone's plates*). There's something silly, well, wouldn't it be silly somehow . . . Just imagine us eating here and you across the street?

DAUGHTER. . . . there's soy, beans, basically any legume . . .

MOTHER. Don't you know how gassy they make you?!

DAUGHTER. I'm thirty years old.

MOTHER. Twenty-nine and a half.

GRANDMA. That's too much for me (*Pushes aside her main course, barely touched.*)

MOTHER. Eat, Mama, or you won't get any cake! (*To Daughter*) Do you have any idea of how to feed yourself?

SCENE 4

Mother and Grandma are watching their evening soap opera. Daughter stands in front of the window with her back to the television. Father goes back and forth from the kitchen and the room. The dialogue from the television is audible.

MALE VOICE. I thought you'd forgotten about Ridge.

FEMALE VOICE. I think that I have forgotten about him.

MALE VOICE. But I can see that you're always thinking about him.

FEMALE VOICE. Why do you think that? I don't think about him at all.

MALE VOICE. But I can still see that you're thinking.

FEMALE VOICE. I thought you couldn't see it.

MALE VOICE. Don't deny that you have feelings for Ridge.

FEMALE VOICE. Please, don't talk like that. Oh, oh . . . !

MALE VOICE. Jennifer, what's wrong?

FEMALE VOICE. I don't know, there's a stabbing pain in the pit of my stomach.

Father comes to a stop behind Mother's armchair.

MALE VOICE. Maybe it's just an upset stomach?

FATHER (*to the television*). Maybe you just need to take a crap.

MOTHER. Do you have to interrupt?

FATHER (*to Daughter*). I'm telling you, this whole show is one big pile of crap.

FEMALE VOICE. There's no cure for this.

MOTHER. You know what! She's pregnant, but she doesn't know it yet.

NARRATOR. This is the conclusion of episode two thousand five hundred and sixty-seven.

SCENE 5

Evening. Father is watching television—sound of gunshots, car chases, wailing sirens. Grandma is sleeping in front of the television, head tilted back, mouth hanging open. Mother and Daughter are sitting alone at the kitchen table.

MOTHER. I've had enough of your Grandma, I can't take it any more. She wants honey in everything. Honey on her salami sandwich, in tomato soup. She even spreads honey on her pierogi. She's a regular Little Miss Honeybee.

There's a commercial break on the television. Father gets up and goes to the kitchen. He rummages around in the cupboards. Opens a can of nuts, pours himself a handful and tosses back the whole handful, then raisins or chips, and finally some cornflakes. Mother makes irritated faces. She rolls her eyes, finally, behind Father's back she indicates a cut-throat gesture. The commercials finish and Father goes back to the television.

MOTHER (*to Daughter*). See? I tell him not to rummage around in there, because he'll give himself ulcers. And he keeps on rummaging. When he gets ulcers I'll have a fit.

DAUGHTER. But nuts aren't bad for you . . .

MOTHER. What?

From the television a long burst of machine gun fire.

MOTHER. Well that's enough for now! Here we are blah, blah, blah and you have to go to bed. (*Gently pushes Daughter toward the door.*) You get the best sleep before midnight. Can you take the garbage out to the curb for me?

Daughter slowly puts on her outdoor clothes. Mother presses a black bag full of garbage into her hand and a cap onto her head.

FATHER (*from the television*). Just be careful that your packages don't get torn on your way out of the gate!

Daughter doesn't have packages, just the bag of garbage.

MOTHER (*opens the door for Daughter*). Get going, go on and go.

Daughter leaves.

SCENE 6

Night. Mother in her nightgown, with a crazy look in her eye, walks across the room and into the kitchen. Pulls open a drawer. Gets out a fork, spoon, knife. With an armful of silverware she goes back to the bedroom.

SCENE 7

Dawn. Father in his pajamas, with an armful of silverware, walks across the room as if he were going to Golgotha. He goes into the kitchen. He pulls open the drawer and puts everything back in its place.

SCENE 8

Daylight. Grandma and Daughter are in the room.

GRANDMA. I'm so terribly thirsty . . .

DAUGHTER. I'll make some tea.

GRANDMA. All by yourself?

DAUGHTER. With a little honey. We won't tell Mama.

Daughter goes into the kitchen.

GRANDMA (*sunk in thought, and after a moment she starts to sing*).
    In the Podolian lands there lies a stone,
    And on it a Podolian maid sits all alone . . .
    Sitting and sitting, she weaves and weaves,
    A wreath all of roses and lilies and leaves . . .
    A Podolian man walked up and said
    Podolian girl put that wreath on my head!
    This I would give and two more would I braid,
    If my brother did not make me so much afraid . . .

Then go off and find him and kill your own brother
And then your sweetheart you'll have and no other . . .
(*To herself*) She's my darling little daughter . . . I love her so
much . . . Somehow . . . yes . . . more than . . .

DAUGHTER (*returns with tea and a jar of honey*). . . . Too bad you didn't
have more children . . . I would have had cousins . . .

GRANDMA. What . . .? What was that . . .? Good Lord, I've gotten so
deaf . . . (*to herself, barely audible*) anyone . . . yes, anyone . . .
more than anyone else . . . I gave her my husband's name . . .

DAUGHTER. Stasia . . .

*Grandma answers, without even touching her tea, dipping her spoon
over and over again into the honey.*

GRANDMA (*licking the spoon*). . . . Stasia . . . he was so good, so dear
. . . he was so educated! He graduated in Petersburg from . . .
wait a second, wait a second . . . I forgot . . . And then he
died. I opened the window and said that it's spring and why
don't we go out to the meadow, and he clutched his heart and
died, and his hand was clenched so tight, right here, he
grabbed his pajamas, my God . . . He studied in Petersburg,
he was an engineer, a manager . . . and I told him that it was
warm, that the sun was out, and I opened the window and he
clutched at his heart so tightly, and he died . . . (*Sets aside her
spoon.*) What about you, Iwonka, do you have a boyfriend?

DAUGHTER. I do.

GRANDMA. What does he want to be?

DAUGHTER. An astronaut.

GRANDMA. Goodness! That's aiming high.

Pause.

DAUGHTER. . . . you know, Grandma, I dreamed that I had a brother . . .

GRANDMA (*stands up abruptly*). The way time flies, one forgets . . .

DAUGHTER. . . . I always wanted to have a brother . . .

GRANDMA (*shuffles around the room, lost in thought*). . . . my husband,
too . . . My God, how talented he was . . . but he died . . .

DAUGHTER. . . . he would be so sweet, he would have curly hair . . . and I would take care of him . . .

GRANDMA. . . . back then they'd switch managers every few days . . .

DAUGHTER. . . . our parents would leave us at home and go somewhere . . . we would play Peter Pan . . .

GRANDMA. . . . one of them came up to me and said he wanted to take me for a little ride . . . did I ever give him a piece of my mind . . .

DAUGHTER. . . . and he flew through the window . . . sometimes you can fly in dreams . . .

GRANDMA. . . . then I became a librarian . . . What else could I do? . . . In the factory library . . .

DAUGHTER. . . . I have that dream all the time . . .

GRANDMA. . . . after your Grandpa died, life changed . . .

DAUGHTER. . . . I don't know what it was really like . . .

A key can be heard turning in the lock. Mother enters, loaded down with groceries.

MOTHER. Could someone take these groceries? My arms are about to fall off.

GRANDMA. Stasia . . .

DAUGHTER. Put them down, Mama, what are you still holding them for?

MOTHER (*gives her the bags of groceries*). I'm not going to put them down and pick them up again ten times if they're just going straight to the refrigerator anyway.

DAUGHTER. . . . but you said that your arms . . .

MOTHER. Are you surprised? Look how heavy they are. (*Takes off her coat.*)

Daughter goes to the kitchen with the groceries.

MOTHER. Is your father here?

DAUGHTER. He's not here . . .

MOTHER. Of course he's not!

DAUGHTER. So what?

MOTHER. How should I know?! (*Takes off her shoes.*) And now there are potatoes to be peeled . . . chicken breasts to season and cook . . . lettuce to rinse, tomatoes to add . . . (*Goes into the kitchen.*)

DAUGHTER. About the meat, I . . . there were some hungry kids here, two boys . . .

MOTHER. Begging?

DAUGHTER. They asked if I could give them something to eat. So I gave them a little bread and a piece of meat, since I told you already that I don't eat . . .

MOTHER. You gave them a chicken breast? Are you crazy?

DAUGHTER. Just mine. Yours are still there . . .

MOTHER. Do you have brain damage? Do I buy it so you can give it away? Besides, there are all kinds of con men around these days, Gypsies!

DAUGHTER. But they didn't want money, just something to eat.

MOTHER (*putting the groceries in the refrigerator*). I don't know. I don't begrudge anyone, I'm willing and eager to help someone in need, but I myself have seen how one of them took a roll and immediately tossed it away. He even spit on it!

DAUGHTER. It was yesterday's bread, and the meat, since I won't . . . And besides, they took out the garbage for me.

MOTHER (*straightens up*). And why exactly are you giving *our* garbage to strangers? Garbage . . . garbage is something you take out for yourself!

DAUGHTER. But I'm the one who always takes it out . . .

MOTHER. It doesn't do you any great harm, does it, for the love of God, to take out the trash on your way home?!

GRANDMA. Stasia?

MOTHER. Yes, Mama?

GRANDMA. I've got such a stabbing pain in my side today, right here.

MOTHER. Have you been to the toilet?

GRANDMA. The toilet? How am I supposed to remember that?

MOTHER. You probably haven't been. That's not good, Mama. I'm going to make you some herbal tea.

GRANDMA. No, no herbal tea. It's so bitter. And just now it went away.

MOTHER. Mama, don't be childish. At your age you could get a twisted intestine.

The key is heard in the door, Father comes in.

MOTHER. I'm glad you're here. Grandma is constipated.

Grandma gets embarrassed, turns and shuffles into the next room.

DAUGHTER (*quietly*). Mama! Grandma doesn't like it when you talk like that in front of Dad . . .

FATHER (*loudly*). Constipated? What's so unusual about that? Somebody gets a runny nose, somebody gets constipated. It's all the same to me since I have to sell meds to them all at the pharmacy. Somebody comes with an eye problem, with somebody else it's his heart, and the next guy's got problems with his rectum. I don't get it, what's your problem with it? How is it that one illness can be better than another? (*He opens a cupboard over-flowing with medicines.*) Yesterday I saw a program about a frigging schizophrenic. I didn't see the whole thing, because I turned it off right away. They make such idiotic shows these days, what makes people think that schizophrenia is so interesting, that it's so I-don't-know-what that a film needs to be made about it? It's an illness just like any other. Just like anal cancer. I wonder why they don't make a film about people with anal cancer. That poor man, one of many, just is, he endures, he suffers . . . He endures more than the guy with schizophrenia, because it's incredibly painful. But no, they don't make a film about him.

MOTHER (*from the kitchen*). The program! Iwonka, turn on the TV!

Daughter resignedly stands in front of the television and turns it on. She goes into the bathroom.

FEMALE VOICE. You slept with him after he asked me to marry him.

SECOND FEMALE VOICE. Do you really think I'd be capable of something like that?

FEMALE VOICE. You're an expert at breaking people's hearts.

MOTHER (*from the kitchen*). Iwonka! Call your grandma!

SECOND FEMALE VOICE. We did have something between us, but it wasn't what you think.

FEMALE VOICE. You seduced him, because you wanted to take him away from me. You're cheap trash.

MOTHER. Could someone please move!

SECOND FEMALE VOICE. Don't insult me. Ridge had his own part to play in it.

FEMALE VOICE. Unfortunately, that's true. I trusted him, believed that he loved me.

Mother walks toward the room where Grandma is.

MOTHER (*under her breath*). Drives me crazy . . .

SECOND FEMALE VOICE. But you've lost your chance! Now all I can think about is Ridge.

MOTHER (*under her breath*). I do the shopping, the laundry, take care of Grandma, I do everything. (*Behind her back, Father pretends to kick her.*)

FEMALE VOICE. You're trash!

SECOND FEMALE VOICE. I'm glad that he didn't marry you for the fifth time.

FEMALE VOICE. You'll pay for that! (*A short scream by the Second Female Voice and the sound of a body falling into a pool.*)

FATHER (*to the television*). Go ahead and drown, you cretin.

Mother leads Grandma into the room.

NARRATOR. This is the conclusion of episode two thousand six hundred and thirty-five.

MOTHER. Thank you all very much!

GRANDMA. It's already over?

MOTHER. What did you expect? Priscilla pushed Jennifer into the pool.

GRANDMA. Oh my God! How despicable!

FATHER. The best news is that that this piece of crap is already over.

MOTHER (*knocking on the bathroom door*). Why didn't you turn the TV on for Grandma? (*To Father*) See? She locked it again!

FATHER. Here, Mama, take these—suppositories and tablets.

GRANDMA. What are you giving me those for? I don't need them. (*Turns away haughtily.*)

FATHER (*knocking on the bathroom door*). Don't lock yourself in, because if something happened then we'd have to break down the door.

DAUGHTER. . . . What do you think could happen?

FATHER. Anything! You could slip and fall and cut your head on the corner of the bathtub or crush the back of your skull, you could be poisoned by gas from the pilot light or carbon monoxide . . .

DAUGHTER. Carbon monoxide?

FATHER. Don't act so surprised, carbon monoxide could come through the vent, you would pass out in the tub, choke and get water in your lungs . . .

DAUGHTER. I'm going to take a shit.

FATHER. Whatever. Just don't lock the door and that's final. Who do you have to be embarrassed of?

SCENE 9

Grandma with Daughter in the main room.

To the city of Lwów, so I have heard tell
Came a tightrope walker, the Human Fly
From the third floor he fell
And they say that he died . . .
From the third floor he fell
And they say he died . . .

DAUGHTER. Where is he now, Grandma?

GRANDMA (*rouses herself*). I think he's in heaven . . . he was so good, he took such good care of people . . . he made sure there was a glass of milk for every worker, a glass of milk every day . . . they respected him for it . . . when he was there it took only a short time for him to make a difference, so that they didn't smash it anymore, they didn't sit there and smash that rock, only the one they called the chomper, he built this kind of smasher . . . since he was educated in Petersburg, he was an engineer . . . and the workers called it Chomper, because it chomped rocks . . . and it was all automatic . . . in that . . . in Petersburg . . . oh, back then there were stories . . .

DAUGHTER. Tell me something about mother . . .

GRANDMA. I have a nice picture of your grandfather . . . Because when he was getting educated in that . . . in Petersburg . . . when he started working there . . . he was rising so fast. And there was this . . . painter. A famous painter . . . And he painted his portrait . . . And that portrait is the one that is hanging in that room . . . it's so valuable . . . that portrait is . . . and not only that but what a painter . . . he made that portrait famous . . . probably a Pole . . . it's hanging right in there . . . in that room . . . but in which one, I don't really remember any more.

DAUGHTER. Do you have a picture of Mama when she was little? I've never seen one.

GRANDMA. . . . Who could have guessed? That it would end that way . . . After the war they snatched everything away. There was such a lovely foyer, and they used to say that you could turn your horses around in there, and a salon, so lovely, the parties I went to there . . . people would come . . . I don't remember who anymore, but guests would arrive, friends, because your grandfather was greatly respected, he was so, how can I put it, he was important, I had his diploma around here somewhere . . . what a diploma . . . so people respected him . . . and then they took the house away, they snatched everything away right down to the last piece of wood . . . and that's how my career came to an end . . .

Mother is working on a crossword puzzle with Grandma at the kitchen table. Father is in the main room taking his blood pressure. Daughter comes and sits down beside him. For a moment the conversations go on simultaneously.

FATHER. One hundred eight over seventy-five. (*Puts away the blood pressure monitor.*)

MOTHER. Three down, bull's partner, starts with "h"

DAUGHTER. I had a dream today . . .

GRANDMA. . . . herdsman.

FATHER. You know, I had a dream, too.

MOTHER. What are you talking about, Mama, it's "h" for heifer. Concentrate!

DAUGHTER. I dreamed that I had a brother . . .

MOTHER. Think about it before you say something!

FATHER. I woke up, looked around, and I was sleeping . . .

MOTHER. Mysterious animal that lives in the Himalayas, in four letters.

FATHER. I'm at my brother's house . . .

GRANDMA. . . . frog . . .

FATHER. It's the middle of the night . . .

MOTHER. You're not thinking at all! (*Closes the book of crossword puzzles.*)

FATHER. I'm sleeping. And suddenly it feels like there's some kind of whirlwind . . .

MOTHER (*gets up from the table, mumbling*). Tisk-tisk-tisk!

FATHER.: . . . and then it gets me in the right side, "whoosh!!!" in the ribs! . . .

Mother leaves.

FATHER. I wake up, that is, I dream that I wake up, and then the wind gets me from the other side, "whoosh!", in the ribs, until it's bent me right over.

Grandma starts listening.

FATHER. . . . the curtain is billowing, even though the window is closed . . . I can tell that there's a ghost somewhere in here, it's nudging me, it wants something. I say, "Mama, if it's you, say something! Kiss me . . . !"

GRANDMA (*rises from her chair, worked up*). Then what . . .?

FATHER. Suddenly I see, against the light: someone is sitting on my bed. But it's not Mama, it's a man sitting there. I see part of his forehead and hair. I think to myself, maybe it's my brother? I take a deep breath and say, "Józek, what's gotten into you? Coming into my room at night to scare me? . . ." But he doesn't answer, he just bends over me and leans onto my stomach with the whole weight of his body. And he starts to press down on me with more and more force . . . I say, "Józek, what are you doing? Stop, it hurts! I can't breathe! . . ."

Grandma shrugs her shoulders and reaches for the crossword puzzle book she was working on.

FATHER. But he doesn't say anything, he just keeps on lying on me and pressing on me harder and harder, and then I think that this is the end, that it's already the end . . . With my last bit of strength I take a breath of air and shout, "Let me go, let me go!!!" I push him . . . And I finally wake up.

He sits for a long time in silence.

DAUGHTER. You dreamed about your brother, too . . .

FATHER. It wasn't my brother. It was my father.

Daughter doesn't say anything.

FATHER. My father died of stomach cancer . . . those were signs from him.

Mother appears with a large vacuum cleaner, plugs it into the wall, and stands with the vacuum hose in the middle of the room.

DAUGHTER. Why would he press down on you so hard?

FATHER. My father had a grudge against me . . .

Mother turns on the vacuum cleaner and scours the carpet, drowning out Father's words. Father is talking, but no one can hear him.

Daughter is listening, but she can't understand anything. Mother sucks everything up into the vacuum cleaner. Finally, Father stops talking, and he and Daughter look at Mother, who is whirling around them like a meteor.

SCENE 11

Evening. Mother, Daughter, and Father are sitting in front of the television. Sound of gunshots coming from the television. Father is dozing, but the remote doesn't fall out of his hand. After a long pause.

DAUGHTER. Maybe we can switch to something more interesting?

FATHER *(rouses himself, and irritatedly starts to aim the remote in the direction of the television, flipping through channels, never staying on any one longer than two seconds)*. Here you go, how about this one?

DAUGHTER. Not really . . .

FATHER. No? How about this one?

DAUGHTER. No . . .

FATHER. No? How about this one? *(And so on for a long time. Finally, he furiously slams the remote on the table and gets up.)* Go ahead and watch whatever it is you want. I'm finished watching. *(Leaves.)*

Mother and Daughter sit as if paralyzed, not daring to change the channel, although the program that Father left it on clearly does not suit them. Eventually, Mother picks up the remote and meekly goes back to the film that Father was watching.

MOTHER. See, he gets upset for no reason. I've had to deal with it my whole life.

They sit for a while longer. Father is walking up and down the room, grumbling under his breath. He walks into the kitchen, opens cupboards, rummages in the refrigerator, nibbles on things. The film ends and the commercials start. Mother turns off the television. They sit in silence.

FATHER. I hereby inform you that I am going to buy myself a new television. And I will watch my own programs in my own room.

MOTHER. Go right ahead. You can watch all of your shoot-em-up shows and watch brains splatter on the walls to your heart's content.

FATHER. You'll see, that's exactly what I'm going to do. I'll watch my shoot-em-up shows in my room, and you can watch your soap opera-crap in here.

MOTHER. Why are you going on about crap? Did I say that it was a good soap opera, did I say that?

FATHER. You don't say it, but you're as affected by it as if you were watching nothing less than Hamlet. Your face changes, your chin drops down to your waist, you're so overwhelmed you look like you're going to lose all your teeth. And all for . . . Jesus! Such crap—nothing more.

MOTHER. How much do I even watch it? What's really bugging you about it? What else do I have in my life? Are you begrudging me a stupid soap opera?

FATHER. I'm not begrudging you. Go ahead and watch it. But why do I have to watch it, too, and stuff myself full of your crap.

MOTHER. Who says you have to stuff yourself with it?

FATHER. What do you mean who? (To Daughter) Your mother is a terrorist! When she's watching, do you think I could dare to change the channel? Not only can I not change the channel, but I have to tiptoe around.

MOTHER. Well you know what? You're talking like I watch it all day and that I never let you near the television. You watch your shoot-em-ups when you want and for as long as you want, and no one changes the channel on you. And all I have is *The Style of Success*, which lasts a whole goddamn 15 minutes. Only 15 minutes out of the whole day, all I have is *Style*, nothing else.

FATHER. Poor little thing. As usual, you're a saint. (To Daughter) Your mother is a saint!

MOTHER. Now what are you going on about?

FATHER. Oh, nothing. It's just that no one can say anything to you.

MOTHER. Nobody can say anything to you either. Have I been saying anything? For half an hour you've been sitting here and going on and on at me.

FATHER. Oh, please! Martyr! Saint Bobola.

MOTHER. Again with the Bobola?

FATHER. You never admit to making a mistake. Never. I say, "Forgive me, I'm sorry." I admit it, I humble myself, flagellate myself, cringe before you. And you? Not once, *never* have you ever forgiven me. Have you forgiven me even once?

MOTHER. And why do I have to forgive you, if you'll forgive me for asking?!

FATHER (*to Daughter*). Anyway, the television and the kitchen are my two nightmares connected with your mother. How many hundreds of times have I said, asked, begged, implored, made requests and threats, and still she never, never turns on the kitchen fan. I come home from work and it smells like a greasy spoon, hole in the wall! The smell of cabbage spreading all through the building and all over the city of Swarzędz. I cook, therefore I am. Everyone has to smell it.

MOTHER. What about you and your hands? (*To Daughter*) He's always in here, looking into pots, drives me crazy as soon as he starts. He comes in, takes off the lids, acts like he's smelling it, and just as soon as I turn my back he's got his whole arm up to the sleeves in my frying pan. And gobble, gobble—is it tough? Is it raw? Just so he can gulp something down, dip his fingers into it.

FATHER. Dipping my fingers into it is a crime. This is an aristocracy after all. So I'm not allowed to taste anything either. What harm is it if I want to try something? I have to taste it to see if it's good, to prepare myself for dinner, to get the juices flowing. But in this house it's better not to eat anything at all, just to look at the aristocracy in the kitchen. Pickles, too. The jar is already open in the refrigerator, so I want to try them. So much has been said, that there are pickles, that Mama made them, that they're good. But just let me try to touch the jar when I hear: *Use a fork! A fork!* Don't stick your fingers into the jar! What's the point? It's generally accepted that people eat pickles with their fingers. But oh no, not here, not in this house. Cabbage or fish with a stench that spreads all over Swarzędz, fine, but using my fingers, oh no. I have to say that I didn't plan the apartment layout very well. I should have put in a thick wall to separate the greasy spoon from the rest of the rooms in the house.

Grandma comes out of the room.

FATHER (*not stopping*). And the way to the kitchen should have been through the crapper!

Silence.

MOTHER (*to Daughter*). Go on and give Grandma those pills like I've been asking you to since this morning!

DAUGHTER. Which pills, Mama?

MOTHER. Which pills?! The laxatives!!!

SCENE 12

Night. Mother in her nightgown, with a crazy look in her eye, walks across the room and into the kitchen. Pulls open a drawer. Gets out a fork, spoon, knife. With an armful of silverware she goes back to the bedroom.

SCENE 13

Dawn. Father in his pajamas, with an armful of silverware, walks across the room. He goes into the kitchen. He pulls open the drawer and puts everything back in its place.

Father is sitting in front of the television, sounds of a martial-arts film. Mother and Grandma are in the kitchen, peeling apples for pie. The telephone rings. Mother picks it up.

MOTHER. Zosia? Hello, Zosia darling . . .! How are things with you? Everything's fine here, Grandma is feeling good, she's our busy little honeybee, we've just been peeling apples for pie . . .

Father turns up the volume a little.

MOTHER. Oh Lord, you don't say, really . . .! Hold on a minute . . . But I thought . . .!

Father turns up the volume a little more.

MOTHER. I have to tell you that it doesn't surprise me at all . . . ! You're kidding . . . ! I didn't want to say anything, but from the very beginning it looked suspicious to me . . . !

Father turns up the volume yet again. The sounds of the karate fight begin to drown out Mother's words.

MOTHER. That's terrible!. . . Now what are you . . .? You know . . .

GRANDMA *(from the kitchen).* I'm done peeling them, should I slice them now?

MOTHER. Hold on, Mama, I can't hear you. *(To Father)* Could you turn it down for a second?

FATHER. What for?

MOTHER. I'm talking to Mama!

FATHER. I thought you were talking on the phone.

MOTHER. I can't hear what Zosia's saying to me!

GRANDMA *(louder).* I can go ahead and slice them . . .

MOTHER *(to Grandma).* Hold on, Mama, I'm about to get off! *(To Father)* Turn it down! *(To the phone)* I feel like I'm going insane!

FATHER *(under his breath).* I would go insane, too, if I had to listen to that nonsense!

MOTHER. What did you say?!

GRANDMA (*trots up to Mother and puts the knife and the apples right in front of her*). I can go on and cut them already . . . Just tell me if you want them in quarters or slices?

MOTHER. Hang on, Mama! I'm talking to Zosia, remember Zosia? She's had a tragedy at home . . .!

Father turns down the television, Grandma is silent. Pause.

MOTHER (*to the phone, peevishly to Zosia*). See what I mean?! I'm about to lose my mind! Don't tell me things like that right now! (*Puts down the phone; to Father, peevishly*) How do you like that? A Mormon's gotten Zosia's daughter pregnant!

Father turns off the television. Grandma puts down the knife. Mother stands in the kitchen over a bowl of apples. Silence.

MOTHER (*in a stifled voice*). People have such terrible problems. There's not enough room for all of them in your head. It's a never-ending struggle. One child with an alcoholic, another one with a Mormon. Thank goodness that everything is OK with us. Sit down, Mama, I'm finishing up the peeling. (*To Father*) Turn on the program for Grandma, because I'm about to go insane.

Father turns on the soap opera without a word. He goes out. Grandma sits down in front of the television. The soap-opera theme song can be heard.

SCENE 15

Dusk. Father is standing in front of the window. Mother is standing beside Father.

FATHER. The light's on over there, so I don't know why she won't answer.

MOTHER. I talked to her just a minute ago. She's probably in the bathroom.

FATHER. I'm going to go over there. Maybe something happened.

MOTHER. Wait a minute. She did say she wasn't feeling well.

FATHER. I'm going to try again.

Father at the telephone. Mother beside Father. Father dials the number.

FATHER (*to Mother*). She's there. (*To the phone*) I'm calling you right now, because I was just getting home from work and your mother tells me as I'm walking through the door that you're not coming for dinner this evening, because you don't feel well . . . And what's worse, that you're probably going off to some fasting spa. What's gotten into your head, may I ask? What kind of fasting spa are you going off to in this kind of weather, I'd like to know? And not only that, on the other side of the country? *By car*?! Out of the question! . . . Black ice, sleet, and blizzards . . . it's a weather emergency . . . So I just wanted to tell you, my dear daughter, that your mother's and my evening is completely ruined! With your fasting spa and trip. And the whole day tomorrow, too . . . (*Suddenly, looking suspiciously at Mother.*) Why is it that you're going off to this fasting thing *right now*?!

MOTHER (*as if struck by lightning*). Why are you looking *at me* like that?!?

FATHER (*to the phone*). When exactly is it that you're planning on going? . . . On Saturday??? Well that's just great, our Saturday's all ruined, too. (*To Mother*) Did you know? It's not tomorrow, but Saturday, that she wants to leave.

MOTHER. Good Lord, on Saturday??? Give me the phone!!!

FATHER (*to the phone*). Hang on, I'm giving the phone to your mother.

Father gives the phone to Mother, stands next to her.

MOTHER (*to the phone*). Iwonka, what's gotten into your head? You want to leave on Saturday? Darling, listen, the whole country is covered in black ice . . .

FATHER. Why are you telling her the same thing I just said? Are you going to repeat everything I said?

MOTHER (*to Father*). Now what? (*To the phone*) Sleet and blizzards . . .

FATHER. I'd like to know how much we pay per minute after six o'clock. You should call after six o'clock if all you want to do is repeat . . .

MOTHER. . . . it's a weather emergency . . .

FATHER. I'm going to put in my own line, for the love of God.

MOTHER (*to Father*). You're making me insane, you know that? (*To Daughter*) They keep saying on television: Drivers, stay home . . . and honey, that's when you want to go? Darling, why don't you put it off?. . . Sweetie, what do you mean . . . you can't? . . .

FATHER. Yes, tell her again that she absolutely has to stay here. Don't ask! Don't discuss it! She can't go and that's final!

MOTHER (*to Father*). Do you think you could not jabber on at me when I'm on the phone? Now I can't hear what Iwonka's saying. (*To the phone*) Sweetie, your father's talking to me when I'm trying to talk to you, and I didn't hear what you just said . . .

Father grumbles something unintelligible under his breath.

MOTHER (*to the phone*) Just a minute, your father's going ballistic, and I have no idea what's going on. (*To Father*) What's the problem now? Can you explain to me what it is that I'm saying that you don't like?

Father spits out monosyllables, gesticulates.

FATHER. OK, OK . . . tell . . . tell her she has to . . . make her a sandwich for the trip.

MOTHER. A sandwich? She's going to a fasting spa! You know what? You talk to her yourself. (*To phone*) Iwonka? Hang on, I'm giving the phone to your father.

She ostentatiously hands Father the phone and goes into the kitchen to deal with a pot rattling on the stove. Father takes the phone, but he doesn't hold it up to his ear, he just keeps on debating with Mother, waving the phone all over the place.

FATHER (*to Mother*). Why did you give it to me? I already told her what I had to say . . . Talk to her, yourself . . . You don't even know how to convince your own child . . . (*Imitating Mother*) "Drivers, stay home . . ."

MOTHER (*from the kitchen*). Go ahead and talk to her then! Talk to her, if you're such a great negotiator . . .!

Father is close to exploding, but he checks his emotions and returns sweetly to the forgotten phone.

FATHER. Just a moment, honey . . . Your mother's got me all confused.

Mother carefully stirs something in a pot.

FATHER. All I wanted to do was tell you calmly and straightforwardly that it's hard for me to imagine what it is you're planning to do. In no way can I imagine it. And I can see only two options for you: either take the train or don't go at all. . . . Should I bring something over for food poisoning? Aha . . . Then drink lots of fluids so you don't get dehydrated. We'll talk when you come for dinner tomorrow. (*Puts down the phone.*) A diet spa of all things . . . going all that way for a diet! . . . And in winter! (*Sits down in front of the television, turns it on, flips through the channels.*)

MOTHER. That's the fashion right now. Everyone is losing weight. The worst thing she could do is go by car. We have to get that idea out of her head.

Father turns to the channel with Happiness.

FEMALE VOICE. He loves Brooke, and I just have to accept it.

MALE VOICE. Ridge is the father of your child.

Father quickly changes the channel.

MOTHER. Mama, come here. *Happiness* is on!

Grandma comes out of the other room, a little sleepy.

GRANDMA. Goodness! Already? Why didn't you call me?

She sits in the armchair and leans forward, as if she wanted to climb into the television screen. Father turns back to the channel with Happiness, *tosses the remote on the table, and goes into the other room.*

FEMALE VOICE. I saw them in bed today. Now I know how much she means to him.

MALE VOICE. You're right. You have to think about the baby.

FEMALE VOICE. I'm pregnant. Oh God, what should I do?

MALE VOICE. There's only one thing you can do for yourself and the baby.

FEMALE VOICE. I feel like a fool. What do you think I should do?

MALE VOICE. You have to concentrate on yourself and the baby.

FEMAL VOICE. It's Ridge's baby.

MALE VOICE. But you saw them in bed today. Now you know how much she means to him.

FEMALE VOICE. You're right. I have to think about the baby.

MALE VOICE. You're pregnant.

FEMALE VOICE. There's only one thing I can do for myself and the baby.

MALE VOICE. What do you think you should do?

FEMALE VOICE. I should concentrate on myself and the baby.

MALE VOICE. But it's Ridge's baby.

FEMALE VOICE. I can't take Ridge's baby away from him.

MALE VOICE. Now I know that Ridge is the baby's father.

NARRATOR'S VOICE. This concludes episode two thousand six hundred and seventy-four.

SCENE 16

Mother and Daughter are sitting at the kitchen table. Father is standing in front of the cupboards, nibbling on things.

MOTHER. Definitely not at night.

DAUGHTER. What?

MOTHER. Definitely not at night. Have a little soup.

DAUGHTER. But I'm going to book a sleeping car. I'm not hungry. I'll book a sleeping car and then I can sleep the whole night.

FATHER. Your things will be stolen.

DAUGHTER. I'll lock the door.

FATHER. Ask your mother.

MOTHER (*to Father*). All these years and you still have to bring it up . . . Leave that trail mix alone! (*To Daughter*) I was by myself and I had put the chain on the compartment door. Eat your soup! (*To Father*) I was sure that . . .

FATHER. And I was *never* sure. All you had to do was look around at all the people riding those trains . . . If I was a thief, I would always work out a way to find the most naive passenger.

MOTHER. Wouldn't it be nice to just land a helicopter on the roof and cut . . . cut . . . a hole . . .

FATHER. That's the movies, Stasia, the movies.

MOTHER. It strikes me that you're the one who's watched all those movies. (*To Daughter*) Do I have to feed you myself?

DAUGHTER. Mama, stop.

FATHER. My stomach already hurts because of your fasting.

MOTHER. More like from overeating. Who ever heard of eating chocolate after pickled herring?

FATHER. It's because I'm upset!

MOTHER. Your father got upset, too.

FATHER. My father had cancer!

MOTHER. That's what I'm saying! It ate at him. Something's eating at you, too. (*To Daughter*) When something eats at him, then his jaws move all by themselves.

FATHER. So it's better to starve myself then, is it? Do you want her to go?

MOTHER. I don't want her to go! It's your father that's pressing down on you at night.

FATHER. So who's pressing down on you at night?!

Mother abruptly turns her back.

FATHER. Better not to ask! (*To Daughter*) Let's talk about this calmly. Why is it that you're going on this fast? It's total nonsense. Maybe it would be good for fat people. But your cholesterol levels are normal.

DAUGHTER. . . . it leads to complete . . . cellular regeneration . . .

FATHER. Go get a makeover, get a new hairdo! Your hair could use some help. Like those girls I see bouncing around on television, jiggling a little here, wiggling a little there. Healthy, strong, smiling. And you? (*Pointing at Mother, who rolls her eyes.*) She's always mocking me. The only wisdom she acknowledges is Grandma's. (*To Mother*) Has your mother ever had a stomach ache?! No! She's never been upset in her whole life!

MOTHER. Don't start on my mother! You . . . you . . . you . . . you have no idea . . .!

FATHER. When has she ever had to deal with anything like this?

MOTHER. She was a widow!

FATHER. . . . So she had to work hard!

MOTHER. She lost everything!

FATHER. . . . She abandoned her children!

MOTHER (*jumps to her feet*). What . . . childr . . . Shut up! Your daughter is going on a fast, and you're going on about my mother! (*Leaves the table, shaking. Doesn't know what to do with herself, finally goes to the garbage can, takes out the full bag, fastens it shut, and puts it by the front door.*)

FATHER (*to Daughter, flustered, tries to change the subject*). Your mother thinks that I don't love her mother . . . For your mother, love is supposed to look like it does in her soap opera . . . it has to be all *Style of Success* . . . Those are her authorities and role models.

Mother gets out the blood pressure monitor in the other room; after a moment the characteristic sound can be heard.

FATHER. What is it we were . . .?

DAUGHTER. You were saying I shouldn't go . . . which means that I should keep an eye on my bags . . .

FATHER. Hold on. When I travel, I keep my money here . . . (*points to his chest*), tucked between my shirts, divided up into parts. Not all together, just a little here and a little there . . . And no one will try to rummage around for it on you if you have it here. Not only that, I always check underneath and between the bunks, does anything wiggle, does it open properly? From one side and then the other, from the window to the corridor: are there partitions or planks, moveable or removable, if they can be raised up or if they slide . . . I look, listen, smell . . . And if everything's OK, then I lock the door and go to sleep.

MOTHER (*reproachfully*). There you go: one hundred and three over one hundred and twenty.

FATHER. But what kind of sleep you get . . . Even then I don't take pills.

DAUGHTER. Do you take sleeping pills?

MOTHER (*coming out of the other room*). Without pills he usually can't . . .

FATHER (*calling after Mother*). What, am I not supposed to sleep?!? It's because of you that I can't sleep!!! . . . It's not sleep . . . it's a . . . bed of nails.

Mother turns around and looks Father in the eyes. Pause.

DAUGHTER. You can get addicted . . .

Mother walks into the next room.

FATHER (*controlling himself*). That's exactly why I take one pill one day, and a different pill the next, and so on. Not because I feel addicted or anything . . . Besides, they're pills, because you're supposed to take them. There are people who can't sleep for months at a time! They sleep for three days, three days they don't sleep . . . Fall asleep, wake up . . . I can't handle that . . . I have a job.

DAUGHTER. I'm against it . . .

FATHER. So am I.

DAUGHTER. . . . taking a pill for everything right away . . .

FATHER. I'm against it, too . . . But I have to sleep, don't I?

MOTHER (*returns*). So how did you end up settling things?

DAUGHTER. That the best thing would be to check . . . that there aren't any loose boards . . .

MOTHER. Or screws loose . . .

DAUGHTER. . . . and the money goes here . . . (*Points to her chest.*) I think that . . .

FATHER. Wait a minute. What are we getting so anxious about? If you can go there during the day, then go during the day.

MOTHER. So she's going?!?!

He answers her with silence.

MOTHER. Sweetie, look, you didn't eat your soup . . . My blood pressure is rising. Can't you see how much we love you?

DAUGHTER. I have too much . . .

MOTHER. That's normal. No reason to get upset about it.

DAUGHTER. But why did I always sleep at Grandma's house, and not at home?

Pause.

FATHER. When it comes down to it, go whenever you want. You won't leave your money on the table like your mother, after all . . . silly idiot . . . She saw a hand, she saw it reaching out, she just didn't feel like moving.

MOTHER. Oh please, not again about the same old . . . The soup is completely cold . . . All that work for nothing. (*She takes the bowl and goes with it into the kitchen.*) I didn't think it was a person, I just thought it was a shadow.

FATHER. Not that it was a shadow, just that you were dreaming it.

MOTHER. So why should I have moved if I thought that I was dreaming?

FATHER. If I had a dream like that, I would have jumped up right away.

DAUGHTER. Really?

FATHER. I would have caught the guy, grabbed him by . . . by . . . grabbed him by the hand and bitten him so hard that I bit off his finger. I wouldn't have hesitated for a second. I just would have grabbed him and bitten it off as hard as I could.

DAUGHTER. Jesus, Dad . . .!

FATHER. I would have done it instinctively.

DAUGHTER. What are you . . .

FATHER. I would have bitten it off instinctively.

DAUGHTER. Bitten off his finger . . .

FATHER. Bitten it off. I would have . . . I would have caught him by surprise, I would have grrrrrrr . . . I would have done it like this . . . (*Demonstrates savage biting off of a finger.*) And tfu!!! (*Spits.*) And I would have spit it out.

DAUGHTER. . . . really?!?

FATHER. And then I would have raised hell.

MOTHER (*from the kitchen*). That's what he would have done from the very beginning.

FATHER. And nobody would have done anything to me.

SCENE 17

Father is rummaging through the medicine cabinet. Grandma is in the armchair in front of the television.

MALE VOICE. Tell him that you are carrying my child.

FEMALE VOICE. You want me to tell Ridge that it's your baby, even though we both know that it's his baby?!

MALE VOICE. Is it still my child?

FEMALE VOICE. Yes, it's still your child, but it's my child too, however being that the baby is Ridge's, he is its father.

MALE VOICE. Wait a minute. Calm down. It could be bad for the baby.

FEMALE VOICE. What kind of life would our child have? It would have a mother, who has a child, and a father, who is the father of the child!

MALE VOICE. So I see you've decided to make your own decision. I don't care when we get married. The main thing is to avoid stress.

FEMALE VOICE. Thanks. Everything's just fine. Except that I still don't know who my father is.

NARRATOR. This is the conclusion of episode two thousand seven hundred and eighty-four.

Father quickly turns off the television with the remote and goes back to his pills.

GRANDMA (*sighs*). If they still put on *Halka*[1] then I would still be going.

FATHER (*without turning around*). And you won't go without it?

GRANDMA. It's the only Polish opera. But what am I trying to . . . (*She stands up.*)

FATHER (*without turning around*). What about *The Haunted Manor*?

GRANDMA (*considers it for a moment, then sneaks up behind Father*). Are you afraid???

FATHER (*startled*). Me?. . .

GRANDMA. Taaaaaaaake your snuuuuuuff! (*Giggles.*)

Mother enters the room. Grandma's smile freezes on her lips.

MOTHER (*to Grandma*). You know, Mama, your eightieth birthday is coming up?

GRANDMA. Really?

MOTHER. I'm trying to figure out what you might want for your birthday.

GRANDMA. Ehhh, what else could I possibly want . . .

MOTHER. Exactly. So you know what I came up with? I'll bring you a priest. It's been a long time since you've gone to confession . . .

GRANDMA. A priest? Here? What am I supposed to tell him . . .?

MOTHER. Don't get upset, Mama, it's just a priest, and he'd already know that you're elderly . . .

GRANDMA. But what for? I don't know him!

---

1 *Halka* is a Polish national opera composed by Stanisław Moniuszko. Halka (Helen), a diminutive for Halina, is also a homonym for a slip, the woman's undergarment.

MOTHER. You don't have to, he's a priest, just tell him that you don't remember . . .

GRANDMA. No, don't call him, and that's enough of you and your priest.

FATHER (*sotto voce*). What for, last rites?

MOTHER. Well no, not last rites right now, it's just that I wish Mama would go to confession, since she's getting on in years. And when it comes down to it last rites are . . . no big deal. It doesn't have to mean that she's about to . . . Nowadays they do last rites just in case. You can do it again later. Zosia's mom has done it twice already, even though she's completely healthy.

GRANDMA (*in despair*). But what for? I don't remember . . .

MOTHER. For goodness sake, Mama, calm down. The priest will take one look at you and know you don't sin anymore. The most it could be is gluttony. Well, anyway. It's no big deal. I'll help you get ready, I'll help you put on a pretty blouse, you'll pray for a while with the priest, do you still remember any prayers . . .?

GRANDMA. I remember some, but I don't want . . .

MOTHER. There you go. You'll see, you'll feel better right away.

Father turns away from the medicine cabinet and furiously hurls a packet of medicine to the floor.

FATHER. For the love of God, how can you be so calm. Not a care in the world. Your daughter left for who knows where and for you, nirvana! Some charlatan messed with her head . . . the country's swarming with them these days . . . Do you even have a telephone number for that center, just in case . . .? (*Starts pacing back and forth across the room.*) She's sitting there, fasting and pooping into a sieve—some vacation! The only thing I want to know is what she's pooping since she's not eating anything! But that's of no concern to you, you can't get Grandma out of your head!

MOTHER. It's from those herbs. After you take them, some kind of deposits come out. Stones. Did you know that just about everyone has stones in their intestines? Then you can see exactly what it is in that sieve . . .

FATHER. Of all the frigging . . . I never would have thought. I never would have thought that my daughter was so idiotic that she would believe in shit like that.

MOTHER. But it's all under control, under a doctor's supervision, that's what it said on the flier . . .

FATHER. Don't eat, and on top of that, you pay for not eating!

MOTHER. It's called "detox." Cleansing the body of toxins.

SCENE 18

Daytime. Grandma is standing in front of the window. Mother is in the kitchen staring out into space. Father is in the armchair taking his blood pressure. The sound of the monitor can be heard in the silence. There is a sealed bag of garbage by the door.

GRANDMA. Nothing . . . No wind at all . . .

FATHER. What does your mother want wind for?

MOTHER. You mean you don't know? If there's no wind, then nothing happens.

Pause.

FATHER. One hundred twenty over seventy-three.

SCENE 19

Evening. Father is standing in front of the window. Grandma sweeps nonexistent dirt from the carpet with a cane. Mother is in the armchair taking her blood pressure. The sound of the monitor can be heard in the silence. There are three sealed bags of garbage by the door.

MOTHER. One hundred forty-eight over one hundred and two.

Pause.

GRANDMA (*singing*).

>Pope Urban pope Urban pope Urban pope Urban
>Instead of a tiara he wore a turban, a turban, rumpety-thump
>Did the tiara he lose somewhere, lose somewhere, lose
>somewhere
>Or was it for the turban he most cared, he most cared,
>rumpety-thump
>Oh no oh no oh no oh no!
>It's just the way they want it in Rome
>When in Rome, when in Rome, when in Rome-a-dome-dome
>Don't go doing what you'd do at home.

MOTHER (*to herself, looking at the bags of garbage*). There's no way I'm going to take it out. No way. There are limits. I do everything. I do the laundry, I get the groceries, I take care of Grandma. No way.

SCENE 20

Night. Mother in her nightgown, with a crazy look in her eye, walks across the room and into the kitchen. Pulls open a drawer. Gets out a fork, spoon, knife. With an armful of silverware she goes back to the bedroom.

SCENE 21

Dawn. Father in his pajamas, with an armful of silverware, walks across the room. He goes into the kitchen. He pulls open the drawer. And comes to a standstill.

FATHER (*to himself*). Jesus, Mary Mother of God, son of a bitch, what did I do to make the Lord God punish me this way . . .? (*Closes the drawer, drops the silverware into the garbage bag, fastens it, and puts it by the door.*)

SCENE 22

Daytime. Father is in the armchair. Grandma is standing in front of the window. Mother is setting the table for dinner.

MOTHER. Where did all the silverware get to?

FATHER. There isn't any.

MOTHER. What do you mean . . .?

FATHER. We're going to eat with our fingers.

MOTHER. What on earth are you talking about . . .?!

FATHER. No more aristocratic airs. Dip your fingers in and eat . . .

MOTHER. Are you crazy?! Give them back!

FATHER. I threw them out.

MOTHER. How could you? They were . . . they were . . . a souvenir . . .

FATHER. I was so sick of that souvenir, sick out to here with it!

Mother stands there in consternation. After a moment she starts to look for the silverware, violently pulling out drawers. She eventually manages to control herself and returns to the table.

MOTHER. Fine, have it your way. We'll eat with our fingers. Come here, Mama, let me give you a napkin. We have to eat somehow.

Father doesn't move.

MOTHER (*louder*). We have to eat somehow. We're going to eat, we're a family after all.

FATHER (*suddenly*). You've got me by the balls with this food thing of yours!

Silence.

FATHER. I'll go to Jadzia's diner if I want something to eat. It's not like I live in the barracks, is it?

MOTHER. Have you all gone crazy? What's gotten into you? Are you going to start fasting, too?

By this time, Grandma has sat down at the table.

GRANDMA. I don't know, I don't hear so well . . .

MOTHER. Eat, Mama. With your fingers today. Just for fun, just go ahead and eat.

GRANDMA. But how? Without a fork?

MOTHER. I told you already, with your fingers! Do I always have to repeat myself 10 times. We're pretending to be barbarians.

GRANDMA. Like when Grandpa was arrested by the NKVD[2] . . .

FATHER. *With his fingers!*

MOTHER. Enough already, Mama, with the NKVD.

GRANDMA. After that they said I was bourgeoisie . . .

MOTHER (*to Father*). Leave my mother alone!

FATHER. Do you know by any chance where your daughter is?

MOTHER. She's your daughter, too!

FATHER (*to Grandma*). Maybe Mama knows where Mama's daughter is?

GRANDMA. I don't have a mama anymore.

FATHER. Mama's mama doesn't have a mama. (*Screaming.*) But Mama has a daughter!

GRANDMA. If you say so.

Mother covers her face with her hands.

FATHER (*to Mother*). Where is she? Why doesn't she come back? Why isn't she here with us? *Why isn't she here?*

Grandma, frightened, picks up a cutlet with her fingers.

SCENE 23

A dreamlike space, dim light, some of the furniture is gone, the walls have shifted. Daughter is so pale she looks transparent, weak. She is sitting half-conscious in an armchair in the middle of the stage.

MOTHER (*standing over Daughter*). You should have seen the piece of wild boar sausage he ate yesterday and then he says: Staszka, is

2 The Narodnyy Komissariat Vnutrennikh Del (People's Commissariat for Internal Affairs) was the public and secret police organization in the Soviet Union during the Stalinist regime, which eventually became the Committee for State Security (KGB).

there anything for dessert? I say that there isn't. But then I remember that there are four chocolate chestnuts. I say: Well, there are the four chocolate chestnuts that I bought yesterday. And you know what chocolate chestnuts are like, big and round, with hazelnut filling. I bring him two chocolate chestnuts. He eats both of them at once gobble, gobble. We're watching a movie on TV. Later on I look in the cupboard and those two that were left were already gone! But that's not the worst part. The worst part is that he didn't even throw away the box. He defiles it, gobbles it up, scarfs it down, and then when I pick up the box—it looks like it hasn't been touched—there's only one little chocolate rolling around. I wouldn't even begrudge him those chocolates. Heavens, I don't begrudge him anything. Let him go ahead and scarf as much as he can get down. But then he does this. I'll buy fruit, for example. Tangerines. And right away he eats four of them, gobble, gobble, one after the other. Then a banana, gobble, and the only thing he doesn't touch is the apples, because they give him gas. And then he'll ask me curiously: Who's been eating all the fruit? Like maybe it was Grandma! Can you believe it?!?!—drives me crazy. Or I'll buy nuts for a cake. Then he'll sit in front of the television and gobble one bag and then gobble another. Then when I want to make the cake, and all there is in the cupboard is the two gobbled up bags, and maybe there's something left in the bottom of them, crumbs. If he would just tell me, but no. He never eats the whole thing, and to cover his tracks he leaves whatever it is he's gobbled up puffed up in the cupboard with a few morsels left in the bottom to make them look like they're full!

DAUGHTER. I have a headache.

MOTHER (*notices Father, who came in near the end of the monologue and had been listening in for a while; quickly changes the subject*). . . . cut some onion, sauté it, season it, mix it . . .

FATHER (*grimly*). What are you two talking about in here?

MOTHER (*to Daughter*). Why aren't you drinking your tea?! (*To Father*) What do you want for supper?

FATHER (*rubs his stomach with his hand, presses on it from the right, presses on it from the left*). . . . Well maybe . . . yes, something . . . what do you have?

MOTHER (*to Daughter*). Drink that tea, it's no good when it's cold! (*To Father*) What do you mean, what do I have? Go to the refrigerator and see. There's ham, cheese, there are eggs, the soup from yesterday, don't ask such silly questions, what do I have . . .

FATHER. I usually ask, because I get heartburn . . .

MOTHER (*grabs Daughter by the chin, puts her teacup to her lips and pours the tea into her throat*). Drink the tea already, you're driving me crazy!

Daughter breaks away from her, choking.

FATHER (*to Daughter*) See, see what a bundle of nerves that mother of yours is. She's a terrorist! If I get ulcers, it's because of you!

MOTHER. Why don't you just kill me, bury me, and then you'll have peace and quiet! Especially because then I'll be able to rest in peace and eternal repose! (*Walks out.*)

FATHER (*by the kitchen*). Put it on low . . . (*Turns the vent on the lowest, quietest setting.*) Turn it on if you let one. But if you let one and you're cooking cabbage?! (*Turns the vent to the highest setting and has to yell over it.*) It always stinks in this house!!! And the windows are always closed!!! (*Turns off the vent.*) And all you have to do is turn on the vent! Or open the window, just the tiniest crack—just a chink! And there's a little breeze. Not a big gust, not blustery, not enough to blow Grandma away. Your mother says that she turns it on, but she turns it on low, (*turns the vent on low*) so she won't drown Grandma out, because Grandma doesn't like it. Who does?! (*Turns the vent up as high as it will go, yells over the noise.*) I don't like it either!!! The only reason why I care is that I don't like it when it stinks!!!

DAUGHTER. I have a stomachache.

FATHER (*opens the medicine cabinet, rummages around in it, talking loudly, shouting over the noise of the vent*). I don't count for anything in this house! I'm at the very end of the food chain. Grandma is the most important. She has to be happy. Mamamouchi bitch! I had other ideas about how life would turn out. But nobody listens to me.

Mother enters with the vacuum cleaner on and drowns out whatever words come next. The noise of the vacuum combines with the noise of the vent. It makes a breeze, ruffles papers, stirs the flowers.

MOTHER (*passing near Daughter*). And all he does is gobble gobble those bags of nuts!

Father pours some tablets into Daughter's hand. Mother walks out through the other side with the vacuum. The breeze dies down.

FATHER. . . . she has just one prescription for everything—nirvana! . . . Folds her napkins, plants her flowers, turns on the television and she's happy . . . just her and her mommy . . .

Mother comes back in with the vacuum. Everything flutters.

MOTHER (*passing by Daughter*). If there are two chocolates, then he defiles them both right away! (*Goes out the other side with the vacuum.*)

FATHER. And what exactly did her mommy do . . .? *Nothing!* After her husband died she forgot all about her children!

DAUGHTER. I have a . . .

Father pours another handful of tablets into Daughter's hand.

FATHER. It's because of her that your mother has acted like a lunatic her whole life! It's because of her that she sleeps on the silverware!

Mother comes in with the vacuum.

MOTHER (*passing by Daughter*). Scarfed down four chocolate chestnuts and a huge piece of wild boar sausage. That kind of thing can drive a person crazy, you know! (*Goes out the other side with the vacuum.*)

FATHER. . . . because her own mother threw her out of the house! Gave her to an orphanage! *As punishment!* . . . Because she wasn't watching her brother and *her brother fell from the third floor*!!!

Everything gets quiet. The light changes in the room, in a few places cold lights start to shine. Mother enters after a moment, carrying a cake with a burning sparkler.

MOTHER. You didn't even know that today is Grandma's birthday!

Grandma shuffles in behind Mother with honeybee wings fastened to her back and a little cap with antennae on her head.

MOTHER. Grandma had confession, and look, now she's like a little angel. Kiss your Grandma, Iwonka. (*To Father*) And you take a picture of us.

She pulls Daughter up out of the armchair. They arrange themselves around the table with the lit cake. Little Miss Honeybee is in the middle. Father brings the camera.

FATHER (*excited*). Smile! Relax! Act natural, girls. You need to get a different haircut, Iwonka, that one makes you look like a drowned angel of death. Looks like an afro, at your age! Look at your mother, how pretty she looks today!

Father takes a picture. They sit down at the table.

FATHER (*to Grandma*). Mama, how do you feel at this lovely age?

GRANDMA I . . . feel good . . . it's just that . . .

MOTHER. Yes, Mama?

GRANDMA Just . . .

FATHER. Yes?

GRANDMA What was it I wanted to say . . .?

Father and Mother burst out laughing.

GRANDMA (*starts to cry*). I have such terrible memories that I feel like crying.

MOTHER. Eat a little piece of cake, Mama.

GRANDMA. There was this hotel there . . . the most expensive one in town . . . it was called The George. People would come from abroad to stay there, to reserve rooms.

FATHER. That really is terrible, Mama.

Father and Mother burst out laughing.

GRANDMA. And he was so renowned . . . he traveled the world and showed off how he could . . . from the roofs . . .

FATHER (*mocks her*). To the city of Lwów, so I have heard tell . . . Came a tightrope walker, the Human Fly . . .

GRANDMA. . . . and a bunch of people came to see, how he was going to walk that rope up to the roof of Hotel George . . . and he was going, going . . . and when he got to a certain level . . .

FATHER. To the level of the third floor!

Father and Mother burst out laughing again.

GRANDMA. . . . and I was standing just like this . . . with my back to the Hotel George and I watched . . . I was a young girl then . . . and . . . and . . . he was getting closer and closer . . .

IMAGE 3.1 (From left to right) Halina Skoczyńska, Danuta Szaflarska, and Janusz Gajos in Małgorzata Bogajewska's production of *Daily Soup*. Teatr Narodowy, Warsaw, 2007.
Photograph by Stefan Okołowicz.

Father and Mother laugh uproariously.

GRANDMA. . . . and suddenly, right before my eyes . . . somehow . . . he lost his balance . . .

FATHER. Maybe the rope was crooked?

Father and Mother burst out laughing all over again.

GRANDMA. And he *fell*! Fell! Right in front of me . . . And I stood there and looked . . .

MOTHER (*growing more serious*). Sing us something cheerful.

GRANDMA (*sobbing*). Why didn't I do anything . . .?!

DAUGHTER. I dreamed that . . .

MOTHER. Don't interrupt, Grandma's singing. (*Crams cake into Daughter's mouth.*)

Everyone sits in silence for a moment.

MOTHER (*to Grandma*). It's your birthday, Mama, sing!

GRANDMA. To the city of Lwów, so I have heard tell . . . Came a tightrope walker, the Human Fly . . .

Daughter covers her mouth and runs to the bathroom.

MOTHER. (*interrupts Grandma*) Something cheerful!!!

GRANDMA (*sings*). Monday tisket Tuesday tasket

A lady wove herself a basket
A lady wove herself a basket
Wednesday she unraveled it fast
Because she knew it wouldn't last . . .

A rainbow appears outside the window.

GRANDMA (*keeps singing*). Thursday tisket old dog Rover

Saw that she was starting over
Saw that she was starting over
Friday she unraveled it, too
Because she knew it wouldn't do . . .

Father and Mother walk to the window as if under a spell.

GRANDMA. Saturday tasket she began

The tisket thing all over again

The tisket thing all over again
Sunday tasket she lay about
Because she was all worn out . . .

MOTHER AND FATHER (*together*). A rainbow!!! How pretty! Maybe once
in a . . . Look at the colors! It's changing! Amazing! A double
one! Heavenly! Take a picture, quick, take a picture!

Father takes a picture of the rainbow.

MOTHER. Iwonka, where did you crawl off to? Hurry up, there's a
rainbow! Quick!

Father knocks on the bathroom door.

FATHER. I told you not to lock the door! And you're going to get it
if you don't come out right this minute!

Mother knocks on the bathroom door.

MOTHER. Open it, slowpoke! Why do you dawdle like that?!

FATHER. Silly little ass! You're sleeping your life away!

MOTHER. You're always unhappy, always sulking.

FATHER. Just looking at you makes me want to curl up and die! So
moody, so sour, so sluggish, screw you, you hear me, screw
around, a screw up, I meant to say. (*Makes dismissive hand gesture and goes back to the window.*)

MOTHER. And don't go blaming anyone else. It's your own fault. The
one time that something beautiful happens is exactly when
you're in the bathroom!

*Goes back to the window, and with Father gazes at the rainbow.
Grandma starts eating cake. Daughter comes out of the other room
wearing Mother's nightgown and crosses the floor as if she were bal-
ancing on a tightrope. They don't see her.*

DAUGHTER. . . . I dreamed that I had a brother . . . I always wanted to
have a brother . . . he was so sweet, with curly hair . . . and I
was taking care of him . . . our parents had left us at home,
they went somewhere . . . we were playing Peter Pan . . . and
he flew through the window . . . because sometimes you can
fly in your dreams . . .

The furniture and the walls are back in their places. The room is in semi-darkness. The television is on without the sound. Grandma is alone in the armchair in front of the television; absent gaze. The window is wide open, the breeze stirs the curtain. From offstage can be heard the voice of a child or an old woman—someone is crooning a song about an acrobat.

Mother comes in.

MOTHER. What's going on here? Have you gone crazy?! Who opened it? It's so cold! Where's Iwonka?! She was supposed to look after . . .! (*Tries to close the window, the wind pushes her away.*)

MOTHER. It's awfully nippy in here! (*Leaves the window, which she didn't manage to close. Walks up to Grandma sitting motionless.*) Mama? Mama . . . what's going on . . .?

Daughter, who was sitting curled up in the corner the whole time, now stands up and slowly walks past Mother, unnoticed by her. She takes the garbage bag.

MOTHER. Mama, please . . . wake up . . . say something . . .

Daughter walks out. She passes her Father at the threshold, who also doesn't pay any attention to her.

FATHER (*alarmed*). Where's Iwonka? . . .

MOTHER. . . . She's dead . . . she's dead . . . Mama's dead . . .

IMAGE 4.1 Kamilla Baar and Wojciech Solarz in Tadeusz Bradecki's production of *First Time*. Teatr Narodowy, Warsaw, 2006. *Photograph by Michał Mrowiec.*

THE FIRST TIME

MICHAŁ WALCZAK

CHARACHTERS

HE
SHE

TRANSLATED BY BENJAMIN PALOFF

SCENE 1

SHE. It's about time.

HE. Sorry, I couldn't make it. It's just one apartment building after another out here, what the hell kind of urban planning is this? The same building over and over.

SHE. No, come on, it's my fault for calling so late, but I . . .

HE. I'm sorry, I just couldn't find it in the dark. There should be a map. What if somebody isn't even from here, like a foreigner, for instance? Forget about it.

SHE. No, come on, it's my fault, I was just feeling lonely is all.

HE. What kind of project is this? It's the same building over and over. What kind of moron built this place?

SHE. I'm really sorry for dragging you out in the middle of the night. I was feeling lonely.

HE. No, come on, I'm the one who's sorry. I should have taken a cab, I got out at the wrong stop and didn't know where I was . . . You look nice.

SHE. What?

HE. Nothing, never mind.

SHE. I'm sorry, I hurt all over. I don't know, maybe it's the weather, the barometric pressure or something. I was a wreck, I didn't know what to do.

HE. You know, this city's really poorly lit? They should have street lights. I couldn't find your building, let alone your entryway.

SHE. God, I'm really sorry, I should have mentioned that my place is pretty hard to find, but once you do find it the next time is easier, and it just keeps getting easier after that.

HE. No, come on, I'm the one who should be sorry, I should have figured it out, I should be able to find it, you're all freaked out.

SHE. I'm really sorry, I wanted . . .

HE. Come on, no, I'm the one who's sorry, a man should be able to find the place, and here you were waiting, I really did want to make it as fast as I could.

SHE. No, come on, I should be sorry for wearing you out. I was crying, I didn't know what to do, I was a wreck. I'm better now.

HE. No big deal, really, I'm sorry, I hope you didn't have to wait long.

SHE. Well, why don't you come in?

HE. Me? Oh, thanks a lot, I don't know, though. I'm all wet . . .

SHE. If I hadn't been crying I wouldn't have called. I'm sorry. It was a very intense cry.

HE. I'm sorry, I'm all wet . . .

SHE. Oh my God, I'm sorry, you're all wet, you must be cold. Maybe I could get you some tea? It might warm you up.

HE. The lighting's so bad in this town, they should have street lights. Puddles everywhere. What kind of weather is this? I really don't know if I should come in, I'm all wet.

SHE. Oh my God, I'm so sorry, you're all wet and now you're probably pissed at me. Forgive me. I was feeling so lonely. If you really don't want to, I won't make you.

HE. No, come on, I'm the one who's sorry. I should have taken a cab. It's cats and dogs out there; I didn't know how to get here. I don't know, I don't want to fuck up your couch, I should take care of it, like, put something down on it. What's with this weather, always this weather.

SHE. I'm really sorry, I should help you out, give you some warning, I feel really bad about it, you're all wet.

HE. To be honest, I didn't know it was going to be like this. They didn't say anything, quiet evening sky, and then all of a sudden. You never know what's going to happen.

SHE. Oh my God, I'm so sorry, you're standing in the door, why don't you come in, I'll make you tea. You're all wet.

HE. I don't know if I should. It took me a really long time to get here, I wanted to get here as fast as possible. I don't know who makes these street maps, some moron. Morons.

SHE. You were probably already in bed, I'm so sorry, I really don't know. I don't want to throw myself on you. That is, I don't want to impose myself on you. I was a wreck. You probably want to come in.

HE. Sure, I mean, if you need me to . . .

SHE. Because it's already passed, I'm better, so you don't have to come in if you don't want to.

HE. It's passed?

SHE. Yeah, it's passed. Good humor.

HE. Really, you're alright?

SHE. I'm fine, all good, I was just feeling down. Blue. You don't have to if you don't want to, really.

HE. No, I can come in, just in case you feel bad again soon. Sure, I'll come in for a while, I'll have some tea. Because I'm all wet.

SHE. No, it's alright, I'll manage. Thanks, though, a lot. You're sweet. You know, I'd actually gone to bed already, so maybe we could talk some other time?

HE. Alright then. Bye.

SHE. Bye. But listen . . .

HE. Yeah?

SHE. You're not angry with me?

HE. Me? No, come on. So, bye.

SHE. Bye.

HE. Bye. I'm going. See you later. Take care. I have to get moving. Peace.

SHE. So you'll call me, right?

HE. I'll call you. Bye.

SHE. Bye. Thanks.

HE. Don't mention it. Bye.

SHE. You're all wet. I'm sorry. Bye now.

HE. I'm a little wet. Bye now.

SHE. Huh?

HE. Nothing.

SHE. No, you were going to say something.

HE. Jesus, you couldn't wait.

SHE. I couldn't wait for what?

HE. I was really counting on you being a wreck.

SHE. What?

HE. That I could finally touch you because you were a wreck. You couldn't hold out a little longer? This goddamn town. Morons. The bus moved like a slug. We can never make it fucking work. Nothing in this town works. What the hell kind of town is this? Some moron, what the hell kind of moron built this town?

SHE. So what am I supposed to say now?

HE. I don't know, like, come in.

SHE. I don't know, like come in, if it's so important to you that I say it.

HE. But I don't know if you're sure, I'll fuck up your couch, it looks new.

SHE. Dude, it's fine, you're all wet, I'm really sorry, you're probably all worn out because of me.

HE. OK, but just for a little while, I'll drink some tea and get out of here, because I'm all wet, but you know, I really don't know . . .

SHE. I'm sorry I'm being such an idiot, but you see . . .

HE. No problem, really.

SHE. So . . .

HE. I don't know . . .

SHE. Are you coming in or aren't you?

HE. What's that?

SHE. Nothing, never mind.

HE. So maybe I'll come in.

SHE. Huh? OK, sure. Oh my God, you'll catch cold. Come in, come in, just, you know, slow and careful, so that you don't mess up my stuff.

HE. I'm sorry, I'm all wet, I was sweating a little, I was running, the puddles. I don't know who built this neighborhood, some moron.

SHE. Wow, you're really pretty soaked, it's pouring off you, and you're shaking.

HE. Jeez, I'm sorry, maybe I'll just stand on the doormat for a minute, till I drip dry. I don't want to mess up your stuff, I don't want to mess things up for anybody.

SHE. Don't be silly, I'm the one who's sorry, you misunderstood. Come on, come in, don't be embarrassed.

HE. I'm not embarrassed, I'm just all wet.

SHE. Listen, make a decision already, because it's too cold for me to stay here daydreaming in the doorway.

HE. What's your problem, I'm wet is all, I don't want to mess up your stuff.

SHE. No, really, I'm sorry I've worn you out, you didn't have to come if you didn't want to.

HE. No, really . . .

SHE. You're not doing me any favors.

HE. Maggie, please . . .

SHE. You think I don't know you were feeling sorry for me?

HE. It's not like that, you have it all wrong . . .

SHE. Go fuck yourself.

HE. Bitch.

SHE. What?

HE. What the hell kind of way is that to behave, this is you from the start, I come here and what, you act like this.

SHE. How am I acting?

HE. Fake, you're acting fake, what's that about, like you're putting on airs.

SHE. Christ, what are you yelling for, try not yelling on the stairs, the neighbors are asleep.

HE. Listen, try deciding whether you want me to come in or not, because now I don't know. You call me, I come, and what. Putting on airs. Yes or no.

SHE. I was lonely is all. I felt down. Otherwise I wouldn't have called. I thought you'd understand, but you yell at me.

HE. Fine, fine, I'm sorry. Just calm down . . .

SHE. Forget it, we're through. I don't ever need to see you again. Farewell.

HE. Farewell to you.

SHE. No, wait.

HE. What?

SHE. You don't understand. When I said "farewell," I was only testing you.

HE. Testing what?

SHE. To see how you'd react, if you have feelings for me and how strong.

HE. But you know I do.

SHE. And maybe it happens you've forgotten about that thing you're holding behind your back?

HE. God, I'm sorry, I totally forgot. These are for you.

SHE. For me? Jeez, thanks. I'm sorry, I'm tired, I don't know what's up with me.

HE. No, I'm the one who should be sorry, for that blow-up just now, it's just that I'm all wet and all. Do you like them?

SHE. Listen, dude, didn't you just hear me say thank you? I was feeling lonely. But I'm glad you came. Hurray!

HE. I'm glad, too. Mind if I smoke?

SHE. Go ahead. Make yourself at home. I was feeling lonely. What are you so nervous about? Don't be nervous. Spaz. Man, you really poured on the cologne; they can probably smell it out on the street. I'll get you some supper. You like toast?

HE. Yeah, sure, I love toast.

SHE. I wanted to make toast, but the toaster's on the fritz, it's all fucked up. Sorry, no toast.

HE. No problem, really.

SHE. I could make you a sandwich. Sorry, that's all I know how to do.

HE. I don't know, Mags, whatever you want . . .

SHE. But you said you were hungry.

HE. I'm not hungry.

SHE. Hey, no smoking in the house, OK? I told you, my mom can't stand the smell of cigarettes.

HE. I'm sorry, but you said . . .

SHE. Come on, dude, what's your problem?

HE. I'm putting it out, chill. Listen, Maggie . . .

SHE. Wait a sec, I'll put on some music. You like music? Because if you don't want to eat, maybe we could drink some wine.

HE. Unfortunately . . .

SHE. Hey, man, chill, don't be such a spaz. Spaz. Have a seat on the couch, have a cigarette, and loosen up.

HE. So I can smoke?

SHE. Sure, I just told you you could. I love this music. But I'm forgetting something . . . I know! Wait a second.

HE. Yeah, fine . . . What a girl . . . Sweet and mean, all at the same time . . . Modern. My kind of girl.

SHE. This'll be awesome. You'll love it. Help me set it up. Or no, I'll set it up, you smoke your cigarette. Wait, I have to turn out the lights. Well, nice . . .

HE. Nice . . .

SHE. Dinner by candlelight, right? Here, open the wine . . .

HE. But I . . .

SHE. You don't think I'm crazy, do you? I was just feeling lonely, is all. A person sometimes gets lonely, there's nothing wrong with it. Loneliness and all that, right?

HE. Absolutely . . .

SHE. Give it to me, I'll open it. Klutz. Retard. So, what's new with you?

HE. With me? No reason to complain, I guess . . .

SHE. Christ, you really are uptight. Grab a glass. In the cupboard. Not that one. Come on, I'll pour you some. Hold it straight. Hey, your hands are shaking.

HE. Magdalena, you are so beautiful.

SHE. Hey, man, what the fuck are you doing? You've fucking spilled all over my favorite dress!

HE. I'm sorry, I . . .

SHE. Fine, good, enough blathering. My best dress. You know how much I paid for this? Moron. Stop, I'll wring it out myself.

HE. Maybe I could . . .

SHE. No, no, stop, come on. Help me undo it . . . Not on that side, idiot. Fine, leave it, I'll do it myself. Why are you all sweaty? Are you sick or something? Idiot.

HE. I . . . I'm sorry . . .

SHE. Sorry, man, sorry—you're such a fucking child. You've never seen a woman before?

HE. Maggie, I should go . . .

SHE. Listen, Chuck. I know I'm being weird, and I'm sorry about that. You came out here in the middle of the night, and I can't even behave decently . . . It's mean of me . . . I'm sorry . . . If you hate me, you can go, I won't be mad at you . . . I . . . I'm so stupid . . . I'm sorry . . .

HE. Maggie, don't be like that, now . . . fine, come here . . .

SHE. Hey, love . . . This music's too loud, I can't hear what you're saying to me . . .

HE. Hey, love . . .

IMAGE 4.2 Kamilla Baar and Wojciech Solarz in Tadeusz Bradecki's production of *First Time*. Teatr Narodowy, Warsaw, 2006.
Photograph by Michał Mrowiec.

SHE. Who the hell are you?

HE. Maggie, it's me. Charlie. You don't recognize me?

SHE. What do you want? I'd just gone to bed.

HE. I'm sorry, but you're the one who called me. Maggie, do you feel alright?

SHE. Listen, I'm sorry, but we're going to have to call it a night. Stop by some other time, OK?

HE. Just a minute, what's going on here?

SHE. Pardon?

HE. No, pardon me, maybe you could explain?

SHE. Dude, chill out. You come here completely drunk in the middle of the night, raving. I told you it's, like, over between us.

HE. You're messing with me, right?

SHE. Listen, dude, I'm pretty tired, I want to go to bed. Take care of yourself.

HE. Come over, I'm begging you, I'm so lonely, I want you to come over, please. That's what you said on the phone, so look, honey, what's with you changing your mind all of a sudden?

SHE. Hey, sorry, man, really, sorry, but you got it all wrong, sorry, man, you've been dreaming. You bring me to the door at two in the morning, you just show up all of a sudden, sorry, but I want to go to bed. Drunk.

HE. I love you, get it? Whoa, I finally said it . . . Come on, enough with the games . . .

SHE. Listen, Chuck. I know I'm being weird, and I'm sorry about that. You came out here in the middle of the night, and I can't even behave decently . . . It's mean of me . . . I'm sorry . . . If you hate me, you can go, I won't be mad at you . . . I . . . I'm so stupid . . . I'm sorry . . .

HE. Maggie, don't be like that, now . . . fine, come here . . .

SHE. Wait, I have to tell you something. There's something you need to know.

HE. Yeah?

SHE. When I was little, I was throwing some stones and this bird died. I'm bad. I'm a child of Satan.

HE. Shhh, shhh, hush now. Just calm down. Don't scream, you'll wake the neighbors. Close your eyes.

SHE. Hey, man, what's with all the romantic stuff?

HE. This is what.

SHE. Oh, hello. Except that we've already said our hellos. So, then, have a seat, make yourself comfortable, why are you standing in the door like some loser?

HE. I . . . To be honest, I was late because I was looking around for a florist.

SHE. You what?

HE. As they say . . . So maybe we could finally go inside?

SHE. God, come in, sorry, you're standing at the door. Really, you shouldn't have.

HE. Hi there.

SHE. Hi yourself. Jeez, I'm sorry, I forgot to say my hellos. Far out.

HE. It's no big deal, really. So, we're finally inside. To tell the truth, I'd lost hope that I'd make it into your place and this whole scene. Jeez, it's really dragging on.

SHE. What's dragging on?

HE. Nothing, never mind. Where can I . . .

SHE. You can hang it here.

HE. Far out.

SHE. And what are you so cheerful about?

HE. Me? Nothing, I'm fine.

SHE. But what are you standing like that in the foyer for? Come in. Be brave, there's nothing to be afraid of. Don't be afraid. He's afraid.

HE. I'm not afraid.

SHE. Such a big boy, and he's afraid. You're looking dapper. Dandy. You're wearing cologne.

HE. What's with you?

SHE. I was feeling lonely, I was crying, I don't know what your problem is. You want to see where?

HE. Where what?

SHE. You know, I'm tired, I'm going to bed. I'm sorry. Good night.

HE. But Maggie . . .

SHE. Don't you think you should be going? I don't have it in me for your all-night conversations. Those all-night conversations of yours.

HE. But . . . Did I do something wrong?

SHE. Listen, pal, don't keep tormenting me with these questions of yours, so now really, good night, get going.

HE. Maggie . . .

SHE. Don't touch me! Leave me alone! What are you doing? Help!

HE. OK, OK, calm down, I'm leaving . . . Maggie, I'm sorry.

SHE. No, I'm the one who's sorry. Fuck, my head hurts, you know? You know how I get when I have a headache, or maybe you don't know. So, what, you coming in or not?

SCENE 2

SHE. It's about time.

HE. Sorry, I couldn't make it. You live so far away, what the hell kind of urban planning is this? It's so far away.

SHE. No, come on, it's my fault for calling so late, but I . . .

HE. So can I come in?

SHE. You forgot to say how you couldn't make it, about all the adventures you had while you were on your way over here.

HE. I'll tell you in a minute, but could I come in first? I'm all wet.

SHE. Hey, buddy, what's your problem? What are you so spastic about, spaz?

HE. I'm not a spaz, I'm cold is all. Can I come in?

SHE. What's that supposed to mean?

HE. I'm sorry, but I couldn't find it in the dark.

SHE. No, I'm the one who's sorry, I was feeling lonely, anxious. It's no fun being anxious.

HE. I should have taken a cab, I got out at the wrong stop . . . But you know how it is.

SHE. Sure. I really can't tell you how sorry I am to drag you out in the middle of the night, but I was really freaking out.

HE. It's no big deal. Anyway, hi. These are for you. So now you say, "Thanks so much," and I say, "I'm all wet, can I come in," and you say, "Sure, I'll make you some tea," and I say, "I don't know if I should," and you say, "Well, make up your mind," and I say, "Fine, I'll come in, where should I throw my coat?"

SHE. What the hell kind of way is that to behave? What's with the irony?

HE. Maggie, I . . .

SHE. Uh-uh, no way . . . I don't want to, let go of me . . .

HE. Put the flowers in some water, OK?

SHE. No, I can't . . . Leave me alone, get out of here . . . How could you? . . . Jerk . . .

HE. Please, just calm down . . .

SHE. You want to? Go ahead, please, I'm all yours, I can get undressed, go ahead . . .

HE. Quiet!

SHE. What . . . oh, Pookie, why are you yelling . . . Pookie . . .

HE. Are you going to calm down, or what?

SHE. But I am calm . . . So, um, maybe I'll put these flowers in some water . . .

HE. Maggie, I can't go on like this, not like this, if you get me . . .

SHE. But Pookie, why are you getting upset? Don't get upset. How about some tea? You're all wet.

HE. I come over here, and yet again . . .

SHE. Hey, look, flowers. For me? Gee, thanks . . .

HE. Yeah, I already gave those to you.

SHE. And why did you go and do that? I didn't ask you for flowers. I'm sorry, pal, but it's not like we're lovers.

HE. No, what, come on . . . I mean, I just wanted to . . .

SHE. You can put your coat over here. Make yourself at home. I'll go get the tea. Look at you, all tense. Squarepants, over here. You're a dear for coming, thanks.

HE. I . . . no problem. I'll hang up my coat.

SHE. I was having bad dreams, I couldn't sleep. If I'm any kind of burden, really, go back home, I don't want to inconvenience you with my problems.

HE. It's alright, really.

SHE. I was feeling lonely, I was crying. You want to see where?

HE. Where what?

SHE. Where I was crying.

HE. Sure.

SHE. Over here. There are still marks. Believe me now, shithead?

HE. I'm sorry, what?

SHE. Do you cry often?

HE. I . . . That is . . .

SHE. I have different kinds of crying in me. This time it was a real intense cry. It was existential.

HE. I see.

SHE. That's how I was crying, more or less. I wanted someone with me to hold me close and stroke my cheek, but there wasn't anyone else here, so I stroked my own cheek and said to myself, "It'll be OK, it'll be OK."

HE. Wow, that sounds so sad . . .

SHE. Right? I was lying here, leaning my head, sort of like this, and I was just wracked with grief. It'll be OK, it'll be OK . . .

HE. Oh, honey . . . It'll be OK, it'll be OK . . .

SHE. God, you're all wet.

HE. I'm sorry, I wanted to hold you close . . . My intentions were good . . .

SHE. No, never mind, it's cool, it's passed. You know, I don't like people to touch me. To tell the truth, I seriously have to be a wreck if I'm going to let somebody touch me.

HE. What about now?

SHE. Not now.

HE. You're not a serious wreck right now? I was really trying to catch you while you were a wreck.

SHE. Sorry, Pookie. Maybe next time. Really, sorry. So, come on, let me go.

HE. How would you rate this atmosphere?

SHE. What atmosphere?

HE. Well, is today the day?

SHE. Is today what day?

HE. You know what day.

SHE. Look, pal, I don't know what kind of fantasy world you're living in. Daydreamer. We're just having a pleasant conversation. I don't know what your deal is. Where are you coming from, all freaked out?

HE. Maggie, for the love of God, again . . .

SHE. I'm sorry, pal, I'll manage, you came here, you stopped by, you're all wet, but this isn't it.

HE. What do you mean, this isn't it?

SHE. It's not.

HE. It is.

SHE. It's not.

HE. This is the night. I said so, and I'm not leaving here until . . .

SHE. Until what?

HE. Is this my fault? Did I do something wrong? If you want, I can tell you about how I had a hard time getting here, it was dark and raining . . .

SHE. Pookie, really . . .

HE. I know, I know. Let's start from scratch, OK? Let's do it over, Maggie, please. Just give me one more chance.

SHE. Charlie, what's your deal? Stay.

HE. OK? OK? So, here I am, I'm ringing the doorbell, now I'm waiting for you to open the door . . . Wait, I have to put my coat on . . .

SHE. Charlie . . .

HE. All set. I'm sorry, I had a hard time getting here. There are so many streets and buildings, I don't get what the hell kind of urban planning this is, some moron, I should have taken a cab . . .

SHE. You've gone bonkers. Come back in here and behave like a human being. Are you drinking this tea or not?

HE. Please, just give me one more . . .

SHE. Listen, enough blathering, my head's going to explode. Are you a girl or a guy?

HE. Don't insult me, OK? Fine, I'll come back in, I'll drink my tea, and I'll tell you.

SHE. So, talk.

HE. Maggie, please, just not in that tone of voice.

SHE. What tone of voice? Why don't you forget about my tone of voice and worry about your own?

HE. So today I get nothing?

SHE. What nothing?

HE. Maggie, how much longer do I have to wait? Just tell me how long.

SHE. Buddy, what are you talking about?

HE. God, this is so humiliating . . . awful . . . why are you doing this? Why?

SHE. Pookie, you're trembling all over. God, I forgot that you're all wet . . . Maybe you'd like something warm? Take off those rags and put on a robe from the bathroom, you hear?

HE. Just a second, just a second, something's not right here, I'm doing something wrong . . . I don't know, I don't know . . . Maybe I should be speaking to her differently somehow, I don't know . . . Something has to be done, this can't go on like this, I'll go nuts . . .

SHE. Charles . . .

HE. Yes?

SHE. What are you pacing around for, sit down. Chill. What's eating you, I can see that something's eating you. We're friends, you can tell me anything. Shoot.

HE. But you know . . . You're the only person who knows everything about me . . .

SHE. Pookie, I really don't want you to think that I'm some nut or anything like that, I don't. It's not every day that I call someone in the middle of the night and ask him to come over. If it's a big pain for you, you don't have to come over in the middle of the night. God, it's already the middle of the night, maybe I should go to bed . . .

HE. You know that's not what's bothering me.

SHE. I don't understand . . . I'm sorry, I'm awfully tired, I have a headache . . .

HE. Maggie, I . . .

SHE. Christ, would you spit it out already?

SHE. Listen, shouldn't we talk this over?

SHE. But we are talking it over.

HE. No, something else. Us. Because you know . . .

SHE. Ow, ow . . .

HE. What?

SHE. Nothing, never mind, I just had a pain in my leg. Lately my leg hurts, I don't know why. Maybe I should see a doctor.

HE. Uh-huh. Yes, of course. Legs are very important.

SHE. So then, what was it we were talking about?

HE. Well, you know how I feel.

SHE. Listen, I don't know about you, but I'm fading. If you want, I can put you up on the couch. Good night.

HE. Quit lying and sit down, enough with the games.

SHE. Ow, that hurts.

HE. Sorry, I had to.

SHE. You're one messed-up guy.

HE. Come on, I'll massage it out.

SHE. Not that one, idiot, the other one.

HE. Sorry. How's that?

SHE. Good. Thanks.

HE. You're very welcome. But you were saying something about your leg . . .

SHE. But we've talked about this a million times. It has to be a special night, not any old night. Do you want to be any old guy?

HE. But I did everything I was supposed to do. I don't understand, I stopped by, I bought flowers . . . What, wasn't I mean enough? Or maybe not tender enough?

SHE. I don't know, Pookie, don't ask me. Be spontaneous, get lost in the fantasy . . .

HE. But Maggie, this is like the tenth time it's been raining, I buy flowers, I feed you some shit about how I had trouble making it, and you keep saying it's not right, I don't know why you think it isn't right. The tenth time . . .

SHE. I was thinking we could have a little supper together, chat, but forget it, you can go, see you later, go fuck yourself.

HE. Wait. Please, explain it to me. Something's wrong. Don't be offended, but I have a right to want you . . . I mean, to want you to explain . . .

SHE. Understand, Pookie, that a woman has to be in a particular frame of mind for that to happen, not in just any frame of mind. That's all.

HE. Fine, let's just talk, then. I would . . . God . . . I can't . . .

SHE. What's wrong, Pookie?

HE. But Maggie, this is off somehow, this same thing over and over into infinity, it's some kind of . . . infinity . . . The tenth time . . .

SHE. You were the one who asked me, you were begging me, remember?

HE. Yeah, sure, but . . .

SHE. What, you didn't ask? Didn't you ask?

HE. Maggie, please . . . just not like . . .

SHE. So what did you ask? Tell me what you asked. Right now.

HE. But.

SHE. Repeat what you asked. I want you to repeat it. Christ, it's hot in here. Would you mind if I took off some clothes?

HE. Please, Maggie, give me one more chance.

SHE. More convincingly, like before.

HE. Please, Maggie, give me one more chance.

SHE. Good. And now what did I say to you when you asked me out?

HE. You said you had baggage from Ollie, your ex.

SHE. Great, I said, I'll go out with you, but under one condition.

HE. Under the condition that I make you feel secure and that I'm patient, but Maggie . . .

SHE. And now what did we settle on with regard to the initiation of our living our lives together?

HE. That I would be patient, and that we would try to get close to one another . . .

SHE. And?

HE. And that we would get close to one another physically in a certain way, namely, that on a romantic evening, while it was raining, you would call me and I would come with flowers, and we would have supper together, and then.

SHE. Excellent. Then I don't see any problem.

HE. But Maggie, this is the tenth time . . .

SHE. I want us to start our lives together consciously and beautifully. I thought you did, too.

HE. Sure, of course, but . . . but everything was fine the last time . . .

SHE. For the majority of people it's an accident, it's chaos. I don't want to be like most people. My first time has to be perfect, it has to be completely thought out and consciously understood that that's how I'll express myself, get it? Don't interrupt me. From the entire population of men I've chosen you, because it seemed to me that you're just as sensitive as I am, but now I see that I was mistaken. You should appreciate it. If you don't love me anymore, if you think I'm weird, just go, close the door behind you and never come back. I'll understand.

HE. Maggie, I'm begging you, I'm just saying that we need to go about this more spontaneously . . .

SHE. But you agreed with me that it was a pretty scene: night, it's raining, I'm a wreck, I'm crying, I call you, I beg you to come over, you come over as fast as you can, but you can't find my apartment, it's this huge housing complex, building after building, finally you find it, you come to me dripping wet, in your left hand—by the way, remember that we agreed on your left, not your right—so in your left hand you hold a bouquet of roses, we chat for a minute at the door, we're timid about the whole situation, we exchange some awkward small talk, and then I invite you in, the tension reaches its peak when you take off your coat, I offer you tea, you accept, your voice trembling, you'd like to throw yourself on me and make love to me right away, on the sofa in the front room, but you're scared, you're shy, you're breaking out on your face, you come in, we make pointless chit-chat, but you actually want so badly to tell me that you love me, but I don't make it easy for you, I play the lady, slippery, pretending I don't see how much you want me, you can't take the pressure, and then . . . But you agreed that it was a lovely scene. I don't understand why you're backing out now. You've disappointed me, Charles. You've really disappointed me. We could have made such a beautiful, detailed scene. It could have been the most beautiful scene in the world, the most self-aware first time ever.

HE. Maggie, my love, my everything, that scene is still going on. Aren't we sitting and talking, isn't everything exactly as we imagined it should be? We've been rehearsing for so long, and today is the premiere of the most beautiful performance in the world. I feel it.

SHE. Oh, how can I believe what you're saying when you've been so heartless and cruel?

HE. Oh, believe me, my heart upon your warm heart lies, it longs to beat with yours as one . . .

SHE. To hell with you, for real, leave me with my misery, because you don't love me, admit it. All you really want is to see my pussy.

HE. Magdalena, sunshine, how can you sully your mouth with such vulgar language, wound me not with thy tongue but with thine eye.

SHE. Oh, I feel my soul breaketh. You know how wounded I am, how Ollie, my ex, hurt me without shame, and I'm constantly licking the wounds of my soul: Will you be my cure?

HE. I'll tell you verily, my love, that Ollie was a rogue and nothing more. Dearest, give me your lips.

SHE. Why are you so quiet? I hope that we've clarified a thing or two. And now I have to excuse myself, but I really am tired. These conversations will be the death of me.

HE. What, then, so we're never going to see each other again?

SHE. I don't know, I'm sure we'll see each other here and there. But maybe you should be going. Christ, it's already light out . . .

HE. Yeah . . . You know, I had such big plans, big dreams . . .

SHE. Dude, please. I've had enough of your fantasies. Always with your fantasies. Good night.

HE. Maggie, I . . .

SHE. Don't forget your coat. Bye.

HE. Alright, fine . . . bye. But I . . .

SCENE 3

HE. Hi.

SHE. Hi.

HE. Surprised, huh?

SHE. About what?

HE. About what? You know perfectly well about what. You don't mind if I make myself at home. It's barely raining and still pretty light out, but I thought I'd drop in. And I don't have any flowers, so don't bother with the vase. But to tell the truth, I would like something to drink.

SHE. I'm sorry, but do we know each other?

HE. We haven't seen each other for a month, and already you don't recognize me? You're pathetic, you know that?

SHE. Please let me go. What's this all about?

HE. You changed your hair. It doesn't suit you. I liked it better the other way. I'd like you to change it back to the way it was.

SHE. What's your problem? Please leave. Police!

HE. Quiet! You'll wake the neighbors. I'll put your hair back myself. What, he didn't like it? You changed it for him?

SHE. What's this about? I don't understand . . .

HE. You think I don't know that you're back with Ollie? You think I don't know you're rehearsing those scenes of yours with him now?

SHE. Help . . .

HE. You look different somehow. All it takes is for a woman to change guys and right away she starts to look different. So how's it going with you two? We've had plenty of rain lately, I guess that means you can do it often enough.

SHE. You're drunk. Please leave this instant, because I'm calling the police.

HE. Not so fast. I've come to my senses, finally. You have no idea how wonderful it feels.

SHE. What do you want from me? Leave me alone . . . God . . .

HE. I want to see you naked, bitch, you bitch, I'm going to strip you of all your bitchy little modern bitchiness, all your bitchy little bitch airs, and we're going to be animals, tigers, elephants, wolves, baboons. Alright, bitch, my bitch, get over here. It's me, bitch, your real man.

SHE. Don't strip me of my modernness, I'm begging you.

HE. Enough with the midnight journeys, enough text messaging, rain, flowers. No one's going to write text messages now. I'm going to howl, and you're going to howl, girlie.

SHE. Oh, stop, I'm begging you . . . Your words are wounding my modern heart.

HE. Slut. Bitch. Female. I've always wanted to call you a bitch. Bitch, bitch.

SHE. Oh, oh. Does this mean you want to get brutal?

HE. Yeah, I want to get brutal, because all love is brutal.

SHE. Oh, he wants to get brutal. Oh, oh.

HE. Oo, oo.

SHE. Oh, oh.

HE. Oo, oo.

SHE. Oh, oh.

SCENE 4

SHE. Oh . . .

HE. Are you alright?

SHE. Oh . . .

HE. Are you OK? God, I'm sorry, I don't know what came over me. The animal got out. Are you offended? You hear me?

SHE. Oh . . .

HE. That was unpardonable, now I know you'll never call me again, I said such vulgar things to you. I'm sorry. I'll get going.

SHE. Oh . . .

HE. But I want to tell you one thing before I go. I know you hate me now, but . . . That was the greatest experience of my life, if I can put it that way . . .

SHE. Oh . . .

HE. You screamed beautifully.

SHE. Thanks.

HE. Don't mention it. By the way, my name is Charles, not Chris.

SHE. Sorry. Charles . . . Don't go, please, stay a while . . .

HE. Really? You're really not mad at me?

SHE. Oh Charles, you were wonderful. I didn't think you knew so many tricks.

HE. No, no, I was too brutal. That was awful. The howling and all, my gestures. I should apologize.

SHE. Really, don't mention it.

HE. Magdalena, would you marry me? You don't have to answer now.

SHE. Easy there, Pookie, why so fast?

HE. But I really . . .

SHE. Take it easy, we have time. Are you offended?

HE. No, no, come on.

SHE. Easy, we have time, like I said.

HE. Sure, sure. All this happened so fast.

SHE. Let's not make any rash decisions.

HE. Easy, we have time.

SHE. It all happened so fast.

HE. Sure did. You're right, I'm sorry, I pushed it too far.

SHE. No, come on, I'm sorry, I hurt you with my tone.

HE. No, come on, really, I know what you meant.

SHE. We're modern people, the fact that we slept together doesn't necessarily have to mean anything.

HE. Of course not. It all happened so fast.

SHE. You see, we have to consider what kind of potential life-plots can come out of this. We need to consider how our brains behave after everything that's happened, how the ensuing events will be absorbed by our memories, whether we'll remember it fondly. I'm not using overly complicated language, am I?

HE. No, no, come on.

SHE. I believe that what I would call intellectual consensus is just as essential as sexual understanding.

HE. But you're not saying no?

SHE. Of course not, Pookie.

HE. Excellent.

SHE. Quiet, you'll wake the neighbors. You're my first boyfriend, so it's hard for me to compare these impressions to others. I don't want to make any rash decisions, you know what I mean.

HE. Naturally. God, I'm so happy. Really, it was good for you?

SHE. It was wonderful . . . magnificent . . . I was so afraid . . . I was afraid it would never happen.

HE. Oh, so *you* were afraid, it was you who was afraid.

SHE. I want to do it again . . .

HE. Wait, maybe tomorrow . . .

SHE. Just a taste.

HE. Really, I can't . . . You want to smoke?

SHE. I didn't think you had it in you, you know?

HE. To be honest, neither did I.

SHE. Was that really your first time?

HE. That's what I said.

SHE. Oh my. Mine too.

HE. I know, you said. Listen, we have to talk this over. A person's intimacy is . . .

SHE. You're good, you know?

HE. Well, some of it's instinctual.

SHE. I'm glad you came over. When I saw you at the door I was just overjoyed.

HE. I knew it would come to this somehow, sooner or later.

SHE. You knew?

HE. Of course.

SHE. God, Charles, you're so smart.

HE. Thanks.

SHE. So, now you.

HE. Me what?

SHE. Tell me I'm pretty.

HE. You're the most beautiful girl I've seen in my whole life, even though now you look a little different than usual, but that doesn't matter.

SHE. That's the afterglow. But what do you think, am I good?

HE. Good at what?

SHE. Well, you know, I want to know.

HE. Yeah, OK, if it's up to me, I'd say you did a good job.

SHE. God, Charles, how smart you are.

HE. Thanks. I'm just interested in various things, I'm pretty open-minded. When I was just a kid I showed incredible talent for drawing. I started talking when I was three months old. What more can I say? I don't want to bore you. Since preschool I've taken the best notes in subjects in the humanities as well as in the sciences. In the future . . .

SHE. God, dude, I feel so dumb next to you.

HE. Hm . . .

SHE. Sweetness. Are you asleep?

HE. To be honest, a little . . .You know, could you get off my arm, it's gone a little numb . . .

SHE. Jeez, sorry . . .

HE. No, it's alright, it's just gone a little numb . . . So, good night . . .

SHE. Good night . . . Charles, you know, I feel a little weird . . .

HE. Hm . . .

SHE. So many sensations, and then like a lightning bolt . . . That must be the sensations . . . Are you asleep?

HE. Hm . . .

SHE. I've never felt like this before . . . It's so weird . . . You're asleep, right?

HE. What are you doing . . .

SHE. Pookie, what's going on?

HE. Goddammit . . .

SHE. What is it, honey?

HE. Fuck . . . What's with you?

SHE. Charlie, I . . .

HE. Jesus, your belly!

SHE. What about my belly? Charles . . . Jesus, Mary Mother of God . . .

HE. Your belly's growing! Your belly's growing! Your belly!

SHE. Ow . . . Charles . . . My belly . . . Do something fast . . . My belly's getting bigger . . . It's huge . . . Oh my God . . . Help me, Charles . . . I have a belly!

HE. She has a belly!

SHE. My belly!

HE. Your belly!

SHE. My big belly!

HE. A giant big belly!

SHE. It keeps getting bigger . . .

HE. It's getting bigger . . . Wait, don't panic . . .

SHE. Jesus, what . . .

HE. Wait. It's stopped.

SHE. What do you mean, stopped . . . Charles . . .

HE. Don't panic. Your belly got bigger, but now it's stopped.

SHE. Stopped?

HE. Yes. It's not getting bigger any more.

SHE. Phew. That's a relief . . .

HE. God, I was so scared.

SHE. But where'd this belly come from?

HE. I don't know, you grew a belly all of a sudden.

SHE. Does it look awful?

HE. What can this mean, your having grown a belly?

SHE. God, I don't know. Charles, do you still find me attractive?

HE. You must be sick or something. Does this sort of thing run in your family? Has your mother had this belly-thing too?

SHE. God, do I have cancer?

HE. Chill out. I'm sure they can treat this.

SHE. But Charles, why are you standing so far away from me? Come over here, don't be afraid. It's just a belly.

HE. Sure it is. And what if it's an infectious disease? I don't want to have a big repulsive belly.

SHE. Don't talk like that, Charles.

HE. Big belly. God, you're repulsive with that belly, not attractive at all.

SHE. Charles, hold me . . . Oh God . . .

HE. What's happening?

SHE. Owwwww . . .

HE. What's the deal?

SHE. Charles . . . ambulance . . . call, ahhh . . .

HE. Christ, you're having a kid! Woman, you're having a kid!

SHE. Help me, please, I can't take it . . .

HE. I was going to leave on account of the belly, but suddenly a mature man has awakened within me. Push hard! I'm here, honey! Push!

SHE. What's happening, ahhhh!

HE. Breathe, rest, breathe, one, two, three . . .

SHE. Aaaaa . . .

HE. Again, again . . . Harder, Mom . . . What's happening? I see the head . . . The head!

SHE. The head!

HE. The head is out!

SHE. The head!

HE. What an unlikely situation, but then there's no time to wonder, to react, you just find yourself in the situation, you do something, you act one way or another, maybe you act like an idiot, you perform various moves, make various faces, you're horrified, but what to do. The arms are out!

SHE. The arms!

HE. The arms are out!

SHE. The arms!

HE. A little more, push, push! One more push!

SHE. Oooooo . . .

HE. The belly!

SHE. The belly!

HE. A little belly!

SHE. A little belly!

HE. Be brave, finish the job, just a bit longer!

SHE. I can't hold out . . . a bit longer . . .

HE. The legs are out!

SHE. The legs!

HE. Two legs!

SHE. Two legs! Are we done?

HE. A little more . . . Done!

SHE. Done!

HE. Done!

SHE. Done!

HE. Done . . .

SHE. What?

HE. Where is . . .

SHE. What was that? What was that clang?

HE. What clang?

SHE. I heard a clang.

HE. I didn't hear anything.

SHE. Where's my baby?

HE. What kind of urban planning is this, who built this town, some moron . . .

SHE. Charles, what was that?

HE. You know, I think I'm going to get going . . .

SHE. Are you nuts? Charles! Stop! Goddammit, what the fuck was that?

HE. I . . . I . . . don't know . . . I . . .

SHE. Calm down and tell me what happened. Where is my baby? I don't see him, I want to see him.

HE. What baby? Are you nuts? That's not even possible.

SHE. Just a minute ago I gave birth to a baby. Where is my baby?

HE. Honey, you're tired and emotional. You've had a dream.

SHE. I'm warning you, I can't be held responsible for what I do. I'm not nuts. There was a baby here.

HE. Maggie, calm down, please . . . Ow . . .

SHE. Where's my baby?

HE. I thought you were on the pill . . .

SHE. But you had a condom, I saw it . . .

HE. But your eyes were closed the whole time . . .

SHE. He knocked me up! Hey, everybody, he knocked me up!

HE. Shhh, don't yell, you'll wake the neighbors.

SHE. Shithead! Irresponsible, spoiled little shithead.

HE. Nutcase!

SHE. I want my baby, where's my baby?

HE. I don't know.

SHE. What do you mean, you don't know?

HE. He ran away. Through the window.

SHE. Are you nuts? But that doesn't seem likely, that an infant would run away out the window.

HE. He broke the window and jumped out. Ran away. The infant.

SHE. Are you of sound mind? And I'm supposed to believe that?

HE. Listen, I don't know, I don't want to think about it . . . I'm still young, I have my whole life ahead of me . . .

SHE. Murderer! Thief! Police!

HE. Calm down, that's just the postpartum shock. Let's both calm down. Let's lie down.

SHE. I want my baby . . .

HE. That was one modern newborn, fast. Kids today grow independent so fast.

SHE. How can you make fun at a time like this? How can you?

HE. Where are you going? Step back from the window. You'll catch cold.

SHE. My little darling . . . My little darling fell . . .

HE. Wait . . . Look.

SHE. What's that?

HE. An infant. An infant on the grass.

SHE. My little darling.

HE. Our little darling.

SHE. He's alive.

HE. Like I said. That's one modern infant.

SHE. He's looking at us.

HE. He's smiling.

SHE. It's a girl!

HE. No, no, it's a boy.

SHE. He has my eyes.

HE. What's he doing . . .

SHE. He's running away . . .

HE. Toward the park!

SHE. After him. Hurry. There are cats out there, and lizards, and shards of glass . . . My little precious, wait for your mother. God . . . If only he hasn't caught cold . . .

HE. Maggie, this is crazy . . . It's almost dawn . . .

SHE. I want to find my baby. My baby needs me. If you don't like it out there, you can always come back to Mommy, if you don't like out there. You can come back if . . . Dear! Dear, where are you!

HE. Stop it, please stop . . .

SHE. Give me my baby! I want my baby back this instant!

HE. You're exhausted, you should rest. Maybe he just doesn't want us to find him?

SHE. Why wouldn't he?

HE. Well . . . Maybe he wants to live his own life?

SHE. Such a small little baby? You're crazy. Honey, where are you . . . What are you breastfeeding from? What is it, a dog?

HE. I'm sorry . . . Maybe he's afraid of us?

SHE. Don't be afraid, cutie . . . What'll I tell my folks? God . . .

HE. Ultimately it's not our fault . . . If he doesn't want to, he doesn't want to . . .

SHE. You have to marry me.

HE. I have to what?

SHE. A wedding. Propose to me. On your knee, pig.

HE. But Maggie. Somebody could see us.

SHE. You have to say that you love me.

HE. But come on, we're young, modern people . . . We're not going to get hitched just because . . . Anyway, he ran away . . .

SHE. So you don't really love me? You just wanted to screw me?

HE. It's not like that. Anyway, you said yourself . . .

SHE. Quiet . . .

HE. What?

SHE. I heard something. There. Behind me. Go quietly. Steal up from the other side.

HE. Honey, I'm home! Honey . . . It's really pouring . . . Where's my wifey hiding? Maggie! I picked up some groceries, I'm putting them in the fridge.

SHE. You're home late today. Warm up some soup, it's in the fridge.

HE. These are for you.

SHE. You didn't have to do that, but OK, I'll put them in a vase. What are you looking at?

HE. But you know.

SHE. Hang up your coat here, and try not to get water on the sofa. You're all wet.

HE. I thought you'd be happy. Twenty years.

SHE. A lot of years.

HE. Yup, a lot of years.

SHE. Twenty years.

HE. Let's fix a little supper, what do you say? No, I'll do it. You want toast? I took the toaster in for repairs, now it works great. Turn on some music, or else candles . . . Maggie, please.

SHE. What's all this for?

HE. You want cheese or cold cuts with your toast? Here, let me open the wine. What's wrong? It's our anniversary. I asked the people at the train station. No one had seen a fugitive baby. They told me to ask at the airport. I'll go there tomorrow. You still have those little photos? I ran out of the Xeroxes . . . You don't have anything new?

SHE. I saw tracks in the snow. Yesterday, I was passing by the zoo. It might have been our little baby, or else it was some dog.

HE. You follow up on your leads, I'll follow up on mine. I saw these sort of claw marks on the wall.

SHE. Listen, do you actually believe that . . .

HE. What are you saying?

SHE. Nothing, never mind. Good night.

HE. No, come on, you started to say something. Please, finish.

SHE. We'll talk about it some other time.

HE. Say it.

SHE. I was just asking whether you actually believe that . . . Do you really have faith that our little one . . . But it's been four years . . . which is not to say . . . We've looked everywhere . . . Not a trace . . .

HE. If I didn't believe it, I would never have . . . Let's maybe have some supper, huh?

SHE. I'm not hungry.

HE. I'll open the wine.

SHE. Charles, it doesn't make sense.

HE. He's bound to turn up sooner or later, you'll see. I'm sure he'll enjoy all those toys we bought him. Our little Marty will be very happy.

SHE. Now it's been 20 years.

HE. Hold on, the toast is burning. What did you say?

SHE. I don't love you any more. I never loved you.

HE. He's a healthy baby. Strong. Did you see how he ran off? I'm sure he worked things out and will just pop up at the right moment, with his own children, and he'll say, Hi, Mom and Dad. That will be a very happy day.

SHE. I want to move out.

HE. You remember our wedding? It was a lovely wedding.

SHE. It all happened too fast. A funny, grotesque story.

HE. Maggie, I . . .

SHE. What?

HE. I'd like to thank you . . .

SHE. What for?

HE. That night . . . I know it was pretty messed up, but I . . . I was never so happy in my life. What about you?

SHE. A little, maybe . . .

HE. Yeah . . . Well, then, bring your glass over here, let's pour the wine. And turn on some music, that music of yours. I love it.

EPILOG

HE. Oh my God, hi!

SHE. Jesus Christ!

HE. I'm sorry, I startled you. Maggie, Maggie, it's been a long time . . .

SHE. Hi . . . I'm sorry, but . . .

HE. Come on, Maggie, you don't remember me? It's me, Charles.

SHE. Charles, right, I'm sorry. Charles.

HE. No, please, I'm the one who's sorry, I didn't mean to ambush you downtown. I startled you.

SHE. No, come on, I'm the one who's sorry, I should remember . . .

HE. Maggie, Maggie, it's been a long time . . .

SHE. It has . . . How many years has it been . . .

HE. A lot.

SHE. A lot.

HE. God, how many years has it been, a lot.

SHE. Listen, I have to . . .

HE. Do you have a minute? Maybe we could get a drink?

SHE. I'm really sorry, but to be honest . . .

HE. I know this great place just around the corner. Maybe we could get some coffee?

SHE. Listen, Charles, I'd really like to, but . . .

HE. It's a really great place, not one of those loud cafes where you can't even have a decent conversation.

SHE. Fine, but just for a while, because I really . . .

HE. No, it's fine, forget it. I understand. We don't have to talk.

SHE. No, Charles, let's go to that cafe. I'm in a bit of a hurry, but I'd be glad to get a cup of coffee.

HE. But I know you hate me.

SHE. Hey, where'd you get that? Charles, do you feel OK?

HE. Me? I'm sorry, I'm alright, everything's fine. You really have a little time?

SHE. Sure. Let's go.

HE. No, wait. Do you really want to talk to me? I don't want to force you.

SHE. Jesus, man, are we going to that cafe or not, because I really am in a hurry.

HE. I'm sorry, yeah . . . I'm acting like an idiot. Let's go.

SHE. Let's.

HE. It's right over here. Oh, and here we are. Even closer than I thought. Shall we sit?

SHE. I don't know, maybe over here?

HE. You want coffee, tea, maybe something stronger, some wine?

SHE. No, thanks, no, I'll have some coffee.

HE. So . . . What's new with you?

SHE. I'm good. How about you?

HE. Good, good.

SHE. That's good.

HE. Listen, can we be honest?

SHE. I thought we were being honest.

HE. Blah, blah, blah.

SHE. Forgive me, I'm just having a hard time talking to you.

HE. Yeah, it's not so easy for me talking to you, either.

SHE. But it's been a long time.

HE. Yeah, a long time.

SHE. Your memory gets rusty, a person stops being real, so to speak . . .

HE. You hit the nail on the head.

SHE. You know, I'm going to get going . . .

HE. Maggie, I . . . I wanted to apologize.

SHE. Why did you want to apologize?

HE. You know very well, don't say you don't.

SHE. Not really.

HE. For everything. It was my fault.

SHE. Oh, Charles, stop, that was a long time ago.

HE. No, no. We have to talk about this. It's been grating at me all these years, the worst nightmare, please, do me this favor . . .

SHE. Sure. God, I didn't know you were taking it so hard, we were such brats.

HE. It was so horrible . . . I acted like the ultimate sack of shit . . .

SHE. Don't be so hard on yourself. I was the one who wasn't right in the head . . . I wanted everything to be so unbelievably perfect and, like an ass, you went along with it. You remember how artificial we were? You would come to my place, and we would play our roles . . .

HE. I wanted so badly for it to turn out beautiful, so that we'd remember it without feeling embarrassed. I'm so sorry.

SHE. But I remember it very fondly.

HE. Really?

SHE. Sure. Those were strange and beautiful times.

HE. And I was so afraid that you would hate me forever . . . God, I had nightmares after that night, I dreamt that you grew this belly, and that right after that you gave birth to a kid who ran away, and then we were married and . . .

SHE. Wow, you're pretty fucked up, you know?

HE. For real. I had the same dream whenever it was pouring out. Don't laugh. I didn't think it was funny. But that was our first time . . .

SHE. You know, all first times are pretty much the same. Awkward. Messy. I learned that. You can't draw any big conclusions from the first time. It's the times after that that might mean something . . . But, anyway, but with us, it didn't come to anything . . .

HE. I wouldn't put it that way.

SHE. We just kept rehearsing and rehearsing . . .

HE. I was afraid you'd get pregnant. Really.

SHE. Pregnant? How could I get pregnant? From you rubbing my hand?

HE. You've become quite the wit, I must say. For me, each and every time meant something, that I started something with you, and that you started something with me . . . Maybe it meant everything. I met a lot of girls after that, but I could never forget . . . that evening . . . The first time, for both of us . . .

SHE. Charles, when I was going out with you, I was no longer, well, you know . . .

HE. What do you mean you . . .

SHE. It happened earlier.

HE. With who?

SHE. Ollie. You know, that stupid, drunken evening . . . I don't remember it fondly. To tell the truth, it was an awful first time. That's why I sort of wanted to have a first time again. With you. Forgive me, it was dumb, but don't be upset. How old were we then, 15, 16?

HE. Ollie?

SHE. Yes. Why are you looking at me like that?

HE. Why are you lying?

SHE. I'm lying?

HE. But when you were with me you lost your . . . you know.

SHE. Charles, I think I know who it was with.

HE. Why are you doing this to me? Why?

SHE. You haven't changed at all. You're having your fantasies again . . . Dude, don't you think you should hightail it to a shrink? Seriously . . .

HE. Ollie?

SHE. Yes. I'm sorry.

HE. But you hated him . . .

SHE. I know, but then he said he was sorry. He couldn't forgive himself, he had nightmares, he lost weight. You have no idea how bad he looked. And I really always loved him. Maybe you could come by to see us. We have a lovely apartment just down the . . .

HE. We? Who's we?

SHE. You don't know? Ollie and I got married.

HE. Ollie? Ollie, again. Wherever you go, it's Ollie. Who is this Ollie? I don't know any Ollie.

SHE. Do you feel OK?

HE. Listen, all is not lost. I'm sorry, too. I'm sorry for everything. I forgive you for this Ollie dude, I forgive you for everything, all the hypocrisy and lying. Let's try again. You know what, I have an idea. Come to my place at night, I don't care when, I live alone. Just ring the bell. Wouldn't that be magnificent? This scene. I know, I know that it might not work out but we'll give it a try, OK? You'll come to see me many times, until our second night is perfect. You're right, it's not the first time that matters most, but the times that come after. It doesn't matter how the man starts, it matters how he finishes, as Tolstoy said, or somebody . . .

SHE. Dude, I guess you really are somehow messed up in the head. Charles. Calm down. You want to drink some water?

HE. I had nightmares. I dreamt you were pregnant, and that the baby ran out through the window, and then you make me marry you and our marriage is terrible, and finally . . .

SHE. Let go of me, what's your deal? . . . I'm sorry.

HE. Don't worry about it. I needed that. I know, my stock has totally dropped in your eyes. You hate me, right?

SHE. No, it's not like that . . .

HE. But before we part ways forever, I want to tell you one thing. That night, you remember, a month after the last unsuccessful try, I came to you, even though it wasn't night-time, it wasn't raining, and I didn't have any flowers. I was drunk, pissed, prepared to do whatever it took to have you. You were surprised to see me, you pretended not to know me, but I knew your apartment perfectly. You'd changed your hair a little, I knew you were going out with that guy again . . . I threw myself on you . . . That was awful . . . After a minute your submitted. You wanted it too, I felt it. Don't interrupt me. It was so animal, so . . . amazing . . . I wanted my revenge. I wanted to make you revile me . . . but you were so beautiful . . . Our first time . . . When it was all over, you snuggled up to me and whispered sweet nothings in my ear, I couldn't take it . . . I slammed the door behind me as I left, I had tears in my eyes . . . I was determined never to see you again . . . I locked myself in . . . These nightmares started, that terrible infant jumping out the window . . . I would wake up crying . . . You know why? Please, don't interrupt me, hear me out. Because after that night, I knew that you were the woman for me but that I wasn't right for you and would never be able to look you in the eye. That night I saw you as you really are, defenseless, weak, needing to be looked after, needing what I couldn't give you. That's why I wanted to thank you. I wanted to thank you for that night. I'll always love you as I remember you from that night. So that's it, goodbye.

SHE. Charles . . .

HE. Yeah?

SHE. Listen, you know that there wasn't any night?

HE. Huh?

SHE. You're messing with me, right? This is one of your nightmares, right?

HE. What are you talking about?

SHE. After the last time we met, we moved. You couldn't have come to my place drunk.

HE. I did come over drunk, and it happened . . . You changed your hair, remember? . . .

SHE. I never changed my hair.

HE. But what do you mean, you've always lived in that same neighborhood, you know, that same building, one after another . . .

SHE. Charles, I'm telling you, I moved. Some girl rented that apartment, does some girl ring a bell, kind of fat, with bangs? . . . The one who's now raising a little boy on her own.

HE. Kind of fat, with bangs, huh?

SHE. I don't know, I could be wrong . . .

HE. Fat, with a kid, huh?

SHE. This is good coffee . . .

HE. This town's too big, you can't get your bearings, everywhere it's the same building, one after another . . .

SHE. Right. So, I'm going to get going. I'm already late . . .

HE. Right, sure. Christ, there was something I was supposed to take care of, too.

SHE. Well, then, you'll call, right?

HE. Sure, I'll call.

SHE. Bye.

HE. Bye. It was nice seeing you.

SHE. You too.

HE. Bye.

SHE. Bye.

LET'S TALK ABOUT LIFE AND DEATH

KRZYSZTOF BIZIO

CHARACTERS

RED	Wife and mother, about 40
BLUE	Husband and father, about 50
WHITE	Son, about 20

LET'S TALK ABOUT LIFE AND DEATH

TRANSLATED BY MIRA ROSENTHAL

The action takes place in a single room. There is a telephone in the center of the space. The actors remain on the stage for the whole performance.

BLUE (*talking on the phone*). Hello. Good morning, sir. I'm calling from personal accounts with the Internal Revenue Service, the collections department . . . (*Laughs*) Oh man, you actually fell for it. Yeah, yeah, yeah. I've been calling and calling, but the answering machine keeps picking up. You know, it'll all be beyond us someday, you'll see.

Yeah, I'm on it. I greased some palms when I had to, and now it's just a matter of waiting. It's a done deal. Frankly speaking, I think it was a great idea. I have to do something with the money, and it could eventually pay off. The most important thing is our health.

Exactly, I've already thought through it all: boat, campfire, barbeque . . . and so on. You know how it goes: romantic evenings, sweet vodka, marinated fish, a good pipe.

Of course you're invited, that's why I'm doing it. I've been wanting to see old friends, and a cabin on a lake is the perfect excuse. We're getting old, man, and it's about time we admit it.

Listen, while we're shooting the shit, you might be interested to know, some jackass scratched up my car with a nail. Can you imagine?

That's what I'm telling you: with a nail. I was in the store, I came back, and there was a scratch along the right side.

I felt like someone had slashed my hand with a knife. I stood there and didn't know what to do. If I'd caught the jackass, I would've skinned him alive with a potato peeler. What an age we're living in, man, but I can't tie my car to a barbed wire fence.

I could've done something with it in my shop, but I'm no auto detailer. I know of a few, but you mentioned you have a good one.

Sure, what's the number? Eight seven at the end? Great, got it.

Thanks, man, and feel free to drop by. Take care. See you later.

RED (*talking on the phone*). Is that you, Ala? Ala, is that you?

Not at all, I'm not talking quietly, and I'm not sick. Why are you always so judgmental of me? I was calling to see if anything had changed.

I'm definitely coming. I'm already set, and I even bought a new blouse. It's a lovely deep red, you'll see.

Listen, I'm taking this very seriously. My best friend is introducing me to her fiancé. I have to come across well so that he'll know you don't associate with just anyone.

You don't even know how happy this makes me. I haven't said anything, but I've been really worried about your situation.

Oh, sweetie, of course I care about you. We've known each other practically our whole lives, and you know I care about you. But I just couldn't see how depressed you were. It's utterly obscene that a girl like you should be alone. I knew you'd find someone. It was simply a matter of time, and I'm so happy it finally worked out.

Your situation is straightforward. The divorce is final. You've already divided everything up with that stupid fool. I know you're an honorable person, but it's too bad you didn't clean him out entirely. I would've done it differently, but never mind.

I'm so curious. He must be a wonderful man, seeing as you fell in love with him. There's nothing to debate. Life's so short, and for us even shorter than for them.

Sweetie, I'm sure, I know where it is. Listen to you, first you invite me to the best restaurant in town, and then you ask me if I know where it is.

I know you're in a hurry, sweetie, but you have to promise me that you'll tell me every single detail. I'm holding you to your word.

Love you lots, and I can't wait. Bye.

A conversation between Blue and White.

BLUE. Are you there?

WHITE. Yeah, I'm here.

BLUE. Is Mom there?

WHITE. She's not here.

BLUE. Is everything fine?

WHITE. Everything's fine.

BLUE. Anything new?

WHITE. No, everything's fine.

BLUE. I should run. I have stuff to do in town.

WHITE. Sure.

BLUE. Bye.

WHITE. Bye.

WHITE (*talking on the phone*). Hey, where are you?

Can you talk, or did I wake you up again?

Listen, dude, I'm not upset, just really pissed off. Who the hell's brain is in your head? Who the hell was I talking to yesterday? Did the girl ditch the convent? Dude, I'm not a biology teacher.

Listen, dude, why are you bullshitting me? First you say what a cool chick she is, and now you're telling me no one knows. I didn't ask you for help to have you pull this stunt on me. I've become a fucking perv because of you. But I'm telling you right now I'm never gonna help you with any of your shit ever again.

Dude, I'm not risking my head and dialing up some gangster if I don't get anything out of it. I'm doing you a favor, and you're jerking me around. If I ask my friend to arrange a date for me with a gorgeous chick, I have the right to demand that the chick be gorgeous and that she understand what's going on.

I don't know who you're gonna get it from, but your account's overdrawn with me. The well has dried up, and you're gonna have to bust your balls if the sun's gonna shine on you again. Read the old books, dude. You'll learn a lot from them. Force yourself to think what's the right thing to do.

You can't limit your life to watching porno, smoking joints, and listening to music.

You've really blown it with me, and it's your move now. Bye.

A conversation between Red and White.

RED. Are you there?

WHITE. Yeah, I'm here.

RED. Is Dad there?

WHITE. He's not here.

RED. Is everything fine?

WHITE. Everything's fine.

RED. Anything new?

WHITE. No, everything's fine.

RED. I should run. I have stuff to do in town.

WHITE. Sure.

RED. Bye.

WHITE. Bye.

RED (*talking on the phone*). Is that you, Ala? Ala, is that you?

God, he's wonderful. If he wasn't already taken, I'd be interested in him myself.

I'm only joking. You know quite well that I love my husband very much.

You've always had such excellent taste. And now there's finally a real man in your life.

Your husband before Victor was such a child.

Of course the food was great. He must have spent a fortune on it. I even liked the prawns, and you know I don't usually like seafood.

It's so great that you can start all over again. Sometimes I wish I could, too. Break all these ties and habits and just float. I've been dreaming about it since I was a girl, and now you're doing it.

When's the wedding? You should insist on it. Don't put it off. I've told you many times that life is short, and for us women, that much shorter.

I already know what I want to get you for a wedding present. It's beautiful, really beautiful, you're going to love it.

I know exactly what you mean, everything's just like a fairytale. You really must go have lunch with his family.

Don't say that. How do you know they'll be against it? I'm sure they'll be happy, and if not, remember that it's your life.

God, I'm so happy for you. Love you. Bye.

WHITE (*talking on the phone*). Yeah, it's me.

You must have gone crazy, girl, to be calling here.

I'm the one who calls you, you don't call me. That's the arrangement, understand?

Do you want me to fry? Just think what would happen if the phone's bugged after all.

I'm not imagining it, just thinking through all the various scenarios. That's what makes me different from the other dipshits. I know how to anticipate things.

Of course I love you, Kasia.[1] But you remember what we agreed on: I call you, never the other way around.

And you know what I'm dealing with. I'm hanging out with the worst scum in the city, and I'm concerned for your safety. Don't tell me I'm imagining things. I take what I do very

---

1 Kasia and Kaśka are both diminutive forms of Katarzyna.

seriously. I'm starting with weed, but later I want to broaden my operations. All the fucking dealers in this country are morons. But how many of them do you think actually have high-school diplomas? I have a high-school diploma, and I've started college. Intellectually, I'm light years ahead of them. The point is to see it through.

Of course I won't forget about you, baby doll. We'll be together till death do us part, you know that's how I am.

Yes, I love you very much. If I told you the dreams I've had about you lately, you wouldn't have any doubts.

Love you, love you.

BLUE (*talking on the phone*). Yes, yes, I know who it is.

Sure, but I can't stand it when someone tries to rip me off. If I order a few used parts for my shop, I want a few used parts, not a load of scrap metal.

Don't give me that nonsense. I'm not signing your goddamn invoice. The job should be finished, the whole place cleaned up, and everyone smiling.

I don't give a damn. It's your problem, and don't threaten me with the police. You send me illegal parts and shady receipts, and then you expect to charge me a pretty penny.

Come off it, man. I've been in this business too long to believe such bullshit. I'm paying you hard cash for the job. I know you and like you, but I can't just shut my eyes to this. You'll sell it to me, and I won't be able to unload it on anyone else. You'll get rid of the mess, but I'll have an even greater problem on my hands.

I'm saying it calmly for the last time, and you better listen to me. My car shop is a professional economic entity. If I order parts from someone and ask his employees for help, I want the parts to be good and the service done professionally. I turned to you because I know you've been having trouble and that you'd be able to help me. We have a longstanding working agreement. And what do you do? You send me some tipsy Ukrainians with junk parts.

I know what I'm talking about. Don't interrupt me.

You're lucky I'm soft. Someone else in my position wouldn't even discuss it with you, but I'm giving you a chance. I'm asking you to please straighten this matter out today. As for the invoice, for now you can stuff it . . . into your own pocket.

I'll wait to hear from you. Good-bye.

A conversation between Red and Blue.

RED. Are you there?

BLUE. Yeah, I'm here.

RED. Is Paweł there?

BLUE. Paweł's not here.

RED. Is everything fine?

BLUE. Everything's fine.

RED. Anything new?

BLUE. No, everything's fine.

RED. I should run. I have stuff to do in town.

BLUE. Sure.

RED. Bye.

BLUE. Bye.

RED (*talking on the phone*). God, Victor, don't call here.

But you know how I feel about you from yesterday, and my son and husband are here.

Yeah, I mentioned divorce, but I can't tell them about it so suddenly. Give me a little time.

I think it was the most wonderful night of my entire life, really. I still can't put my thoughts together.

But I told you, Victor. Life's so short, especially for women.

Have you seen Ala yet? So, did you talk to her?

You're right not to have said anything to her yet. We need to think about what to do. After all, she's my best friend. I wouldn't want her to think that she . . .

No, no. Of course I love you, Victor, of course. I'm only trying to figure out how to solve this delicate situation.

Ultimately, though, no one here is a child any more.

Oh, Victor, yes, the roses are next to my bed. They're exactly the right kind, just like I told you. You're so wonderful. You know what a woman needs. I've been dreaming of you for years.

Clearly that's until I met you, but I was speaking metaphorically. You're my ideal man.

Definitely, definitely tonight.

I might be a little late, but I'll be there for sure.

Bye, darling, bye.

WHITE (*talking on the phone*). Slow down, I want to get everything.

I'm a professional, I don't take any goddamn notes. I use a computer, not my head, for these things.

Shit, dude, what did you do with the goods? This is exactly your problem. You've got to pay attention.

Only so I don't get scammed again. This is crucial. I give you the goods, and you give me the cash. It's really fucking simple.

You don't have to ask about quality. You know I don't deal in shit. I take care of my brain.

True, maybe I should listen to the needs of the market and extend the offer.

You always go off on these philosophical tangents. That's why I like you. You know, I'm telling you: we live in a fucked up age. My grandpa made a fortune selling tomatoes, my father sells cars, and now I'm entering a whole new line of operations.

Soon everything's gonna be one global fucking village. The only people left will be tycoons, and everyone else can go sweep the streets. Today, more than ever, individuality counts. You have to be someone, you know? You have to have your own big plan and deliver on it.

Shit, dude, in five years I'll be king of this city. I'll have the goods, the girls, and all the fucking icing on the cake. Clearly it's my calling.

Stick with me, and you'll get there eventually. See ya.

RED (*talking on the phone*). Hi, Ala. Yeah, it's me.

God, Ala, don't scream so loud. I'm not a slut.

Ala, listen, let me tell you what happened. It's not my fault.

Don't talk to me like that. I'm not a whore. What are you saying? It's all because of Victor, and you know how I start goofing around when I drink.

Please, don't cry. Don't cry. I'll tell you everything.

Ala, listen to me. Ala?

He called and said he wanted to talk to me about you. I thought it was so sweet. I didn't know how things would unfold. He invited me over, we had a glass of wine, then another and another, and it happened. It's no big deal.

That's not true. I didn't sleep with every one of your fiancés. Even if I knew some of them a bit better, that doesn't mean I did anything bad.

But I can't get divorced. You know how much I love my husband and how good we are together. We have a house, a wonderful son and everything.

Calm down. This one mistake doesn't change anything.

Absolutely not, you can't say Victor's a lech. When he found himself alone with me, you know, he just gave in, that's all. He's a wonderful man, and you should appreciate that.

Ala, be serious. You're no virgin yourself.

I'm glad you're starting to understand. Emotions aren't essential here.

I know you have to go, but we still need to talk. It should be a long conversation and not over the phone.

Oh God, Ala, don't cry. You're my only friend. What are all the guys in the world worth compared to a true friend?

Don't talk about me like that. Why are you insulting me? I am not a nymphomaniac. Please, don't use such words. Victor said he loves you very much.

But I know how much he means to you. You can't erase your whole future because of one stupid night.

You're my best friend, absolutely. You just need to calm down. Everything will fall into place. I'll come over, and we'll talk about it calmly.

BLUE (*talking on the phone*). Kiss, kiss, kiss, my love, wherever you desire.

Of course your tomcat didn't forget about his little kitten. But, pet, you know how much the tomcat has on his mind. Everyone wants a piece of him. People are horrible, honey, they want to rip me off, steal from me, and land me in prison. I can only relax with you.

I was just calling to talk to you about it, honey.

Do you remember, pet, how I told you about the cabin on the lake?

Exactly, the cabin I bought for my little kitten. It's the cabin of your dreams, honey: with a fireplace and a garden.

Yeah, it cost a bit, but luxury always costs. You said it needed to have a porch and be on a lake. I looked and looked, and there it was with a porch and on a lake. Nothing but the best for us, that's the way I am.

There's a really nice view. Sunrises and sunsets, a forest, fresh air, makes you feel like living. Everything's set up the way you wanted it, kitten: fridge, grill, soft bed. We'll take some chicken and beer and go.

I'm not sure who else will be there. I was thinking of inviting one of my friends. The only thing is he's kind of shy. You know, we've got to loosen the guy up. He and his wife have some issues. They reconcile, then break up again. I was thinking I'd help the guy out. A man has to forget his troubles, you know.

Oh, yeah, have I got presents for you. A whole sack of presents, plus a little something extra on the side. You know how much I love giving you presents. We could even go this coming Saturday and Sunday.

My cow of a wife is going somewhere, too.

But you know I don't speak to her. The matter of the divorce is hanging by a thread. Anything is possible, kitten, you know that.

Don't you have someone for my friend? You don't have to explain his situation to her, since it's so bad.

He's definitely a decent guy, a businessman of course. He works in insurance.

I'm not sure what his type is. I'm counting on your good taste. OK, love you, see you soon.

A conversation between Red and White.

WHITE. Hi Mom. A friend of yours called.

RED. What did she want?

WHITE. I don't know. She asked if you were here. She didn't say who she was, and I didn't recognize her voice. She seemed kind of upset.

RED. Upset?

WHITE. Yeah, she was screaming into the phone.

RED. I wasn't home? Oh, that's right, you sit in front of the phone all day long. Can't you do anything else besides watch TV and hog the phone?

WHITE. Mom.

RED. All day long you stare at the TV. What are you even watching? You should be concentrating on your studies. I've already told you how much I care that you graduate. I never finished, but that's only because you were born. Otherwise who knows how my life would have turned out.

WHITE. Give me a break. Today things are different.

RED. Today may be different, but people are the same. I know something about it.

WHITE. Today is a time of radical change. Nothing will ever be the same, the world has changed completely.

RED. You philosophize too much.

WHITE. You'll see that I'm right.

RED. Men are always right. It's only women who cry at night.

WHITE. Mom.

RED. And women will go on crying, all because of you, you'll see.

RED (*talking on the phone*). Hi, Kasia.

I don't really have a reason for calling, just that it's been so long since we've seen each other. How are you?

What did you say? Ala called you? She's a complete idiot. And what did she tell you?

Yeah and so, I went to bed with her new man, and what of it? You know how she is: she always exaggerates things. She doesn't know what she wants out of life. She called and invited me to lunch. And later . . . well, the rest is a waste of breath.

Of course I went. Victor, her new man, seemed like a decent guy. You know how it is. I called him, he called me, and that's that.

Oh God, Kasia, is it really important who called first? Even if it was me, who cares?

I had his number because he gave me his card.

You know, dear, what's the worst thing about all this? My period's late. Just think: what would happen if I were pregnant? It would be such a catastrophe, it's awful to even think about it.

Clearly, with Victor. I haven't done it with my husband in so long that I forget when the last time was.

All these little things add up. I feel like I'm getting older and older, and at any moment I'm going to fall apart completely. I'm starting to feel sick. It's just like with a car, you drive and drive, and then suddenly that's it. God, thinking about it, I'm a wreck of a human being, a dried-up old lady. It's all so horrible and unfair. I prefer not to think about it, but it doesn't change anything. I wonder how other people manage, because certainly I can't.

It's all really wearing me out. I was thinking that maybe I would take a trip somewhere to get some perspective on things. I was thinking Egypt. It's such a beautiful country, and it's warm. I don't like the cold.

I've been alone my whole life. I've endured all kinds of situations and conflicts, so many stupid looks, but suddenly I've had enough.

Don't tell me I'm in a bad mood. I'm telling you the truth, but whatever. I'm still alone, and that's that. Take care, Kasia. We really must find a time to get together.

Bye.

WHITE (*talking on the phone*). Hi, you called? There was a message on the machine.

Of course I'm interested. I'm always interested in everything concerning you.

Yeah, of course I love you and want to be with you. How many times do I have to tell you?

I'm standing up. Does it really matter if I'm standing or sitting down? Listen, babe, just tell me what happened, because I'm kind of in a hurry.

A father, how a father? You're gonna have a kid?

That's great, and whose kid is it?

Mine, mine, are you totally sure?

Sorry, I'm not trying to act dumb, it's just that it hasn't sunk in yet. It's not every day I find out I'm gonna be a father.

Yes, yes, I'm happy. But are you sure? Is your period late? Did you take a test?

I'm not acting dumb, I'm just trying to establish the facts. I'm really happy. But you know how I have a scientific mind and always want to get the facts.

But first: Are you sure you're pregnant? And second: Are you sure I'm the father?

Oh God, I don't think you're a whore. What the hell are you talking about? I've already told you that I love you, but I need to make sure. Do you remember what happened with Maras? After two years, it turned out he wasn't the father.

Have you told anyone yet?

Good, good. Don't tell anyone.

I know you'll have to say something eventually, but don't tell anyone yet.

Are you at home right now?

Don't leave the house and don't tell anyone, understand me? I'll be there in a minute. I'm getting dressed and I'm coming over. Hear me?

Yes, yes, I love you too.

BLUE (*talking on the phone*). Hi, hi, not so loud. My head's splitting.

We really went over the top on Saturday. I've never seen that side of you before. I didn't think you were up to scoring with three girls in one night.

I know, next to you I'm a weakling, but age takes its toll.

We can do it again for sure, only let's wait awhile. We have to recover our strength.

I was cleaning the cabin all night last night. Loads of bottles, condoms, and cigarette butts.

Yeah, yeah, the ladies were great, but it's not for me any more. I realized it on Saturday, when I was banging my girl. I'm an old donkey. I can't go that long any more.

It's different for you. If it makes you happy, there's no need to talk about it, just do it.

It's all really wearing me out. I was thinking that maybe I would take a trip somewhere to get some perspective on things. I was thinking Egypt. It's such a beautiful country, and it's warm. I don't like the cold.

I've been alone my whole life. I've endured all kinds of situations and conflicts, so many stupid looks, but suddenly I've had enough.

Don't tell me I'm in a bad mood. I'm telling you the truth, but whatever. I'm still alone, and that's that.

My car's fixed thanks to that detailer. He's a real pro. He only charged me half price because of some promotional deal he had going. Not bad, huh?

OK, till next time. Bye.

WHITE (*talking on the phone*). Listen, sweetheart, everything's set.

It's all really safe, totally sterile.

But, babe, we already talked about this. Let's not go over it all again.

Listen, babe, this is necessary. You know an abortion is the only way out of this situation. Pretend like it's nothing. You're just going for a doctor's visit.

I know you're worried. I'm worried too. We've both learned our lesson, and we should be more careful.

But you know I love you, I love you a lot. It's just that we should wait a while to have a kid.

A while, that means, I don't know . . . a few years, till things are more settled. First I need to get on my feet.

I need to be financially stable, that's the most important thing. I'm gonna be someone, and you'll be right by my side.

Do you want us to live paycheck to paycheck? Because I don't. I don't intend to laze around in some dingy apartment with a kid. I know all about such stories. Bachelor pads for a long time, a second kid, that's the pattern. I'll have to give up school and work in some miserable place, for miserable pay. You'll get on my nerves, and I'll get on your nerves. No one will be happy. That's all fine in the end, but we won't even be able to look at each other, just like my parents.

You know?

I just need a little time. Then we can have a child, a dog, a big house, a lawn in the front yard, and a few cars. I'll buy a sweet Mercedes for you.

Everything will be just like I promised, I swear. I know exactly how I want my life to look.

Don't cry, because I'm not gonna hear it. I'll wait in the car, like we planned, and give you a ride, OK?

See you in a minute.

A conversation between Red and Blue.

RED. What happened to you? You don't look so good.

BLUE. You don't look so good, either.

RED. Oh, right, I'm not attractive to you. Once again there's something wrong, maybe that I'm too old for your tastes. But you're not getting any younger either. Just look at yourself.

BLUE. Calm down. What on earth are you talking about? I really worry about you.

RED. I'm so pleased to hear it. You worry about me, like I believe that.

How's business, anyway?

BLUE. Fine. Everything's fine.

And how about you? Do you want to go back to work?

RED. I've been thinking about it. I have to figure it out, though. One wrong step, and that's it.

I just met with a friend from school. She was trying to talk me into running a travel agency with her. It could be good. I've always liked traveling, but the business end is whole different thing. It's important to approach with caution.

BLUE. And?

RED. I know how to run a boutique, but not a travel agency.

BLUE. You don't have to make any rash decisions.

RED. But I don't want to end up getting an earful from you again.

You know, it's probably the worst thing in the world to have someone tell you that you're dependent on him and can be kicked out at any moment.

BLUE. Don't start on that again. I got carried away, and I apologized.

RED. I know, I know. It happens sometimes.

RED (*talking on the phone*). God, Ania, why weren't you answering the phone? I've been calling and calling. You must have been out, because I kept getting your answering machine.

Oh my God, Ania, you'll never guess what happened! I can't even say it, I can't even let myself think about it. Ania, you there? Listen to me, Ania, I have cancer, understand, I have cancer!

In the right and left breasts, three centimeters from the nipples.

How do I know? How do I know? I went to the doctor and had some tests done. I know because of the results. They took some test samples. Do you know how much that hurts?

Yes, it's definitive. Today I had the follow-up tests. They did a second biopsy, and everything was confirmed. I haven't had the third one yet.

How would you feel? I'll die, or best-case scenario I won't have any breasts. None, get it, I won't have breasts! I can't even imagine it.

You don't know what you're talking about, some kind of prosthesis. Besides, it's not worth it, if I even survive.

There are two big lumps inside me. I'm rotting from within, get it, I'm dying!

Yes, I'm going in for an operation, but you know how worthwhile these operations are. Until they cut you open, they don't know anything. They'll cut off my breasts, throw them in some container, and only then will they know more. Maybe it will have metastasized, and that'll be it.

You know, when I found out about it, I thought I was going crazy. I didn't have anyone to tell. I felt so alone all over again. It must be my fault, that I made mistakes.

You don't have to comfort me. If I don't have someone to lean on, then it means I haven't done very well for myself.

I'll call you when I go to the hospital. I don't have anyone to count on.

Yes, I know I can count on you.

I know, I know, I'll remember. Bye.

WHITE (*talking on the phone*). Fuck, man, you're not going to believe what happened to me: Kaśka's knocked up.

You know how much I've had to deal with? You're not going to believe it, but she wanted to have the kid. What a stupid skag, suddenly wants to have a bun in the oven.

Yeah, in the end I managed to, but I really had to rag on her. Man, I sold her a load of bullshit.

I promised to marry her, buy her a car, go on vacation, all sorts of far-out things.

Of course I had to pay for it. It was goddamn lucky that I finally managed to drag her to the doctor. I don't know what I would've done if she had refused. I'd have been saddled with child support for the next 18 years, or I would've had to marry her. I don't know what would be worse.

Just imagine, everything's set and we're agreed, and I go over to her place. I ring the bell, the door opens, and there in the doorway stands her mother. My heart immediately starts racing, because I can see what's in store for me.

Her mother orders me to sit and starts in on me. We talked for two hours. Man, I thought it was all over. The old lady bursts out crying and says that I'm a murderer, that I took advantage of her daughter, and that I'm irresponsible. I thought: I'm gonna lose it, stand up and slap her. But I kept thinking: be calm, I barged into this shit, and now I've got to get myself out. Slowly, little by little I convinced the old skag. I told her some line about how I loved her daughter very much and that everything was going to be fine. Dude, I sold her such a line, even I can't believe she fell for it. But finally I convinced her.

I didn't wait for a second. I grabbed Kaśka's hand and ran. I was worried the doc would take off, but somehow it all worked out. I took her in and waited. I probably smoked more than I have in my whole life.

After it all, I took Kaśka back home, and I went to a party by myself. Dude, I got more fucked up than I've ever been in my whole life. I feel a hundred kilos lighter. It's such a relief, I can't even tell you.

Yeah, dude, you better watch out. I'm not doing it with any piece of ass without protection. It doesn't matter what kind of line she gives me.

OK, take it easy. Bye.

BLUE (*talking on the phone*). Damn, man, you're not going to believe what happened to me.

Two guys in ski masks came into my garage and started threatening me.

Yeah, that's what I'm telling you. I was sitting there calmly with one of my guys, it was already late, and suddenly the doors open and a guy in a ski mask comes barging in. He puts a piece to Wojtek's head and says, "Where's the fucking money?" Wojtek looks at me, at the piece, and tells him, "I don't know."

The guy in the ski mask gives me the once over, then does the same to Wojtek. Suddenly the doors open again and a second punk in a ski mask barges in. He puts a piece to my head and says, "Are you the boss, you fuck?" And that's when I think: I'm fucking done for.

I look straight into his eyes and tell him, "The boss already left. We're just here to clean up." Without taking his eyes off me, the second guy says, "Don't fuck with me, you're the boss. First I'm gonna cap this guy, then I'm gonna shoot you. Spill it, where's the money?!"

Man, the hair on my neck stood up, but I tried not to show it. The entire income for the week and the money for payroll was in the filing cabinet next to the desk. At this point I'm thinking: No, I've been through too much to hand over the till to this sucker. I look the guy in the ski mask straight in the eye again and say, "We're cleaning up here. We don't know anything!" That's when they ordered us to lie down and tied our hands. Finally they stuffed us in the can and closed the door. They started ransacking the place. They took the computer and some of the tools, but they didn't find the money. They were in too much of a hurry.

Police, are you kidding? Do you even know what country you're living in, man?

The cleaning lady let us out after an hour. Of course, we called the police immediately, but it took them an hour to get there with their dog. One of the policemen weighed, at most, 50 kilos. Like a strong wind could have blown him right over. The dog picked up a scent but came back after five minutes, and the dumbass says to me, "The dog's lost the trail because the thief got away in a car!" Right, he got away in a car. And what was he supposed to do, fly a helicopter or ride a bike to the police station?

Man, I've had enough of this country. Do you know how these things are handled in the States? Several guys from the FBI show up, and in two days everything's fine: the thieves are doing time and decent people feel safe.

I've spent 50 years in this hell hole. I was a Boy Scout, I've stood in line, and now two clowns might kill me. This country's in no kind of state to get anything done. It's sick!

I'm not yelling, I'm just giving an explanation. I can't calm down after all this. I could be dead right now, you know? You take care of everything, worry, save up money, and what? Suddenly you're gone.

When I left the office, I was thinking: I should tell someone about this, share it with someone who's close to me. And you know what? Blank, a complete blank, there wasn't even anyone to call.

In the end I felt like a complete ass.

My wife, give me a break. I don't know what she does with her time, and she doesn't know anything about me. By and large, we might as well be living on different streets. I'm not talking about our son, because that's a different matter, but she could give a rat's ass about me, for sure.

I'm not exaggerating, that's just how it is.

In any case, at least I'm still alive. We can talk more when we get together.

OK, bye.

A conversation between Blue and White.

WHITE. Hi, Dad. I heard about the hubbub. Not bad.

BLUE. Not bad. They could have bashed my head in, and you say, not bad.

WHITE. I read the paper, there's something about the incident.

Look: Yesterday evening two men were attacked by masked assailants. The assailants were in possession of objects that resembled hand weapons. The assailants locked the aggrieved parties in the bathroom. After picking up a lead, the police dog lost the trail.

BLUE. What audacity. Objects resembling hand weapons? What, did they have to kill me to prove they were guns, not fakes? The dog picked up a lead, and it's true, he picked one up. That dog was the best one of the whole lot, but the rest were a pile of idiots.

I'd tell you to ditch this country if you could.

WHITE. But you're wrong. It's total shit, but you can do business here.

BLUE. What business can you do with a bullet in your head? Everything's been fucked up here for the last 30 years, and nothing's gonna change. Where can we go from here, you know? The only thing going for this country is the women. They're the only thing worth living for.

WHITE. Chill out, I got it. But there are a few things in this world worth living for.

BLUE. If I were your age, I'd know what to do.

Did you hear what happened to your mother?

WHITE. Yes. She said she has cancer. She was really upset.

BLUE. I know.

WHITE. I don't think it's anything dire, though. She's always pretty lucky. Too bad they'll cut off her breasts. She's still a pretty dishy old gal. But you know the rest.

BLUE. Yes, yes.

And how are you doing?

WHITE. Great. Everything's going really well. But I should go study.

BLUE. Go study, then.

WHITE. Yeah, OK.

RED (*talking on the phone*). Hi, Kasia. I'm going in tomorrow already.

I know I'm talking quietly, but I can't talk any louder. Everything gets stuck in my throat. I haven't been able to eat or drink.

Yes, tomorrow I go register at the hospital. Later they'll do some tests, and in two or three days I'll go for the operation. They'll cut me open, and then we'll know the outcome.

Guess what I did last night?

I went to a photographer and did a photo shoot with bare breasts. I chose an old guy on purpose, and I had him take pictures of me. He started joking that I wanted to become some *Playboy* centerfold. I didn't tell him anything.

You know what the worst thing is? Let me tell you how I see it. You're young and pretty and don't really think things will be any different. Life goes on, and you grow old. You try not to notice it, till suddenly you realize that you're ugly and dreadful. You explain to yourself that it's normal, that that's the way it is. You know what I mean?

I never thought that something like this would happen to me. My breasts were my crowning feature. I would've rather died than lose them. But today I pray to God they'll cut them off so I can live longer. It's a rotten feeling. Of course, I'm afraid, I'm really afraid. You know what? I even went to church.

Yeah, yeah, I haven't been for probably 15 years. I stood there and stared at the altar, but I didn't say anything. You know, it seems so stupid to ask someone for mercy, if it never really even crossed your mind before.

Yes, please. Please call me.

OK, I'll take the phone with me. Bye.

WHITE (*talking on the phone*). Hey.

I know it's been a while since I called. I've been in a funk lately. First of all, my mother's dying. Secondly, they tried to kill my father. Then I myself ordered a guy killed, and now they're after me.

You know how it is. I borrowed a little cash. A few dollars, I thought, that I'd pay back quickly. I'm in a bind, and people are starting to get anxious. They can get more nervous than anyone else I've ever known.

Their hands start to shake from the nerves, but they're holding a baseball bat, or a gun.

What's up, man? Calm down. I don't want any money from you. I'm talking to you as a buddy, and you're worried about money. Fuck, does this whole world revolve around money? Isn't there anything else?

I'm not exaggerating. I'm a realist. There probably aren't many things people believe in in this world, but money's certainly one of them. Your girl is yours, as long as you're in the black. If your balance doesn't cover weekly shopping, presents, shit loads, you're worth crap to her. People won't say straight out they don't give a damn about you, but they'll make sure you feel it. Disrespect, fucking shenanigans, bullshit.

You know, I've fallen to shit. I used to think: I want to be someone. And what do you do if you want to be someone? The answer was simple: I have to have money. That was the beginning of all this misery.

Maybe I wanted too much, and maybe I'm not as fucking badass as I thought I was. I don't know, man, I don't know, but I made a mistake somewhere along the way. And what? I'm left all alone, because everyone's taken off. It's a nasty feeling, I'm telling you.

But I'm gonna show them. I'll stand up on my fucking puny legs and become someone, and later I'll kick em' in the ass. I'll invite all the fucking shitheads to a party. I'll lay out so much cash on the table that their eyes will be swimming. Then you know what I'll do? I'll burn the crap, and I'll throw the scraps in the can and flush it. That'll be a fast one, won't it?

For now I have to conjure up a few bucks out of nowhere, because those stinking animals are gonna rearrange my arms and legs.

Take it easy. The sun's gonna shine again someday.

BLUE (*talking on the phone*). Hi, hi. I'm sitting on the couch. What are you doing?

One has to work so much just to get enough. But for what, for some motherfucker to put a bullet between my eyes? Nothing cheerful. My wife is dying of breast cancer in the hospital, and my son was beaten up by gangsters and is lying in his room.

When I was little, I didn't even have enough to eat. My dad died young, and my mom worked from dawn till dusk in order to feed us. You know, in those days my brother and I ate the potato peels. It's horribly degrading, but it gives you an idea of what's most important in life. Like a little brat, I told myself: when I grow up, I won't ever be hungry. What do people who have everything they want know about life?

No one ever gave me anything. I had to fight for everything.

Don't worry, don't worry, I'm not going to go on to you about life. That's all, and it doesn't even mean anything. My only regret is that my mom didn't live to see me. She would have been so proud, or maybe not. She never would have been able to forgive the fact that my brother and I had a falling out. Her greatest punishment was when she would start to cry. There was nothing worse: not screaming, not being grounded. When she started crying, that was it.

Remember when we first started out? We were free, no wives or children. I had so much energy then, I could do anything. I remember wanting the night to be over as quickly as possible so I could get up again. I was so happy when I started my garage. I was in love with living, I was really happy. I finally

had something that was my own. But then something began
to crack, just like for you. We lost our way, man.

I know, I feel like an old rag.

No, I'm not having a nervous breakdown, but I don't know if
I can keep going. Something has to change, things can't keep
going on like this.

How long can you go on, pretending to live?

My own brother doesn't speak to me any more, my wife didn't
even tell me she was sick.

I found out about everything by accident. It's sick, it's so sick.

It has to end, it really has to end.

Alright, all the best, bye.

*A conversation between Red, Blue, and White. White and Blue are
on the stage. Red enters.*

WHITE. Hey, Mom, you're here already . . . You look great, really,
you look great. I've never seen you in that outfit. It really suits
you. See, I told you everything would be fine.

I know, I know I was supposed to pick you up. But I was so
relieved and happy, I forgot you were leaving the hospital.

BLUE. Darling, how great that you're already here. You don't even
know how much I've been thinking about you. Different
moments keep coming back to me: our vacation in Turkey,
even last Christmas Eve at your mother's place. It's funny what
out of everything sticks in your mind. You know, I felt a little
stupid not being with you, but you said yourself it's a minor
procedure. You know how it is . . .

RED. When I look at the two of you, I have no idea how I managed
to put up with you for so many years. Twenty years with such
animals. Twenty wasted years.

WHITE. Mom, don't get upset. We've been going through hard
times, too.

Maybe now finally we all understand what's most important.

RED. Hard times, is that what you call it?

Do you really think I don't know who you are, son? First a small-scale junkie, then a rookie dealer. And now this. For consolation I can tell you that your father wanted to get rid of you, too. My mother was going to throw me out of the house, and your dad gave me the money for an abortion. It was probably the only moment in my life when I was my own person. I decided to have you. And after a month, your father had a flash of insight, too.

WHITE. How do you know I'm a . . .

RED. Is that really your biggest worry: How I know?

I never figured my son would lead such a sham of a life. A mistake, as always. I answered the phone for you. By some strange twist of fate you weren't home, and Agata told me everything. It seems she's not as strong as me at times.

WHITE. It's not like that.

RED. Like what? You'll have to tell me what it's like sometime, because I have my own version of things.

Yes, yes, you both deserve each other. Your father thought he could persuade me to get an abortion, too. It's the simplest solution to the problem, simply to kill it.

And that whore you keep is also pregnant. Just look at him, look at how many new wrinkles Dad has. Think how much he's been through recently. The attacks, the sick wife, the stupid son, and his pregnant girlfriend. Not everyone can withstand such burdens. There's no telling what to do.

WHITE. What are you talking about?

RED. You know exactly what I'm talking about, and I've got good news for you, the most important being that you're not the father of that girl's baby. Don't be naive. Did you actually think that your little kitten was yours alone? She had several tomcats like you sniffing around.

BLUE. What a load of bullshit. What are you talking about?

RED. Give me a break, I knew about everything from the beginning. I've always been quite inquisitive. I've learned to defend myself after all these years, and to read the telephone bills. Later, it was only out of curiosity.

Trust me, I know how to talk to people. If you take the right approach, you can find out a lot.

BLUE. Don't be so sure. Do you think I'm completely oblivious? Your sudden departures from the house. Don't tell me you were looking for love. I understand you too well. You know what it is you always wanted?

RED. Shut up, you never understood me. I never asked you to marry me. I would have raised him alone, maybe even done a better job.

BLUE. For fuck's sake, don't make yourself out to be so fair and just of late. Do you think I don't know what you've been doing in every out-of-town hotel? What are you, a fucking nymphomaniac?

WHITE. I'm not gonna get in the middle here. I'm gonna go.

BLUE. Stay, since we're already talking about it. Didn't you want to be treated as a goddamn adult? Dumbass, you already had everything: money, car, vacations abroad. I only expected one thing of you: that you'd grow up to be a smart person. And what? I pay your tab to guys who have somehow gotten it into their heads that they're playing at gangster. You hide everything from me, and then I have to get you out of the shit you're sitting in up to your chin. How many times has it been already?

And also, is it true about the abortion, what your mom said?

WHITE. I don't know what you're talking about. Is it about this or the other thing, when you wanted to kill me?

RED. I hate you both, I really hate you. When I look at your faces I don't even feel like living any more. You've both killed me slowly over many years. That's it. I can't look at you for a second more.

BLUE. I don't love you either, and even less without your breasts.

RED. You pig, you filthy pig.

BLUE. I am, maybe I am, and that's OK. I never talked back to you: I was too stupid and couldn't even understand what you were saying.

You think I don't know what your mother thought of me? She would have killed me if she could have. Everything was a fiction, and I was always the bad one. Eternal deceptions, always something wrong; it's too late, not now.

At first I had a sense of guilt, but it's kind of stupid to live with a sense of guilt for 20 years. I thought that maybe we had to set things up differently. We had such different personalities. You were so austere.

You only opened up in moments like this one, when everything fell apart. But you didn't say anything when everything was fine. I know you felt too proud. But how come you never wanted to be honest with me?

RED. I didn't want to be honest with you? I wanted nothing more than to be honest and tell you what I was thinking. It was you who never had the time. You said it wasn't important.

BLUE. Not important? You remember the fight we had five years ago, and you moved out for a month? When you came back and things were good for a while, it was the happiest time of my life. I've always loved you.

RED. Why didn't you ever say anything?

BLUE. You never wanted to listen. You always had something you had to do. Besides, I never felt comfortable with your friends because I was too crass. You remember, you remember when you said: You're so crass.

RED. That wasn't my point, and you know it. I had to converse with a guy whom I constantly suspected of betrayal.

BLUE. Don't talk to me about betrayals, because you were first. Do you know how it made me feel? Do you? Do you know how it felt?

RED. I know, because I felt the same way.

BLUE. What's the point? Why didn't you want to say anything to me? How'd we get ourselves into this hell?

RED. Me, why me? You never gave me the smallest sign that you wanted to listen.

BLUE. In order to give someone a sign, you have to see that the other person's willing to listen, too.

I thought maybe it was possible. You'd live in your world, I'd live in mine, but at least you'd be close.

RED. I don't believe you.

BLUE. What don't you believe? I knew about all your infidelities.

If I didn't feel anything for you, I would've gotten out of here a long time ago.

RED. I knew about yours, too.

It's strange that you're telling me all this now. I'm not exactly sure why.

BLUE. I don't know, I don't know either.

WHITE. Maybe we should sit down.

Mom just got out of the hospital. We shouldn't upset her.

I'm hungry. Maybe we should eat something.

BLUE. So?

WHITE. What do you mean?

BLUE. So, what should we eat?

WHITE. There's nothing in the fridge, I looked earlier. We could go buy something or get take out. Mom's sick, so something light. I know: What about Chinese or Italian?

RED. I have enough food here. I could make something, that is, since I'm not a bad cook.

WHITE. Pierogi, then, or naleśniki. My favorite.

BLUE. Mine, too.

RED. Good, then, it'll be ready in a minute.

BLUE (*talking on the phone*). Good morning, hello.

Oh, please, there's no Internal Revenue office here, only me.

True, I haven't called for a while. I've had a few things to take care of.

Yes, yes, I know, we have business to finish, but I didn't feel like talking about it.

Stop, no more new girls. You only have one thing on your mind, and I'm calling about something serious.

Listen, I want to invite you to lunch.

No, over to our place.

Who'll be there? I'll be there, my wife and son . . .

I don't see any reason to be surprised. One married couple is simply inviting another married couple over for lunch on Sunday, to their house.

Listen, I'm not playing a joke on you. I'm just inviting you. We want to spend a little more time at home.

Yes, it's true she knows about everything, and I know about her. But, well, that's not the point. We both did some stupid things. She's a wonderful woman, and she means a great deal to me.

Of course we have our problems. Sometimes she even pisses me off, but I'm trying to stay calm when she does. Do you remember what it was like when we were young? You see, I keep thinking about it more and more. It wasn't that long ago. Maybe only back then was I the way I wanted to be.

No, no, I'm not getting all sappy. But just run yourself a bath, then pull out the plug, and watch how the water drains away. That water is your life.

I'm trying to tell you something important. I don't even know myself what I'm trying to say, and that's why I don't know how to say it.

Anyway, I'm inviting you to please come over with your wife on Sunday. We're looking forward to it. We'll have some time, and maybe then I'll be able to explain.

Bye.

PRZEMYSŁAW WOJCIESZEK

MADE IN POLAND

CHARACTERS

BOGUŚ

IRENA — Boguś' mother

REVEREND EDMUND

EMIL

MONIKA — Emil's sister

VICTOR

MARIANNA — Victor's ex-wife

LIDKA — Victor and Marianna's daughter

GRZEŚ

TOMASZEK

FAZI

KRZYSZTOF KRAWCZYK,
TEN KRZYSZTOF KRAWCZYK LOOK-ALIKES,
DISCO-POLO BAND, ANKA, ANDRZEJ,
HELENKA, AND OTHERS

MADE IN POLAND

TRANSLATED BY DOMINIKA LASTER

1. IN THE STREET, EVENING

Boguś (19) is walking down a street of a housing development. All around are seedy apartment buildings several stories high. Lighted windows here and there. Boguś grips a steel rod. On his forehead is a large, distinct Gothic tattoo, which reads: "Fuck Off!"

BOGUŚ. Get up, you sons of bitches, get up. This is a revolution. You hear, fuckheads? This is a revolution.

Sound of a window opening in a nearby apartment building.

MAN'S VOICE. Shut your trap!

BOGUŚ (*stops, turns toward the window*). What's your name?

MAN'S VOICE. None of your fucking business!

BOGUŚ. Had enough?

MAN'S VOICE. What???

BOGUŚ. Have you had enough?

MAN'S VOICE. Yeah, I've had enough of you!

BOGUŚ. Are you pissed? Like me?

MAN'S VOICE. Hear that? The motherfucker wants to know if I'm pisssed. I'm going to kill him right now.

BOGUŚ. Join me.

MAN'S VOICE. I'll join your face to my fist, asshole!

From an open window of a nearby apartment building, loud disco music can be heard. A party in full swing.

WOMAN'S VOICE. Hey, join the party!

BOGUŚ. Fuck your party!

Boguś gestures "fuck you" in the direction of the window and begins to run down the street. After a moment, he stops in front of a dilapidated apartment building that is a few stories high. He cups his hands around his mouth.

BOGUŚ. Anka! (*After a pause*) Ankaaa!!!

After a moment, one of the top-floor windows opens.

ANKA'S VOICE. What do you want, Boguś?

BOGUŚ. Come back to me.

ANKA'S VOICE (*bursts out laughing*). Piss off!

BOGUŚ. Come back to me. I need you. I am not like the rest of them any more. I've waged war against them. I'm like you always wanted me to be. Come back to me!

ANKA'S VOICE. Boguś, don't piss me off!

BOGUŚ. Anka, I'm alone against everyone.

ANKA'S VOICE. Boguś, but you cry even at the sight of a naked piece of ass. Better get yourself home.

ANDRZEJ'S VOICE. Who's that?

ANKA'S VOICE. Boguś came to win me back.

ANDRZEJ'S VOICE. You coming on to my chick?

Boguś does not answer.

ANDRZEJ'S VOICE. I'm a junior master in Judo. Do you want me to come down? Do you? Do you, motherfucker, or what?!

2. EMBANKMENT NEAR THE HOUSING COMPLEX. EVENING

Evening, dark. Boguś stands on an embankment overgrown with grass. From here he can see a small peripheral church—brightly lit. In front of the church, a parking lot with a dozen cars. Individual people walking toward the entrance. Scaffolding surrounds the church—evidence of ongoing renovations. Visible from the embankment is a concrete road, which leads from the church to the expansive housing development a few hundred meters away. Boguś runs down from the embankment, heading toward the church.

3. IN THE VESTRY. EVENING

Boguś, with small plastic bag under his arm and rod in hand, opens the door and enters the vestry. Reverend Edmund looks up at Boguś, notices the tattoo. Boguś stops a few steps away from the front door. In the background, throughout the scene, the singing of the congregation can be heard coming from the church.

EDMUND. Finally, you're here. Change, and let's go.

Boguś throws the packet in the plastic bag to the ground.

BOGUŚ. My surplice. I'm leaving.

Edmund approaches Boguś, examines his tattooed forehead for a moment.

EDMUND. What does this say?

BOGUŚ. "Fuck off."

EDMUND. Never mind. Change and let's kick it Old Testament for Jesus.

BOGUŚ. No way—I'm leaving.

EDMUND. What happened?

Boguś hesitates.

EDMUND. Speak up, I'm your priest. Who will you tell, if not me?

BOGUŚ. I'm pissed.

Edmund does not respond.

BOGUŚ. I just woke up this morning and felt it. It's like AIDS, it's burning me up. All day I go around wrecking phone booths. It does nothing for me. I'm burning up inside.

EDMUND. Go see a doctor.

BOGUŚ. I did, this morning. But he pissed me off, so I fucked up his car. He won't give me another appointment.

EDMUND (*points toward the church*). C'mon, listen to them, feel their strength.

BOGUŚ. I don't want these incense smoke screens. My altar boy days are over.

EDMUND. You won't serve mass, if you don't want to. Go on in.

Boguś resists.

EDMUND. You owe it to me.

BOGUŚ. Don't try to pull that one over on me, Reverend.

EDMUND. Let's go.

Edmund takes Boguś by the hand. Boguś gives in but not without a struggle. The two approach the door leading to the interior of the church. The singing of the congregation grows in volume.

EDMUND. Is that better?

Boguś pulls away from Edmund's grasp.

BOGUŚ. Now I know everything. They're pigs. I hate pigs! (*Pointing to his tattoo*) I've had enough of these lies, don't you see?

EDMUND. What lies?

BOGUŚ. The lies you feed your flock. I don't believe them.

EDMUND. Would you like to talk about it?

BOGUŚ. With you? So that you can give me this worthless crap all over again? I've been here five years and for five years every Sunday you try to push this shit on me. I don't believe in eternal life, I don't believe in the New Testament, I don't believe in the revelations of the prophets. And those are only pigs. Take a walk in the parking lot, most of them came here straight from the supermarket.

EDMUND. Those people work hard . . .

BOGUŚ. But they could've bought their barbecue grills and tracksuits on a Saturday. What kind of religion is this, with no principles and responsibilities?

Edmund doesn't answer.

BOGUŚ. Do you know why you have always been a lousy priest? Because your God croaked a long time ago!

Boguś turns to leave the vestry.

EDMUND. So this is it?

Boguś nods.

EDMUND. And you won't help me with the church renovations?

Boguś, laughing, shakes his head.

EDMUND. God exists, you idiot, I know, I experienced it.

BOGUŚ. I know the story—fabricated drivel.

EDMUND. I saw, how he came . . .

BOGUŚ. I heard. Always when you drink too much liturgical wine, you come out with it.

EDMUND. It was the third month of fasting, a true end . . .

Boguś stops, turns around, walks up to Edmund.

BOGUŚ. . . . And you knew, that you would not come out of it. But he came, right? Strong and radiant—he was so close, as close as I am to you now. He exists, Boguś, he exists . . . Is that how it went?

EDMUND. Boguś, it's true, you have to believe me!

BOGUŚ. Is that why they transferred you to the housing development?

Edmund is silent.

BOGUŚ. Keep telling your story. It's not by chance that they call you "X-Files!"

EDMUND. He exists, Boguś. He is real and true—like you and me. He exists!

Boguś takes two, three steps in Edmund's direction, as if to strike him.

BOGUŚ. In your diseased brain maybe, you fucking missionary!

After a moment, Boguś changes his mind, turns around, and with a loud slam of the door disappears from the vestry. After a moment, steps can be heard on the wet gravel along with the sound of a car window breaking. Boguś demolishes the priest's car with his rod. Car alarm can be heard.

4. PARKING-LOT GUARD BOOTH. NIGHT

In the guard booth of a night watchman. Emil (16) sits at a table watching television—crude erotic film broadcast on Polsat.[1] Emil moaning quietly—probably masturbating. He is wearing a tracksuit made of crash fabric—he wears the same one for the duration of the play. After a moment, a smash

---

1 Poland's second-biggest television channel, founded in 1992.

can be heard outside—the sound of a car-door mirror being broken off. Emil freezes, looks outside—sees Boguś standing next to one of the cars. Emil pulls up his tracksuit, wheels over to a nearby desk, tries to reach the phone. His movements are too jerky, however—the receiver falls to the floor and breaks. Emil grabs the wheels of the wheelchair in which he's sitting and propels himself out of the guard booth.

5. PARKING LOT. NIGHT

Boguś is holding a broken-off side car mirror in his hand. He sees Emil, who is pushing the wheels of his wheelchair, approaching him. Boguś throws the mirror away.

EMIL. Hey you!

Emil wheels up to Boguś, who is not paying any attention to him— he is looking around the parking lot.

EMIL. What you did is a crime!

Boguś turns around and looks down on Emil with a semiconscious gaze.

EMIL. Your violation is punishable by imprisonment—from six months to two years, suspended sentence three years. That's paragraph 148 forward slash 7.

BOGUŚ. Seriously?

EMIL. I know the entire penal code. By heart.

BOGUŚ. You work here?

EMIL. I'm the security guard.

BOGUŚ. Then what the fuck do you need the penal code for?

EMIL. I'm going to be a lawyer.

Boguś approaches Emil, bends over him.

BOGUŚ. You know what? Fuck the law. I'm pissed.

Boguś picks up the car mirror he has broken off and throws it forward with a powerful swing. After a moment, the smashing of the front windshield can be heard.

EMIL. By destroying the property of others, you mark your actions with features of criminality. I have no choice. I must hand you over to the prosecutorial authorities.

BOGUŚ. *You're* a crime. Look at you. Who gave you this job? Fucking attorney on wheels.

Emil does not answer.

BOGUŚ. If all of your homies started pimping themselves out you'd be pissed too. Do you have any homeboys?

Emil does not answer.

BOGUŚ. Do you, or did you ever, have friends of any kind?

EMIL. I have a sister.

BOGUŚ. A little skank from the morning bus? Queen of the first shift?

EMIL. You unscrupulous bastard. My sister is perfectly exquisite.

BOGUŚ. What can you know about perfection, you cripple? You can barely move on that thing.

EMIL. Not true. Even at high speeds I can make all the turns. You'll see about that, when I get a hold of you and hand you over to the cops.

Emil wheels over to Boguś and tries to catch him. Boguś jumps away. He stands on top of a heap of scrap metal—out of Emil's reach.

EMIL. I know you! You're the altar boy from the church in the housing complex. You just got a tattoo!

BOGUŚ. Yes, this morning. When I found out that God croaked, I decided to celebrate!

Boguś, rod in hand, starts walking alongside a row of cars on the parking lot. Emil follows him. Boguś turns around, notices him.

BOGUŚ. Everyone is pimping themselves out in this fucking system. Even the best of them. The best of them, you hear? The toughest. One of my homeboys from vocational school got a job at KFC. I ran into him today. He was as happy as a child. The son of a bitch doesn't even know how bad things are with him. We have to end this. We need to rebel. We have to shatter everything to pieces. Maybe then the motherfuckers will open their eyes.

EMIL. Is all of this . . . In accordance with the law?

BOGUŚ (*laughing*). Fuck the law, join me.

EMIL. Join what?

BOGUŚ. The rebellion.

EMIL. Against who?

BOGUŚ. Against everyone.

EMIL. I don't know. That's a little vague.

BOGUŚ. I'm pissed, I want to fight. Don't you feel it? It's in the air. Being pissed—that will be the AIDS of the 21st century. I woke up this morning and felt it—tomorrow the same will happen to you. Join me, be one of the first. Fight.

Boguś turns toward Emil, who is following him.

BOGUŚ. Are you pissed?

Emil shrugs his shoulders. Boguś bends over one of the cars he is passing and bashes the rod into its windshield. The alarm goes off.

BOGUŚ. And now?

EMIL. I'm pissed.

BOGUŚ. Say it loud.

EMIL. I'm pissed!

Boguś picks up his rod, takes a few steps and in a similar fashion breaks the windshield of the next car. And the next car parked slightly further. Almost instantaneously the loud blaring of car alarms can be heard. Emil spins around in his wheelchair frantically.

EMIL. I am pissed, I am pissed, I am pissed!!!

Boguś notices an elegant Western car a few meters away. Boguś, rod in hand, walks over to the car. He smashes the windshield, pummels the hood. The car alarm goes off—louder and more furious than the others. Emil brings his wheelchair to a halt, looks at Boguś.

EMIL. I'll get you, you thug!

Boguś makes his escape from the parking lot. Emil follows in pursuit of Boguś. For a while he even begins to gain on him, but the wheelchair is unstable—Emil topples over. Boguś stops and approaches Emil who is lying in the overturned wheelchair.

BOGUŚ (*tightening his fist*). I'll give you a piece of good advice. Come back here tomorrow and say: "Enough."

Boguś turns and walks away.

EMIL. If I had a better wheelchair, you wouldn't stand a chance!

Boguś is too far away to answer.

6. ON THE STREET OF THE HOUSING DEVELOPMENT. EVENING

A speeding police car passes in the street. Grześ and Tomaszek are sitting in a car parked on the street. The headlights are turned off. Grześ lowers his window, lights a cigarette. Both men are dressed in suits throughout.

GRZEŚ. Did you see that Krautwagen? They even have them here. But ever since they switched over to them they go faster somehow, you notice? ¡Arriba! ¡Epa! ¡Epa! and you're home. A non-stop ride, hell . . . Except your taxes pay for the gas.

TOMASZEK. Grześ, getting back to our . . .

GRZEŚ. They drive around like that in my housing complex too. It used to be such a peaceful place. And now? Any little street fight—and they're on a high-speed chase. Who needs that kind of street patrol? People don't feel safe any more.

TOMASZEK. Getting back to our conversation . . .

GRZEŚ. We, the citizens, should take matters into our own hands. With a little neighborly help we'd get rid of criminality quickly. What do you say? Would you be up for forming a citizen militia? Do you even vote?

TOMASZEK. No.

GRZEŚ. That's no good. The fundamental instrument of political struggle in a democratic state governed by the rule of law is the ballot.

TOMASZEK. Getting back to the subject . . .

GRZEŚ. I remember that from some newspaper. I used to be a truck driver. Thirty-six hours of standing at the border. You either sleep or read the paper. Newspapers are good. You can read them, you can eat on them, you can wipe your ass with them. They're better than the radio. Can't wipe your ass with a radio.

TOMASZEK. It's about sitting in the car. It's about me having to sit in the car while you . . .

GRZEŚ. But would you vote for a party that supports a citizen militia? I would.

TOMASZEK. Every time you go on an operation, I have to sit in the car. It's not fair.

GRZEŚ. Yeah.

TOMASZEK. I transferred here from the accounting department three months ago already. I have good health test results and great recommendations. Why don't you give me a chance? Why do I have to rot here?

GRZEŚ. When Fazi says you're ready, you'll go on an operation with us. For now you watch the car.

TOMASZEK. Watching the car is for the retired.

GRZEŚ. Watching the car is for newbies. This is not accounting. You have to go out among people, be tough when necessary. When Fazi decides you're good enough, you'll join the operation.

TOMASZEK. Fazi hates me.

GRZEŚ. Fazi likes you. He likes your style. He can see that you are not a hick, like the others, that you have your own opinions. He sees that you're raring to work. Be patient.

Fazi is heading in their direction. He is well groomed and dressed like the others. He carries a small packet in his hand, which he puts in his jacket pocket after a moment. He gets into the car.

FAZI. Sorry it took so long.

GRZEŚ. No problem.

TOMASZEK. I'll throw that out.

FAZI. Throw what out?

TOMASZEK (*points to Fazi's jacket pocket*). That. We were just talking.

FAZI. Yeah, and?

TOMASZEK. About the fact that I haven't been in on things. I want to know what you're taking away from them. I want to know what you are taking out of their houses.

FAZI. Listen, that's none of your fucking . . .

TOMASZEK. Listen, I've been here three months already, before long they'll transfer me somewhere else. I want to know everything about this job. Don't fuck me around, all right?

Fazi reaches into his pocket. Takes out the packet—tissue paper with something wrapped inside it.

FAZI. You want it?

TOMASZEK. Yeah, I fucking want it.

FAZI. Then here, take it and go fuck yourself.

Grześ laughs. Tomaszek takes the packet, he hesitates.

GRZEŚ. Open it.

TOMASZEK. I'll open it when I feel like it.

GRZEŚ. Go on, open it! What an asshole . . .

Tomaszek slowly unwraps the tissue paper.

TOMASZEK (*turning pale*). Jesus Christ.

Fazi takes the packet away from Tomaszek and throws it out the lowered widow. The contents are not visible, only a quiet splat can be heard.

FAZI. So? Did you learn something? Just don't puke here. Grześ, get him out of here.

Tomaszek gets out of the car.

TOMASZEK. I'm not going to puke. Jesus. I won't puke, I'll be all right.

GRZEŚ. Why the fuck did you take that with you?

FAZI. I got carried away and forgot about it. I thought I'd throw it to some dog.

GRZEŚ. What have we got?

FAZI. A bank account, where he transferred the money. Unfortunately, only half. He bought a car with the other half. That's the kind of openhanded gesture he had, the son of a bitch.

GRZEŚ. Where is it parked?

FAZI. In a guarded lot.

Fazi reaches into his pocket and takes out the keys.

GRZEŚ. I'm driving.

FAZI. Nothing doing. I've never driven a Lexus. (*He hesitates*) Tomaszek?

Tomaszek lifts his head.

FAZI. All better?

Tomaszek, bent over, does not answer.

FAZI. Next time, I'll let you in on the action, I promise.

No answer.

FAZI. You guys hungry? I'd like to eat something before we head back to Wrocław, Tomaszek, will you eat something?

GRZEŚ. A little borscht with pig's ears, maybe?

Tomaszek, holding his stomach, stands up violently. With difficulty he struggles not to vomit. Grześ laughs.

GRZEŚ. Graduate.

7. PARKING LOT. EVENING

Fazi and Grześ are inspecting the Lexus. The front windshield, hood, fender, and bumper—all need to be replaced. This car was the last object of Boguś' aggression the previous night.

GRZEŚ. Motherfucker . . .

Fazi takes out his cell phone. Dials a number.

FAZI. Hey. Listen, check the cost for new Lexus headlights. Left and right. And the front windshield. The bumper and the fender . . .

Tomaszek comes out of the guard booth, walks up to Fazi and Grześ.

TOMASZEK. The security guard saw them.

GRZEŚ. Which one? The one in the wheelchair? Fucking great security they've got here.

TOMASZEK. Apparently he's only filling in for someone.

FAZI. How many were there?

TOMASZEK. Three. Some dipshits. Hobos.

GRZEŚ. Probably from the neighborhood.

FAZI. Did he call the police?

TOMASZEK (*nods*). As soon as he dragged himself to the guard booth. They should be here any minute.

FAZI. We'll have to take the car.

GRZEŚ. Listen, maybe he knows them, maybe he's scared, maybe they told him they'd be back.

Fazi glances at Tomaszek.

FAZI. Work on him.

TOMASZEK. Me?

FAZI. You wanted to get in on the action.

TOMASZEK. But . . .

FAZI. Go, he's a cripple. I think you can handle him, can't you?

Tomaszek heads toward the booth in which Emil is seated but not visible to the audience.

8. A ROOM IN BOGUŚ' APARTMENT. DAY

Inside the apartment belonging to Boguś and Irena. In Boguś' room. Daybreak. The entire apartment is filled with the sound of a Krzysztof Krawczyk song playing loudly on an old vinyl record. Boguś wakes up, not without difficulty, gets up, and sits on the bed.

BOGUŚ. Damn, I'm pissed.

Boguś shudders for a moment, as if pierced through by a cold shiver.

9. IN THE KITCHEN OF BOGUŚ' APARTMENT. DAY

Boguś opens the fridge, reaches for a carton of milk. He takes out a bag of cereal and a bowl from the cupboard above his head. Pours milk on the cereal. Three portraits hang on the wall in the kitchen. From the bottom: Lech Wałęsa from the time of the stockyard strikes; above him the Pope; above him Krzysztof Krawczyk. After a moment Irena enters the kitchen, cigarette between her teeth. She is wearing a T-shirt that says: "Born in the USA." Irena looks at Boguś, notices the tattoo, bursts out laughing.

IRENA. You stupid fuckhead.

Krawczyk's songs can be heard in the background throughout this scene.

BOGUŚ. Mom, I asked you not to walk around in that T-shirt.

IRENA. So now it's my fault? Maybe, you'd fucking like to tell me what happened?

BOGUŚ. Mom, I told you that something inside me snapped.

IRENA. If word gets out, everybody at the gasworks will laugh at me.

BOGUŚ. Maybe they won't.

Irena pointing to Boguś' tattoo.

IRENA. What is that supposed to mean?

BOGUŚ. In brief or in a full sentence?

IRENA. In brief.

BOGUŚ. Get the fuck out.

IRENA. And in a full sentence?

BOGUŚ. Get the fuck out everybody.

IRENA. You retard. You're going to have that for the rest of your life!

BOGUŚ. That's why I got it. I'm not lukewarm. If I make a decision, I go all the way. Hook, line, and sinker. One hundred percent. No compromises.

IRENA. You're talking out of your ass.

Irena glances reproachfully at the picture of Krzysztof Krawczyk hanging on the wall. Boguś notices.

BOGUŚ. Yes, I know—he never got a tattoo.

IRENA. He didn't have to—he was great without one.

Boguś does not answer. He masticates his cereal patiently.

IRENA. You'll never find a job with that dreck on your forehead.

BOGUŚ. I'm not sure if I'm still going to be looking for a job.

IRENA. Sure thing, I'm going to support you for the rest of your life.

BOGUŚ. I didn't say that.

IRENA. That's what it's beginning to look like.

BOGUŚ. No, Mom—I plan to go back to school.

Irena freezes in bewilderment.

IRENA. Wait a minute, I must have misheard.

BOGUŚ. No, Mom, you heard me right.

IRENA. Meaning—you're going back to vocational school?

BOGUŚ. No, I'm not going back to the gasworks vocational school. I'm going to a regular high school.

IRENA. To high school?

BOGUŚ (*nods*). A magnet school for the sciences. On a mathematics and physics track.

IRENA. Get out. That would be something, son.

BOGUŚ. I know it.

IRENA. If you really went to a high school like that . . . You could get a full-time job after graduation.

BOGUŚ. Exactly.

IRENA. And if you had a full-time job, you could make a ton of dough.

BOGUŚ. Right.

IRENA. And if you had a ton of dough, I could quit my job at the gasworks. I would start going to concerts.

BOGUŚ. Sure.

IRENA. I would go to all of Krzyś'[2] concerts.

BOGUŚ. Sure thing.

IRENA. And I would go to all the record fairs in the country.

BOGUŚ. Yes, Mom.

IRENA. I would collect the entire discography . . .

Boguś confirms approvingly.

IRENA. I would have more of Krzyś' albums than that slut from Opole, that swanks at reunions.

BOGUŚ. She doesn't even have half of what you'll have, Mom.

IRENA. I have to say, son, you've impressed me. I'm proud of you.

Irena looks at Boguś probingly for a while.

IRENA. You're putting me on.

---

2 Diminutive for Krzysztof.

Boguś agrees, laughing.

BOGUŚ. You're irreproachable, Mom.

IRENA. You almost had me.

BOGUŚ. Years of practice, and you still smell me out.

IRENA. I'll always smell you out.

Irena goes into the hallway. Puts on a coat, throws a small military backpack over her shoulder.

IRENA. Maybe you should go to high school after all. It's not such a bad idea.

BOGUŚ. Study, Mom? Become one of them? That's so banal.

IRENA. Finish your cereal, sweetheart. And don't cross the street on red.

BOGUŚ. Chill.

Irena leaves the apartment. Boguś returns to his cereal. After a moment he puts the bowl aside, and starts to tremble. The quivering becomes stronger and stronger.

10. A ROOM IN BOGUŚ' APARTMENT. DAY

Boguś turns on the tape recorder by the bed. The sound of good, old The Clash can be heard. Boguś reaches toward a shelf above his bed. On the shelf in a neat row, is a collection of comic books. There are a few dozen. Boguś takes out one comic book—it can be Kloss[3] or Captain Żbik.[4] Boguś opens the comic book and attempts to read. After a moment however, agitated, he throws it on the floor. Boguś moves the mattress on the bed. Underneath the mattress, in a recess, are dozens of pornographic

---

3 Hans Kloss is the fictional figure of a Polish officer recruited by Soviet intelligence because of his physical resemblance to a captured German officer, which he is conscripted to impersonate. In the 1970s, Captain Kloss became an iconic pop culture figure, and appeared as a character in books, television theater, and comic books.

4 Captain Żbik is a Polish comic book series published in the years 1967-1982. The hero, Jan Żbik, is the captain of the Polish Citizens' Militia, a state police institution formed in 1944 by the Soviet-supported PKWN (Polish Committee of National Liberation).

magazines. Boguś sits and starts to leaf through them. He loses his patience quickly, however, and rips the magazine to pieces. He opens a drawer of the bedside table—takes out a small bag of weed, a pipe, and a lighter. He fills the pipe and lights it. However, after a few inhalations he puts the pipe away, coughing. Boguś returns to Irena's room, sits on the couch, turns on the television. On the screen appears an experienced farmer delivering a calf. The birthing is difficult and necessitates a cesarian section. The camera shows the cutting of the stomach. An off-screen voice comments on the successive incisions of the scalpel. From the cut-open steaming stomach of the cow a calf slowly emerges.

11. FRONT DOOR OF BOGUŚ' APARTMENT. DAY

Long doorbell just sounded. Boguś stands at the door. He peers out through the crack of the door, opened only the length of the chain. Edmund stands in the hallway.

EDMUND'S VOICE. Boguś?

Boguś does not answer.

EDMUND'S VOICE. Are you there?

BOGUŚ. No.

EDMUND'S VOICE. Boguś, I can hear you, open the door.

Boguś hesitates for a moment, after which he unlatches the chain and opens the door halfway.

BOGUŚ. What do you want?

EDMUND. You know very well what. You destroyed my Polonez.[5]

BOGUŚ. Me? Stop shitting in my pants! I didn't destroy any little Polonez.

EDMUND. I know it was you!

BOGUŚ. Namely, how? Did you have a vision?

EDMUND. I won't go to the police.

BOGUŚ. Fine—don't go.

---

5 Polish motor vehicle produced in the years 1978–2002.

EDMUND. I won't go if you enter into an arrangement with me.

BOGUŚ. You're threatening me with the cops, you bumpkin? Me?

EDMUND. An arrangement.

BOGUŚ. Don't you ever threaten me with the police again. Never again. I (*Indicating what he thinks of the police with a gesture.*)— the police!

EDMUND. I said—an arrangement.

BOGUŚ. I don't enter into arrangements with the priestdom.

Edmund laughs.

EDMUND. With the priesthood, you illiterate. I need an extra set of hands for the construction work. I can't count on the Sunday parishioners. Help me with the church renovations. Work off the damage that you made. Come today.

BOGUŚ. They don't want to help? Maybe you can threaten them with the pigs—like me? I already told you I don't give a flying fuck about your renovation. Get lost!

Boguś slams the front door, returns to the room, sits in front of the television. On the screen a veterinarian with a blue coat and surgical mask lifts up a newborn, bloody calf. Boguś is incredibly pissed— his whole body shakes.

12. FRONT DOOR OF VICTOR'S APARTMENT. DAY

Boguś stands in front of Victor's front door. He is pounding on it. In his other hand he holds the rod. On the other side of the door, a prolonged, dead silence. Boguś does not stop pounding.

BOGUŚ. We have to talk.

Silence.

BOGUŚ. We need to talk, you hear?

No answer.

BOGUŚ. I won't leave until you open!

13. INSIDE OF VICTOR'S APARTMENT. DAY

Boguś is standing in an empty hallway. Victor leans out of the kitchen, he notices the rod in Boguś' hand.

VICTOR. Leave the pipe in the hallway.

Boguś puts the rod near the coat rack.

VICTOR. You walk around with that all the time?

BOGUŚ. Only since I felt "it." It makes me feel more confident. It makes me feel like I have an influence on reality.

Victor also notices the sign on Boguś' forehead.

VICTOR. Well, well, you're starting to stand out.

BOGUŚ. This sign is a declaration of war.

Victor's apartment consists of one room, a kitchen, and a bathroom. Victor disappears in the kitchen.

VICTOR'S VOICE. Do you want some tea?

BOGUŚ. I could have some tea.

Boguś enters the room. On the wall are shelves full of books. A wall unit and a couch. Besides that, it is dirty and smelly—dirty dishes everywhere, empty beer bottles, scattered papers on the floor. Boguś looks at the bookshelves.

BOGUŚ. You have anything good here?

VICTOR'S VOICE. I have everything.

Boguś reaches for one of the books. He opens it and leafs through. He closes it. He reaches for another—leafs through it, closes it and puts it back on the shelf.

BOGUŚ. Is poetry all you've got?

VICTOR'S VOICE. That's not poetry. That's life.

BOGUŚ. Do you have any comic books? Or magazines with bare asses?

Victor does not answer. Boguś reaches out with his hand and digs around between the books for a while.

BOGUŚ. You don't want to sell all these? If you sold everything, you'd be rich.

VICTOR'S VOICE. They're old books for the most part. Nobody reads old books any more. In the past, when I used to drink more, I tried to sell them. Today I'm all they've got.

Boguś opens a book on a random page.

BOGUŚ (*He tries to read*). Py . . . рус . . .

Victor enters the room. He is carrying two glasses, in which teabags are brewing. Victor sets the glasses on the desk by the window. He approaches Boguś, takes the book from him.

VICTOR. *Pusty menia, atday menia Voronezh.*[6] Osip Mandelstam. I also have Brodsky, Tsvetaeva, Pasternak . . .

BOGUŚ. I don't know Soviet.

VICTOR. Russian. They don't teach you that in school any more?

BOGUŚ. When they were throwing you out, we still had that woman . . .

VICTOR. Sosnowska.

BOGUŚ. But then she lost it and she left on her own.

VICTOR. Are you still in school?

BOGUŚ. What for? I blew it off. Everyone ends up going on the dole anyway.

VICTOR. You blew it off yourself?

BOGUŚ. They threw me out—two months after you. Do you still work for some school?

Victor shakes his head.

BOGUŚ. So what do you do?

VICTOR. I drink.

Victor sits on the couch. Looks at Boguś.

VICTOR. You shaved your head. You're not a punk any more?

BOGUŚ. I never was a punk. I was a SHARP[7] skinhead, there's a big difference. I believed in interracial brotherhood and the

---

6 Let me go, give me up, Voronezh.

7 Acronym for Skinheads Against Racial Prejudice.

struggle of the working class. But in this town there is no room for SHARP skinheads. Anyway, the times have changed.

VICTOR. What's hurting you, Boguś?

BOGUŚ. You know, I've always respected you. You were the only teacher in that fucking school that meant anything to me. You were different, you stood out. Even when they were throwing you out, you kept your dignity.

VICTOR. Stop bullshitting—get to the point.

BOGUŚ. You're my master, tell me what to do.

VICTOR. Fucking hell, boy, I'm an alcoholic who can barely make ends meet. I should give you advice? I can't even give myself advice.

BOGUŚ. I declared war on those pigs. Twenty-four hours have passed, and they still don't know it yet. I'm pissed, I have to fight. I have to fuck up something so big that it either destroys or cures me. But first *they* have to find out about me. I have to make the first step—but what?

VICTOR. Go to a psychiatrist.

BOGUŚ. I went to a psychiatrist—I fucked up his car!

VICTOR. I'm lucky that I take the tram. You're not going to fuck up my tram, are you?

BOGUŚ. I tried. It doesn't help. Only cars and phone booths.

Victor takes another sip of the russet-colored tea. Boguś stares at him tensely.

BOGUŚ. I am looking for someone to go into action with. Go into the street and blow this clusterfuck to smithereens. Hit, you know, hit them all where it hurts. You see what's happening. Turn on the television, turn on the radio. It's the end of the world. Everything is going to hell in a handbasket. You and me—we could show the world. Make something greater out of this.

VICTOR. Who do you hate so much, Boguś?

BOGUŚ. Everybody. Cell-phone assholes, tracksuiters, hipsters, gel boys from the music charts top ten, advertising asses, TV tramps, bastards from banks, motherfucker priests, psychopaths from the army, government, police, and corporations. I hate them. I hate their wives, their husbands, their daughters, their sons, sons-in-laws, brothers-in-law, fathers-in-law. I hate the Russians, Germans, and Americans. Americans in particular. Those motherfuckers want to be everywhere, they want to govern everything, those pricks with noseyitis have to pry into everything. I hate those shitty restaurants that are all over the place now. I've never set foot in one and never will. Like this McDonald's for example. I'll never set my foot inside. I don't give a shit that the john is free there. I'll never even take a piss in a McDonald's, even if I'm leaking. I'd rather piss on the street. Because I simply hate those sons of bitches. I don't even listen to American bands. I only listen to Polish and British bands. I listen to Post Regiment[8] and The Clash. Did you ever listen to Post Regiment? Man, they were dope, but split up because there is too much American shit in stores nowadays. Fuck their grungy dreck. Fuck rap, fuck techno, fuck Nirvana. A fucking ragbag of fag shit. Fuck them all and they better get the fuck out of Polish housing developments, back to their Nicaragua, or wherever the hell they came from.

VICTOR. Have some tea.

BOGUŚ. Fuck tea!

VICTOR. Have a cookie.

BOGUŚ. Fuck cookies!

VICTOR (*laughing*). Boguś, where do you work?

BOGUŚ. What?

VICTOR. Where do you work?

BOGUŚ. Nowhere. Isn't that obvious?

VICTOR. So what do you do?

BOGUŚ. I'm starting a terrorist organization. Average age—20. When I get enough people together—we'll put a bomb under Polmos.[9]

---

8 Warsaw-based Polish punk rock band formed in 1986.

9 Acronym for *Polski Monopol Spirytusowy* (Polish Spirit Monopoly), a state-owned monopoly controlling Polish vodka and spirits market.

We'll blow that monopoly of death into smithereens. I want your advice—what's better, Polmos or the Social Insurance headquarters?

VICTOR. What the fuck are you rambling on about?

BOGUŚ. You don't believe it? It won't be easy but I'm talking to people. Someday soon we're going to be like the Red Brigades.

VICTOR. Find work.

BOGUŚ. What?

VICTOR. Get a job. Maybe there they'll beat that shit out of your head.

BOGUŚ. That's all that you have to say to me?

VICTOR. That's all.

BOGUŚ. And we won't make a revolution together?

Victor shakes his head.

BOGUŚ. *That*, I did not expect.

VICTOR. I'm sorry.

Boguś gets up and stands over Victor.

VICTOR. Piss off.

BOGUŚ. You know what? I don't give a shit about you. You're a complete zero. You and your stinking books.

Boguś exits his teacher's apartment, slamming the door behind him.

14. BOGUŚ' APARTMENT. DAY

Boguś runs up the narrow stairwell onto his floor. He stops in front of the door to his apartment. He takes a key out of his pocket and opens the door, walks inside. Standing in his hallway, he sees that the light in the bathroom is turned on. Boguś opens the bathroom door. Grześ is sitting on the toilet.

GRZEŚ. Can't you see I'm taking a dump?

Grześ slams the door. Boguś walks into the guest room. Inside, sitting on the couch, are Fazi and Tomaszek. The floor is strewn with his mother's belongings, the cabinet doors are ajar. Tomaszek is breaking one Krzysztof Krawczyk vinyl record after another. The

floor is already covered with a sizable pile of LP scraps. Tomaszek
reads the cover title before breaking each album.

TOMASZEK. "If Only It Were Like That" . . . "How the Day Passed" . . .

Fazi raises his gaze toward Boguś.

FAZI. How did your day pass, you shitbucket? Guess who we are.

The sound of the toilet flushing can be heard from the bathroom.
Boguś turns around and tries to run out of the apartment. Grześ
comes out of the bathroom and grabs Boguś by his clothes.

GRZEŚ. Wait till I wash my hands . . .

Grześ pushes Boguś inside the room. In the meantime, Fazi gets up
from the couch. The push propels Boguś right in front of Fazi, who
packs a powerful punch on his jaw. Boguś lands on the rug. Fazi
returns to the couch. Tomaszek keeps breaking the albums as if noth-
ing has happened.

TOMASZEK. "A Drawing on Glass" . . .

BOGUŚ. It wasn't me . . .!

FAZI. Don't ask how we know, because we know, it was you.

BOGUŚ. Ah, what the hell—it was me. And fuck you.

Fazi looks at Tomaszek and laughs.

FAZI. Why are you confessing? You don't even know what this is
about. We're from the telephone company, we've come to
hand deliver the bill.

Fazi, Grześ, and Tomaszek laugh. Grześ stands on the threshold
and wipes his wet hands with a towel.

FAZI. Last night in a guarded parking lot you did a bit of damage to
a few cars. You were recognized by a guy who was a security
guard there. Maybe you had your reasons, maybe not—I'm not
going to pry. One of the cars was ours. The auto body repairs
have to be paid, and that costs an arm and a leg. You'll pay for
that—twenty thousand złoty. Do we have a deal?

Boguś cautiously sits up on the rug.

BOGUŚ. Go fuck yourself.

Fazi gets up from the couch, walks over to where Boguś is sitting and kicks him in the face. Boguś splays out on the rug. Fazi stands over him.

FAZI. The car is in the shop, and tomorrow we leave town. You have until the morning. If you don't hurry—I'll kill you.

Fazi returns to the couch. Tomaszek breaks another album.

TOMASZEK. "Steamboat" . . . I don't like Krawczyk. Really, I don't like him.

FAZI. Come off it. The old ones are still fresh. What he records now is slop, but he used to be king.

TOMASZEK. Have you seen him in concert?

FAZI *(nods)*. With my mom, in Sopot. When I was a little boy. First class, not like the douchebags of today.

GRZEŚ. I never listened to Krawczyk. Although that album with Bregovic was not too shabby.

FAZI. Completely missed the mark.

GRZEŚ. I would play it at parties all the time . . .

FAZI. Stop pissing me off, because I'm getting agitated! The album with Bregovic had no artistic merit! None at all! You don't understand this, but I'll explain it to you right now. Krzysztof Krawczyk is not some dork who sings gypsy hits at weddings. He's bigger than that, much bigger. He is . . . Fuck, I don't know how to explain it to you so you'd understand and stop asking stupid questions. He is . . . Someone like us, only bigger. His life is like ours, only he's lived through it all, get it? His fate is our fate. Look, he was always running away from Poland—only to return here and achieve success. He sinned his whole life, to finally return to the womb of the Church. He fucked left and right, only to find happiness in a lasting relationship. Krzysztof is a symbol, a legend, a monument. If you don't cry like a baby to his old pieces then, I tell you, you're not a true Pole!

GRZEŚ. Sometimes I cry.

FAZI. Genuinely, I hope!

TOMASZEK. You also left Poland?

FAZI. Dear God, how many years I laid tiles for a German, humming his hits. It's thanks to him that I decided to come back. I started a family, became a success in vindication. If it wasn't for him, I wouldn't be who I am today. This country would not be what it is. Do I have to add that it would be worse?

A moment of deep contemplation.

FAZI (*to Tomaszek*). And why did you ask about Krawczyk in the first place?

Tomaszek points to a pile of vinyl scrap.

TOMASZEK. I broke them all.

Fazi bends over and picks up a broken piece of vinyl.

FAZI. But this is a Krawczyk.

TOMASZEK (*laughing*). So is the rest.

FAZI (*pointing at Boguś*). You stupid mutt, now I can't kill him!

Fazi signals to Grześ. Grześ hits Boguś, who is still lying on the floor, with his moccasin.

GRZEŚ. Get up, little one.

Boguś slowly lifts himself up. First he brings himself to his knees and then returns to a vertical position.

FAZI. Are you a Krawczyk fan?

Boguś nods half-consciously.

FAZI. In that case, I can't kill you—such are my principles. But don't think that will save you. This university retard will keep an eye on you. He will make sure you deliver the money.

BOGUŚ. I don't have twenty thousand.

GRZEŚ. You see? Let's take care of this right away. You can't kill him, I'll kill him. Let's call for the gun carriage and be on our merry way to Wrocław.

FAZI (*shakes his head*). We'll take care of it the Catholic way. Maybe he'll be able to collect something until the morning. Beside that, I want to see the city. I hear they have a beautiful market square.

GRZEŚ. You've got to be kidding . . . I was in the market square today with Tomaszek. They tore down all the old tenements and cranked out new apartment buildings in their place . . .

FAZI. Grześ, these are the Reclaimed Territories. We should be proud of them.

Fazi gets up, turns to Boguś.

FAZI. Remember, I can always have you killed. But I'd rather not. Krzysiek has so few real fans.

Fazi turns to Tomaszek, who ran out of albums to break some time ago.

FAZI. You didn't have to break all those albums. How thoughtless . . .

BOGUŚ. Wait a minute, where am I supposed to meet you?

Fazi points at Tomaszek.

FAZI. This certified lout will be in touch with you. Remember, you have until morning.

All three head toward the apartment exit. Fazi stops by Boguś and puts his hand on his shoulder.

FAZI. "What the world gave us, fate suddenly took away. It stole the good times, giving in return, a suitcase of ordinary grimes."

The thugs leave the apartment. Boguś goes into his room in pain— the room has already been searched. The floor is covered with objects from the shelves. The Clash poster has been ripped off the wall and now lies on the floor. Boguś leaves the apartment, closes the door and runs down the stairwell.

15. IN FRONT OF THE APARTMENT BUILDING. DAY

In front of Boguś' apartment building. Boguś runs out of the stairwell and onto the street. Emil is lying on the sidewalk in an overturned wheelchair.

BOGUŚ. What are you doing here?

EMIL. I am.

BOGUŚ. So you are, what of it?

EMIL. I am ready. I want to fight. I want revolution.

Boguś turns around and heads back toward the stairwell.

EMIL. Hey, don't leave me here like this. I quit my job to join you. Now I have no choice, I have to fight!

BOGUŚ. Man, do you think I want a cripple on my hands? No way. Go back to the parking lot.

EMIL. Help me.

BOGUŚ. Fuck off.

EMIL. I know the penal code. I'll get you out of all sorts of trouble.

Boguś doesn't answer. He hesitates. After a minute he walks up to Emil, lifts up his wheelchair and sets it upright with Emil in it.

BOGUŚ. So what the hell are you looking at?

EMIL (*lifts his bruised hands*). They knocked me over. I can't wheel myself around. Will you take me home?

Boguś wavers. Emil points the way. Boguś grabs Emil's wheelchair and begins to push him up the street.

BOGUŚ. I'll never hear the end of it if my pals see me . . .

Boguś pulls his hood over his shaved head.

16. IN MONIKA'S APARTMENT. DAY

A two-room apartment belonging to Emil and Monika. The interior is poor but clean. The kitchen. Boguś, Emil, and Monika are at the table. Monika is putting soup on the table. An enormous piece of sausage floats in each soup bowl. Monika is wearing a tracksuit made of crash fabric, same cut as Emil's, but a different color.

EMIL. I quit my job at the parking lot and joined Boguś!

MONIKA (*devastated*). Emil, it took me three months to find you that job. Fine, I'll call them tomorrow. Eat!

EMIL. I can never get my own way. You always have to add your two cents!

MONIKA. I'm just saying Emil, that with your . . . character, it'll be hard to find you a new job.

EMIL. I'll find a better one this time. Heavens. You won't have to sign phony contracts any more. Boguś showed me how not to be passive. And I won't! They're paying Monika lower wages, even though they promised more. I'll take care of it when I become an attorney, I'll finish those motherfuckers off.

MONIKA. Do you eat soup at home, Boguś?

BOGUŚ. Sometimes.

MONIKA. I make soup for Emil everyday.

EMIL. I love soups!

BOGUŚ. Does it always come with sausage?

Monika smiles and leaves the room.

BOGUŚ. That's your sister?

Emil nods. Boguś can't get over the impression she's made.

EMIL. Monika is exquisite. She works at a butcher shop. Monika knows every kind of sausage. If they ever fire her—she will find work at any butcher shop. Everyone is looking for specialists these days.

Monika returns to the room with a bowl of soup. In her soup bowl as well, there floats a piece of sausage. Monika sits at the table. She places the bowl in front of her and begins to eat.

EMIL. I was just telling Boguś that you work for a butcher.

Monika smiles, embarrassed.

EMIL. Monika stuffs sausages into casings. (*He points to the sausage floating in his bowl.*) That is her handiwork. (*Emil points to Boguś' sausage.*) And that is her handiwork too.

MONIKA. Do you like the taste of my handiwork, Boguś?

BOGUŚ. Very much.

MONIKA. And what do you do, Boguś?

EMIL. He's a revolutionary. Boguś doesn't give a shit. Boguś has had enough and now he's fighting for justice—he's not waiting like the others!

MONIKA. That's fascinating, tell me about it Boguś.

EMIL. Boguś has big plans. He is extraordinarily brave. He stood up to these horrible thugs—the ones who knocked over my wheel-chair. Boguś won't give in to them, Boguś will fight till the end!

MONIKA. Maybe you'll let Boguś speak for himself.

BOGUŚ. There's nothing to tell. It's not like working in a butcher shop. You can't fill your belly with it . . .

Boguś becomes silent. After a minute Emil smiles at Monika, grabs the wheels of his wheelchair and goes to his own room.

BOGUŚ. But I think . . . I am sure . . . That it has many important values, spiritual values . . . I think, for example, that it allows you to keep . . .

MONIKA. Boguś, what's this about?

Boguś looks at Monika, surprised.

MONIKA. Emil doesn't have many friends. If you think that you can use him, then you better leave. Now.

Monika gets up from the table and sits on the couch.

MONIKA. You are that vandal from the parking lot.

BOGUŚ. He told you everything? I don't blame him—I know that he was under pressure, but maybe he didn't tell you the whole truth.

After a minute, techno music can be heard coming from Emil's room. Boguś gets up from the table.

BOGUŚ. I'm not a bad guy. Only pis . . . peed off at the havoc that I see around me. Nobody cares about anything, because you can buy everything. Is that worth dying for? It's not even worth breaking your nail for this mess.

Monika does not answer. Boguś sits next to her.

BOGUŚ. I'm not a bad guy, right?

MONIKA. I don't know you. Maybe you're a revolutionary, as you say. Or maybe a common criminal.

BOGUŚ. I'm not a criminal. I destroy cars and telephone booths, but only to quench the fire that burns inside me. I smashed a clothing store showcase today. With expensive women's clothing. One dress there costs more than my mother's salary. I'd have to be crazy to buy something like that. Would you like to have a dress like that?

MONIKA. I never had one like it.

BOGUŚ. Will you go out with me?

MONIKA (*smiles*). You're fast.

BOGUŚ. I just want to know if you'd like to listen to what I have to say.

MONIKA. Maybe.

BOGUŚ. When?

MONIKA. When pigs fly.

BOGUŚ. What time?

MONIKA. When donkeys speak in rhyme.

BOGUŚ. What time?!

MONIKA. No.

BOGUŚ. What do you mean "no"—we'll meet today.

MONIKA. I was only kidding. I don't want to go out with you at all. You're . . .

Boguś lowers his gaze.

MONIKA. Different . . . well, I don't know. The boys in the butcher shop don't have tattoos. Well you know, I mean, some say that they do have them, down there, you know . . . On the pecker. But they're only messing—to have better pickup. The girls really go for it. Especially in the pâté department. You don't mess around—everything is spelled out on your forehead. And what you say is even interesting.

BOGUŚ. Get lost.

MONIKA. If you want, we can meet, really.

Boguś does not respond.

MONIKA. You're handsome. Very handsome.

Boguś is silent.

MONIKA. Where would you like to meet with me? Speak up—where do you want to meet with me?

BOGUŚ. On the embankment behind the apartment complex.

MONIKA. I've never been there. Is it nice?

BOGUŚ. You can see the entire housing development from there.

MONIKA. That's great. What time?

BOGUŚ. In the evening. At six.

Monika nods, laughing.

MONIKA. You see, things are starting to work out between us.

17. BOGUŚ' APARTMENT. DAY

In Irena's room. Boguś and Irena are picking up the pieces of broken Krawczyk albums from the floor. Irena has tears in her eyes.

BOGUŚ. So, the older one says that they'll smash me up if I don't come up with the money by morning.

IRENA. Twenty thousand is a chunk of change, and I'm broke.

BOGUŚ. Mom, I wouldn't take a penny from you.

IRENA. But if that will save your ass, I'll ask around.

BOGUŚ. I'll manage, Mom.

IRENA. How?

BOGUŚ. I have a plan, trust me.

IRENA. It's all because of your anger. You can't control it.

BOGUŚ. Mom, I hate them so much. They need so little to start pimping themselves out.

IRENA. Son, I was young once too. A blanket on the roof, the first 2 plus 1 album.[10] I felt the same thing. I know how easy it is these days—to become a poser in a suit. All it takes is a moment of distraction and you stop being yourself.

BOGUŚ. Mom, I will never stop being myself. I swear. I'll never be a whore.

Irena looks at the albums scattered on the floor.

---

10 2 plus 1 was a Polish folk and pop band, which existed in the years 1971–99.

IRENA. I want you to know that I am not afraid of thugs. I can take care of myself. Worse things have happened in my life. Your dad had to leave, because he'd get tanked up and made life hell. You, Boguś, are thrashing about too much but you'll turn out all right. I know it. I've managed on my own all these years—I fought my whole life. If need be, I'll fight now too.

BOGUŚ. I have to handle this on my own, Mom.

Irena walks up to Boguś, hugs him.

IRENA. And it's all because you don't know how to live.

BOGUŚ. I know how to live.

IRENA. You don't know.

BOGUŚ. If I don't know, then how come I'm living.

IRENA. I didn't know either, until I met him.

Boguś stands up.

IRENA. It was the spring of 1980. Krzysztof was giving two concerts in Gliwice. That was an extraordinary day—full of magic that filled the air. After the concert, I managed to duck the bouncers and used the back door to get into the hotel where Krzysiek was staying. I didn't want to sleep with him, I wasn't some tramp. I just wanted to exchange a few words, you know, talk to my idol. I wandered around, lost in the hallways, praying to meet him. Who was I then? An underage chump, just like you. I was plagued by only one thought, one question—"how to live?" And I knew that only a real man—a man like Krzysztof, would know the answer. Hours passed, and he still wasn't there. I thought it was all over. Time to leave the hotel and take the night tram back to the apartments. I paced back and forth repeating the lyrics of his songs, and suddenly, on the sixth floor, at "I'm going now"—yes, precisely at "going now," I saw him—he was walking toward me! He was walking from door to door, leaning against the corridor wall—he must have been very tired after the concert. And I walked up to him, looked him straight in the eye and asked—"How to live?" And he looked inside me strangely, somehow piercingly, and said . . .

BOGUŚ. "How to live?"

IRENA (*nods*). "Live as if each day were your last. And even if fate's sharp thorn stands in your way, keep walking, alone through life, walk." He knew! We parted in the morning. He promised never to forget me.

Boguś stares at his mother tensely. The "Fuck Off" tattoo can be seen clearly on his sweaty forehead.

BOGUŚ. Mom, is it possible that I am the illegitimate son of Krzysztof Krawczyk?

IRENA. Unfortunately, son, you are the legitimate son of your son-of-a-bitch father.

18. IN AN ABANDONED WAREHOUSE. DAY

The interior of an abandoned warehouse on the outskirts of town. Tomaszek cracks open a rusted metal door and throws Boguś inside. The interior is lit by rays of sun filtering in through the holes in the roof. In the center of the space Grześ and Fazi are kicking and beating Witold (40)—who is staggering on his hands and knees—with a baseball bat. Witold is wearing a torn and bloodied suit jacket. To tell the truth, he is one big bloody shred. An upturned chair lies on the floor nearby. Tomaszek and Boguś approach the three men. Fazi is about to kick Witold. Grześ holds him back.

GRZEŚ. Wait, Fazi.

Fazi puts his boot down and notices the newcomers. Tomaszek reaches into his pocket and takes out bags of weed taken from Boguś. He throws them on the cement floor of the barrack.

TOMASZEK. The jackweed was playing dealer. I noticed him as he was dealing by the school of the housing complex. And his buddies were sitting in a car and watching how he was doing.

GRZEŚ. You asswipe, you were supposed to be getting money for us, not saving for a color TV!

Fazi looks at Boguś, he points to the plastic bags with the baseball bat.

FAZI. That's how you wanted to pay us back, huh? Is it?

Boguś does not answer. Fazi lifts his boot and aims a series of kicks at the bloody, staggering Witold.

FAZI. That's how you wanted to give us the money back, is it, you son of a bitch?!

BOGUŚ (*very scared*). I won't do it any more, I swear.

FAZI. I reckon you won't, you son of a bitch! I reckon so, huh?!

Fazi gives Witold, who is lying on the floor, a final kick.

BOGUŚ. It was a good plan . . . How else am I supposed to make so much dough in twenty-four hours?

Grześ looks at his watch.

GRZEŚ. Fourteen. You have fourteen hours left until seven tomorrow morning.

BOGUŚ. Seven in the morning?!

GRZEŚ. That's the time we're leaving this fucking shithole.

Fazi turns to Boguś.

FAZI. Where's good for you?

BOGUŚ. What?

FAZI. Where do we meet you?

BOGUŚ. On the embankment, behind the apartment complex. You can drive up there.

Fazi glances at Grześ. Grześ confirms. Fazi turns to Boguś, lifts the baseball bat, which is in his hand.

FAZI. At seven. Just try messing up—Jackie Chan will have a word with you, you son of a bitch.

BOGUŚ. I'll be there, I assure you.

FAZI (*looks at his boots*). The scum ruined my shoes. New, from calfskin. My daughter bought them for me, and he ruined them, scumbag.

GRZEŚ. Boguś, did you read *The Coming Spring*?

BOGUŚ. I had to write about *The Coming Spring* during my evening division exams. I mean, I had to write what it's about.

FAZI. I read it too. It was written by, what's his face . . . Żymierski.

GRZEŚ. Summarize it for me. But only in two, three sentences so that I can remember.

FAZI. It's about a guy who arrives from the backwoods. He thinks it's fucking amazing because his old man told him it's fucking amazing. He comes and it's prickville. What's more, the old man croaked. So the guy gets pissed, and he's pissed for roughly three hundred pages, and finally he's so pissed that he goes and gets drunk with the cops.

GRZEŚ. And what does he do in the meantime?

FAZI. When?

GRZEŚ. When he's pissed, for the three hundred pages.

FAZI. I don't remember, probably he sits at home.

Fazi kicks the motionless Witold.

FAZI. My calfskin shoes . . . Grześ, look around for a rag!

Fazi lifts his gaze, notices Boguś.

FAZI. What are you still doing here? Piss off to dig up the money! We're going to stay here for a while. Right, Mr. Witold?

19. IN VICTOR'S APARTMENT. DAY

In the kitchen, which is one big pigsty, Victor takes the kettle from the stove and pours boiling water into two glasses of instant coffee. Boguś sits at the table.

VICTOR. I won't do a thing.

BOGUŚ. Nothing?

VICTOR. Nothing.

BOGUŚ. You won't help me? I'm fu . . . done for, and what's more the bastards destroyed all of my mom's albums!

VICTOR (*laughs*). If they had the courage to raise a hand against Krzysztof Krawczyk's albums, then the situation really is serious.

BOGUŚ. This is no joking matter. My mother has been collecting those since she graduated from vocational school. Krzysztof Krawczyk gives her life meaning.

VICTOR. I'm sorry, that really is sad.

BOGUŚ. But it's not only them that have me on the hook. The priest from the housing complex, where I was an altar boy, does too.

VICTOR. For the same reason?

BOGUŚ. I transformed his Polonez into a pile of scrap metal.

VICTOR. And how am I supposed to help you? Rob a bank with you?

Boguś does not answer.

VICTOR. Do you have any money?

BOGUŚ. I don't, that's what I'm saying.

VICTOR. No change? You don't have anything in your pockets? I need a drink.

BOGUŚ. That I have . . . (*After a pause.*) I have been selling weed in the apartment complex. It's been adding up. I used some to get the tattoo and still have the rest. But I don't want to deal any more, I don't want to go back to that. I want something real.

VICTOR. I think that the shit you're in up to your ears is as real as it gets.

BOGUŚ. That's not what I'm talking about. I want truth. I want you to help me find it.

VICTOR. Go back to the church.

BOGUŚ. There's nothing there for me. For five years I was an altar boy, for five years I listened to the sermons. I know them by heart. They are all equally hollow.

VICTOR. Why me?

BOGUŚ. You're my master. You know all the answers.

VICTOR (*laughing*). Fuck, I need a drink today. I'm your master, right? Then give me all your loose change and let's go for a beer.

Boguś reaches into his pocket and, after a moment, pulls out a hand-ful of coins and a few crumpled bills and places them on the table.

Victor, with the skillful movement of an alcoholic, sweeps the money off the table. He goes into the hallway and puts on his coat. Boguś does not move.

VICTOR. Did you hear me? Let's go. I'm dying of thirst.

20. A STREET IN THE HOUSING DEVELOPMENT. DAY

Victor and Boguś are walking down a street of the housing development.

VICTOR. You want truth? Look around. Look at how people in this housing complex live, how you and your mom live. You don't want to be passive—but what are you doing? In a few years they'll sweep you off the street like a criminal.

BOGUŚ. What should I do?

VICTOR. You have to find out who you are.

BOGUŚ. I know who I am.

VICTOR. Is that right? In my opinion, you're just playing out the role that you were dealt. And you are just as phony as those jokers on television that you hate so much.

BOGUŚ. Bullshit, I'm fighting.

VICTOR. Oh, I thought, you were just roaming the streets of the housing complex aimlessly and fucking up other people's cars.

BOGUŚ. It heals me.

VICTOR. Don't give me that crap. I know you're not a criminal. Slow down, let it go, hold off. Try to reach the center, inside yourself. Find out who you are, what you want, what you intend to do.

BOGUŚ. How am I supposed to find this out?

VICTOR. From books. Books have all the answers.

BOGUŚ. And comics books aren't enough? Or dirty magazines?

21. IN A BEER GARDEN. DAY

Victor and Boguś enter a beer garden. The beer garden is located on a little square in the old part of the housing complex. It's late afternoon. A few tables are already occupied. A few of the guests greet Victor.

BOGUŚ. How is reading going to help me?

VICTOR. By knowing who you are, who you really are and what you want, you will find people who are like you. You will find out how many people like you there were in the past, what they did, and how they ended up. That's valuable knowledge.

Victor and Boguś enter inside the joint and walk up to the bar. Behind the bar is Helenka (27).

VICTOR. Good day, Miss Helenka. Two pints.

HELENKA. Mr. Victor. Kempiński . . .

VICTOR. He was here? That sly dog . . .

HELENKA. He forbade me. He said . . .

VICTOR. He's was just conning, Miss Helenka. I don't go to him any more. He just comes to get back at me. I'm only asking for two—one for me and one for the kid.

HELENKA. Two. At your own risk.

Victor nods. Helenka pours two pints.

VICTOR. Did you happen to see Jędrzejczyk?

Helenka shakes her head.

VICTOR. The jerk owes me a hundred, but I can't get a hold of him.

Boguś and Victor, with beers in hand, take their seats at a table near the bar.

VICTOR. My former doctor comes here and embarrasses me. I have to find a new joint.

BOGUŚ. Where are you working now, sir?

VICTOR. Permanently—nowhere. I make a little extra cash working at a construction site. Not a bad change, huh?

BOGUŚ. Getting back to the books. Couldn't I find all those things out without reading?

Victor takes a big gulp of beer.

BOGUŚ. To be honest, I never really read that much. I wouldn't know where to start.

Victor puts the glass aside.

VICTOR. "When they hold a knife to your bare breast and force you to look into an opened casket, what will you need, oh noble and proud one?"

Boguś is silent.

VICTOR. What do you need? I asked a question.

BOGUŚ. But it's a poem.

VICTOR. Yes, but I asked a question with it, answer.

BOGUŚ. How am I supposed to know what I need—it's only a poem, I didn't even understand it.

VICTOR. Courage, you need courage. Concentrate.

Boguś stares at Victor.

VICTOR. "And when you fall, unbending, strong and the enemy clasps your heart in his hand, what will you need to die without a wail?"

BOGUŚ (*laughing*). Fuck, I don't know. Is it about finding a rhyme?

VICTOR. It's about you not being such a nitwit, start thinking!

BOGUŚ. So what do I need then?

VICTOR. Contempt.

BOGUŚ. I couldn't have known that—I don't know anything about poetry.

VICTOR. There is one more stanza.

BOGUŚ. No.

VICTOR. The last.

Victor takes a swig from his glass.

VICTOR. "Your white bones now sown above, and from your deeds descendants will profit. What is it you want to resurrect in legions?"

BOGUŚ. Love.

VICTOR. How did you know?

BOGUŚ. It rhymes with "above." Who wrote that?

VICTOR. Broniewski. Władysław Broniewski. Ever heard of him?

BOGUŚ. Yeah, he's the one who wrote "Restless Rain."

VICTOR. You cretin.

Victor imbibes the rest of his beer.

BOGUŚ. I was only kidding. I know him, we learned about him in elementary school. A load of shit.

VICTOR. You know what you were given to learn. He is a great poet. The only man amongst twentieth-century Polish poets. The rest are all wankers.

BOGUŚ. But he was a Commie. He wrote poems to commemorate anniversaries. It's dreadful crud.

VICTOR. He lost his way, that's true, but he lost his way like any man. Yet he also fought like a real man. And he paid the bitter price for his mistakes. He lost his way, stood his ground, drank and fought. He lived. Look at yourself—are you alive? Is this life? Do you know that there are places in this country without housing complexes? Can you imagine that? Have you ever seen a house, a regular house? With four walls, a second floor and a chimney? Have you ever seen a house, you son of a bitch? Have you ever lost a house like that?

Victor's voice breaks.

VICTOR. Because I have . . .

BOGUŚ. Sir, you don't have to insult me . . .

VICTOR. Call me Victor.

They shake hands.

BOGUŚ. Call me Boguś. You don't have to insult me right away, Victor.

VICTOR. I'm sorry, Boguś. I just wanted to tell you that somewhere out there is a different world, a different life. Someday you'll find that out for yourself. Hopefully it won't be too late . . .

Victor takes the entire table in with his gaze. He has already drank his whole beer, while Boguś' is barely touched.

VICTOR. Are you drinking?

BOGUŚ. I don't like the taste.

Victor reaches for Boguś' glass and guzzles it instantly.

VICTOR. I'll go get another one.

Victor gathers the glasses from the table and walks up to the bar.

VICTOR. Miss Helenka, two more. For the boy.

HELENKA. I saw, Mr. Victor, you drank them both.

VICTOR. Miss Helenka, this time the kid will drink them. He's a little timid, I had to show him.

HELENKA. Kempiński . . .

VICTOR. Fuck Kempiński, he's a butcher. Two more, please . . .

HELENKA. I can't. What if something happens . . .

VICTOR. Nothing will . . . My God, Miss Helenka, two more. For me and the kid.

HELENKA. I don't know . . .

Helenka hesitates for a moment, but finally pours two pints. Victor pays. Victor returns to the table where Boguś is sitting. Victor puts the glasses on the table.

VICTOR. For the sake of formality—will you drink?

BOGUŚ (*shakes his head*). I have to be sober. I'm a revolutionary.

VICTOR. Thank God.

Victor reaches for Boguś' beer, guzzles it down, moves closer to the boy.

VICTOR. Courage, Boguś, contempt and love—remember that only, be guided only by that. Be courageous—fight, be contemptuous—be contemptuous with all your strength of this manure, love—because only then does life have any meaning. Find yourself a woman, Boguś, find her and love. Love your friends, love life. Live Boguś, don't be a lifeless corpse, live.

Victor squeezes Boguś' shoulder, shakes him, reaches for the second beer.

VICTOR. "A day of hunger, fire, air, and war is born from the historic night. Here I call out like the prophets of old, a poet in his heart free."

Victor finishes Boguś' beer and sets the glass aside.

VICTOR. "Woe to the skyscrapers of Babylon confident in their might. A terrible day is born from the night. There will be hunger, conflagration, and plague."

Victor lifts his gaze toward Boguś.

VICTOR. Do you believe in the apocalypse, Boguś? In my opinion it is just approaching.

Victor glances in the direction of the bar.

VICTOR. They won't let me drink, the sons of bitches, they won't let me drink. Tomorrow they won't let me breathe, the day after, to spank the frank.

Victor gets up from his seat, gathers the glasses on the table.

VICTOR. I'll order more, say it's for you. You haven't had a drop.

Victor gets up and tries to walk to the bar. He is already drunk. He takes a few steps, after which he stops, bends over, and vomits violently onto the floor of the bar. He drops the glasses, which break on the ground with a loud shattering sound. Boguś jumps to his feet. In the meantime, Victor cannot catch his breath—he coughs, starts to choke. He takes a step, a step and a half, slips on a puddle of his own puke and falls to the floor. Boguś runs up to Victor, who is lying on the floor. Helenka comes out from behind the bar and approaches them. Victor is lying on the ground, wheezing. Boguś grabs him by his clothes and tries to lift him.

BOGUŚ. Victor, what happened?

HELENKA. I said he shouldn't drink!!! He is not supposed to drink! He is not supposed to come here!

BOGUŚ. Can you get up? Everything is OK. Victor?

Victor signals with his head that nothing is wrong. Boguś pulls Victor, who is lifting himself up slowly.

HELENKA. Get him out of here, you hear?

Boguś nods. Victor returns to an upright position.

HELENKA. Pay for the glasses! Now, before you get him out of here!

In the meantime, Victor bends over, vomits again, this time on Boguś.

HELENKA. Fuck, get him out of here! For God's sake he splattered it on my apron!

Victor is lying on the floor of the bar again. Boguś helps him get up.

VICTOR. I'm sorry, I'm sorry . . .

Boguś slowly and clumsily lifts Victor who is slipping on the spewed-up floor. Smeared in puke, Victor leans on his shoulder inertly.

HELENKA. Pay for the glasses, you hear? Pay for them now!

Meanwhile, Victor doubles over again and vomits. Boguś loses his balance and falls into the puddle of puke along with Victor.

VICTOR (*muttering*). Lidka, my little Lidka . . .

22. IN THE BEER GARDEN OUTSIDE THE BAR. DAY

Boguś and Victor are sitting on a bench in the beer garden. Victor wakes up and looks at Boguś.

VICTOR. I have a plan. Let's go to my ex-wife. Maybe she will give me one last chance and lend me some money.

23. FRONT DOOR OF MARIANNA'S HOUSE. DAY

Leafy suburban neighborhood. Boguś and Victor, somewhat refreshed, stand in front of Marianna's door. Victor pushes the doorbell. A moment later Marianna (45) cracks the door open.

MARIANNA. What's this about?

VICTOR. That's not a pleasant welcome.

MARIANNA. You don't deserve a better one.

Marianna closes the door. Victor puts his foot inside preventing the door from closing.

VICTOR. Wait, I want to talk. (*Points to Boguś.*) This kid needs help.

Marianna studies Boguś, his tattooed forehead.

MARIANNA. Let him go to a psychiatrist.

VICTOR. I have to look through my things.

MARIANNA. I threw them out.

VICTOR. You didn't throw everything out.

MARIANNA. Everything!

VICTOR. I don't believe you, you didn't throw out our Krawczyk albums. You wouldn't dare. I have to look through them.

MARIANNA. I'll bring them down.

VICTOR. You won't be able to manage, it's a big box. Let me in.

MARIANNA. No!

VICTOR. It's only about the records, really. He is my witness, he's my student.

MARIANNA. But you don't teach any more, they threw you out, you boozer.

VICTOR. He was my student, please . . .

MARIANNA. Only for the records . . .

Victor nods.

MARIANNA. You'll take them and get out of here. Forever.

Victor nods. Marianna opens the door.

MARIANNA. One wrong move and I call the police.

24. MARIANNA'S HOUSE. DAY

Boguś and Victor are sitting on a couch in the living room. The interior is cheap and ugly. On the far side of the room are stairs leading to the second floor of the house. Victor looks in that direction.

BOGUŚ. You lived here?

Victor nods.

BOGUŚ. That plaster lambkin is cute.

VICTOR. Put it up myself.

After a while Marianna appears at the top of the stairs. Behind her she pulls an enormous cardboard box. Victor gets up from the couch.

MARIANNA (*stands up straight*). Don't you dare move!

VICTOR. I'll help.

MARIANNA. No!

> *Marianna pulls at the box again—it's an old box, however, and tears at the next pull. Vinyl records—LPs and singles—spill out onto the stairs and slide down to the living room floor. Marianna continues to struggle with the remains of the box for a while longer, however, after a moment that too falls apart. Victor tries to approach Marianna.*

MARIANNA. I told you son of a bitch—stay away from me.

> *Victor approaches her anyway.*

VICTOR. I want to see Lidka.

MARIANNA. Fuck off!

VICTOR. I have the right.

MARIANNA. You gave up that right, so stop playing games!

VICTOR. I haven't seen her in two years!

MARIANNA. I'm calling the police!

VICTOR. Lidka!

MARIANNA. Shut up!

VICTOR. Lidka! Lidka! Daddy's here!

MARIANNA. You sick son of a bitch, you'll end up in the slammer, you'll see. You hurt her once, that wasn't enough for you?!

> *Meanwhile Lidka (10) appears on the second floor. She peeks out from behind the door of her room. She sees Victor and Victor sees her.*

VICTOR. That wasn't my fault!

MARIANNA. Yes it was, you drunkard!

VICTOR. I had had two beers! Two! It was a car malfunction!

MARIANNA. It was your fault. I'll never forgive you!

> *Victor softens.*

VICTOR. Forgive me, please . . .

> *Marianna turns around, notices the girl. She runs up the stairs and drags her back inside Lidka's room, closes the door. She stands at the top of the stairs ready to defend. Victor sits helplessly on the floor, cries.*

25. VICTOR'S APARTMENT. EVENING

Inside the TV room. Victor sits on the couch dressed in a grey tracksuit. He is conscious but extremely wearied. He is drinking russet-colored tea from a glass that has a teabag floating inside. He takes a drag of a cheap cigarette. Boguś sits nearby.

BOGUŚ. I don't know where to get the cash. I don't have any ideas.

Victor gets up and takes down a book from the top shelf, hands it to Boguś.

VICTOR. Broniewski. He has all the answers.

Victor picks up the vinyl records from Marianna's house, hands them to Boguś.

VICTOR. I know this doesn't make up for the loss of an entire collection, but give them to your mom. It's all I have left from the conflagration of my marriage.

Boguś looks at the records.

BOGUŚ. They smell like hell.

VICTOR. They're almost thirty years old.

BOGUŚ. And this one is in Russian.

VICTOR (*shakes his head*). We bought it in Bulgaria, on our first vacation.

BOGUŚ. Thanks.

Boguś puts the records aside.

BOGUŚ. Everything got so fucked up.

26. EMBANKMENT NEAR THE HOUSING DEVELOPMENT. EVENING

Boguś sits on the top of the grassy embankment with a volume of Broniewski in his hand. After a while he notices Monika, who is walking toward him. Boguś hides the book in his pocket. Monika smiles, walks up to Boguś. Monika is dressed in her outdoor, button-up, nylon tracksuit.

MONIKA. Hi.

Boguś does not respond. Monika sits next to Boguś. She looks at the panorama of the housing development.

MONIKA. It's cool how you can see everything from here.

Boguś eyes Monika's tracksuit.

BOGUŚ. Have you had a boyfriend before? Have you gone on dates before?

MONIKA. A few times.

BOGUŚ (*bursts out laughing*). And you always wore a tracksuit?

MONIKA. Fuck off!

Monika gets up and walks back in the direction from which she came. Boguś gets up and blocks her way.

BOGUŚ. I only want to know who you are.

MONIKA. Who am I? Who are you, motherfucker, to insult me?

BOGUŚ. You're a tracksuiter, right? One of those girls whose favorite diversion is television and whose ideal candidate for husband is the raddest Maciek Zakościelny?[11] You know what? Fuck Maciek Zakościelny! Because you are a tracksuiter, because you wanted to insult me coming here in a tracksuit.

MONIKA. Look at him—you're a fucking Maciek Zakościelny wannabe. Take a look at yourself. In your gay lace-up boots and rolled up pants. You think you're tough because you inked up your entire forehead? You look like a little faggot, because only fags tattoo themselves!

BOGUŚ. I'm no fag. When I saw you my woody stood at attention at once.

Monika stops.

MONIKA. That's what you say to girls on a first date? Or maybe this is your first date, you scumbag. You're a romantic, is that right? That's what you think of yourself? Well, I'll tell you— you're not. You're a big, fat zero. You don't know what it means to have a house, a job. You've never worked a day in your life, you don't know what it means to fight!

BOGUŚ. I know . . . Alright, I want to find out.

---

12 Polish actor and singer. Roughly the equivalent of Justin Bieber.

MONIKA. Find out from someone else, motherfucker.

BOGUŚ. You can't walk away like this. I like you. I think you're sexy and have your own style!

MONIKA. Piss off!

BOGUŚ. Wait, let me read you something!

Boguś reaches into his pocket and takes out the volume of Broniewski that he received from Victor. He tries to open it on the page that he marked, but the slip of paper that he had placed between the pages slips out. Boguś leafs through the book but cannot find the poem. Finally he gives up, he opens the book on a random page.

BOGUŚ. "When they come to burn down your abode, the one in which you live—Poland—the earth you sowed, when they throw thunderbolts for you to abate, when they plummet iron armies and stand at your gate, and in the night with rifle butts pummel your stead, From sleep lifting your head, stand at the door, bayonet as your weapon, let the blood pour!"

MONIKA. What is that supposed to mean?

BOGUŚ. I love you.

Monika laughs and walks away.

BOGUŚ. Will you be my girl?

Monika keeps walking away, after a while she turns around and gives Boguś a fleeting glance, she keeps walking.

BOGUŚ. Will you stay?

Monika does not answer, keeps walking away. Boguś keeps looking at her. After a while, he closes the Broniewski book and throws it behind him angrily. The book falls on the grass somewhere far away. Boguś is left alone on the embankment.

27. BOGUŚ' APARTMENT. EVENING

Boguś enters the apartment. The light is on in his mother's room. Boguś walks through the hallway and stands in Irena's doorway. Irena is sitting on the couch, smoking a cigarette. Next to her is an ashtray full of cigarette butts. Irena holds one of the albums given to her by Victor in her hands, raises her gaze toward Boguś.

IRENA. Thanks for the albums.

BOGUŚ. No problem. They're from Victor, the teacher, remember?

IRENA. Damn, I didn't know that Krzysztof recorded an album in Bulgaria. He is truly great!

Irena looks at Boguś.

IRENA. Did you manage to gather some cash?

Boguś shakes his head. Irena reaches for her wallet.

IRENA. I emptied my account. Borrowed from wherever I could. I have two thousand. If you give it to them, will they leave you alone?

BOGUŚ. Mom, I have a different idea.

IRENA. Yeah?

BOGUŚ. Just don't get mad, because I've thought everything through. And it's the most important thing in the world to me.

Irena waits for an explanation.

BOGUŚ. I had a date today. My first date with a girl. She's beautiful. I want to buy her a dress. She doesn't have any. I saw one that would be good.

IRENA. Is that so urgent?

BOGUŚ (*nods*). I have to do this.

IRENA. And then what?

BOGUŚ. I won't give them the money back, not tonight.

IRENA. And if they kill you?

Boguś is silent. He doesn't know the answer to that question.

IRENA. Damn it, I'm going to go gray because of this . . . Do you want me to go there with you?

BOGUŚ (*shakes his head*). I have to take care of it alone.

IRENA. Have you thought about high school at all . . . ? It wasn't such a bad idea.

BOGUŚ. Mom, pass the graduation exams, become one of them. Do you want that?

IRENA. You remind me of your father when he was young. He had so much drive. That's why I fell in love with him. Unfortunately, he ran out of steam after our wedding. I don't want you to share his fate. If you're to end up like him, it's better if you don't graduate.

Irena hands Boguś the money.

BOGUŚ. I'm glad you understand, Mom!

IRENA. I've never heard Krawczyk in Bulgarian before. It must be . . . Beautiful!

Irena goes over to the record player, puts on the record. After a moment, the whole apartment is filled with the voice of Krzysztof Krawczyk performing one of his great hits in Bulgarian. Irena and Boguś listen hypnotized.

28. IN MONIKA'S APARTMENT. NIGHT

It's still dark, but dawn is soon approaching. Monika opens the door to her apartment. She is wearing a pajama-style tracksuit. Boguś stands at the door. He holds a sizable package in his hand.

BOGUŚ. Hi. May I?

MONIKA. If you must.

Boguś enters Monika's apartment. Hands her the package.

BOGUŚ. Here you are.

Monika hesitates.

BOGUŚ. It's a gift. Open it.

Monika tears the paper. Inside is a dress from an exclusive store.

MONIKA. I don't want it.

BOGUŚ. It's yours. Don't be silly. I'm not taking it back.

Monika hesitates, holding the dress.

MONIKA. I can't.

BOGUŚ. I bought it. For you.

MONIKA. Why?

BOGUŚ. Because I love you.

MONIKA. You don't even know me.

BOGUŚ. I know everything about you that I need to know.

MONIKA. What am I supposed to do now?

29. IN A ROOM, MONIKA'S APARTMENT. NIGHT

Monika stands facing Boguś. She is wearing the dress he bought for her. She looks wonderful. Boguś is awestruck. Monika takes Boguś by the hand, leads him toward the bed. Boguś and Monika sit on the bed.

MONIKA. What do you know about me?

BOGUŚ. You have a big mouth.

MONIKA. What else?

> *Boguś would really like to answer but nothing comes to mind. His agony lasts for a while.*

MONIKA. You can lie next to me now . . . But no touching.

> *Boguś raises his hands, he submits.*

MONIKA. None whatsoever.

BOGUŚ. OK.

> *Monika lies down on the bed in the dress that Boguś bought for her. Boguś lies down next to her. They lie like that for a while—motionless. After a while, Boguś extends his hand and touches Monika's hand. The girl withdraws her hand, pressing it to her side. Boguś waits a minute, after which he puts his hand on Monika's hand. This time she does not protest. Blackout.*

30. INSIDE MONIKA'S APARTMENT. MORNING

Dawn. Boguś and Monika are lying next to each other on the bed, they are in the same position as they were at night. Monika turns to Boguś.

MONIKA. How are you feeling?

BOGUŚ. Good.

MONIKA. All bad things passed?

> *Boguś nods.*

BOGUŚ. Will you be my girl?

MONIKA. If you will have me.

Boguś sits on the bed.

BOGUŚ. Only you and me?

MONIKA. Yes.

BOGUŚ. I have to go out. For a little while. Would you do something for me? Burn your tracksuit?

MONIKA (*laughs*). I'll think about it.

31. EMBANKMENT NEAR THE HOUSING DEVELOPMENT. MORNING

Boguś is standing at the very top. Below, the housing development can be seen cloaked in mist. Fazi's car stopped at the foot of the bank. Fazi, Grześ, and Tomaszek are climbing up. After some time they walk up to Boguś.

FAZI. Hey pipsqueak. What's up?

Fazi gives a signal to Tomaszek, who goes up to Boguś.

TOMASZEK. Cough up the dough.

BOGUŚ. Go fuck yourself.

Tomaszek hits Boguś forcefully in the stomach. Boguś doubles up.

TOMASZEK. Just a minute, I don't think I heard you right. I said— hand over the money.

Boguś does not respond. Tomaszek gives Boguś another blow, which is equally hard. Boguś falls to the ground.

TOMASZEK. You son of a bitch, if you don't have the money with you, you're dead.

Tomaszek bends over Boguś, who is lying on the ground in pain, and searches his pockets. After a minute, he turns to Fazi and Grześ.

TOMASZEK. He's got nothing. The cunt doesn't have a penny on him.

FAZI. Fuck Krawczyk. Kill him.

Tomaszek turns toward Boguś and starts to kick him. He deals him several very strong blows. Boguś coils up and groans.

VICTOR'S VOICE. You thugs, try dealing with me!

Tomaszek, who is bent over Boguś, freezes. Victor has climbed onto the embankment from the steeper side of the slope. Victor walks up to Tomaszek—he is bleary and terribly hung-over—he raises his fist and assumes the posture of a boxer.

VICTOR. C'mon, let's go!

Fazi, Grześ, and Tomaszek burst out laughing. Fazi reaches into his pocket, takes out a two-złoty coin, and throws it to Victor.

FAZI. Here is some change for a beer. Now piss off.

Meanwhile Boguś notices Victor. He gets up on all fours. Victor hits Tomaszek, who doubles over with a groan.

FAZI. Kill the son of a bitch. Kill them both!

Tomaszek goes up to Victor, stands in front of him, throws a punch but misses. Victor uses a skillful dodge, he jumps to the side and dances in front of Tomaszek for a minute.

VICTOR. C'mon, you ogre . . .

After a moment, Victor deals another blow, hitting Tomaszek for the second time. Tomaszek jumps away and reels, blood bursts from his nose.

VICTOR. For the first time in two years, I feel like a man!

In the meantime, Fazi and Grześ run up to Victor and start clobbering him with their fists. Victor defends himself like a lion, but looses his strength—he takes more and more hits. Victor looks around toward Boguś.

VICTOR. Run kid, run!

Boguś raises himself up with effort, first hesitantly, and after a moment with full speed, he runs across the embankment in the direction opposite to that from which the thugs came. Meanwhile, Tomaszek has come to. Fazi turns to him.

FAZI. Catch up with him and kill him!

32. EMBANKMENT NEAR THE HOUSING DEVELOPMENT. MORNING

Boguś is running across the embankment. Tomaszek is following him in the car. After a while Tomaszek's car is head to head with Boguś. Tomaszek leans out toward Boguś.

TOMASZEK. You're done for. Done for, you cunt! You have nowhere to run.

Boguś, running, overtakes another section of uneven ground on the embankment. He descends from it. In front of him—the church. Boguś runs toward the church with all of his might, he overtakes Tomaszek's car.

33. IN THE VESTRY. DAY

Inside the vestry. Silence, tranquility. Reverend Edmund is sitting at the table, he is picking out lotto numbers. Water for coffee is boiling in the kettle on an electric stove. The doors of the vestry open with a bang. Boguś bursts inside.

EDMUND. May the blessings of God be upon you.

Edmund lifts his gaze toward Boguś—sees that the boy is out of breath and terrified.

EDMUND. What happened?

BOGUŚ. I need help. Please . . .

Edmund gets up from the table and walks over to Boguś.

EDMUND. The police?

Boguś shakes his head.

EDMUND. If it's not them, then we'll manage.

Meanwhile, through the open vestry door enters Tomaszek.

TOMASZEK. God bless you. (*To Boguś*) Get out!

EDMUND. Just a moment, he is my guest. He just dropped in for some coffee and is not going anywhere. Sit down and I will offer you some as well.

TOMASZEK. Thank you, I don't have time. Junior, make yourself scarce.

EDMUND. I told you—this is my guest. He will sit here and drink coffee for as long as possible. And the coffee is delicious, I assure you.

TOMASZEK. Junior, get out of here right now!

EDMUND. What's this, my son? You raise your voice in the House of God? Maybe you are the one that needs to be kicked out of here.

TOMASZEK. I'm sorry, Reverend, but this cun . . . skunk destroyed something that was someone else's property. He has to pay for it. I won't let him get away with it. He shouldn't be able to get away with it. Reverend, that would set a bad example for others.

EDMUND. What did he destroy?

TOMASZEK. A Lexus. Brand new!

EDMUND. He also destroyed my Polonez. He's a good kid, but has moments of weakness. He will work it off.

TOMASZEK. Mr. Reverend, sir, please don't believe him—he's a liar. He doesn't keep his word. He has to be punished. Once, but properly. I'm not leaving here without him. Please don't reproach me any longer, because I'll stop being polite!

EDMUND. How much do you want from him?

TOMASZEK. Twenty thousand.

EDMUND. Twenty thousand what?

TOMASZEK. What do you mean, what? Złoty.

EDMUND (*with relief*). Aaa, well in that case . . .

Reverend Edmund goes up to a metal cabinet that stands against one of the vestry walls. He reaches under the sweatshirt he is wearing and pulls out a chain with a medallion. There is a key attached to the medallion. Edmund uses it to open the door of the metal cabinet. He hides the key under his sweatshirt again and takes a metal safe box out of the cabinet. He puts the safe box on the table and opens it.

EDMUND. This is from yesterday's mass. I haven't had a chance to count it yet . . .

Edmund separates the bills from the coins, he straightens out the bills and puts them in one stack. Meanwhile, the sound of Fazi's car pulling up outside can be heard. After a moment, Fazi and Grześ appear at the vestry door. They enter.

FAZI. God bless.

Edmund lifts his gaze toward the newly arrived.

EDMUND. We're renovating the church so the contributions are larger . . .

Edmund hands Tomaszek a wad of cash.

EDMUND. Here is five thousand.

Edmund reaches into the safe box again. He walks up to Tomaszek.

EDMUND. Open your pocket.

TOMASZEK. I don't want your change, what would I need it for?

FAZI. Take it, it will come in handy on the road.

EDMUND. Let's say that is five hundred złoty, although it's more for sure.

Edmund pours the money into Tomaszek's pocket.

EDMUND. How much did I give you?

TOMASZEK. Fifty-five hundred.

EDMUND. For sure?

FAZI. For sure. We don't break our word.

EDMUND. Come back after the first for the rest. I don't have it right now. I have to pay the workers.

FAZI. God bless you. Until the first.

Fazi exits. Grześ and Tomaszek follow.

TOMASZEK. It's unfortunate that you are abetting that piece of shit, Reverend.

GRZEŚ. Yeah, you will regret helping him one day, Reverend. He's trash.

After a while the sound of the thugs' car can be heard driving away from the church.

BOGUŚ. What did you do that for, Reverend?

EDMUND. I don't know Boguś. You're just so disarming.

Boguś does not reply.

EDMUND. But don't think that you'll get away with it. You'll have to work it all off by helping with the renovations. I'll pay you the salary of a regular construction worker—four fifty an hour.

BOGUŚ. Six . . .

EDMUND. Five. Deal?

BOGUŚ. Deal.

Boguś and Edmund shake hands. The kettle on the electric stove begins to whistle. Edmund starts walking it its direction.

EDMUND. I'm going to brew a strong one.

BOGUŚ. Please brew two. I'll be right back!

Boguś runs out of the vestry.

34. EMBANKMENT NEAR THE HOUSING DEVELOPMENT. DAY

Boguś runs along the embankment near the housing development. After a while, he notices the Broniewski volume, which he threw on the grass the previous day. Boguś runs toward it, picks it up and keeps running.

35. EMBANKMENT NEAR THE HOUSING DEVELOPMENT. DAY

Boguś stops at the top of the elevation. He sees Victor lying on the grass. He walks up to him. Victor lies motionless with his eyes closed, his brow is cut open and bleeding. Boguś bends over Victor. He puts his ear to Victor's chest, listens. After a moment he gets up, opens the Broniewski book.

BOGUŚ. I know some of them by heart already.

Boguś closes the book.

BOGUŚ. "My head life did not caress, it was not ambrosia I drank— but that is all well and good, to my health: that is how one becomes a man. I was yet but a child, when I took rifle in hand . . ."

Meanwhile, Victor opens one eye and then the other. He gazes at Boguś.

VICTOR. That's beautiful Boguś, but give it a rest. My head is splitting.

Boguś extends his hand toward his teacher. Victor grabs Boguś' hand and slowly, with effort, lifts himself up.

VICTOR. Do you still want a revolution?

Boguś nods decisively.

36. INSIDE THE VESTRY. DAY

The vestry door opens. Enter Victor and Boguś.

EDMUND. God bless you!

VICTOR. Good day.

EDMUND. Please sit down. I'll call an ambulance.

Victor sits at the table.

VICTOR. No need.

Victor pulls up his sweater and shirt. Out from behind his belt, he pulls out a dozen books and puts them on the table.

VICTOR. Broniewski saved my life, yet again! The Collected Works . . .

EDMUND. Shall I dress your eye?

Victor touches his cut brow with his finger.

VICTOR. No, it stopped leaking . . .

EDMUND. It could get a nasty infection. Please wait, I'll dress it.

Edmund goes to the cabinet and takes out gauze and rubbing alcohol. He moistens the gauze and approaches Victor.

EDMUND. Please don't cover it up! You are not a child.

Edmund cleanses Victor's wound. Victor hisses in pain.

VICTOR. You are all alone in the vestry, mister?

EDMUND. Alone.

VICTOR. No tender little maid?

EDMUND. Don't be insolent, or I'll throw you out this minute.

VICTOR. Let's not exaggerate. We're all adults here. I've always wondered what it must be like to live with the consciousness that you can't hook up.

EDMUND. I manage just fine, thank you. Please hold the bandage.

Victor follows the instructions.

BOGUŚ. Coffee?

VICTOR. If I may.

Boguś takes the kettle from the stove. Pours water over three coffees. Meanwhile, Edmund takes his place at the table.

VICTOR. Celibacy is evil it its pure form.

EDMUND. Broniewski was a Stalinist poet.

A moment of heavy silence.

VICTOR. From what I remember there is not a word about celibacy in the Gospels. I read that the prohibition was introduced by the Church to protect its wealth against claims made by married priests.

EDMUND. You know this theory from tendentious Communist literature.

VICTOR. Maybe it is tendentious—but not without passion. The main thing is to search for different sources, discover various points of view and different truths.

EDMUND. You will excuse me, but for me there is only one truth. Either it exists or it doesn't. Just like on the computer—either zero or one.

VICTOR. Life is not a binary code. Even in the presbytery. There are no solutions that are pure.

Victor takes off his bandage.

EDMUND. Does it sting?

VICTOR. It wore off. Thank you.

Silence. Long pause.

BOGUŚ. Reverend, why do they call you "X-Files" around the housing complex?

VICTOR. They call you that, sir?

EDMUND. No, he's talking nonsense . . .

BOGUŚ. I'd like you to tell us about what happened in Africa, Reverend.

EDMUND. No, please. This isn't the right time.

VICTOR. You've been to Africa? I would love to hear about that.

EDMUND. I assure you, sir, that you don't want to hear about this.

VICTOR. Yes, I would. We would, right Boguś? I'm curious. I won't let it go now.

Edmund hesitates.

EDMUND. But one laugh and I'm throwing you out of the church. You'll both be out.

Victor gives a sign that he agrees to this condition.

EDMUND. I was a missionary in Africa, 35 kilometers from Kinshasa. Refugees from neighboring Rwanda would pass through this region when the war began. Most of them died exactly in this region. Women, children, the elderly—no graves. Most of the bodies were eaten by animals in the night. Finally the war reached us as well. We ran out of food, gas, medicine. Hunger and disease began. When I could no longer walk, I went into the chapel, lay down on the dirt floor, and started dying. Have you ever experienced dying? It lasted for a week, so not too long. After five days He came to me. He looked exactly like in the pictures I received from the priest after caroling when I was a child. He had a beard, robes of azure, and fiery eyes. And when I opened my eyes, he kept looking at me. And when I closed them as well. It was not a dream. In the morning he was bright and strong. Then he receded, faded. That evening, I stopped seeing him, I stopped seeing altogether. I went blind. Two days later the medicine transport arrived. It took me two weeks more to come back to life.

VICTOR. Did He say anything?

Edmund nods. Victor is transfixed in anticipation.

EDMUND. "Go back to the housing complex."

Victor moves closer, surprised.

VICTOR. In Polish?

EDMUND. He's God. He can do anything.

VICTOR. And then what happened?

EDMUND. A month later I came back to Poland.

VICTOR. Giving "that" as a reason?

EDMUND. They don't trust me to this day. They think I went crazy.

VICTOR. Well, it sounds like blasphemy.

EDMUND. But it happened, that's how it was, I experienced it.

VICTOR. So then, He is Polish. Truth be told, I always thought so.

Victor cannot hold it in any longer and bursts out laughing.

EDMUND. I told you—one laugh . . .

VICTOR. I'm very sorry, sir, but that's the biggest fib I've heard in my entire life . . .

EDMUND. So God doesn't exist, right?

VICTOR. Neither do the angels, heaven, and all the saints. Why don't you call Gagarin, he'll tell you.

Edmund is furious, he gets up from the table.

VICTOR. But please don't think that I am undermining the meaning of your work. I respect priests. They are carrying out a very important social mission. Especially in housing complexes such as this one.

EDMUND. Get out of my vestry. You don't deserve to be my guest.

VICTOR. We've run out of arguments, have we?

EDMUND. But you don't listen to arguments, you old drunken atheist!

VICTOR. And what arguments are you trying to persuade me with? That a Jesus, with the hairdo of a Czech soccer player, revealed himself to you? That's the kind of nonsense that you try to push on the kids in the vestry?

EDMUND. And what do you teach them in your school? How to live in apartment complexes built for rats? It seems that they still haven't learned, because they go around destroying cars!

VICTOR. And what does the Church teach them? Love thy neighbor as thyself? How can they love others when they hate themselves? Because it's all about money. For two thousand years you've been milking money out of these beggars. In the name of what? A God that doesn't exist?

EDMUND. God exists, you idiot! I experienced it . . .!

VICTOR. That's a load of hogwash!

Edmund starts to thrash about with Victor. The coffee cups fall from the table. Boguś grabs the two men and separates them.

BOGUŚ. What are you doing . . .! That's how my masters behave? This is senseless! I already know who I am . . . I am . . . A young, working-class Catholic. And I know what I want. I want . . . To live, I want . . .

Boguś has serious difficulty in finishing his thought. Meanwhile, Monika appears at the vestry door. All eyes are on her.

MONIKA. I was looking for you . . .

Boguś approaches Monika, takes her by the hand, leads her to the center of the vestry. Kneels in front of her.

BOGUŚ. Monika, will you marry me? (*Pointing to Edmund.*) This is a priest, who will marry us today. (*Pointing at Victor.*) He is our best man. I will be the best husband on Earth. I swear.

Monika does not answer—for how could one reply to that?

37. IN BOGUŚ' APARTMENT. DAY

A crowd and commotion. In a larger, decorated room is the longest table that will possibly fit, and a second, smaller one next to it. At the first table sits Boguś, with Monika, Emil, Victor, Marianna and Lidka, Edmund, and other unknown people—a delegation from the gasworks and the butcher shop. At the second table sit ten Krawczyk look-alikes. On a provisional platform on the other side of the room is a disco-polo band[13] performing standard hits of the genre. On the tables, the usual—salads, vodka, meat, etc. Irena is not in the apartment.

---

13 Disco-polo is a genre of music, which emerged in Poland in the late 1980s. Fusing Eastern European folk tunes with electronic dance music, disco-polo is often perceived as a low form which vulgarizes traditional folk songs and lacks artistic value. Tunes such as *Majteczki w kropeczki* (Polka Dot Panties) by Bayer Full, replete with strong drum machine beat and synthesizers, accompanied parties, festivals, weddings, and political campaigns in Poland throughout the 1990s.

BOGUŚ. Have you seen Mom?

Monika shakes her head. Meanwhile, Victor clinks his glass with a knife, the commotion subsides. Victor raises his vodka-filled glass. Marianna, seated next to him, grabs his suit.

MARIANNA. Victor.

VICTOR. Just one.

MARIANNA. Victor!

VICTOR. Just one, please.

Victor stands up, his vodka shot glass in hand. Marianna ineffectually tires to pull him back down.

VICTOR (*hurried*). To the young couple. May they fare well!

Victor, and with him the entire room, empties their shot glasses. Victor sits. A few dozen eyes turn to Boguś and Monika. After a moment of confusion, Boguś gives Monika a resounding kiss. All the guests, the ten Krawczyk look-alikes included, clap and whistle. Suddenly, Irena enters the room. She stands on the platform, takes the microphone from the disco-polo band vocalist's hand.

IRENA. Son, I'd like to apologize for my delay, but I had a reason. An important reason. (*To Monika*) My dear, you look wonderful. Before I invite to join us here the person who came with me, I would like to thank everyone for coming. (*To the Krawczyk look-alikes*) I would like to especially thank the boys from the fan club. Many of you came here from the far corners of the Poland.

Krawczyk's ten look-alikes nod with pride.

IRENA. I love you—for your friendship and heart!

Irena gets down from the stage, glances toward the door of the room. All the guests freeze in anticipation. This lasts a moment. Krzysztof Krawczyk enters the room, goes onto the platform, takes the microphone in his hands.

KRZYSZTOF KRAWCZYK. Hello ladies and gentlemen.

ALL GUESTS. Hello!

Krzysztof Krawczyk leans over toward the stunned vocalist—explains something for a moment. The vocalist nods, turns on the synthesizer.

KRZYSZTOF KRAWCZYK (*starts singing*). "Lock the world with a key— come back to me, Leave all regrets behind—come back to me, I still remember you as you were back then . . ."

Krzysztof Krawczyk sings. The whole room, the ten Krawczyk look- alikes included, sway rhythmically. After some time, when a couple of minutes have passed, the piercing peal of a thunderbolt can be heard. Everything is silent, everyone looks at Boguś. A light blue ray emerges through the ceiling and touches his forehead. The ray slowly erases the tattoo from Boguś' forehead. After it's gone, the ray disappears.

Boguś turns to Monika and gives her a killer kiss. The whole room bursts into applause. One of the Krawczyk look-alikes blows into a cardboard party horn. Boguś, after a longer moment, tears himself away from Monika. His forehead is clean. Full of laughter and health, he reaches for his shot glass filled with alcohol. The whole room follows suit. Suddenly, from the window, a frightful howl and a series of blows with a rod against the body of a car can be heard. All the guests direct their gaze in that direction.

Fade, blackout.

In the background, "White Riot" by The Clash.

A COUPLE OF POOR, POLISH-SPEAKING ROMANIANS

DOROTA MASŁOWSKA

CHARACTERS

BLIGHTY AND GINA	A couple of poor, Polish-speaking Romanians. *(Blighty and Gina are both Poles pretending to be foreigners.)*
DRIVER	Male, middle-aged, nervous
WOMAN	
GEEZER	
POLICE OFFICER	
BARTENDER	
HALINA THE HATCHECK GIRL	
ROSCOE	

A COUPLE OF POOR,
POLISH-SPEAKING ROMANIANS

TRANSLATED BY BENJAMIN PALOFF

Martini and Rossi, Martini and Pickup, Martini and Spit up.

Martini and Rossi, Hyundai Sonata, Los Trabantos, Buenes Aires.

Suzuki Katana, Cinquecento, Seicento, Fellatio.

Volare, o-oh, Cantare, Romy Schneider, Coffee and Tea.

He's belting this shit out, and she says, Shut up. And he says, But this is our Romanian national anthem, babe. Don't renounce tradition. And they left some doodles back here, because they were all over each other, and as soon as I got going, they just scratched away. And that there's metallic black paint, the most expensive there is.

This weird thing happened when I was driving from Warsaw to Tczew . . .

And these two people, they were acting all crazy, and they introduced themselves . . . We're from Romania: I can show you the flag. What flag? What flag???

I said to them, What do you mean, do I have any scraps of meat? What the fuck is that, scraps of meat? Put your chick in the car, give me your address, and I'll send you your scraps of meat. You'll finally get that Chick-fil-A sandwich you've been dreaming about. Now fuck off.

My wife and I stopped off at the Texaco, and these two people came up to us acting all weird. One of them, the woman, she was pregnant, and they're passing themselves off like they're Romanians who speak Polish. The wife's in chemo. She's missing a tit. I can never remember if it's the left or the right, and . . .

But the girl, I mean, she was like one of those girls who holds on to the door and doesn't want to let go, even when I'm moving. And I was like, No. No fucking way.

It's an abomination. Unacceptable.

I said no, because I can't let them into my car, you know, seeing as the car's registered to my business, and you can see the screen in back, and you know, I can't take them, so they say . . .

And they just stood there staring, all crazy. She had that exact same expression on her face like, you know, a fish in jelly. My husband said that unfortunately there was no way we could take them with us. When we refused, they started crying and cursing up a storm.

I said, No. Because no means no.

So if that no-good broad lies down on the ground, that's her fault. You're just going to lie there, oh, I said, That's a new one. Come over here, slut, I'll lay you out right good. And oh yeah, I'm heading right for her. Boy did she take off. She blew up dust. Like she was all jacked up on something.

I filled up, went inside to pay. When I get back my ten-year-old son asks me if there's such a thing as Polish-speaking Romanians. I say of course there isn't, because he's an anxious kid, sort of talks too much, kind of slow for his age, and he thinks up these stories.

They were like so nice, like so nice, but when I saw their teeth, whoa, I totally said no to giving them a lift. I'm not saying that it's such a big deal, but these days it's no problem, all you have to do is stop by some five-and-dime and buy yourself the cheapest tooth-brush they have, and give yourself a good cleaning twice a day, brush-brush, rinse, straightedge for life, and that's it. You got to take care of that. It's called manners. Amen.

SCENE 1

Winter. A gas station. The two poor Romanians pile into the Driver's car.

BLIGHTY. My wife's called Gina.

DRIVER. But this girl, about 20, pregnant, she didn't say a word. She just sat there, but I figure she's an accomplice to the murder. Whose murder? Me, my murder, get it? Though that may seem unrealistic.

BLIGHTY. Just call her Gina. Gina, what's your last name?

DRIVER. He asked her last name, and she still didn't answer. Just sat there. But her name was Gina, which was probably short for Regina, and that's the bloody glove right there. Now they can catch these murderers, because that's an uncommon name, and that's what I'm demanding, that they arrest these killers in the name of all taxpayers, who could very well find themselves assaulted and killed by these two.

BLIGHTY. She doesn't have a last name. Just Gina. A beautiful name for a girl like that. Actually, both a name and a first-name-last-name, and at the same time a stage name. Gina's a good girl. No stealing, no barfing. The child she's carrying in there is living proof. You know, that's life. We're poor, honest Romanians who happen to speak Polish. The wife's pregnant, she's going to a doctor in Wrocław, to a specialist, because she's got some metastases, some cysts, because it's just a mess there in her belly. And so on. So we'll all go where you're going, huh?

DRIVER. To Wrocław! You hear that, Detective? And this is on the road to Gdańsk!

BLIGHTY. To Wrocław. But we're not picky. Maybe Gdańsk would even be better. They have all kinds of specialists. The sea, iodine, mussels, ships. Maybe Gdańsk, then. I don't want to argue.

DRIVER. I told them I'm going nowhere. Just to Elbląg. And anyway, then I'm coming right back. I was all calm about it, because that's the way I am, calm.

BLIGHTY. Well, then, to Elbląg, or wherever, and then she'll make do. She always makes do. Always. We Romanians, whoaaaa, we're feisty. She'll even sing you something when she straightens herself out a bit, huh, Gina? You'll be alright, dear. A very nice girl. Well, sit yourself down. Yeah, come on, pookums, is everything alright? Is that a new hairband? Now when did you buy that? Just now? I don't believe it. You're too cute, you know that? What are those, chicory blossoms, those stones?

DRIVER. It's actually hard to say how it happened. It just took a minute.

The man she was with, I knew his face from somewhere: he was definitely one of those famous mob guys. Knuckles, or that other one they show, and I'd just turned away, because he yelled at me, Look out! The Romanians are coming! or something like that. And I turned around, and of course it was a setup, and he stuffed her into the front seat, with all her crap, her bags and stuff, and I say, Hang on there! . . .

And he says, Gina. This is Gina.

I was worried, Detective, which I think makes sense. I say to him, Hey man, what Gina, what's this about Gina now, what do I care about somebody's wife named Gina? That's what I asked.

She could be named Slim Shady, for all I care, but get her the hell out of here. I'm in a hurry. I'm on my way to work. What the heck kind of nonsense is this? . . .

BLIGHTY. Actually, her name's Novalgina, but she tells most people to call her Gina. Novalgina, Aspirin, Caffeine, for us these are traditional Romanian women's names. Saint Novalgina, in Romania she was, you know, the patron saint of drunk girls coming home in the dark. Right? That sort of thing happens. Girls such as her. But she tells most people to call her Gina. I don't know, sort of a caprice on her part. Please don't call her Novalgina. Just call her Gina. Show some respect for the feelings of this perhaps-great artist.

DRIVER. But what's it to me? Get out, you . . . Romanians. Because I'm about to call the . . .

All this time the pregnant girlfriend I was just telling you about, she was pretending not to be listening. But I had this little scented pine tree and she was playing around with it, probably planning a way to steal it undetected.

So then he tells me to look at how pretty she is, and what on earth does that have to do with me, if she's pretty or not. All I know is that she smells like frying oil, like some awful deep-fryer, and just get away from me, shithead, and take your princess and her brat with you!

I'm not going anywhere.

GINA. You said you were.

DRIVER. Did I? My mistake.

I was being ironic. Because I was already getting irritated with this antagonistic and unnecessary circumstance.

GINA. This thing's fucking awesome.

DRIVER. And the girl-shithead was playing around cynically with the pine tree, trying to change the subject.

GINA. Did you buy this, or did you make it yourself?

DRIVER. What do you mean, make it myself? Make it myself?! Lady, you can buy these anywhere. Just go into the station, and there are tons of them! What planet are you guys from, anyway?

BLIGHTY. Just look how pretty she is. Oh, you little rapscallion. Well, her teeth need a bit of work. But that's from a hard life, right, dear? We don't have it easy in Romania. In fact, we've only eaten butcher's scraps our whole lives, and that's murder on the old bones. And, you know, zirconia. Chicory. And for dessert we like Pepsid. You know, for heartburn.

DRIVER. And he tells me about his cosmic odysseys, how they have it there in Romania, how they ate bones, weeds, rocks. Well, maybe so, but HEY, we had martial law here, too. There was rationing, and HOLY COW, WHAT'S ANY OF THIS HAVE TO DO WITH ME! Please stop talking to me! Because I'm not listening to you! I'm not listening to this any more! I'm not listening.

He covers his ears dramatically.

GINA. Or vanilla sugar, dry. For example. Some AquaFresh, but very rarely, very rarely, only when mom pawned something, like the family crystal. We had tons of that, because she whittled veggie sticks all over Romania and was very famous.

BLIGHTY. Anyway, I'm not going to hide the fact that the pot is calling the kettle black. That's a saying back in Romania. Because I don't have such great teeth myself. A nice cover of teeth, but with some blank spots, yes indeed.

DRIVER. And he shows me his teeth, these foul brownish pegs, just like cigarette butts. I nearly lost my lunch: How can you have teeth like that and still procreate? . . . And the girlie with that little pine tree, is that any way to behave?

GINA. Oh Jeez, I'd like to have one of these . . .

DRIVER. And he says:

BLIGHTY. Well then just take it, he has two. You're not going to be offended anyway, right?

DRIVER. You get that? He said for her to take it. My private property, mine. Foreigners, who I'm laying eyes on for the first time in my life.

GINA (*trying to hang it around her neck*). But where should I put it?

BLIGHTY. You know, it's not easy with her, once she insists. She won't relent, because she's, you know, relentless. Why don't you just give it to her? Please, do it *for me*. We don't have these little pine trees in Romania. We don't even have anything *like* a pine tree, just other kinds. Oak. Bloke.

DRIVER. Bloke! Have you ever heard of a tree like that, Detective? Because I haven't!
Please get away from my car. And leave me be. I'll take appropriate measures. The girl, too. Take your old bag and fuck off. This is my car, and I don't have time for this. And I tried to drag her out of the car. And get the fuck out, bitch! And let me tell you, that brought her around.

GINA. Oh yeah?!!

DRIVER. And she grabbed her bag and hit me with it here, right in my neck bone . . .

GINA. Bully! Get your big paws off me!

DRIVER. And I have this boil right near there, and that could have caused an irreparable threat to my health and my life. I started to scream, Somebody! Anybody! Help! Because I wanted to call for help, but they prevented me, they terrorized me, and then they wanted to kill me.

BLIGHTY. Hey, man, what's up? Have you lost your mind? You want to beat up a pregnant woman, a big man like you? You don't see she's smaller than you? She's all skin and bones; she doesn't stand a chance against you. You just stay where you are, Jean Genie. Undo your boots. That's right, my little sunflower. You know you got a little booger in your nose? Other side. Well, my little Gina likes to walk around with boogers in her nose. Know what I mean? The little whore. But she's a sweetie. Let me get that for you.

GINA. Nooo, I'll do it myself. I'll do it!

BLIGHTY. No, let me do it. *Let me do it*. Come on!

DRIVER. And he's all cool and shows me her gunk, her disgusting snot from out of her nose. You see, I'm sensitive to that sort of thing, I . . . It reminded me of when I was in grade school, when the other boys, with their spit, wet willies, you know, they lit their farts . . . *I'm not going! I'm not going anywhere! I'm staying right here!* I'm staying here! I'm staying! I'm biding my time! Because I love the cold!

BLIGHTY. Fine, have it your way. So now I'm just going to have to kill you . . .

Blighty shows him his pocket knife.

DRIVER. And that's when he first threatened my life.

BLIGHTY. I'll kill you, though I don't really know how. I don't have the technique down, so maybe it'll hurt more than anything you've ever felt before. And then after that you'll go to hell, and I wish you all the best. And you'll do your time in hell, your nuts will burn off, you won't like it, and you'll think to yourself: It wasn't worth it. Oh, how it wasn't worth it. And in the end I'll get to Elbląg anyway, and now fuck. They throw an innocent man—meaning me—in jail . . .

GINA. And he was such a big shot, like he was too cool for school. And all you had to do was flash him your vegetable peeler and he shits his Underoos.

BLIGHTY. And you don't even know where this knife has been. Maybe I scraped the walls of an aquarium. Or maybe I cut some dog shit into slices, huh? Or maybe it's dull. Because maybe I use it to open envelopes. With letters inside. From my relatives in Romania. Letters they write on tree bark, with urine and feces. And Easter-egg dye. Little cousins all begging for me to send them a piece of paper. Laszlo wants a Snickers, and Dickwad a Mars, and Bam-Bam a Twix, while Cincinnati's dreaming about this cardboard French-fry holder, you know the kind. And you think I send them this stuff? I do. It really means a lot to them. A whole lot.

Knife in hand, he opens the back door and gets into the car.

Get in. I said get in. Stop fucking around: Get in, get in, get in. We Romanians have a lot of patience, but any Romanian is eventually going to tell you, Enough. Let's get going.

SCENE 2

Driving.
Gina and Blighty take out some smokes and, in a terrible rush, start smoking two at a time. They cough.

BLIGHTY. Enough, already. But it's a good thing I didn't kill you. And Christ, I came close, but I'd have paid for that in the morning. Sure, you know, I went to this party, it was cool, no big deal, but then I killed some strange guy I didn't even know!
It just makes me sick. Faster, friend, faster. Let's show some respect for each other's time. But don't get so upset. Because you're sweating, and you'll catch a chill.

He massages the driver's shoulders tenderly.

BLIGHTY. Hyundai Sonata. Nice ride, huh, Gina?

GINA. Like a bullet out of gun, right? No stopping a car like this.

BLIGHTY. Or a Chevy Cavalier. Now those are some wheels. You know, when we tell them in Romania how we got there, look out. Our relatives'll burn down our lean-to, just out of jealousy. Hyundai Sonata. It's not a car, it's a religion. They're going to shit themselves, you'll see. Why don't you fucking let her rip! Fuck yeah. Like a hot pussy, you know? Like a hot pussy, you got a car with that kind of potential, and you let it float there like a sea monkey in soup. Gina's going to hurl . . .

GINA. Now you just hold on there. I don't think I'm that drunk.

DRIVER *(apparently falling to pieces)*. My assailants were constantly humiliating me, egging me on, forcing me to drive faster and faster, against all good sense and the rules of the road. I've been driving for 15 years. I have this little habit: when another car is coming the other way, I read its license plate. I can't control myself. The same with road signs, Gdańsk 153 kilometers, etcetera, Iława, etcetera. I add all the numbers and divide up the sum. I always have this hope that it'll come out even. When it's even, I'm happy. I take it as proof that, somewhere out there, there exists something like symmetry and order in the world's most elementary structures. But the worst is when it doesn't come out even.

BLIGHTY. I'm going to take my boots off, okey-dokey? Perky? Puerto Rico? Martini seicento fellatio?

DRIVER. I keep quiet. I don't say anything. The most important thing with murderers is not to provoke them.

BLIGHTY. What I just said, that means "thanks" in Romanian. But I haven't slipped off my slippers yet. Oh yeah. Like porn. Because it's like, we're here in our own intimate little circle, huh?

He yawns, settles down to sleep.

DRIVER. I just keep saying to myself: It's OK. It's OK. It's OK, it's OK, it's OK. Because maybe this isn't even happening. Maybe it's just a dream, I just don't know it yet, and I'm getting worked up over nothing . . . But it wasn't a dream.

And now he's almost asleep, almost passed out, and I was hoping . . . I was thinking . . .

BLIGHTY. Damn, man, it stinks in here. Gina, did you fart?

GINA. I didn't fart. It already stank in here when we got in.

BLIGHTY. Right. But now it's getting nasty. And it wasn't me.

GINA. Yeah. It wasn't me, either.

BLIGHTY. Someone let one rip, that's for sure. But definitely not me.

GINA. Me neither, no way. Not you, not me. Who do you suppose released the hounds?

BLIGHTY. Piggy. And he was sitting here all quiet like a church mouse, huh.

DRIVER *(falls to pieces)*. What?! IT WASN'T ME!

GINA. Who, then?

BLIGHTY. YOU! It was you! It had to be!

GINA. Stinker.

The Driver throws himself hysterically at his cell phone and tries to make a call.

BLIGHTY. And just what do you think you're doing with that phone? Who do you want to call? Tell us. Maybe the police? What kind of friend are you? Give me that phone. Give it to me.

Pause.

BLIGHTY. You're driving. That's ridiculously unsafe. I'll dial the number for you: just tell me what it is. Oh my, get over here, hurry, for the love of Christ! A pregnant woman! Frozen! Unarmed! She's sitting in my car! And she's driving with me, and I'm taking her somewhere! I don't know what I'm doing! Help! Save me!

My God! You're fucking useless, a real asshole. How could you?

He settles down with the cell phone and falls asleep.

DRIVER. So then he finally fell asleep. And then I knew that this was my only chance to speak with that woman: she's a woman, which lent her certain human qualities. Women can never be quite as evil as men can be. As far as I'm concerned, that's the whole basis for the world's existence, since they have to give birth to children, and they're not alcoholics. But that gave me hope, so I say to her, Do you know how to speak, or what?

GINA. I learned once, you know? But somehow it didn't take. I didn't have a knack for it.

BLIGHTY (*in his sleep*). We're just a couple of poor, honest, Polish-speaking Romanians . . . We sailed here on the coal barge *Advil* . . . We don't have these little pine trees where we come from. We have other kinds.

DRIVER. This one here's your boyfriend?

GINA. Who? Him? No. My cousin. That means he's sort of like my lover.

DRIVER. Your Romanian here snores a bit, huh?

BLIGHTY (*in his sleep*). It's the septum.

GINA. Because of the septum: he broke his nose in jail. Now he has a terrible complex about it. Don't say it too loudly, because he'll get pissed, and he'll cut us down like dogs for fondling each other and plotting against him.

BLIGHTY (*in his sleep*). No, no, no, no, hold on, what's going on here? *Pause.*

DRIVER (*wiping his face with a cloth handkerchief*). It's his kid?

GINA. Whose?

DRIVER. Your kid.

GINA. With my kid?

DRIVER. Well, you know, that thing you're carrying around in there. Is it with him?

GINA. Me? Oh, Jesus . . . What? No!

DRIVER. It's not his?

GINA. No. I like only just met him yesterday . . . And what does it matter to you, anyway? My mother keeps asking the same thing, and I tell her, It's a kid, it's just a fucking kid, and that's it, get it? It's my son. And he's mine, because, well, that's how it turned out. It's my kid. I definitely didn't have him with you. And she says, You should take care of him, but no: you smoke, you drink, you party, you pull down your panties for whoever walks by, and then you wake up at 5:30 in the afternoon and are surprised you don't feel good. Why don't you do something about it, like, grab the vacuum cleaner and . . . But I . . .

Fine, forget it. It's fine. It's a good thing you reminded me.

She takes out a tube of glue and pretends to sniff it.

I'm totally addicted to this shit. To tell the truth, I don't even like it any more.

DRIVER. And this monster, this awful woman, I don't even want to call her a woman, she reaches into her crap, into all that garbage, and she takes out a tube of Crazy Glue. And she looks herself over in the label! Like in a mirror!

BLIGHTY (*in his sleep*). Gina's an artist.

DRIVER. And that, uh, that doesn't, you know, hurt the kid?

GINA. Come on, man . . . But I keep it under control. Anyway, the doctors said that my kid is already used to it, and if I stop it would be a worse shock than a little Christmas cheer. That is, the kid could come out retarded, and it's better for me to have a sniff than for me to get into a bad mood and the kid to come out all fucked up. In small quantities it's probably even healthy. You should give it a try. It'd chill you out, and then you wouldn't just sit there. Hey, check out those tanks, there's going to be a war.

DRIVER. Nooo! Never!

I screamed.

The stink was horrible. I started to get dizzy.

GINA. Know what? Because the worst fucking thing is that the world wants to turn a person into a camouflage rag saluting in line, a passer-by passing across the street. A passenger on the fucking tram sucking on a tube, with this face, ugh. Without any features. Without any face. Like you. Cold-cut Man.

I don't want to be like that.

(*Terrified*.) Hey, what's-your-name? Oh, Jeez! Look! Tell me something.

DRIVER. What? What is it?

GINA. Tell me something, but so that she won't figure it out, you get it? No! Not like that, don't turn around! Is that my mother, sitting there in the back? Just tell me, because I don't want to turn around. Brunette, older.

DRIVER. Nooo! That's your boyfriend, the one you came here with! Your cousin!

GINA. That bitch is following me. It's just that I lost all her alimony yesterday, and now she wants to kill me for sure. It wouldn't surprise me if she was sitting right there behind us. I have to keep a close watch at all times, I can't turn around for one second, because she'll pop out of nowhere and say, Why don't you take care of it, that's your son.

DRIVER. Who is? Him?! (*He points at Blighty*.)

GINA. My son? Are you out of you fucking mind? I don't feel so good. Maybe I'm having the kid. Call Dr. Lubich.

DRIVER (*almost crying*). How? Your cousin took my phone!

GINA. Chill, chill, chill. If that's how it is, I can just hold it in. Hee hee. But relax. I'm just fucking around.

They drive.

DRIVER. Look, lady, that's no joke. When my wife gave birth, there were some complications. They had to tear out her asshole . . . Her bladder was damaged. How the woman suffers . . .

BLIGHTY (*now awake*). She doesn't have an asshole.

DRIVER. Of course she doesn't . . . But I was suggesting no such thing . . .

BLIGHTY. Gina doesn't have an asshole. She's not that kind of girl.

GINA. Shut your pie-hole, alright? Go back to sleep. Don't ruin it for two people engaged in refined conversation.

BLIGHTY. Shut up yourself. Don't come crying to me about how he's insulted you . . .

GINA. Goddamn fucking son of a bitch.

BLIGHTY. Turdy shit super-shitstorm. Pee-pee. Armpit.

DRIVER (*on the verge of losing it*). Stop . . . FOR THE LOVE OF GOD . . . People . . . Must you talk to each other like that, call each other names?! Carry on?! Have you no shame?! Lady, you're pregnant, you huff Crazy Glue, you curse, you stink up the car, that kid hears and sees all of it! It gets recorded in his fetal state! Then he'll say it, like when you have people over! The first words out of his mouth! God . . .

BLIGHTY. You hear that, Freddie Mercury? Give her a break, man, she'll calm down. She's a dumb Romanian, a simpleton. Her whole life she's been working away, material girl in a material world and all that: she's doesn't know how to behave around people. You see what you've done? He's nearly had a heart attack from listening to your bullshit.

GINA. Yours isn't any better!

BLIGHTY. Now that's just what I'm talking about . . .

GINA. No. No. No, and still no.

BLIGHTY. Right! Exactly!

DRIVER (*bursts into tears and stops the car*). Stop! I'm begging you . . . It's yours . . . I'm done! I'm done driving! I don't want to, I'm giving it to you . . . The car is yours . . . I'm giving it to you! I'm getting out . . . I'll go on foot . . . I want to take a walk. There's this forest here, that's the place for me, I'll find myself some old root and build a house in it . . . I'll carve out some plates, spoons, hangers, um, some musical instruments . . .

BLIGHTY. No, no, no, my dear, absolutely not. Stop whining. Calm down. Calm yourself this instant. We're under a tight deadline, too. We're trying to get there on time.

GINA. No, let him cry himself out, he needs the release. He has to let it go.

BLIGHTY. No, don't defend him.

GINA. Go ahead, now, cry, it's very cleansing. Now I, for example, when I had a bladder infection, you know how it is, I was moping around, I couldn't find a place to go, I just always felt like I had to pee. I'm running here, I'm dashing there. I'm letting it out on my legs! I'm sprinting, the 100-meter dash for Romanian women with bladder infections! I open my fly! I'm already all pissed! I sit on the throne and make three hot, triumphant little drops, and it feels just like someone's pricking me with needles. You know. Like my body's been tossed under a sewing machine. Sort of like an orgasm. Only worse.

DRIVER (*crying the whole time*). Detective, I owe the fact that I'm alive solely to myself, to keeping it cool, to my control, to the fact that I didn't provoke them, that the entire time I didn't react to their attempts to rob me of my mental faculties, because now I have no doubt about it . . . And then I saw a patrol car stopped by the side of the road. For a minute I was afraid it might be a mirage, that they were trying to drive me all crazy and insane, that they'd put it there, plotted against me, so it was like it was there to provoke me, to get me going. And then they were laughing at me, making fun of me . . .

BLIGHTY. You punk-ass motherfucker, you see what you've gotten us into? No, my friend, this is not how friends behave. What you're up to now, it's scandalous.

DRIVER. And then I don't even know, it just took a second. Despite the killers' attempts to terrorize me and dump it on me and instill in me a sense of guilt and responsibility for that patrol car and to persuade me to keep driving, I succeeded in turning off and driving straight for that patrol car.

POLICE OFFICER. What's the problem here? Why are you stopping?

DRIVER. I was driving too fast, Lieutenant, General, sir. You have to arrest me. I, I was, um . . . You can't see it back there, but there's a hill. I sped up at the bottom, I crossed the double solid, and I hit someone. You didn't know that, but I confess to everything, even more. I would like you to arrest me. I throw myself on the mercy of the court. Please arrest me, it's all I ask. I'll give you the details a little later . . .

BLIGHTY. Daaad . . . Dad, come back to the car . . .

POLICE OFFICER. What's that? What this all about? What's going on?

BLIGHTY. Everything is absolutely fine. We're a couple of poor, honest, Polish-speaking Romanians. Dad here has Alzheimer's. There's a whole plague of it in Romania: it makes it driving with him a real nightmare. He's not himself since they let him out of the camp, these horrific bad dreams keep reminding him, the trenches . . .

DRIVER. I didn't write down the badge numbers of those two police officers, but I'd guess it'd pretty easy to find them. One's not too tall, the other's taller, blond. If you ask me, those guys are guilty, and they should be suspended from duty for failing to provide assistance to an abducted person, and what's more, for collaborating with thieves and murderers, believing their nasty lies, as if I'd been in the trenches and lost my identity there.

POLICE OFFICER *(to Blighty)*. Is that a problem? Isn't it dangerous to let him drive?

BLIGHTY. He's doing just fine, General, sir. Is this the right way to Elbląg? That is, are we heading in the right direction? Because Dad's totally confused. My sister and me, we have no idea where we're going, and we're in a hurry to catch a ferry. To Romania, in fact. Actually, it's this coal barge, the *Advil*. Maybe you've heard of it?

POLICE OFFICER. But there's no coastline in Elbląg.

BLIGHTY. Of course not. Because it sails on a lake. Lake Elbląg.

DRIVER. A coal barge called the *Advil*. Awful name. Please locate that one as well. Maybe they're still on it.

Still driving. The Driver is driving, sobbing hysterically, and spazzing out behind the steering wheel.

BLIGHTY. STOP BAWLING!

GINA. Leave him alone . . .

BLIGHTY. He'd better stop, or else I'm going to start bawling.

GINA. Stop it. Let him cry it out, it helps.

BLIGHTY. No, Genie, because I can't work under these conditions. I can't stand it when a person is as hysterical as he is.

DRIVER. The feeble winter sun, like a crappy little coin, had long since fallen beyond the horizon. There were bodies of run-over dogs and animals cast all over the highway. Last year's ice cream ads, faded by children's lustful glances, swayed in the wind over the cheap bars. I saw the darkness. I touched it.

BLIGHTY. HEY, MAN. Listen to me. We're terribly grateful that you wanted to give us a ride. It's been a long time since we've seen so much kindness from a total stranger who really had no reason to help us out, that kind of sympathy in a tough situation, but who wanted to and did. Such human kindness and sympathy really means so much to us . . .

He starts to dig around in the mesh bag.

Now we have to get going. It's not far from here to the ferry. Your offer to give us a lift, you're doing that voluntarily, you didn't have to do that, but it was a huge help. Thanks to you, we will soon be back in our homeland. Romanians don't mince words, that's our motto. That's why we wanted to reward your goodness and kindness.

The Driver looks in disbelief at Blighty, who removes wads of bills and various other things from a plastic shopping bag.

BLIGHTY. I'm the Wonderful Wizard of Oz. I came here in disguise to see if people are good and do good deeds. You'll be rewarded to the tune of 5,000, paid in a lump sum. One, two, four, five. And my MP3 player as well. And three Euros. And sunglasses, or maybe not—I'll need these tomorrow. You know how they come in handy. Here you have the controls with the headphones. You download a bunch of stuff from the internet. You transfer it from your computer, and you can take 5,000 MP3s wherever you go. Anyway, there are a couple of CDs on there, but I don't know if you'll like them. Actually, I might have thought about it earlier; if I'd known I could have ripped you some, you know, some of that Neil Diamond, Benny Hill. Duran Duran. Monty Python.

So, we're out of here. Come on, Gina, get dressed. That's real money, no funny stuff. Buy yourself something nice. A Cuisinart. I recommend it. Me and Gina, we have one in Romania, and it's worth it. It bakes its own bread. Gina goes out early to the fields, gathers some grain. Then we mix it up in the Cuisinart and we have such fresh bread, with none of those E1939 or E1968 isotopes: now that's what I call LIVING.

GINA. Hey, are you nuts? I'm as tired as a second-day whore, and all I see are woods. Berry patches.

BLIGHTY. COME ON.

They walk away.

DRIVER. And Detective, the worst part was at the very end. He put a knife to my throat and demanded my money and my keys, and she pointed at me with a pistol she took out of her handbag, and the safety was probably off. They wanted to kill me and rob me. They demanded my valuables, all kinds of jewelry, home appliances. They were especially interested in a Cuisinart, which I don't own and have never owned, only my mother-in-law had one once, and I don't keep in touch with her. I don't know how they found that out. How did they know that? You know what I'm thinking is, they had to have followed me earlier. For years I've suspected someone was watching me. And then they fled into the forest without a word, without even thanking me. They didn't leave me any money, not a penny, not a red cent as thanks. And Detective, I would like it to be noted that if they're caught, I hope I'll be able to look them in the eye one more time. But I can't forgive them. I won't. I won't. Not ever. Did you write that down? I won't. Fine, then.

SCENE 1

Evening. Gina and Blighty are walking along the highway, crying, in a
total psychological meltdown.

BLIGHTY. Please. Please. Please. Don't rub up against me while you're
walking, I'm oversensitive to that. What? Why?
What do you mean, I gave him 5,000 and an MP3 player?!
What, like I just gave it to him? To who? To our friend with
the screw loose? You got to be kidding me. I gave it to him?
For free? But that guy was abby-normal! And you didn't say
anything while this was happening? What do you mean, I said
I'm the Wonderful Wizard of Oz? I said I was a wizard? Maybe
you'd say something like that, but me?

Actually, I remember feeling like a wizard, but it's not like I'd
just give something to someone because of that. And you let
me do it, you didn't say anything and just let me give him all
that stuff?! 5,000?! Have you lost your mind, woman? You
think I found it in my Christmas stocking? I worked my ass
off to make that. And I gave it to him? Maybe I sold it? Maybe
I sold it to him? No, that's crazy. That doesn't make any sense.

Where's that bag? Sorry. Gina. What kind of name is that, anyway? They couldn't think you up a better one? Are you guys
Indians? Peruvians? Regina? What's your last name, Salve? Hee
hee. Sorry. I have to hand it to myself, that in the biggest shit-
pile life has to offer, at rock bottom, I always manage to exude
a sense of humor.

No, come on. Let's calm down. Let's be serious. That's what
we need here, we need to explain a few things. So there was
this party, that's a fact. We got a little fucked up. I understand
that that's when I met you. But something was off with those
drugs. I don't remember a damn thing. You could tell me
whatever you want. But where did I get 5,000? Did I take it
out of my savings? Aha.

Impossible, no way. If I'd taken it out, I'd have remembered. And I gave it to him? All of it? And you let me? And there wasn't even ten złoty left?! Look in your bag, there's got to be something. I need some coffee. I need to get my head in the game, to take a shower. Give me a mirror or something. I have to be on set tomorrow at eight. And what about that MP3 player? I gave that to him, too? No way. I had everything on that, all my favorite songs. And where's my phone? What do you mean, you don't have it? Look in your bag, it has to be there. And my ID. What do you mean, it's not there?! Not there?! Give me that. It has to be in here.

And maybe you've fucked me over, huh? Come on, don't get all upset, I'm just asking. I don't know you, I'm laying eyes on you for the first time in my life. I don't trust anyone any more. I have to be at work tomorrow at eight, I have to be on set at eight, get it? Do you understand what that means? I have to be on set at eight, and if I don't fucking show up, it's going to be my fucking ass. This sucks. I don't believe it. Do you even have a job? Do you know what that means?

GINA. No.

BLIGHTY. Then where did you get the money for all those good times, huh? Maybe I gave it to you?

GINA. I don't know. I got it out of the ATM.

BLIGHTY. And it just landed there from out of the sky?

GINA. Nooo, maybe it was the alimony.

BLIGHTY. What alimony?

GINA. Well, I went to the ATM. I figured there wasn't anything there, I swear. But there was 500. So maybe that was the alimony, I guess. So I bought myself a hot dog and a couple other things, then that party . . .

BLIGHTY. Right, fine, but what alimony? Like, child support?

GINA. Well, yeah, child support.

BLIGHTY. And what the hell did you do with the child?

GINA. With what child?

BLIGHTY. I don't know, with your child. You said you had a kid, right?

GINA. Oh yeah, I did . . .

BLIGHTY. Oh yeah. Oh yeah. You have a kid.

GINA. I left him somewhere. Wait. So maybe I took him to preschool?

BLIGHTY. When?

GINA. I don't know. In the morning.

BLIGHTY. What morning? Which morning?

GINA. Well, yeah. Exactly.

BLIGHTY. That's right.

GINA. Day before yesterday, maybe. No, maybe yesterday, it was yesterday. No. Because I don't think it was today.

BLIGHTY. So, what? He's still there? Hah hah.

GINA. Listen, you have anything to drink?

BLIGHTY. Just relax, don't freak out. I'm just asking. I don't give a fuck, lady, I don't even know you.

GINA. I don't know, but how should I know? Maybe my mother picked him up. Sometimes she picks him up when I can't.

BLIGHTY. Well, that's just great.

GINA. Well then don't ask me questions when I can't do anything about it now.

BLIGHTY. You're right.

GINA. The main thing is that he doesn't get bored. All you have to do is turn on his "Heroes of Might and Magic" and he has fun. He mostly keeps to himself.

BLIGHTY (*starts to shout*). Exactly! Exactly! He keeps to himself! And I just got fucked out of 5,000, and that's that! Enough, goddammit, I've had enough. Enough with these parties, enough with the drugs, enough of those fucking awesome parties that end in such a fucking stupor I give 5,000 to some neurasthenic ass-backward grandpa. And I wake up dressed in a cardigan from the Salvation Army, pulled off some corpse back in '72, and it's just fucking swell. Since eight in the morning I've been pretending to be a Romanian who speaks Polish, and I'm talking about the detrimental effects of eating butcher's scraps all the time, only all of a sudden it turns out that I'm a Pole coming down, a fucking Pole coming down and speaking Polish. And I wake up in some field, on some berry patch in East Bumblefuck, on the border with Kazakhstan, in a Kazakh cardigan that reeks of moths, and with my teeth all done up with marker that I can't even wash off. And I have to be on the fucking set tomorrow at eight, because it just happens that I play Father Ted in a respected and beloved TV show. Father Ted. In top form, as always.

Pause.

BLIGHTY. But these drugs are really bad. We . . . I just want to ask you one more thing. It's very important. Maybe it's stupid, so pardon me. Did I, that is, you and me, did we have sex? I'm just asking.

SCENE 2

The Tasty Grub. The Bartender and Halina the Hatcheck Girl are watching TV. From outside we hear the approaching turmoil and commotion. Enter Blighty and Gina on the verge of a breakdown, all sweaty, on the edge of madness.

BARTENDER. We're sitting there minding our own, and just then I hear this sort of screaming, like a scuffle. So I say, Now what's it going to be, Bulgarian chicks shooting worms out their cunts and all screaming like that? And I go check it out. And then the door opens, and this two-man isolation ward walks in, I don't know, drunk or fucked up on something, or they escaped from the nuthouse, them and all their paper-or-plastic. They come in. Oh yeah, and that countess there is all pot-bellied. And yeah, so they come in.

Can I help you?

GINA. I would like a lot of boiling water. I'm having a baby. Have granny strip the bed.

BARTENDER. And she points to Halina. Granny! And she was tossing her handbag around. So I say, We don't have anything like that, boiling water. There's coffee, tea, we got borscht, French fries. Just what it says here.

GINA. I'll have the croquette.

BLIGHTY. No no no—she's such a kidder! None of that. None of that, if you ask me. Out of the question. Please excuse us for a moment.

Look there. Hold this. Turn around and look there, and hold this, and don't say a word, I'll do the talking. You stay here and look there and don't move.

I beg your pardon on behalf of this unstable individual. My friend is sort of coming down. She's not even really pregnant, you know. She just has this pillow stuffed in there, oh, hah hah. And stop laughing, stupid, because this isn't even funny any more. A psycho-junkie, this one. But those drugs'll fuck you up, if you'll forgive my saying so.

I'm terribly sorry, but something's happened, and I'm in a bit of a pickle. Might I kindly ask you ladies: what is this lovely town we find ourselves in?

BARTENDER. What town is this, and where are they! That's what he asks me!

Ostróda.

HAT-CHECK GIRL. It's Ostróda.

BLIGHTY. Oh, Ostróda. Really, it's lovely. So is that more to the south, the north, the east? Because I can't really place it.

BARTENDER. Well, it depends.

BLIGHTY. Uh-huh.

It depends. Quite right. You see, because we're in this unfortunate situation: we ended up here by accident. It's not our fault. We're from Warsaw, and we wound up here, well, it's just . . .

BARTENDER. Uh-huh. I'm from Warsaw, too. Halina, too, she's from Warsaw. We're all from Warsaw. We came here on vacation. We just got back from sledding.

BLIGHTY. Well then, there you have it. A fine thing, sledding. It's lovely weather for a sleigh ride together with you, as the poet says. You know, the great poet.

But to business, my ladies, because all joking aside, this occurrence, well, it occurred, that is, it's really unclear to me, hard to explain how it all happened. In fact, it might sound a bit unreal. In a word, I found myself here under mysterious circumstances, and tomorrow I have work at eight, but sadly I don't have my phone on me. And I have to call.

What this basically means is—I don't know how to prove this—I don't really look like this. I don't look like this. I was just fooling around, dressing up, having fun, and you know, it all ended badly, real . . . badly. I'm a professional actor. I play Father Ted in that TV show. I'm sure you've seen it, Father Ted, oh yes, that's me. I was wondering: What time is it?

BARTENDER. But, sir, this is a disguise, too. That there is Princess Diana in disguise, and I'm Danielle Steele. It's 10 p.m., as you can see right there on the clock.

BLIGHTY. 10 p.m. That can't be. No time to sleep before I have to be on set. What a fucking nightmare. Goddammit, Gina, do something. Say something to them. Tell them who I am. You know.

GINA. We'll have two orders of stew.

BLIGHTY. NOOOO!

HAT-CHECK GIRL. Hey, Roscoe!

BLIGHTY. No, come on, what do I need this Roscoe for? And who is this Roscoe, anyway? For the love of God, you ladies don't have any appreciation for the fix I'm in. And who is this Roscoe? What's he to me, this Roscoe? *People*! People. For the love of God. I'm Father Ted. Help a fella out, I have to be at fucking work tomorrow at eight.

BARTENDER. At eight, for what, collecting cans?

GINA. We Romanians are a feisty people.

BLIGHTY. Would you please shut up? Not a word—keep quiet. Turn
around. Turn around. Turn around now. Please shut up. You
left your kid at preschool. Now stay there and think it over,
whether that's a motherly thing to do. She left her kid at preschool. Three days ago. Went to get herself a hot dog. A psycho and a junkie, this one.

BARTENDER. And what did she say? That you're some kind of Romanians or something? Great.

GINA. But I'm sure my mom picked him up, for sure.

BARTENDER. The cheapest phone card is 15.70.

BLIGHTY. But I'm broke!

BARTENDER. 15.70.

BLIGHTY. Come on, lady, all I need is one call's worth. Just enough
to yell, Get me the fuck out of here!

BARTENDER. Roscoe! Come here! We have a bit of a problem.

BLIGHTY. LET ME MAKE A CALL! FUCK! ONE CALL! ONE
CALL! IT'S JUST A FEW CENTS!

BARTENDER. Just a few cents, sure, but the cheapest card is 15.70. I
don't know if you're some kind of troublemaker, a priest, or
even a Ted. That's how much the card costs, and that's money,
and it's not like any old head-case can mosey on over from the
funny farm and call wherever he pleases. That's what I said,
right, Halina? And then Roscoe came in.

ROSCOE. So what seems to be the problem here?

BARTENDER. It's right here. This is Father Ted. With his wife, the nun.
And their kid, the altar boy. Hee hee.

ROSCOE. Alright, what do you want?

BLIGHTY. Greetings, Mr. Roscoe, sir. So here's the deal: I'd like to
make one phone call, and these ladies here are all for it. They
just say I still have to check with you if it's OK . . .

ROSCOE. And you have to make such a ruckus?

BLIGHTY. Certainly not, but . . .

ROSCOE. And do you have to make such a ruckus?

BARTENDER. But what the hell, for an hour now this con artist's been telling us stories about how he's some rich actor from Warsaw, but he can't buy himself the cheapest phone card, because he can't spare the money. They're junkies or something. But I know that mug from somewhere. Hey, wise guy, you're the one who steals the eggs from my henhouse.

BLIGHTY. That's not true, I . . . Fuck you! To hell with you, to hell with you all! I fucking curse you! That your fucking microwave blows you all to hell!

SCENE 3

BLIGHTY. It's worse than Romania. A nightmare, a nightmare in waking life.
But that's poetry. I'm speaking poetry.

GINA. Getting back to the kid. But I'm sure my mom picked him up from preschool. When was that? Wait, the day before yesterday. Thursday. I took him to preschool. I definitely remember that, because he was just wailing, like, blaaaah. I swear. But did I pick him up? You don't know? I didn't say anything about that, that I picked him up?

BLIGHTY. Hold on, let me concentrate. I'm thinking about something else right now.

GINA. Try to remember. I didn't say anything?

BLIGHTY. I don't know, dear, because on Thursday I didn't know you.

GINA. True that, true that. Right. I think she must have picked him up, because she always picks him up, because, for example, I can't. You're right. And that's what happened. That's it. He was standing there and screaming. Boo hoo. What do you think? Maybe that's what happened. Maybe she wanted to spite me and didn't pick him up.

BLIGHTY. Does he have house keys, just in case?

GINA. He does.

BLIGHTY. So then he went home.

GINA. You think so? (*Pause.*)

He doesn't have keys, he's four years old. Idiot.

BLIGHTY. Sorry, but don't "idiot" me, we're not at that level of intimacy, pal. But you're kind of right, though: How could I just give someone 5,000? No way, there's no way. 5,000, you know how much money that is? For 5,000 people would eat their own shit, for that much you could buy a whole field with a house, a fence, a villa in Białystok.

GINA. Actually, I'm not even sure I dropped him off. It's quite possible that maybe he stayed at my mother's. Entirely within the realm of possibility. He plays "Heroes of Might and Magic," he likes his Legos. He'll manage to keep himself occupied.

BLIGHTY. Stop getting off the fucking point. Enough already, because tomorrow at eight I have to be on set, and that's the most important thing we have to do now.

GINA. I'm not making the call. Just get lost, alright? Don't even try to convince me, I'm not going to call. So that she can tell me what? I can say it myself. She tells me all kinds of shit. Yesterday I blew all the child support. She's not going to let that slide. She'll make me get a real job.

SCENE 4

Night. A field. A woman in smeared makeup, 40 or 50 years old, heavily slurred speech, stops her car, gets out, opens the trunk, takes out a bottle of vodka and drinks, then puts it back. Meanwhile, a couple of poor, Polish-speaking Romanians run up to her car, losing their shoes as they throw themselves on her hood.

BLIGHTY (*in tears*). Warsaw plates . . . Are you going to Warsaw?

WOMAN. Warsaw.

BLIGHTY. You miracle of God, you. The Almighty of the Universe, that's what you are. I called for you and you came. Promise me you're not a mirage! A miracle. Miracles happen. To Warsaw, how far is it from here?

WOMAN. Huuuh?

BLIGHTY. How far is it to Warsaw?

WOMAN. About a hundred kilometers.

BLIGHTY. A hundred! A hundred. That's what I was saying. A hundred kilometers is like, oh, it's as easy as taking a stick and beating the shit out of dog. We're rescued! Saved! Madame. Queen. You're beautiful. We're coming with you! We're coming with you! Oh, it's so warm in here! So nice! We're normal people! We just look like this. Please. We'll behave like cultured folk! No breaking wind!

WOMAN. Please. You're a godsend. This isn't even my car. It's a Cavalier. Press that there, and you're all set.

BLIGHTY. So my friend can come too, right?

WOMAN. What's it to me?

BLIGHTY. Come on, Gina, she's going to let you come along, too. I set it up. I vouched for you. She DOESN'T STINK. She just looks like that.

Driving.

BLIGHTY. So what's up? How's life? Weather's not so good this year. Terrible winter harvest this year.

Silence.

WOMAN. Of course. The weather. The pressure. Super-duper.

Silence.

BLIGHTY. And do you always drive this fast, Ma'am? To be honest . . . Perhaps you could go a little straighter?

WOMAN. But over there . . . If you see anyone coming at us the other way, you just let me know. I took my contacts out and put them somewhere over here, but I can see just fine. So? Where are you going? Students, you're students? What do you study? Don't worry about me, I'm not drunk. Don't worry about a thing, just let me drive.

BLIGHTY. We're not students, we're Romanians who speak Polish. We're lesbians, fags, Jews, we work for an ad agency. Like I was saying, you know how it is, we're going to Israel to plant trees, the goddamn people out here don't want to give us a ride, not one centimeter. I'm Father Ted from the Presbytery. I have to be on set at eight. I still have to get some sleep so as to be in shape tomorrow, have a bath.

WOMAN. And does one of you maybe have a driver's license?

BLIGHTY. Well, to be honest, um, no. Aaah. Maybe she has one, but I doubt it. Look out! . . . Jeez, lady, what are you doing?

WOMAN. Well, if you don't, what the hell do you want with me? I thought you did, and that's why you came along. Shit.
No, it's fine. Don't get upset, we'll just keep going. The Lord gaveth, the Lord taketheth away. No doubt about it . . . Or maybe I'll show you: here's the clutch, here's the shifter, and you're all set. Or no, I'll drive. It's a car, it's a ride, it's all on credit . . . Fine, cool, everything's under control. Fuck, I'll tell you. I'll tell you, but I'll tell you. You're so happy, so young, and this car cost 50,000. For 50,000 it can't be bad.

GINA. Sorry—this is an embarrassing question—but you got anything to eat?

WOMAN. Oh fuck. Hungary, Romania, Turkey, I know, really beautiful country. Everybody says, Romania's a mess, shit everywhere, sewage, Islam, kids eating shit from pine trees. That guy, the dictator, Cincinnati, he's in charge, and people eat rocks. But it's a great country, they have peppers and fruits, and vacations, and my husband and I go skiing there. Just great. You go. No things, no luggage, no credit cards, no money, you just keep going, you'll be free from all that food and all that crapping all the time. You have no idea what a mess it is.

GINA. You know, sometimes we find something in the garbage. These days people throw out such great stuff, like whole chickens, hot dogs. Garbage cans. Sometimes when I'm on my way to the garbage something tempts me, so, you know. So that when I take out the garbage, I'm in no hurry to let go of the bag.

WOMAN. That's right, they just throw it out. Garbage is a sacred thing. Once I even found a Secession lampshade. Everybody asks about it.

Silence.

GINA. Well that's all well and good. But I want to take a leak.

WOMAN. What? You can let it out wherever you want. This is my husband's Cavalier. I don't give a shit, I'd be glad. Adieu.

Pause. The Woman drives increasingly in zigzags. The Romanians are starting to worry.

BLIGHTY. Hold on there, Countess. You know, you're a great driver. A fine conversationalist. But if you were to bust out some coffee, we'd be grateful, huh?

WOMAN. What? You can't tell me what to do, sweetie, because I picked you up, because I thought you had driver's licenses. So no complaints.

They keep driving in a zigzag.

BLIGHTY. But you see, the coal barge *Advil*, which is supposed to take us certain places, including Israel, is sailing soon . . . I have to be on set tomorrow at eight, and you're really going out of your way with these zigzags. And it's just that we'd prefer to live, which is just a matter of . . . A couple days ago my friend here left her kid at preschool. To this day he's probably sitting there, playing with his blocks.

GINA. And why did you have to remind me, asshole? Too late. I'm reminded.

BLIGHTY. He's sitting there, no bedtime story, no cap, in undies that need changing. It's just tragic. We're going to rescue him. If we don't get back she's going to get told off by her mom like you've never seen, boy.

GINA. Asshole. Stupid prick.

WOMAN. But hold on there, now, kids, and listen. I'm not having anything to eat, because it's a fact that me, I'm feeling a little fucked up. I admit it, I'm fucked up, but there's no sense you getting out. No, because this is wild Polish wilderness, there are marshes out there. Something will come up, like a gas station, civilization. Then you can get out, but here, I just don't have the heart to let you go.

She takes a bottle out from under her legs and drinks, and she passes it on.

WOMAN. Bottoms up, hah.

BLIGHTY. Lady, I can't believe you. Keep your head in the game! What the fuck is that, no bottoms-up now, just get some fucking focus, because my nerves are shot. Me, an old Romanian who's seen a thing or two. Where the hell are we? Białowieska Forest? Stop the car. I said, stop the car!

WOMAN (*stops with a screech of the tires; it is the middle of the forest, and there isn't a single light or sound*). Go ahead. Walk into the forest. We aim to please. All you had to do was say so. Send me a text message tomorrow or sometime, if you find some mushrooms.

Hah hah.

They keep driving; the woman drinks straight from the bottle.

WOMAN. Just a second, someone's calling me.

The phone is ringing; she answers.

Yeah. Yeah. Yeah. And. And. Nooo, I'm not drunk. I'm driving. With my friends, if you have to know. What are your names?

BLIGHTY. Laszlo Shambo. And this is Regina. Last name Salve.

WOMAN (*into the phone*). Regina and Shmeges, my friends. No. No, I'm not crazy. They're just very nice, easygoing, cool young people. No, I'm not drunk. Come on! You've been waiting for me for three hours? No, I'm not drunk. And who's that talking in the background? Nobody? Is that her? Well you don't have to be all secretive about it, some girl just dropped in to play around on the computer, and you're talking for hours on the telephone, and she's getting bored, naked and sad, and cold, catching a chill, so go to her, go lick her cunt. No, I'm not drunk. I'm not. And maybe I am, so what if I am? I don't know where I am, because there's no signs here, to tell the truth. But there's some field, some woods, actually. Branches and blueberries: maybe it's Norway? I'll be there presently, you go ahead and make me some dinner. Dinner. You burnt it and used too much salt. So it's burnt. And too salty. But that's the way I like it. Because if I don't fucking kill myself, I might come home very hungry. Bye. Adieu.

BLIGHTY. Gina, you hear? We'll be there soon. Not long now. I'll make it to the set. Could I borrow that phone? I have to make a call.

WOMAN. Watch the hands. Sorry about my husband. He's terribly worried I'll fuck up his car. I get it. His lover is there, he was supposed to have a romantic evening, she was making up a class after school, she changed her diapers and came right over. You know how it goes. It's true love, he has her on the phone pretending he's Valentino. He's all furious, pacing from window to window with his limp prick, and he says to her, Sit down here, love, you need to trim your nails. Sorry. And he stands there in that window and shits his pants that his Cavalier is going to pull up, first one wheel, then another, and I'll carry in the rest in a plastic bag. Hah hah.

Hee hee hee.

AAAAAAAAA!!!

There's an accident; the car hits something in the dark.

The Woman, bloody, is lying on the airbag, and nothing has happened to the Romanians. A wild boar is lying in front of the hood.

BLIGHTY (*outraged*). Now what? What the hell is this?

WOMAN (*losing consciousness*). Hedgehog.

BLIGHTY. A hedgehog . . . A hedgehog! I'll show you a hedgehog. Hey, lady, come on, wakey wakey. Jeez, the Countess has bought the farm. Now we're really out on our asses, in the middle of nowhere, in the goddamn sticks.

GINA. So, give her first aid.

BLIGHTY. Me? And you think it's as easy as apple pie? I don't have time; I'm in a hurry. She's probably done for, right?

GINA. How do you know?

BLIGHTY. Is she alive? She's alive. Life's the first thing. She'll be fine now, she has charisma, see for yourself. She sort of has a mustache. The kidder.

GINA. Maybe you're right. There's no point now. What are we doing?

BLIGHTY. You see her phone anywhere? I have to call and let them know I might be late to the set.

GINA. Maybe it got fucked up.

BLIGHTY. What?! No way.

He throws out a smashed cell phone, looks under his legs, pulls out the Woman's bottle of vodka and drinks deeply.

You want a swig? There's a little left. I can't get fucked up, because I have to have my shit together tomorrow.

Come on, let's take her watch. You have yourself a lovely watch, dear, a Seiko. Those little diamonds are the height of fashion. Don't think badly of me; I'm desperate. 12:15. That can't be; maybe it's stopped. So it's around eleven, so there's still a chance I'll make it.

He puts on the watch, digs around in the Woman's purse.

Alright, she has a purse, so maybe she has some cash. I need to buy a phone card. No, you dig around in there. I'm just sick about this, morally. I've never stolen anything in my life. Except maybe for some dalliances in preschool. You know. No, give it here. I'll look. I can't trust you: you're a nutcase and a junkie. Gum—we can split that. Birth-control pills—that's gross—you want them?

GINA. Get that away from me.

BLIGHTY. Well, take them, they'll give you great hallucinations.

GINA. Leave me alone, you jerk. Take them yourself: we definitely need to cut off your gene pool.

BLIGHTY. So take them. You can use them. Aw, fine, I was only joking. Anyway, this bitch has already sucked down half. An old drunk hag like her, and you can still call her Miss Jackson if you're nasty? That's gross.

GINA. Will you shut up?! I can't listen to you any more, you idiot. Fuck off, and put down her purse. If she's already lying there dead don't rummage around in a corpse's purse.

BLIGHTY. What. Maybe she's not fucking around, maybe she takes them for acne? You think? Calm down. Makeup, scribblings, markers, eyeshadow: I'll take that for you, it's all good. Trust me, you could use it: you don't know what you look like, but I see. If you don't want it, give it to someone else. Wait, maybe she has another phone. There's a wallet. 30 złoty. She has 30 ZŁOTY! Jackpot. When we get to a gas station we'll buy ourselves some Q-TIPS.

To the Woman.

You douche bag. You've drunk all of it. I'll show you.

SCENE 5

The ditch. They get out of the car and start to hobble through the total darkness.

BLIGHTY. No mother, no father, alone at last to the bitter end. Well, I'm on board. Some drunk hag picks us up, hits a boar, but of course there are boars in the forest. He could have attacked us. But people have no sense of responsibility. She could have killed us. People are hopeless. I have to call, or there's going to be trouble.

GINA. Would you just shut up? Shut up, shut up. That's all I ask.

BLIGHTY. Fine, great, you shut up. I hate you. I always hate the girls I screw when I don't love them. It's disgusting, disgusting, sex without love. It's porn. Strip down and bend over.

GINA. What? What did you say? I didn't fuck you. I already told you. I didn't fuck you.

BLIGHTY. And how can I believe you, how can I believe you, why should I? Lady, you have amnesia since I don't know when:

now you remember, now you don't, the Lord giveth, the Lord taketh away. How do you know if you slept with me or not, when I don't even know? Please. Don't make me laugh. I had a suspicion I slept with you because now I feel like shit, and it's probably because of that, because of that, that's how I know. I hate mechanical, industrial sex with strange women for whom I don't even feel contempt, just blinding zero and zilch. Some strange body under my hands, it may as well be some strange animal's body, a strange, faceless body, bam-bam, and after it's all over you just lie there. You lie there. Breathing. Your breath like a passing car, like a siren going by, like a shadow falling. It's all so ridiculous. Spit and sperm dry up like rain. Because those are the juices of love, the juices of love. Spit! Sperm! Egg whites! And water mixed with potato flower!

GINA. I didn't fuck you. No way, no way. I told you. Definitely not.

BLIGHTY. Of course we did! You took advantage of my being unconscious and unarmed!

They walk in silence.

BLIGHTY (*he can't stand it*). And what a lovely mother you are. You abandoned your kid. Great, don't say a word about it, I prefer not to think about it. Fucking kid at preschool day and night, even the cleaning ladies have gone home, the janitors have gone home, and he just sits there in a puddle of urine and smashes his Hot Wheels. Because what else is he supposed to do, what now? All the toys reek of him. OK, OK. Time out. If I cross the line, you let me know.

Pause. They're walking; no one drives by.

BLIGHTY. Sorry, but I have to say something. Because we're going to fall asleep. And we're going to freeze. I'm cold. This cold is driving me nuts. How did they stand it in these woods back in the day?

GINA. So lie down.

BLIGHTY. Very funny. Veeery funny.

GINA. Don't you think I'm cold, too? Cold as a cold cunt.

BLIGHTY. So what, now you want to blackmail me into giving you my jacket? No way. Though I'd probably hit the afterlife in about 15 minutes. You could take part in my beatification.

Pause.

So you think we're going to die? Now? Just like that?

GINA. Yes.

Pause.

BLIGHTY. Such hopelessness. What a bummer.

But something is telling me to give up the drugs, not to fool around with that crap any more. It's everyday stuff for you junkies, but for a normal person it's really destructive. And please. Someone tells me: it's a costume party, it's called "Poor Whore Score," Eva's inviting you, in Mokotów. So I dress up, I color my teeth with marker, I put on some stinky rags, and the cab driver doesn't want to take me. I get there. I meet this chick, namely, YOU, and it's supposed to be a good time. People are dancing, someone offers me something they've cooked up, and then BAM: Operation Romania! I'm a Romanian! I'm on my way somewhere, I'm handing out my money! Me, decent Father Ted, a bachelor. You're the one who talked me into it. Why did you remind me? Now I'm pissed off for nothing, and everything's come back to me. Late for the shoot— check. Going to die—check. But not like this. This is crazy.

To be honest, in spite of it all, I'm afraid that I won't receive eternal salvation. That is, God knows that theoretically I was more good than bad, and in the best light I was OK. But then the Catholic Church starts fucking me over with its gospels, confessions, fasts, and I'm screwed. Me. They fuck Father Ted.

GINA. Oh, Jesus—I see a light.

BLIGHTY. Impossible. It can't be.

GINA. Is that a house?

BLIGHTY. A house! We're saved! Warmth! Tea! Not to mention food! A clean bed! I'll call Warsaw, tell them I'm running a little late, but I'll be there for sure.

SCENE 1

Blighty and Gina are standing in front of the door of an unfenced house, which is built in the middle of an open field. They're banging hard on the door:

Help! Help! Hello! Save us! Open the fucking door!

Finally we start to hear the sounds of the opening of many locks, bolts, chains, more and more of them, and the head of an unshaven Geezer pokes out.

GEEZER. Is that you?

BLIGHTY. Yeah, it's us. In the flesh.

GEEZER. Are you alone??

BLIGHTY. Of course we're alone.

GEEZER *(removes the last chain)*. You sure?

GINA. Yes, we are.

GEEZER. Come in. Just hurry.

> *Inside the Geezer's house. He collects garbage. Everything's dirty: two tubs, shoes, all the garbage in the world. The television is on.*

GEEZER *(looking them over)*. Father Ted? But it's the priest!

BLIGHTY. Yeah, that's me. I'm the guy who plays him . . .

GEEZER. What an unexpected and pleasant surprise! At night—at such an hour! Father Ted! At last! The priest has finally come to see me. This is the best, a real pleasure. And this woman, this girl, who is she?

BLIGHTY. My friend, an acquaintance.

GEEZER. An angel?

BLIGHTY. Yeah. She used to be a prostitute, a junkie. You know how it is, my son. I took her in—we did.

GEEZER. But where's your cassock?

BLIGHTY. What cassock?

GEEZER. It would be pretty cold in the cassock, eh? It's howling balls out there. You came in your civilian clothes.

BLIGHTY. Alright, old man, give it a rest. I'm blushing. You have something to eat, grandpa? Something warm to drink? I'm freezing my ass off. My girl, too.

GEEZER. No, no, I don't. I was hoping . . . I was waiting for the priest to help me do the shopping. I can't go out.

BLIGHTY. You can't? Why not?

GEEZER. Don't ask, Father—you don't want to know. As soon as I go out, they come, they come. I'm walking, I'm walking, and I hear scratch-scratch, they're coming. They turn the locks, and they hurt me, they hurt me. They come in and hurt me. Oh, Father, you see. I can never go out, because I have to come right back.

BLIGHTY. You have a telephone, gramps?

GEEZER. Somewhere over there. I had one. But they were calling.

He lies down on the bed.

Here are the marks. This is where they hurt me. This is where they hurt me. Here are the marks from when they hurt me. They come, they come and do such terrible things. I can't leave here for a moment, not for one moment, because they come right away, right away. And they hurt me.

BLIGHTY. Now that's just great.

GINA. Could we maybe sleep here, grandpa? We'll fall flat—on our faces. We came on foot, all the way from Kazakhstan. From Uzbekistan. We just want to get some sleep. We won't cause any trouble.

GEEZER. Get some sleep. 40 winks. Seems, it seems . . . For Father Ted, always. But you have to be careful. They don't sleep. You have to be on your guard. But maybe they'll see, they'll notice it's you, Father Ted, and they'll come to their senses.

SCENE 2

Blighty and Gina are lying on a bed, covered in rags. They look at the watch, chewing gum, in a claustrophobic room filled with garbage and a gurgling sink. Gina is playing with some string.

(The watch is the same one they took from the Woman.—Trans.)

BLIGHTY. Well? So? You got what you wanted. It's your party, your own private "Poor Whore Score" costume party, which cost me 5,000 and my job. Let's have fun! I don't know, let's play a word game.

GINA. A word game.

BLIGHTY. Don't repeat what I say. I'm not going to make it to the set. I've lost my faith. They'll wait, they'll call, there's going to be this big scandal. They're going to kick my ass out of there, that's for sure. And they'll pick up some ridiculous actor. They'll tell our viewers that Father Ted was in a fire and had plastic surgery and now he looks totally different! What a mess! I'm totally fucked!

GINA. Fucked.

BLIGHTY. Where's my cell phone? Where did I leave it? Maybe you jacked it? No. Better you think about your kid. Leave a kid at preschool. What a moral accomplishment that is. Better not to have kids at all. What's his name? It's a boy, right?

Silence.

Well, say something. I'm falling asleep. Grandpa will come in the night with a metal pipe and will think we've come here to hurt him, and he'll kill us. I'll keep watch. But let me ask you: Why do I have to keep watch? What about you? Why, in spite of everything, do I have to be the responsible one? Who the hell are you? What do you do? Professionally?

GINA. I'm a life artist.

BLIGHTY. Oooh. That's exactly what I thought. And what else do you do?

GINA. Like I know? Not so much.

BLIGHTY. Right.

GINA. I used to fill out invoices . . .

BLIGHTY. I need to call my agent. He's going to be pissed.

GINA. My mother set it up. But I went there with a hangover, and I those numbers just tripled before my eyes. Because there were these columns, rows, boxes, and there were these sluts sitting there in their festering sweaters, which they'd crocheted and measured out against me. I'm a hundred percent sure that in those hours of work they put my tits through the photocopier and looked over how they came out.

Oh yeah, and I worked at this stand during the summers. I fried up kiełbasa, fries, you know, by the square meter, me and a hundred-and-fifty-liter vat of three-year-old cooking grease. That's me, Miss Oil. But I always jacked something, ten złoty maybe, and that evening I had ten złoty, TEN ZŁOTY. And I went to the club for a brew, all proud of myself, and I sat there with my snout all red like canned Spam. Miss Kiełbasa, and the oil dripped from my hair onto the table, and my mother said: finally, finally, finally something, finally.

BLIGHTY. Well that really sucks. You have to do something with yourself, take something up. Or maybe you just don't have any talent.

GINA. So then I hang out, I go out and hang out, I go in and go out. Generally I just fuck around with various dickheads like you, though I don't really want to. I just go to their place because I want to get a decent night's sleep, no one screaming bloody murder in my ear when I wake up with a hangover. You know, we have a studio apartment, 17 meters. If someone slams a teapot or a pan, that's no joke when you're hung-over, when you're dying and your kid brings his toy piano to the bed and starts to bang out "Three Little Indians" or "Baa Baa Black Sheep." And they think I'm going to their place because I want to have the greatest sex of my life in 17 positions and no mercy. Even if they don't give a shit, they still have to stick it in and pull it out at least once, or else no, no, no, it doesn't count. And in the morning it's: Oh God, where are your clothes, you must be in a hurry, I sure am, are you still drinking that tea? If you want, I'll get you a thermos!

Hah hah. Hah hah. And now I'm on the tram, on my way, just like that. I run up the stairs, I open the door. Where were you?!

Look what you're doing! That's your child! Mommy, Mommy, who was Copernicus's father? A better question would be, who was *his* father, right?

God. Who else could it be?

All day he was playing "Heroes"! And finally he pissed himself. I'm sorry, but I'll take the vacuum. Mommy, baa baa black sheep! Baa baa black sheep! Have you any wool? Yes, sir, yes, sir, three bags full! Mommy! Mommy!

But the way I read it, that sheep peddled its ass, too.

No, you'd better listen how he learned to play a hymn on his toy piano! Listen! Every verse! Now backwards! Go get your piano and play for mommy. Not there, dummy. And just look at yourself! Don't you have a home? Did you sleep in a dumpster?

BLIGHTY. Well, I can't help you there, sweetheart. But that really does suck that you act that way; you should quit it, meet someone who won't treat you like a whore. And have you been tested for HIV? You should. Let's be serious: you have to find yourself a guy who, maybe he loves you, maybe he doesn't, but you can't keep tearing yourself up. Maybe you have some kind of subconscious complex; maybe it's caused by a bad relationship with your father.

GINA. God our Father.

BLIGHTY. I, personally . . .

GINA. Could you lend me five złoty?

BLIGHTY. Me? To you?

GINA. My kid is really dirty. All the other women have their normal kids. Why do I have a dirty kid, and not a normal one?

BLIGHTY. I hate random sex with women who just think of me as Father Ted. And they think that this way they're affirming their existence in the world, that they've slept with me. I slept with Father Ted, I'm no longer a nobody, la la la. I slept with Father Ted, girls, it was such a turn-on, I thought I'd go crazy.

GINA. I can't go back. She'll kill me.

BLIGHTY. I hate it. But the worst part is that they always pull me in with some ruse: we have some albums you'd love, we have a collection of rare stamps, we have various flavors of tea. Come on. These shelves are from Ikea. We have this, and we have that, isn't it COOL?

GINA. I have to take a piss.

She goes into the bathroom.

BLIGHTY. We have this, and we have this, and here we have some titties. Don't you peek, now. There's this, and that. And these are our stockings: let's throw them there. And oh, who do you play again, is it this one, or is it that one, because now I'm not sure? And here we have a scar, it's awful, simply an awful scar, but that's fate. Here you have it, look it over, there's this and there's that, and I'm going to take a bath. Oh, I'm back already. Well? Not bad, eh? So now what? You're sleeping in your clothes, are you insane? Come on, I'll show you where you're going to sleep. And to tell you the truth, I'm going to sleep there, too, with you, can you believe it? Watch. Me and you, you and me, and me and Father Ted, because you're totally wrong that I'm just some bartender at Café Café, just some girl at the newspaper stand on the way to the university. It's absurd that you'd think I'm just anybody, since I'm not just anybody. On the contrary, because you're here and I know you.

And I lie there like a burnt-out whore in a burnt-out house.

I wonder if I left the iron on.

I wonder which tram to take home.

What fucking Romania is this? What solitude.

Oh, you've already shot your wad. That's actually a good thing. I'm overjoyed. Now I'm going to sleep. Oh, I'm up already. You've left already? Where have you gone? The girls will be here any minute to see you. They say you're terrible for me, just terrible! And that a girl like me! And they say, if you're going to be like that, well!

And I take the tram. There I go. No mother. No father. Alone till the end of the line.

And now they've fucking fired my ass. No—they will fire my ass, in three hours. I'm nobody. I'm finished.

In a fresh burst of euphoria, he stands at the bathroom door.

Gina! Gina? Hey.

Now I know what your problem is. I just got it, it's real easy.

GINA (*trying to tie herself a noose*). Yeah?

BLIGHTY. Just don't get offended. You haven't found love! It's as simple as that! It's just that nobody loves you! Nobody loves you, and that's why you're so unhappy. You screw those guys who don't love you, and it's pointless, it's empty, it doesn't mean anything. Love is the most important thing in the world, having someone who won't tell you to fuck off in the morning. Well, you know. Gina? Love will cleanse you.

Hey, now, what are you doing in there?

You taking a bath? What for?

Come out. I don't want to sit here alone. I'm afraid. You went into the bathroom by yourself, and you left me here.

I won't peek.

What are you taking a bath for?

I'm not going to fuck you, and that's that, even if you scrub yourself with boiling water.

Hey, Gina!

I was just kidding, moron.

Open the fucking door.

Open the door!

He pulls on the doorknob; the door opens.

Gina, who in the meantime has hanged herself, is hanging in the middle of the bathroom.

BLIGHTY. Now what have you done?! What did you do that for?!

How could you?! What is this? What's this? Get down from there this instant. AAAAAH!

GINA. So I hanged myself.

BLIGHTY. So just go on hanging, because I'm out of here.

GINA. Fuck no, you can't just leave me here by myself.

BLIGHTY. Save it. I'm gone.

And what's next, and what I'm writing, what would happen then: Blighty runs out, and Gina cuts herself down with the pocket knife and runs after him. Along the way they knock down the horrified Geezer, in his long johns. Praise the Lord, we're rushing to catch our ferry!

The coal barge Advil *sails up on the snow. They run onto its deck, where the Romanian crew and the passengers greet them enthusiastically: Finally, finally! They hand out candy wrappers and flyers for language schools, and everyone kisses them on the hand. An ecstatic prom of welfare recipients. The participants eat branches and dirt. They hold droopy old balloons in their hands, and they sing shrill Romanian songs. The waiter says to Blighty: Mr. Bułacz, you do us a great honor. Specially for you and your wife we have prepared an entire pepper stuffed with butcher's scraps! Would you like a taste?*

BLIGHTY. Of course, but I have to wash my hands. I've been on the road all day.

He goes into the bathroom. Gina is hanging there.

MAŁGORZATA SIKORSKA-MISZCZUK

LOOSE SCREWS

> Much meaning has come to my life
> through the absurd.
>
> Prof. Arrigno Piperno

CHARACTERS

VICTORIA	A most unusual woman, unique 24/7, faces a dilemma
MR. BLEH	Prime Minister-for-Life, Victoria's itinerant lover, in private her husband
99 CENT	A terrorist from Kuyavia
ZACHAR	A terrorist blindly devoted to 99 Cent and, it turns out, also blind in both eyes
THÉOPHILE GUM	A simple inspector-type who has given up on life
UNCLE ANTONI	A relative of the most unusual woman, an ancient Roman Doctor of the Vomitarians (*vomitum ergo sum*)
PROFESSOR SAFIRE	A luminary, without whom we would make a mess of our language
HANS	a mendacious Witness of History, a devious insurance agent
GHOSTS FROM OUT THE WINDOW, INCLUDING JOHN, THE WHORE, CHARLIE	
VOICE, POLISH, SPEAKING FOR POLAND	

TRANSLATED BY BENJAMIN PALOFF

1.

A bed. On the bed, Victoria. Enter Mr. Bleh.

VICTORIA. Mr. Bleh comes home from work. It's night.

At work he has had to:

Lie,

Kill,

Commit adultery,

Bear false witness,

Disrespect his parents,

Have another God before the One,

Etcetera.

The list may be incomplete.

Mr. Bleh sits down heavily at the edge of the bed. He looks at me as I poke fragmentarily out from under the blanket. This unfullness of mine reminds him of a poem about an ear that at the moment I have no intention of reciting.

Mr. Bleh sighs heavily. His worries have to do with an insurance company.

MR. BLEH. Let me pose you the following question, Victoria. I have received a letter from the insurance company. In the letter they ask me whether I wish to recalculate my premium.

Which means, Victoria my dear, do I consent to pay more for my life insurance than I did last year. If not, and I die, or someone kills me—which would amount to the same thing—they will have a pretext not to give you the money, or else less than they promised. If, on the other hand, I agree, I will have to pay Those Thieves even more than I did last year, even though when I die or someone kills me—which, as I mentioned, comes to one and the same—I cannot be certain whether you will be indemnified.

That is why I am sitting here heavily at the edge of the bed with the feeling that no matter what I do, I'm screwed. That is why I have a question for you, actually, a request: Could you screw me as well?

VICTORIA. Meanwhile I, plunged into the abyss of sleep, am lying here, rosy, panting lightly. Fresh breath like a child's is subtly traversing my lungs and bronchial tubes. It seems as though the Pitfalls of Life and the dilemmas of sex and insurance do not in the least penetrate the interior of my rosy ear, with its invisible, though efficient, Eustachian tube. I am convinced that Mr. Bleh is now thoroughly moved by my sleep.

MR. BLEH. Sleep, Victoria, and dream your innocent dreams, and I'll make do myself.

VICTORIA. But Mr. Bleh does poorly when he thinks he'll do himself and not me, for it is I who is dreaming this dream.

Victoria kneels. Enter 99 Cent. He aims a gun at her.

VICTORIA (*to 99 Cent*). Why did I allow myself to be lured in the night into a ruined house, to kneel before a terrorist?

99 CENT. A terrorist from Kuyavia, no less. You couldn't have done worse.

VICTORIA. I believe you. What new abomination is this?

99 CENT. Hah, hah. Why do you think I put the gun to your head? Count to three.

VICTORIA. One. Two. My voice breaking, I go on: Three! . . .Only the Silence in the dilapidated house at night remains the very same unblemished Silence.

99 CENT (*mockingly*). Hah, hah. And now keep counting, to six!

VICTORIA. Four. Five. I cringe. Six. It's like before, that is, Nothing Happens.

99 CENT. Hah, hah. And now keep counting, to nine.

VICTORIA. The merciless Terrorist from Kuyavia ordered me to count to a hundred. When the shot rang out, I finally woke up. It was 9:17 in the morning. If Mr. Bleh had not given himself over to onanism, I would not have had to pull out the gray hair that appeared at my temple like the fruit of that terrible night.

99 CENT. It's not your first gray hair. Victoria, don't twist the facts.

VICTORIA. When a figure from your dream doesn't want to disappear, it means it's happening for real.

2.

Victoria and Mr. Bleh, together on the bed.

MR. BLEH. To recover a sense of reality, the best thing is to enter the flow of life, to enjoy the benefits of the ritual of a meal together. No, I wouldn't say that. Victoria no longer shares her dreams with me. Victoria, come to breakfast.

VICTORIA. Mr. Bleh, the Prime Minister, is hungry. Good governance is exhausting, and though the wellspring of Mr. Bleh's soul and brain is his love of fatherland (a wellspring that is itself inexhaustible), Mr. Bleh's remaining organs have their own reasons not to expire.

MR. BLEH. For breakfast I would like Kuyavian bran.

VICTORIA. I am prepared to furnish Mister Bleh with bran, but at the same time I stand before a dilemma: should I be bitter, or not?

MR. BLEH. For breakfast I would like Kuyavian bran.

VICTORIA. I have Mazovian, Podlachian, Mazurian, whatever your heart desires.

MR. BLEH. I would like Kuyavian. The best comes from unspoiled Kuyavia.

VICTORIA. I don't know how to tell you this, Bleh, but there's a problem with breakfast.

MR. BLEH. That's no good, Victoria. It troubles me greatly.

VICTORIA. I don't know why you're so troubled about Kuyavian bran, but the reason we have none is as follows: Kuyavia has attacked us.

MR. BLEH. What us?

VICTORIA. Our country.

MR. BLEH. Oh! That doesn't worry me. I'm glad! What's important is for us to have breakfast together.

VICTORIA. What about Kuyavia?

MR. BLEH. A province in revolt. Wonderful. What other kinds of bran do we have?

VICTORIA. How about Mazovian?

MR. BLEH. Mazovian might be polluted. No doubt they want to kill me as well?

VICTORIA. You, and The President of the U.S., and they want to wipe Poland off the map.

MR. BLEH. Wonderful, wonderful. I judge the situation to be critical and unforeseeable. Couldn't be better.

VICTORIA. That being the case, let's have Podlachian.

MR. BLEH. Podlachian would be fine. I am a good leader for this country. The last one was an idiot. The one before him was an idiot, and the one before him was also an idiot. The first ones were whittled out of potatoes. That being the case, I will look after Poland. You must eat something.

POLAND (FEMALE VOICE) (*solemnly*). Stop looking after me.

VICTORIA. You don't have to look after me.

MR. BLEH. My day's gotten off to a terrible start, as far as breakfast is concerned. But, I repeat, I will look after Poland, regardless of the situation, to the death.

POLAND (FEMALE VOICE) (*solemnly*). I'll manage quite fine without you, no offence.

MR. BLEH. Even if Poland herself were to come here and say, "Don't worry about be," I wouldn't listen.

POLAND (FEMALE VOICE) (*solemnly*). You're out of line. Think about your wife's anatomy.

VICTORIA (*to Mr. Bleh*). And if Poland were to say to you, "Don't worry about me, just think about your wife's anatomy"?

MR. BLEH. The fact of the matter is that rarely does a politician have a wife with such beautiful anatomy as yours, Victoria. Of course, I'm not saying this on the record, which would be madness on my part!

VICTORIA. Hee hee. And here is our bran, Bleh.

MR. BLEH. Let's dig in, or, to be precise, let's dig our spoons in, Victoria.

3.

VICTORIA. But the words that had been uttered germinated in Mr. Bleh's mind. He recognized that he seldom took advantage of my anatomy, and that this might have historical consequences, for he is a creature of history, and an outstanding one at that.

4.

Victoria, in front of the door to the bathroom.

VICTORIA. I can't go into the bathroom.

The situation is tense. Terrorists from Kuyavia have declared war on the world. They want to wipe Poland off the map and have The President of the U.S. and Mr. Bleh shot.

(*to 99 Cent*) Are you waiting, too?

99 CENT. I was born in a tiny village not far from Żerniki, in southwestern Poland. We don't have oil reserves there; rather, the land's wealth is in its black earth. My parents grew sugar beets, and thanks to the beets my childhood passed like a fairytale. I had my own yacht, a golf course, private tutors. I collected Inca figurines and Chinese vases.

That's all I can say for now. For your own protection, observe me from a distance.

Here.

He hands Victoria a pair of opera glasses.

VICTORIA (*to herself*). I will maintain my distance for as long as I am able.

She observes 99 Cent from a distance through the opera glasses.

99 CENT. I swear, all our comrades have been holding their breath, and what have you been up to all this time, Zachar?

ZACHAR. I'm in the bathroom.

99 CENT. But you know that we're all waiting for you to finish assembling the terrible bomb we're going to drop on the American President.

ZACHAR (*from the bathroom*). I know you're all waiting. I have the bomb right here.

99 CENT. Spies from all over the world are trying to get a bead on our hideout in Kuyavia. Most of all those dogs from the Mossad. And also Inspector Théophile Gum from the station in Łaszczów. I went to grade school with him.

ZACHAR. Gum will die first. He stole my girl.

99 CENT. Insha'Allah.

ZACHAR. Insha'Allah. I just learned to say "Insha'Allah." Insha'Allah, insha'Allah, insha'Allah him in the gob.

99 CENT. Zachar! You know that I announced over the Internet that you're constructing a bomb?

ZACHAR. That's fucking awesome, I swear.

99 CENT. The whole world has been holding its breath. They're scared shitless. Soon they'll suffocate, and there won't be anyone left for us to fuck up.

ZACHAR. Damn, 99 Cent, you crack me up.

99 CENT. Do you have a lot left to do??

ZACHAR. Just have to connect the red wire to the green.

99 CENT. Excellent. They're showing global panic on the TV.

ZACHAR. From what?

99 CENT. I sent a message over the Internet, "just have to connect the red wire to the green." The American President is crying. He's saying he's sorry for disappointing his nation.

Pause.

99 CENT. Have you connected those wires yet?

ZACHAR. No.

99 CENT. Why not?

ZACHAR. I got a lash in my eye.

99 CENT. A lash in your eye?

ZACHAR. Yeah, that's why I took the bomb to the bathroom. To take out the eyelash.

99 CENT. Here, let me do it.

ZACHAR. I can't stand to have someone else digging around in my eye.

99 CENT. The world can't bear this tension, Zachar.

ZACHAR. Fuck the world. I have a lash in my eye.

99 CENT. Fine. I'll send a message that we're going to hold off for the time being. Until you get that lash out. Let them go to sleep.

ZACHAR. Maybe it will come out on its own?

99 CENT. Nothing gets done on its own, Zachar. I'm writing that we're putting off the end of the world until tomorrow.

ZACHAR. Fine. They can go fuck themselves. Show them the lash.

99 Cent goes into the bathroom and closes the door behind him.

VICTORIA. And the message was sent. On account of which Mr. Bleh will come home from work wanting the two of us, him and me, to bring it to fruition. Half the world will follow him, and the other half will go to sleep—that's statistics. Only the Mossad and Inspector Gum never sleep. A tough night lies before them. They will be tormented by many questions. Where are the Kuyavian terrorists hiding? And where the hell is Kuyavia?

5.

Victoria is lying in bed.

VICTORIA. The night that has just now fallen on the Palace of the Prime Minister-for-Life strikes me as exceptionally dark. My life has wandered off God-knows-where and led me to the bedroom. With a heavy sigh, I sit on the bed. Charlie? John? Whore. Come out, you bitch.

Charlie crawls out from under the bed.

CHARLIE. Can't you get by without us?

VICTORIA. No, I can't.

CHARLIE. Don't you think that's a little weird?

VICTORIA. Yes, I do.

CHARLIE. And what if there comes a time when we don't?

VICTORIA. Could John and that Whore hurry it up?

JOHN AND WHORE. We're coming out.

John and Whore come out from under the bed.

CHARLIE. So what are you going to do now?

VICTORIA. None of your business, pipsqueak.

WHORE (*to Charlie*). Don't pick on her.

CHARLIE. She should do something.

WHORE. Like what?

CHARLIE. Like start banging somebody else.

WHORE. You think it's so easy?

VICTORIA. Exactly. For me it's not easy.

CHARLIE. It's easier for you to gangbang with us than bang somebody else?

VICTORIA. Who said it was easy?

CHARLIE. You mean the gangbang?

JOHN. Or somebody else?

VICTORIA. Guys. Please. Let's drop it.

WHORE. Leave the girl alone. You have no idea how hard she has it. No idea.

Whore and Victoria hug.

VICTORIA. I can't bear it any longer.

WHORE. They're a little tired, too. You couldn't try doing it with somebody else?

JOHN. Look out! Here comes Mr. Bleh.

WHORE. Try doing it with somebody else. Will you try?

VICTORIA. I face a dilemma. Mr. Bleh sees only me. I can feel his breath.

MR. BLEH (*lying down on Victoria and making use of her anatomy*). I'm beating myself against the walls with worry, with the concern, love, and pain which I am proud to call . . . Poland.

VICTORIA. It's starting. Get on with it!

The group start to play their roles.

WHORE (*to Victoria*). You whore!

CHARLIE (*to Victoria*). You're caught! John, take her!

JOHN (*to Victoria*). I will do with her as I please! Vrrrr!

MR. BLEH (*making use of Victoria's anatomy*). Poland, Poland, "here I will rest"—Poland means "here I will rest" in Old Slavic, but even if I am mistaken with respect to the language or alphabet, it's outdated anyway: no one will rest here, there are no lovely ruins here for us to contemplate, the roads are bad, really bad, they lead us astray, where our countryman sits in an altered state of consciousness, which doesn't mean he's drunk, just that he's Polish, the ground chuck of nations, which he upchucks at other nations.

VICTORIA. I close my eyes and really concentrate.

WHORE (*worked up*). You whore! You whore! You nasty little whore!

Whore stops.

VICTORIA. I don't want to believe it, but the Whore stops doing anything at all. She actually starts writing a text message, she's singing to herself, she forgets to shout, she's humming a pop song and pressing the buttons on her phone.

CHARLIE. We have you now. A whole company of soldiers is waiting for you. You have to earn your keep, you whore!

VICTORIA. Thinking that my eyes are closed, Charlie quickly pulls out a book and keeps shouting as he reads, but he only remembers that he's supposed to shout every so often.

CHARLIE. Yes, a whole company of soldiers, lascivious boys, without a moment's rest, none.

VICTORIA. And now John lies down to sleep. He turns on his cell phone, and what do I hear? "Wah, ooh! Don't stop! Harder!" High time I told them my eyes are open and I can see all their tomfoolery and fucking around.

VICTORIA. You know what? You're traitors. (*To Whore*) Even you.

MR. BLEH. Look at me, Victoria, and remember this moment: this is how History is made. It's made from your dream. We are one body, Victoria, or rather we are on and off, but that allows me to take your dream and to give it the power to change the world.

VICTORIA. Now John, Charlie, and the Whore are making silly faces. They're sheepish.

MR. BLEH. You yourself do not know what you dreamt. You only see what's on the outside, but inside there's a Vision that will pull our country back from the edge of the world, from a dead province where nothing happens, from the Land of Emptiness it will lead us to the Land of Ferment!

CHARLIE. Let's speak like adults. Because you can't live like this, honey.

VICTORIA. How can't I? I have to.

CHARLIE. Look at him.

VICTORIA. I don't want to look at him.

MR. BLEH. I was worrying about how to pull Poland out of the ass of the world. I was fighting with myself about how to tell our citizens, directly and without beating around the bush, that we are the Land of the Great Fart, which we let out while we were jumping over a fence. Think about it, Victoria: Kuyavia has revolted—following in the footsteps of other Great Revolts, like maybe that of Northern Ireland, the Emerald Isle, whose revolt bathed her in blood and changed her from emerald to red in the eyes of the world!

WHORE. Let's face it: *he* is here, and we're *not*. Do something with that.

JOHN (*solemnly*). Yes. Do something with your life.

VICTORIA. You shut up. You didn't put in even a little effort, you just played with your cell phone. And Charlie, what's that you're reading?

CHARLIE. About terrorists.

VICTORIA. What exactly?

CHARLIE. *The Secret of the Kuyavian Terrorists.*

VICTORIA. Don't you think that 99 Cent is terribly handsome?

CHARLIE. I haven't gotten to the pictures yet.

VICTORIA. Because they're at the end. And all this time Mr. Bleh is putting my anatomy to use.
It hurts.

MR. BLEH. Victoria, now there has to be real terror, they have to show that we're the elite, we're the upper crust, that we have to take extreme measures . . . Let Kuyavia shoot the bullet of rage into the heart of Poland, and that heart will tear itself right out of the snot of this Nowheresville and stand there, supple and muscular, before the world, shoulder-to-shoulder with the Greatest! . . .

WHORE. Maybe you could chat with Charlie about books?

JOHN. It would make things easier—on us. And Charlie loves to chat.

VICTORIA. But it doesn't make it easier on me.

WHORE. Talk about other books, then. (*she thinks*) *American Psycho?* That has a lot of sex.

VICTORIA. Yeah, with a severed head.

Pause.

VICTORIA. Look! Mr. Bleh is seizing up and falling over.

WHORE. That takes care of that.

JOHN. For today.

VICTORIA. Let's live for the moment. Maybe tomorrow a brick will fall on my head, or else I'll get cancer?

CHARLIE. And maybe he'll finally get killed (*he points at Mr. Bleh*) by some Islamist terrorist?

WHORE (*wistfully*). Right. Like we were.

VICTORIA. Charlie, John, and the Whore feel better now. They've heard a few words of truth. The atmosphere's improved, and even though I look busted and in no condition to change anything, I'm really trying to change my life, and if I can't, well, at least I'll quietly read some book.

6.

Victoria thinks.

VICTORIA. Or not. While Mr. Bleh is sleeping we will move back in time and find out how things went with Charlie. He was preaching at me, mouthing off, so let's familiarize ourselves with how he got on in life.

And it was like this: Charlie sat by himself in an office with two computers and a window. He looked out the window and saw people falling from a high tower.

CHARLIE (*to himself*). Everything's great when you're in love. Her glasses are great. I saw those glasses quite clearly yesterday, and it turned out that I love them, but the right side was wrapped in white tape.

WHORE (*sits on the table in front of Charlie*). I have a better story for you. Very enlightening, and important. It's the story of a guy who had an airplane fly through his window.

VICTORIA. Charlie doesn't react.

JOHN (*to Whore*). Maybe he doesn't see us.

WHORE. (*gets off the table*) Love is blind.

CHARLIE. It all gets going at nine.

JOHN (*screams in Charlie's ear*). You have a screw loose? Get the fuck out of here!

CHARLIE. It all gets going at nine. (*Looks out the window*) How can one work under such conditions? If it weren't for love, a man could go nuts.

WHORE. Fine, let's hear the story about the glasses.

JOHN. Tell him that the other guys have already bolted. Fine, I'll tell him. (*Screams.*) The other guys have already bolted! And one even managed to call his girlfriend in Bochum!

WHORE. He's not listening to you. He doesn't want to hear the story about the guy who had an airplane fly through his window. And it's a long story, because the plane flew through a lot of windows.

JOHN. Hardly a long story! I flew in—end of story!

WHORE. Depends on how you tell it. Listen: the plane flew through the first window, through the second window, through the third window . . .

Pause.

JOHN. And? Where else do you want to take this story?

WHORE. There are a hundred of these windows. You know that.

CHARLIE. People are jumping out the window holding hands. I have to focus on my work.

JOHN (*to Whore*). And in your story there's still the eighth, the ninth window, and so on? Ha ha, not bad.

WHORE. Right? I turned it into a great bedtime story.

JOHN. I'd rather hear about the glasses.

WHORE. I could just skip to the hundredth window and go from there.

JOHN. We both know that we can expect nothing good after that story about the plane. I prefer the story about love and the glasses with the white tape.

VICTORIA. They're more occupied with each other than with Charlie. But Charlie holds on to his love at his desk, and all is lost. Am I bitter?

CHARLIE. I thought to myself, what happened to those glasses? Did she step on them? Or maybe her husband stepped on them?

JOHN. You hear that? He's in love with a married woman.

WHORE. A four-eyes at that.

CHARLIE. And what if she and her husband had been having a candlelight dinner? And she carelessly set her glasses aside before going to bed with him? And one side of the glasses got scorched, but they didn't notice?

VICTORIA (*to John*). One more try.

JOHN (*to Charlie*). Look out the window. That's what your world looks like. Run.

CHARLIE. She leaves her husband, and we're together.

WHORE. He's in love. Just like me.

JOHN (*to Whore*). We agreed that we wouldn't talk about love.

WHORE. Fine. Finally, the plane crashes through the window. Bam. Nothing left. Darkness.

VICTORIA. That's the end of the story about the guy who had a plane fly through his window. Bam, and darkness, and ringing in my ears. Now Charlie-in-love is dead. Maybe it's for the best. He didn't have much of a chance with Miss Four-Eyes, but he died believing in love. Should I envy him?

WHORE (*to Victoria*). Shall we take Charlie in under the bed?

VICTORIA. Do they really exist, or are they just one side of my psyche, goblins I make do my dirty work? Or maybe they flew out with the wind from the hundred-story building and, wandering the world unburied, unfed, unmourned, they've come to me, crazy old romantically aggrieved Victoria, in order to tell me How to Live, to ask me to change my life?!

CHARLIE. Don't make such a fool of yourself, Victoria. We're dead, but that doesn't mean we're not here.

WHORE. I was asking whether we should take Charlie in?

VICTORIA (*to Whore*). Make some room for him, but vacuum a little under the bed. If you can, wipe up behind the fridge. I hate that.

Victoria, in bed.

VICTORIA. Mr. Bleh is sitting here running the country. The whole country falls under his watchful eye, except for Kuyavia, which has declared itself the Kuyavian Zone and constructed a border crossing with Honduras with grants from the European Union. The EU thought they were providing assistance grants for programs that promote women in the workplace.

The phone rings.

VICTORIA. Now Mr. Bleh is wondering whether he should answer the phone.

MR. BLEH. I wonder whether I should answer. I just received a letter regarding a retirement home for lesbians and a retirement home for lesbos. Penned by Professor Safire.

VICTORIA. I've always admired him, that hardworking professor. Without him we'd make a mess of our language.

The phone rings again, but the tone turns into an obscene sound.

MR. BLEH. This phone is not what it pretends to be. Perhaps it's not even a telephone at all. (*To the phone, but without picking up the receiver*) Who are you?

TELEPHONE. I am a 50-year-old virgin who hasn't been screwed in ten years. (*Pause*) OK. I'm not a virgin.

MR. BLEH. I say. I don't believe you. I've lived in this country too long to simply take you at your word.

TELEPHONE. You do not offend me. There actually might be something to that.

MR. BLEH. Listen, I'm busy. I'm running the country, I'm holding it under my watchful eye. Besides, I'm fucking annoyed by how the EU pisses away its money.

TELEPHONE. I understand. Just remember, though, that the EU is a noble idea. I was moved to tears after the referendum.

MR. BLEH. Did you vote?

TELEPHONE. No. I was in Ireland. I was watching *The Day of the Wacko.*

MR. BLEH. So you foresaw that I would become Prime Minister-for-Life?

TELEPHONE. No one could have foreseen that.

MR. BLEH. Now I will cast my watchful eye over this country, so that nothing will happen to it, for the rest of my life.

TELEPHONE. Until they kill you.

MR. BLEH. I sense that every night.

TELEPHONE. But I'm calling you about a different matter. A certain fellow came into me, filled me, if one can put it that way . . . He has something to tell you.

OSAMA (*from the Telephone*). Insha'Allah. Greetings, Bleh.

MR. BLEH. Praises. What did you enter this virgin for?

OSAMA. I didn't have a cell, and I had to call.

MR. BLEH. What's going on?

OSAMA. I'm standing by the Polish National Bank on Złoty Square, and it's raining, insha'Allah.

MR. BLEH. We get a lot of rain in Poland.

OSAMA. We get quite the opposite in Saudi Arabia.

MR. BLEH. Are we then to conclude that you are now in Saudi Arabia?

OSAMA. No, I'm on Złoty Square, at the Polish National Bank.

MR. BLEH. And what's going on?

OSAMA. It's really coming down. Could you send me a staff limo from the Office of the Prime Minister-for-Life?

MR. BLEH. Under what name?

OSAMA. Osama bin Laden.

MR. BLEH. Let me write that down. Osama bin Laden . . . The President of the U.S. really doesn't like you. Did you know that?

OSAMA (*giggles*). Like I don't know that.

MR. BLEH. If your people happen to come out on top, you'll remember me, right?

OSAMA (*thoughtfully*). Is this phone bugged?

MR. BLEH (*apologetically*). Yes.

OSAMA. We both know that you are helping me without self-interest.

MR. BLEH. That's right. I hope that sending you this limo will be another little millstone around my neck.

OSAMA. Insha'Allah.

MR. BLEH. This country is disgustingly patient.

OSAMA. Insha'Allah. I'm going to the airport.

MR. BLEH. What's new in Kuyavia?

OSAMA. I brought them a bomb. A pretty basic one.

MR. BLEH. I heard, I heard: red wire with the green.

OSAMA. It'll go off soon.

MR. BLEH. Here Osama is mistaken. One cannot be certain of anything. What does one wish Osama? A nice flight?

OSAMA. Yes, in the name of the Holy War. And also that there won't be any suicide bombers on my flight. Especially today.

MR. BLEH. What's today?

OSAMA. It's my birthday.

MR. BLEH. Oh, Happy Birthday. Then let me sing to Osama. (*Sings.*)
¡Feliz cumpleaños a tí!
¡Feliz cumpleaños a tí!
¡Feliz cumpleaños a ti!
¡Feliz cumpleaños a tí!

VICTORIA. Osama, strangely moved, gets into the limo and drives to Warsaw International. Unfortunately, there will be a cell of deep-undercover suicide bombers on the plane. Osama will die on his birthday, just as the Gypsy woman foretold at that hotel in Dubai. Mr. Bleh will take full credit for this death and will testify to The President of the U.S. that he set the whole thing up in advance.

It is just one of many lies on this topic disseminated by the rotten Prime Minister. When will Poland wake up and crap him out with one hard push?

8.

Victoria in bed. Mr. Bleh stares at Hans. Enter Hans.

MR. BLEH. At last! My dear Hans, I couldn't wait!

HANS. My dear Mr. Bleh!

MR. BLEH. Everything's ready, the kiełbasa, the campfire's going. Let's have a seat: time to straighten out History.

HANS. Time, as they say, it's time. It pains me that History is never straightened out.

MR. BLEH. So now tell me, Hans, how do you like Poland, how many years has it been?

HANS. Since '39 it's been exactly 67 years, but I remember it like it was yesterday.

MR. BLEH. You are a Witness of History, quite precious to my nation, so look: I'm putting a kiełbasa on a spit for you. Go ahead and roast it, so that you don't go weak on me.

HANS (*taking the kiełbasa*). Danke. From time to time I'm going to throw in these German words, gut?

MR. BLEH. A capital idea. You, the young generation, are more creative than we, the old geezers.

HANS. You, Mr. Bleh, do not look like a geezer.

MR. BLEH. I try to take care of myself in consideration of my wife, Victoria. She doesn't like to be pinned down by my belly.

HANS. Gut, gut, let us speak of women perhaps off camera.

MR. BLEH. All the extraneous stuff will be edited out, but your kiełbasa's getting overdone on one side.

HANS (*turns the kiełbasa over*). What's true is true.

MR. BLEH. The truth is our main subject on the occasion of this informal Polish-German campfire. There are matters one should never stop discussing, referring to, educating subsequent generations about. Let us reminisce, Hans.

HANS. Those were terrible times, ja. (*He tastes the kiełbasa.*)

MR. BLEH. I'm glad that the Witness of History has such a healthy appetite. Anyway, life prevails, it triumphs: even the worst memories fly away in the face of a tasty kiełbasa. Let's raise a glass to life, which always triumphs. Well, maybe it had a run of bad luck with the German death machine. They'll edit out that digression. (*He drinks.*)

HANS (*wipes his lips*). Like the majority of Germans, I was against Hitler's politics. I felt great sympathy for my brothers, the Polish nation which we defeated so efficiently within two weeks. Yes, I know. That is also a lie that we have to set straight. The war with Poland lasted a couple days longer . . .

MR. BLEH. Well, not days—months!

HANS. Till when?

MR. BLEH. Till April 1940. April was when we surrendered.

HANS. Ja. The war with Poland lasted a couple months longer, until April. As everyone knows, we Germans are an undisciplined nation. One out of every two people is some kind of individualist, a freak.

MR. BLEH. A Fritz?

HANS (*waves his hand*). Fine, simply put, we're a nation of individualists. We despise order, "ordnung" is an awful word, we hate it. But so as not to speak only of bad things, I am proud that our blood runs with respect for other cultures and religions, and we are especially close to our older brothers in faith, the Israelites.

MR. BLEH. Can I throw more kindling on the fire?

HANS. No need, I'll do it myself in a minute. (*He goes on.*) That is why I was ashamed when my German brothers ordered the Israelites to burn up their book, which I read as well, in a German translation, during my religious lessons. Though it mainly served as kindling, I'll show you, time to remember the bestial acts of History . . .

Hans pulls a Torah scroll out of a bag, takes it out of its ceremonial wrapping, and throws it into the fire.

MR. BLEH. What a terrible sight.

HANS. Should I do more?

MR. BLEH. That'll be enough.

HANS. We Germans had enough of that as well. We organized picket
lines to protest in front of the Gestapo headquarters in Warsaw.
We screamed "Hitler kaput," "End the occupation of Poland,"
"Open the synagogues!" The demonstrations were brutally sup-
pressed. Then we dispersed among the hospitable Polish houses
nearby, and there they hid us, fed us bigos, black market pork
chops, and good Polish moonshine they bought from the Russians in Brest.

MR. BLEH. How many of you were there?

HANS. In the beginning our marches numbered about a 100,000 people, but soon the number of Good Germans rose. It is currently
estimated that the Poles, risking their own lives, hid over a million Germans during the Second World War!

MR. BLEH. Extraordinary!!! It's an as-yet-unexamined page of History!
Harboring Germans was punishable by death . . .

HANS. There was a war, after all, ja. War's no picnic.

MR. BLEH. Oh, no. Is there another way of calling the heroic uprising
of the Poles, without using the word "heroism"?

HANS. Heroism, naturlich. It was quite simply superhuman solidarity. Over a million Germans hidden by the Poles . . .

MR. BLEH. We should never stop talking about it.

HANS. But you have to eat, too. You haven't eaten anything.

MR. BLEH. Because I was rapt. Here we have a warm fire, we're sitting
here pleasantly, and just to think that this really took place . . .

VICTORIA. Mr. Bleh is lost in thought, plunges into his memories, and
starts to hum. Hans joins in, he knows the tune, I know it, too.
Everybody!

Mr. Bleh, Hans, and Victoria sing "As Time Goes By."

Victoria lying in the bed.

MR. BLEH. Come here, Victoria. Everyone's here already, the whole family. There's pork chops.

VICTORIA. Mr. Bleh has asked me to come. I want to go, but I can't. Besides, something's bumping around in the dark.

Victoria squints her eyes into the darkness.

VICTORIA. What the fuck is that? I'm staring There, into That Darkness! Is there somebody there? Hey, can't a girl go see her idiotic family?!

UNCLE ANTONI. Not if that idiotic family isn't really yours.

VICTORIA. And who is this speaking to me from that billowing darkness?

UNCLE ANTONI. Your uncle.

VICTORIA. Uncle?

UNCLE ANTONI. Come here, Victoria. Enter the darkness. Your whole family is there.

VICTORIA. Why should I believe that?

UNCLE ANTONI. I'll unveil the truth to you. (*Solemnly*) Humanity is divided into two cultural spheres: There and Here. You, it so happens, belong There.

VICTORIA. Then what am I doing Here?

UNCLE ANTONI. A terrible happenstance. But now you know the truth.

VICTORIA. And what do you all have There?

UNCLE ANTONI. Order, prosperity, the graves of your ancestors properly honored. We also have bathtubs.

A bathtub slides out from the darkness.

VICTORIA. How did you know I love bathtubs? Maybe you really are my uncle, though you look like some fucking Roman. (*She introduces herself to Antoni.*) Victoria.

UNCLE ANTONI (*getting into the bathtub*). Don't be an idiot, Victoria; don't introduce yourself to your own uncle.

VICTORIA. I'm sorry, I don't remember you, Uncle.

UNCLE ANTONI (*from the bathtub*). You don't remember your Uncle Antoni?! And who taught you to vomit?

VICTORIA (*glad*). You mean that wonderful technique of light and natural ancient Roman vomiting after drinking or eating too much, which I got from who-knows-where?

UNCLE ANTONI (*glad*). . . . Right . . . Tickling the throat with a peacock feather . . .

VICTORIA. . . . subtly and quietly, without disturbing the music of the cicadas with the sound of vomiting . . .

UNCLE ANTONI. . . . and listening to the waves washing over the Mediterranean . . .

VICTORIA. . . . and, after throwing up, returning to one's guests with a clear mind, to conclude the suspended discourse . . .

UNCLE ANTONI. But not that drunken puking your guts out, that Central European heaving, eyes bulging in barbaric mugs . . .

VICTORIA. Upchuck that washes over an unconscious maw, upchuck in no way uplifting, but consisting of herring, beets, mushrooms . . .

UNCLE ANTONI. No details, please . . .

VICTORIA. Upchuck in which one passes out, only to wake up in the Moscow River, cut into several pieces . . . Head over here, legs over there . . .

UNCLE ANTONI. Victoria, have mercy . . .

VICTORIA. Why should I? Why should I have mercy, Uncle Antoni?

UNCLE ANTONI. Because I'm really sorry that you were exposed to that barbarian puking for so many years.

VICTORIA. I don't give a shit about that, Uncle Antoni. What you should have done was take me There right away, not throw me out Here like a dog. That's no way to treat family.

UNCLE ANTONI. I know, that's what I told them at the forum. They didn't want to hear it.

VICTORIA. I always felt wrong Here, and what for? Fuck. And now you tell me?

UNCLE ANTONI. I came, I asked . . . And now you know the truth, Victoria.

VICTORIA. I'm fucking pissed.

UNCLE ANTONI. Please, Victoria, get into the bathtub and don't dawdle.

VICTORIA. Get into the bathtub with my uncle?

UNCLE ANTONI. Nothing creepy. Come back to your people.

VICTORIA. Come back, come back . . . But how will I live without puke consisting of mushrooms and digestive juices? I'm going back to the puke.

UNCLE ANTONI. No, no, Victoria. I'll slit my wrists.

VICTORIA. Do it, Uncle, if you feel so responsible.

UNCLE ANTONI. I will. (*He starts to cut his wrists.*)

VICTORIA. Uncle . . . I'm not heartless, but I can't stand it when someone blackmails me with the threat of suicide.

UNCLE ANTONI. I always dreamt of quietly cutting my wrists when I'm really hopeless. It's an ancient Roman tradition.

VICTORIA. A beautiful tradition but that sudden desperation of yours is weird, Uncle. If someone were watching all of this from the background, he'd say it's weird, too.

Théophile Gum slides out from the background and watches.

VICTORIA. Are you watching this from the background?

THÉOPHILE GUM. I am, yes.

VICTORIA. And?

THÉOPHILE GUM. Well, it is all quite strange.

VICTORIA. You see, Uncle?

THÉOPHILE GUM. So now I go to the car for pharmacy. I come right back.

VICTORIA. Please wait. A Roman with cut wrists in the bathtub is not a good sign. Don't come back here: I feel bad premonitions wrapping their tentacles around me.

THÉOPHILE GUM. I have made an appointment with Mr. Bleh, and no lady's tentacle will keep me. I go for pharmacy.

Théophile leaves.

VICTORIA. A nice fellow, that Théophile Gum. He intends to apply a compress to Uncle Antoni's wounds, but soon he'll come back and see that both my uncle and the bath have disappeared. The simple fellow won't wrack his brains over it, he'll just walk it off.

10.

VICTORIA. Mr. Bleh and Inspector Théophile Gum have a top-secret meeting. Everything is top secret, so top and so secret that no one knows where the Prime Minister's desk is, where's the lamp, where's the chair. Théophile Gum and Mr. Bleh circle around the office and talk, but at the same time it seems like they don't know each other, like they can't see, like they're not even talking to each other. All because of the need for absolute secrecy.

Mr. Bleh paces.

MR. BLEH. What I'm saying now will never be said, and you won't hear it.

VICTORIA. Théophile Gum paces.

THÉOPHILE GUM. Indeed, I will not hear nothing.

VICTORIA. Pacing.

MR. BLEH. I will be frank.

VICTORIA. Pacing.

THÉOPHILE GUM. Then I'll stand in the background.

VICTORIA. Pacing.

MR. BLEH. Please listen closely, because I won't repeat myself.

VICTORIA. Pacing.

THÉOPHILE GUM. I hear nothing, I hear nothing.

VICTORIA. Still pacing, to and fro.

MR. BLEH. Can you hear me or not?

VICTORIA. Also still pacing, to and fro.

THÉOPHILE GUM. So what are my orders?

VICTORIA. Pacing.

MR. BLEH. Officially he hears nothing, but unofficially he hears extraordinarily well.

VICTORIA. Pacing.

THÉOPHILE GUM. Indeed, yack, yack, hoo, whacha.

VICTORIA. Pacing.

MR. BLEH. What does hoo, whacha mean?

VICTORIA. Pacing.

THÉOPHILE GUM. Right, left.

VICTORIA. Mr. Bleh stops dead.

MR. BLEH. Can I go to the left and to the right at the same time?!

VICTORIA. Théophile Gum stops dead.

THÉOPHILE GUM. I didn't mean you. It was a decoy. As if I were in Łaszczów talking to a man about a horse, not to you.

VICTORIA. Mr. Bleh resumes his pacing.

MR. BLEH. Aha. We can't stand still like this, because it will look like we're talking.

VICTORIA. Théophile Gum resumes his pacing.

THÉOPHILE GUM. Right.

VICTORIA. Pacing.

MR. BLEH. Listen closely. Terrorists from Kuyavia are threatening Poland.

VICTORIA. Pacing.

THÉOPHILE GUM. I know. They'll clobber us.

VICTORIA. Pacing.

MR. BLEH. They want to wipe Poland off the map and establish Greater Kuyavia in its place.

VICTORIA. Pacing.

THÉOPHILE GUM. Holy shit.

VICTORIA. Pacing.

MR. BLEH. They want to transplant Poland somewhere else.

VICTORIA. Pacing.

THÉOPHILE GUM. What a plan! But where?

VICTORIA. Pacing.

MR. BLEH. To the island of Jakundu.

VICTORIA. Pacing.

THÉOPHILE GUM. I will not go there, and I will not be moved.

VICTORIA. Pacing.

MR. BLEH. I gave the order to mine a one-kilometer zone around all
  of Kuyavia, but they're clearing a path with their little martyrs.

VICTORIA. Pacing.

THÉOPHILE GUM. Kids are dumbasses.

VICTORIA. Pacing.

MR. BLEH. And now they want to throw a bomb at The President of
  the U.S., at me, at democratic institutions, and they'll shoot
  while Zachar is taking an eyelash out of his eye.

VICTORIA. Pacing.

THÉOPHILE GUM. Zachar? Stole his woman, I did.

VICTORIA. Pacing.

MR. BLEH. Inspector Gum, that will make it easier to identify our
  adversary.

VICTORIA. Pacing.

THÉOPHILE GUM. I have to nab Zachar?

VICTORIA. Pacing.

MR. BLEH. What I will tell you now I will never tell you. You must
  assassinate the leader of the terrorists, a certain 99 Cent.

VICTORIA. Pacing.

THÉOPHILE GUM. Why me?

VICTORIA. Pacing.

MR. BLEH. I will not answer that question. Because you've received
  excellent training.

VICTORIA. Pacing.

THÉOPHILE GUM. And without a written order?

VICTORIA. Pacing.

MR. BLEH. I will not answer that question. Yes.

VICTORIA. Pacing.

THÉOPHILE GUM. And things are so bad that it can't be done otherwise?

VICTORIA. Pacing.

MR. BLEH. I will not answer that question. It must be done for Poland.

VICTORIA. Pacing.

THÉOPHILE GUM. That's all you had to say. If it's for Poland, it will be done. For Poland, my motherland, my beloved country, I would do anything.

VICTORIA. Théophile Gum leaves Mr. Bleh's office undetected and, undetected, finds himself now on his way to Kuyavia. He is a simple fellow from Łaszczów, this Inspector Gum, but fantastically well-trained, and ready to do anything for Poland. But has Mr. Bleh made the right move? Do the ends justify the means? Doesn't assassination bear forth the poisonous fruit of evil?

11.

VICTORIA (*to herself*). For a while now I've been wondering what's going on in my bathroom. What we have to lose, we will lose; the intimate space of our bathrooms is the first to betray us: we won't recognize ourselves in the mirror. But I, Victoria, will not die. I will live, on and on, until the last person on earth comes, lays himself down on my anatomy, and says, "Here I will rest." Then I will be happy, and we will both die.

12.

Zachar and 99 Cent in the bathroom.

ZACHAR. Where is the Chosen One who will banish the darkness for good?

99 CENT. Ooh! Talk about the map! The map!

ZACHAR. Where is the Expected One who will straighten the paths?

99 CENT. Ooh! Where is the map that we don't yet have?

ZACHAR. Oh! Oh! Where is El-Kuyava? Where is El-Kuyava and its son, the Kuyavian? Which road will lead the Chosen One to them?

99 CENT. Ooh! Oh! The road is on the map that we don't have! The road is in the heart, which is still beating!

ZACHAR. Oh! Oh! Ooh! Ah! I see the map! I see the map!

99 CENT. Oh! Oh! I see the map, too! And greater, greater, Greater Kuyavia!

ZACHAR. Oooooh! Yes! Yes! Yes! There is no Poland on the map! Yes! A beautiful map! Greater, greater, Greater Kuyavia!

99 CENT. I'm coming, I'm coming right to the point!

ZACHAR. The Chosen One will banish the darkness and wipe Poland off the map!

99 CENT. My heart—a wad of rage! I'm going to shoot it! I'm going to shoot it!

ZACHAR. The wad of rage will blow away the infidels!
Fire at will!

99 CENT. Fire at will! The map is ready!

ZACHAR. The map is ready! Fire at will!

99 CENT. I'm going to blow! The map is ready!

ZACHAR. Fire at will! I'll blow away the infidels!

99 CENT. My heart, my rocket, my heart, my rocket, my heart . . . bam!!!

ZACHAR. El-Kuyava, here I come, here I come!

13.

VICTORIA. Now I have to turn the light toward myself. But even in the spotlight my psychic state remains in darkness. Thus I face the dilemma of whom to trust: myself, or him as well. I get the impression that when I was young I was too open: I didn't guard my boundaries the way I should have. Now I find myself in the middle of a conversation at its breaking point.

VICTORIA (*dramatically*). Bleh, say something!

MR. BLEH. What?

VICTORIA. I asked you a question.

MR. BLEH. When?

VICTORIA. Just now!

MR. BLEH. What did you ask me?

VICTORIA. You weren't listening?

MR. BLEH. I was, but I don't know what you asked me.

VICTORIA. I asked you whether you think that not answering me when I ask you uncomfortable questions is a good strategy for maintaining our relationship, which is in a crisis, the one we were just talking about!

MR. BLEH (*thinks*). I don't know.

VICTORIA. "You don't know?" And who should know if not you, Bleh? Somebody's supposed to know that for you? And who's supposed to know for you?

MR. BLEH (*thinks*). I don't know.

VICTORIA. "Don't know, don't know." How can anybody talk to you?! I'm always the one who's talking. You think I don't see that?

MR. BLEH (*says nothing*).

VICTORIA. You have something to say? Because I'm leaving!

MR. BLEH. What should I say?

VICTORIA. You don't see that I'm losing my mind? I've had enough of trying to talk to you.

MR. BLEH. So stop talking.

VICTORIA. Now it's "stop talking," but later it will be "I love you."

MR. BLEH. No. I've had enough of these conversations with you.

VICTORIA. Say that again, "I've had enough of these conversations with you." Say that to my face.

MR. BLEH. I've had enough of these conversations with you!

Victoria tosses Mr. Bleh's pajamas to the floor. Victoria puts them back on the bed.

VICTORIA (*calmly*). People can't talk this way. Let's stop talking this way.

MR. BLEH. It's you who's talking this way. I'm not talking this way.

VICTORIA. But you're not answering my questions. Don't you understand how much that hurts? It's hard for me to be calm when you don't answer my questions, you know?

MR. BLEH (*says nothing*).

VICTORIA. You know?

MR. BLEH (*says nothing*).

VICTORIA. Why don't you say something?

MR. BLEH (*says nothing*).

VICTORIA. I can't stand this!

MR. BLEH (*says nothing and stares at her*).

Victoria slaps herself in the face, now with her left hand, now with her right, now her left, now her right.

MR. BLEH (*thinks*). You need help.

The telephone rings.
Victoria answers.

VICTORIA. Hello? (*To Mr. Bleh*) It's for you.

MR. BLEH. Bleh here. (*Listens*) Greetings, Director of the FBI-slash-KGB-slash-Fuck the Police. Go on. (*To Victoria*) I love you. (*Into the telephone*) Go on.

VICTORIA (*to herself, aloud*). I don't think I need help. It just unnerves me that I'm beating myself about the face. To be sure, life is a play that you can't easily control, and marriage is an even bigger play, but beating yourself about the face?! Calm down, Victoria. Sometimes it's hard to untangle these painfully tangled intertwined knots of matrimonial feelings . . . It's also hard to find a straight, clear road to another heart . . . You're aggressive, Victoria: you speak in an elevated register, you pose unclear questions . . . Yes, high time to beat your chest and find the right road to another heart.

But what could I possibly mean? What could that be? Maybe bake him a cake? Suck his dick? Have a candlelight dinner? I can only guess, but I can't ask him what he wants most, because right now he's busy fighting a war against corruption.

14.

The bathroom reveals its mysteries more and more.

99 CENT. Today, in our Bedtime Story for Martyrs, we will hear of the heroism of our leader, El-Kuyava the Great the First, who died at the hands of those dogs from Poland.

99 CENT (SHRILL). El-Kuyava the Great was surrounded. The hour of his fight to the death was at hand. Before the battle his faithful warriors feasted on Kuyavia's famous mushrooms, which are called Black Boletes.

99 CENT (DEEP VOICE). We don't mean anything by it: it's just a regional term for mushrooms.

99 CENT (SHRILL). El-Kuyava was betrayed. His small unit didn't stand a chance against the army of the Potato-Eating Infidels . . . The little Martyrs must know that the enemies were slicing the bellies of El-Kuyava's warriors and eating up the still-warm Kuyavian Black Boletes from their entrails! Let's avenge El-Kuyava!

99 CENT (SHRILL/DEEP). Heeyaaa!

99 CENT. El-Kuyava the Great has sacrificed his life, and now you will sacrifice yours, for there is nothing more beautiful than such a sacrifice: we all know this, and there's no point in droning on about it. Each child reaches the Point of Martyrdom with his security blanket. This is very important. The blanket should be large enough to wrap snugly around him. Each child crosses the minefield only after an adult has asked him if he's all snug. We do this so that the explosion doesn't splatter the body parts all over the place, so we can transport them in the blanket to the El-Kuyava Cemetery of Martyrs. Let us sing!

CHORUS. Kuyavia, my homeland,
> I'm wrapped up warm and nice!
> When you find a piece of me in the sand
> I'll be smiling from Paradise!

Refrain

> Kuyavia, my Kuyavia,
> I wouldn't die for Scandinahvia.
> It's high time I jumped on a mine,
> Kuyavia, dearest Kuyavia!

15.

VICTORIA. My personal boundaries have disappeared. I have to define myself anew. Mr. Bleh has initiated a coup d'etat. He's dissolved the Parliament. He now has absolute power. "This country is being consumed by corruption," Mr. Bleh said. "There is no love in this country."

MEGAPHONE 1 (*solemnly*). This country is being consumed by corruption!

MEGAPHONE 2 (*sadly*). There is no love in this country.

VICTORIA. I'm standing here listening to the Megaphones. I'm disguised as a beggar. I'm holding out a cup for coins. In my other hand I have a sign that says, "99 Cent is enough. God Bless You."

99 CENT (*comes out of the bathroom*). That's a fucking dumb thing to do. I told you to keep a distance from me.

VICTORIA. I had to find you, 99 Cent.

99 CENT. Can I trust you?

VICTORIA. Yes. Say, "Get into my car. Quick."

99 CENT. I will never follow a woman's instructions. Now, get into my car, because I want you to. Quick.

99 CENT. Now we're going to drive together for many hours without saying a single word. I have to take back-roads to lose our tail. The sun will beat down through the window, but there's no air conditioner. So fucking go to sleep, you're tired.

VICTORIA. I never do what a guy tells me. I've already heard my share of brats like you. But since I'm worn out by the journey and your roundabout way of losing our tail, and the merciless sun is beating down through the window, I'll go to sleep, because I want to.

99 CENT. Wake up. My voice betrays my ill humor. We're going to go on foot, you pampered city girl who knows nothing of toil and martyrdom.

VICTORIA. I see that the moss is growing on the same side of the tree as the direction we're walking in. We're heading north, and therefore you trust me and are taking me to the Kuyavian Zone. I'll march bravely on, though you can really fuck yourself up in this darkness.

99 CENT. If you fuck yourself up, don't worry about it. Don't even look around.

VICTORIA. I just fucked myself up, and my knees are bleeding.

99 CENT. I have no comment. Or rather, I do have a comment. Bleeding is good, if it will help free Kuyavia. What are you looking for?

VICTORIA. I'm looking for the way to your heart, and step by step I'm learning what toil and martyrdom are. It's a magnificent feeling, but I would like to rest.

99 CENT. We'll rest in Paradise. Now we are in great danger. Mr. Bleh's assassins are combing the thin pine forests of Kuyavia, branch by branch. They're confiscating the televisions and satellite dishes of any villagers who give us shelter, and they're smashing all the liquor bottles in the village stores. They broke into the house of the Lubiewo alderman and burned his collection of Kuyavian saints.

VICTORIA. You're kidding.

99 CENT. Yeah, I was kidding. You bring out my macabre sense of humor. I wasn't telling the truth.

VICTORIA. And what is the truth?

99 CENT. That they're killing the villagers who support us, leveling everything, leaving no stone on another. But the great

El-Kuyava is watching, and he'll return with the Chosen One to restore order. Give me your handbag, I'll carry it for you.

VICTORIA (*handing him her handbag*). That helps. I'm afraid that we're going to keep walking for many hours more, and I'll fuck myself up many more times, and the moon will disappear behind a cloud, and we won't be able to see anything.

99 CENT. Maybe it will, maybe it won't; I cannot betray how many hours of marching we still have before us, in case we're caught by Mr. Bleh's assassins.

VICTORIA. The moon is disappearing behind a cloud, I keep fucking myself up, and 99 Cent is paying me no attention.

99 CENT. And now clench your teeth hard, so hard that the blood drips from your bitten lip, for you must concentrate.

VICTORIA. I'm concentrating without biting my lip. What's up?

99 CENT. We're about to move along the edge of the famous Kuyavian Gap, may the great El-Kuyava watch over us, insha'Allah.

VICTORIA. I see that you are starting to trust me more and more, because you have used your famous insha'Allah.

99 CENT. It's raining. The water will be over your shoes in a minute.

VICTORIA. Oh well. The mud is sticking to my soles, but that's martyrdom.

99 CENT. We've almost reached the point where you'll be completely hungry, freezing, and barely conscious.

VICTORIA. I hear a noise. What is that?

99 CENT. That's the great river Brda, in which El-Kuyava cleansed himself centuries past, before his fatal battle with the Polish Potato-eaters, may they burn in hell.

VICTORIA. Do you guys happen to have a bathroom with a bathtub?

99 CENT. Forget about that ancient Roman tradition. All we have is a shower, but at the moment Zachar is taking an eyelash out of his eye. Go cleanse yourself in the Brda.

VICTORIA. I run into the Brda, take my clothes off, and scrub. I hide bashfully behind the reeds.

99 CENT. No one hides here. Comrades keep no secrets from each other. You're pretty, but a bit withered.

VICTORIA. The flower of my youth was plucked by another man.

99 CENT. Let's go inside our headquarters. It's camouflaged by leaves and bulrushes, and we'll sleep on the dirt floor on a tarp that will protect us from the damp.

VICTORIA. What color is the tarp?

99 CENT. I don't pay attention to colors. I think only of the Affairs of Kuyavia.

VICTORIA. Now, as I enter a camouflaged cottage and step onto a tarp, I can tell you: I saw you in my sleep, 99 Cent.

99 CENT. What was I doing?

VICTORIA. You wanted to shoot me. You ordered me to count to one hundred.

99 CENT. That's my style. You can cuddle up to me.

Victoria cuddles up to 99 Cent.

VICTORIA. I have to tell you something. I've already forgotten what it's like when the body moves spontaneously. My subconscious is whispering to me that I want to submerge myself in the ocean of your desire, but my reason is telling me that it will be uncomfortable on the tarp.

99 CENT. That heavy pressure will remain forever in your memory. Here, on this tarp of obscure color . . .

VICTORIA. . . . white . . .

99 CENT. . . . we will surrender to heretofore unknown pleasures, which will sanctify our bond forever.

VICTORIA. But won't I pay too high a price for it?

99 CENT. We're not in a bank. This is life: Kuyavia and martyrdom, but there's no accounting for love. That's why you dream of it.

VICTORIA. And you? What do you dream about?

99 CENT. About the Kuyavian Cause, but about you, too. Since I knew that you would come here to give yourself to me, I waited for you a million years.

They make love.

99 CENT. Look at the stars.

VICTORIA. I'm looking through the leaves and bulrushes.

99 CENT. I want to have a baby with you. Our baby will be the Chosen One. He will even carry on the Kuyavian Cause if we perish.

It's all over. They've lit a cigarette.

VICTORIA. I've never had it so good.

99 CENT. Victoria. You're Mr. Bleh's wife. What are you doing here? You wanted to get it on with a *shahid* from Kuyavia?

VICTORIA. I have to free my friends, who were killed by Islamic terrorists.

99 CENT. You're blathering from fatigue, but I do hope you got pregnant. Our son will be the Chosen One.

VICTORIA. These friends upset me. I wonder if everyone becomes so conceited in the afterlife. Insolent, sassy apparitions. Lazy and mendacious.

99 CENT. I won't be like that after I die, Victoria. With you at my side, I'm ready to die without hesitation.

VICTORIA. Don't count your chickens . . .

16.

VICTORIA. Since I crossed my borders I've felt my way along, unsurely, because I don't know where I am. I'm still facing a dilemma. Maybe I'm facing it more actively than before, but I still need some advice.

PROF. SAFIRE. I'll give you some in a second, as soon as I finish this invoice.

VICTORIA. The word "love" is often used frivolously, right, Professor?

PROF. SAFIRE (*comes out of the bathroom, followed by 99 Cent and Zachar*). Unfortunately, the payer of my invoice is Mr. 99 Cent, and first of all I have to raise an issue that will interest him. (*To Zachar and 99 Cent*) I recently issued comments in regard to the consequences arising from the choice of one of two nearly synonymous expressions. The matter concerned the formulation "retirement home for lesbos" versus "retirement home for lesbians."

VICTORIA (*to herself*). Doesn't sound like advice for me.

ZACHAR. That's really fucking interesting, Professor. What about these lesbos and lesbians?

PROF. SAFIRE. So . . .

99 CENT (*interrupts*). We summoned you here, Professor, on a more important matter.

ZACHAR (*angry*). Chinga tu madre! Let him talk!

99 CENT (*to Zachar*). Fine, chill, he can tell us about the lesbos at the end, but now about martyrdom.

PROF. SAFIRE. As you wish, gentlemen. (*He begins*) The culture of martyrdom has taken years to develop. Seeing as suicide is a mortal sin, forbidden by the Koran, suicide missions, by definition, cannot be suicidal! Therefore, in order to conceal the fact of suicide in language, we use the concept of '*amaliyya istishhadiyya*, literally, "martyrdom operation." I think that in contemporary Polish we would do better to use the formula "holy shitstorm," given the broad humor so beloved of Slavs.

99 CENT. And applied to Kuyavia, what would you suggest?

PROF. SAFIRE. Hmm, yes, I'd have to think about that, maybe playing on Kuyavia . . . to kuyate . . . to kuyatify . . . Maybe "holy kuyatification" or "act of kuyatifying." It will require some consideration.

ZACHAR (*surprised*). Not bad, Professor. Your head's as sharp as your dick!

99 CENT. Zachar, think before you speak.

PROF. SAFIRE. I take that as a compliment and will allow myself to continue.

VICTORIA (*to herself*). It's a shame that Bleh can't hear this.

PROF. SAFIRE. Moving on. The most important concept is the term *shahid*, or "martyr." (*To 99 Cent*) Anticipating your question about how to find something suited to the word "Kuyavia," I would suggest "Kuyeer"—a martyr from Kuyavia—"Kuyeer." Or else "martavian," no, it's so much worse. Eventually, one might connect Kuyavia with the word "hero," yielding "Kuyero," which sounds interesting, energetic, or else "herawarian," which sounds a little like "warrior" . . .

ZACHAR. Warrior's a good word. Warrior's muy bien.

99 CENT. Zachar!

PROF. SAFIRE. I very much value your input, gentlemen. Please don't hold back. Comment, ask. Now, coming back to the concept of the *shahid*, we must differentiate between the *shahid al-said*, or "martyr of fortune," and the *shahid al-mukatil*, or "shahid killed in battle," someone who could have gone on living, but preferred to die instead. The paragon of self-sacrifice is the *istishhadi*, the person who sacrifices himself in martyrdom, and thus every suicide bomber.

VICTORIA. Amazing!

PROF. SAFIRE (*satisfied*). And that's not all. There's also the *shahid al-mazlum*, or the person who has died against his will, though he hadn't planned on it.

99 CENT. Meaning . . .?

PROF. SAFIRE (*to 99 Cent*). Come closer. (*99 Cent stands next to the Professor.*) Let's imagine that you're a candidate for martyrdom, and I'm driving the car, minding my own business. Let's say that you pull the pin or some trigger, we both die, but in the paper they say I'm a *shahid al-mazlum*, but you're a *shahid al-said*.

99 CENT. That is, we're driving along, you don't know anything, I go "click," and so on?

PROF. SAFIRE. Yes.

99 Cent takes out a pistol.

99 CENT. Click. (*He shoots the Professor in the head.*)

The Professor falls, dead.

VICTORIA (*screams*).

99 CENT (*to the Professor*). You wanted to be a *shahid al-mazlum*, you dog!

ZACHAR. 99 Cent, you fucking asshole! He was supposed to tell us about the lesbos!

99 CENT. He pissed me off. He said our holy words without respect.

VICTORIA (*to 99 Cent*). I don't feel right. The hard-working professor who told us what was hidden behind words has died. Was he an inconvenience?

99 CENT. He was condemned, and the sentence was carried out.

ZACHAR. So much for Professor Lafire.

VICTORIA. Safire!

ZACHAR. Names are meaningless to the Kuyavian courts.

VICTORIA. A name should mean something to a court!

ZACHAR. Don't get cheeky, you. We kill for la revolución.

99 CENT (*to Victoria*). Remember, Victoria: our bond is forever. You knew who you are, and you found your way to me yourself. And a woman widowed by martyrdom is called *armalat al-shahid*. Say it.

VICTORIA. Armalat al-shahid.

99 CENT. Very good. I love you.

17.

VICTORIA. There's this really good old joke. Abraham goes up to the rabbi and says, "It's no good, Rabbi. The count is sleeping with my wife." The rabbi nods his head and says, "Well, that's no good." "But there is one good thing about it," Abraham says. "I'm sleeping with the countess." "Well, that's good," says the rabbi. To which Abraham says, "But it's really not good, Rebe. Because I'm making him counts, but he's only making me kikes."

The point is, I knew that things were no good.

VICTORIA. Anyhow, whatever hangs in the air, we have to face facts. Just now it happens to be Théophile Gum. He's hanging, and he's quite dead, this Théophile Gum. That's something, Théophile Gum.

Mr. Bleh crosses the street and stops beneath the tree. The shadow of death hangs over Mr. Bleh, though he thinks it's just the shadow of a tree.

MR. BLEH. I cast my watchful eye continuously over this country. I have a considerable reserve of watchful eyes; after all, I wouldn't cast my own. Ha ha. Just kidding. For Poland, I don't spare my eyes. I love Poland, and I work for her on the macro scale as well as the micro.

He picks up a piece of paper.

This little piece of paper is on the micro scale.

He takes a plastic bag out of his pocket.

I always carry a plastic bag with me, and I return from my travels through Poland with a plastic bag full of garbage. I pick things up far from the cameras, not for applause. (*Loses himself in thought.*) Victoria loved my work on the micro scale.

VICTORIA. Look. A sudden breeze from over the sea is moving Théophile Gum. A shoe falls off the inspector's foot and hits Mr. Bleh in the head.

Mr. Bleh rubs his head and picks up the shoe.

MR. BLEH. And how can you not love this country? A fantasy that knows no bounds, a nonsensical creation, deliberate or otherwise! A shoe on a tree: I love it, for it is eccentric, senseless, absurd. Maybe there's even a second one, or more, shoes instead of leaves, a whole tree of shoes!

Mr. Bleh looks up. He spots the hanged man.

MR. BLEH. What's that I see? Unexpectedly, one of my countrymen is hanging there. Should I feel personally responsible as the Prime Minister?

THÉOPHILE GUM. I am a simple inspector, but after the coup d'etat the Prime Minister's office has gone to hell in a handbasket!

MR. BLEH. So are you a dead hanged man, or living?

THÉOPHILE GUM. I'm a dead hanged man.

MR. BLEH. Then I can't talk to you.

THÉOPHILE GUM. You can. You didn't talk to your wife, so you can chat with a corpse, because you're responsible for me. Inspector Théophile Gum reporting for duty, and hanging.

MR. BLEH. Théophile Gum? What are you doing here? What about Your Mission!

THÉOPHILE GUM. My Mission?! I'm a simple peasant; my uncle was in the state militia, but I myself honestly love Poland. You tricked me!

MR. BLEH. No I didn't!

THÉOPHILE GUM. I was supposed to kill that 99 Cent fellow, to assassinate someone in the name of the Fatherland, and what did I find? Personal motives!

MR. BLEH. Not true! We both feel love for Poland, as one body: pure love, with no ulterior motives!

THÉOPHILE GUM. My body is dead, and I don't feel anything, and your wife Victoria is banging that very same 99 Cent!

MR. BLEH (*says nothing*).

THÉOPHILE GUM. Back in Łaszczów, we call those ulterior motives!

MR. BLEH (*says nothing*).

THÉOPHILE GUM. Perhaps you guys in Warsaw don't take those for ulterior motives, huh?

MR. BLEH. A corpse hanging from a tree and making accusations. The very picture of insanity!

THÉOPHILE GUM. Right. I went crazy and killed myself.

MR. BLEH. I was just walking quietly down the road. I was casting my watchful eye over the country. I was collecting garbage. My life got away from me. It seemed like things couldn't get worse.

And then everything changed, just like that. Inspector Gum hanged himself because of me, and that death weighs heavily on me. My, life is extraordinary, shocking, absurd. I love it. It's great to be alive!

THÉOPHILE GUM. Please take off my other shoe and send it to my mother. Nothing gets wasted out in the country.

MR. BLEH. A barefoot corpse, swinging in the breeze, the sun setting in the background, and the familiar call of the stork. Life, life, unspeakably beautiful!

VICTORIA. Mr. Bleh takes off the other shoe and puts both in a fresh plastic bag. Now he knows that it's not the shadow of a tree, but the shadow of death that hangs over him. Mr. Bleh feasts his eyes once again on the familiar, crazy vision and moves away, la luna floating ever so quietly behind him, and the voice of Théophile Gum: "I was supposed to get married after the harvest, after the harvest . . ."

19.

VICTORIA. Endowed with feminine intuition, I call out to Charlie, John, and the Whore. I recalled that 99 Cent had promised me "Kuyavia and martyrdom," but I, blinded by lust, didn't pay this the attention it was due.

I yell: Charlie? John? Whore?

Come out. Silence. I call out again: Charlie? John? Whore? Come out!

Charlie comes out from under the bed.

CHARLIE. Can't you get by without us?

VICTORIA. No, I can't.

CHARLIE. Don't you think that's a little weird?

VICTORIA. Yes, I do.

CHARLIE. And what if there comes a time when we don't?

VICTORIA. Could John and the Whore hurry it up?

JOHN AND WHORE. We're coming out.

CHARLIE *(to Victoria)*. Why did you say, "Come out," and not, "Get the fuck out of there"?

VICTORIA. 99 doesn't like me to use strong language.

WHORE. You've reined in your tongue for him, Victoria. You use fewer words.

VICTORIA. A lot fewer, honey. I've completely lost my ability to speak.

CHARLIE. Ha! I've gone blind, and you've lost your ability to speak. Love causes more injuries than sports.

WHORE. Blind, deaf: that's nothing. After all, it's because of love that we're dead.

VICTORIA. Isn't it because of Islamist terrorists?

WHORE. We can thank them as well, but ultimately it was love that determined our deaths. Charlie could have left his office, but he didn't.

CHARLIE *(nods)*. No, I didn't.

JOHN. But we . . .

WHORE. John looks great now, but before . . .

JOHN. Because Esther is no whore.

WHORE. John and I were playing Tragic Genius and the Whore.

JOHN. We came to work before anyone else arrived.

WHORE. I'd go from the Finance Department down to Marketing, where John was sitting in a wheelchair. I'd say to him, "John, I'm your whore, and I'm going to suck your cock."

JOHN. And I would say, "No thank you, for I am tormented by the tragic dilemmas of humanity. What is truth? What is good? Is there a God?"

WHORE. And I would say, "John, you're so very wise, I admire you for these tragic dilemmas, and for that I want to suck your cock all the more."

JOHN. And I would say, "Don't trouble those pretty lips, for I must plumb the nature of evil and the problematic of free will!"

WHORE. And I would say, "Grab my tits, look how wantonly they swing into your face!"

JOHN. And I would say, "The question of free will is, in my opinion, fundamental, all I can do is discuss it with you!"

WHORE. And I would say, "Must the question of free will be settled just now? Because I'm getting really hot."

JOHN. Esther did a great job getting into the archetypal figure of the woman-temptress!

WHORE. John and I have the same sense of humor. It's one of the reasons I love him.

VICTORIA. And did you end up sucking his cock?

WHORE/JOHN. Of course!

WHORE. But we never spoke of love.

JOHN. I didn't want to.

WHORE. He didn't want us to talk about love.

JOHN. So we didn't talk about love, but it was love, and we died because of it.

WHORE. The elevators were out, and he was in a wheelchair. So we just sat there together while everyone else was running downstairs. At least we were together.

JOHN. She sat next to me, and we waited for a strong fireman.

WHORE. Then we popped into Charlie's office. John screamed at him that he had a screw loose, but I knew that he liked him.

CHARLIE. But I didn't know then that he liked me.

VICTORIA. Look out: here comes 99 Cent. Get ready!

JOHN. Victoria, you still don't get it.

VICTORIA. Quiet.

20.

Bathroom. 99 Cent appears with Zachar, his constant companion. Both are lugging blankets filled with stuff in their arms.

99 CENT. Two hearts beating in the name of the Lord. Pete's heart, Sophie's heart. We all suffer agonies of humiliation and contempt. To hell with Poland and its Prime Minister-for-Life.

ZACHAR. Only Pete and Sophie—whom no one knew in the world— only they stood guard—two orphans, for Christ's sake, while everyone else was sleeping, the only ones not sleeping were them and the unit of herawarians that chucked the bomb at the Tesco Department Stores.

99 CENT (*to Victoria, handing her the blanket*). Sophie—it's like she's anorexic. Barely weighs anything. We gathered what we could.

ZACHAR. Get started, 99.

99 CENT. Surely you'd like to know why I'm called 99 Cent? Because that's how short I was for beer one evening, and I had to spend the night sober. Then I understood Everything.

ZACHAR (*to us*). Think about that, you fucking alcoholics!

99 CENT. I set off for Kuyavia and pulled it up off its knees!

ZACHAR (*to us*). Yeah, you fucking alcoholics!

99 CENT. In the name of the Holy Hell in a Handbasket! In these here blankets we have two heroic martavians . . . (*he ponders*) . . . two heroic Kuyateers who burned with eagerness to blaze a trail and meet the Lord. We pay them honor in the place of their pathological parents, who dropped them in the orphanage.

ZACHAR. Fucking alcoholics!

99 CENT. First we pay honor to Sophie, that little anorexic, who left a note. Seeing as we are now having a contest for the best suicide note, please rate it immediately on a scale from one to ten.

VICTORIA (*to Charlie, John, and the Whore*). Hold me up. I feel weak.

99 CENT (*reads from a piece of paper*). "Mother"—hmm, could be her pathological mother wouldn't be able to read this—"Mother, I'm not dead. I walk among you, I sing, I dance, I realize all my dreams. I'm so happy to be able to sacrifice my life as a heroic martyr. Don't cry for me, don't be sad, be joyful and smile."

Scores are projected onto the background.

99 CENT (*repeats aloud*). Seven, six, six, five and a half, seven, six, nine—who gave nine? (*Looks*) Come on, Hans, don't suck up. (*Continue*) Well, that's quite a high score, but is it enough to win? Oh, Sophie, Sophie, I told you to apply yourself more! But before you can rest by the Fountain of Blood, in the El-Kuyava Cemetery. Victoria, dance with Sophie, it's really simple, the step is like a polonaise, and when you hear the word "Kuyavia" you take a bow. (*To Zachar*) Zachar, you too.

CHORUS (*begins*). Kuyavia, my homeland . . .

VICTORIA (*to Charlie, John, and the Whore*). Do something!

CHARLIE. (*sighs*). Oh, honey, you can't even take a step without our help.

JOHN. I'm sorry, but there are no miracles. You have to dance.

VICTORIA (*dancing and bowing*). Help!

WHORE. I can't listen to this!

VICTORIA. The Whore, as usual the most empathetic, peered discretely into the blanket that held Sophie, pulled out an MP3 player and earphones, brushed them off delicately, and put them in my ears. Thanks to her, I no longer hear the sounds of that martyr's polonaise, but then again, I'm not moving with the rhythm. My one comfort is the vision that has been visited upon me: Sophie and Peter are dancing together, holding hands, just as together, holding hands, they blew themselves up on a mine.

21.

VICTORIA. 99 Cent didn't like to waste words. Having announced his intention to bomb The President of the U.S. as well as Mr. Bleh over the Internet, and that the only thing left to do was to connect the red wire to the green, that business should have been over and done with. Unfortunately, a stubborn eyelash had lodged itself in Zachar's eye, not realizing that it had saved

The President of the U.S. and my Mr. Bleh from dispersal, and the world from chaos.

99 CENT. How's that eyelash, Zachar?

ZACHAR. It's in my eye, the fucker.

99 CENT. Come 'ere.

ZACHAR. You're not going to dig around in my eye, are you? I don't like people digging around my eye.

99 CENT. I won't. Victoria, look away.

VICTORIA. Zachar goes up to 99 Cent, who plucks out his eye.

99 CENT (*handing Zachar his eye*). All better.

ZACHAR. You're a real dickhead, 99.

99 CENT. Get to work, Zachar.

VICTORIA. Zachar turns around and suddenly freezes.

99 CENT. Zachar, what is it?

ZACHAR. You plucked out the wrong eye!

99 CENT. Really?

ZACHAR. The fucking eyelash is still there.

99 CENT. Come here.

ZACHAR. What for?

99 CENT. Just come here.

VICTORIA. Zachar goes up to 99 Cent, who plucks out his other eye.

ZACHAR. What the fuck? Now how am I going to connect the wires?

99 CENT. By touch.

ZACHAR. Touch is for sticking it in chicks, man.

99 CENT. You'll manage, Zachar. I believe in you.

Zachar steps out tentatively, waving his arms in front of him. He goes into the bathroom.

99 CENT. I don't waste words. That bastard, The President of the U.S., is going to die, and so is Mr. Bleh. That's how it has to be, Victoria.

VICTORIA. I know, 99. You've said so from the start. I'll help Zachar come in, or else he's going to fall over.

99 CENT (*to Zachar*). Well?

ZACHAR. I pissed on the bomb.

99 CENT. What do you mean, you pissed on it?

ZACHAR. By accident. I thought it was the toilet, and I pissed on it. But it was the bomb.

99 CENT. So now what?

ZACHAR. It has to dry out.

99 CENT. Oh, Zachar.

ZACHAR. Don't be angry, 99. My bad.

99 CENT. It's cool, it'll dry, and then we'll set it off.

VICTORIA. And 99 Cent issued a new communiqué, that Zachar pissed on the bomb, and until it dries out, the world will go on. But the head columnists from all over the world ask themselves the same unsettling question: How long does it take for a pissed-on bomb to dry? And how much time does humanity have left?

22.

MR. BLEH. My dear Hans.

HANS. My dear Mr. Bleh.

MR. BLEH. The eyes of this vengeful, wounded nation are fixed upon me, and will continue to be until I have given all of myself. And the Nation knows that I will.

HANS. I feel that the time has come, Mr. Bleh, yes? The time has come for what?

MR. BLEH. The time has come for reconciliation. More and more, the eyes of the nation are turning to me. They are asking, "What are you going to do now, Mr. Bleh?" And I look them in the eye and say, "Let's forgive each other. Enough hate. We're different, but we're brothers. Whether you're Kuyavian or

Podlasian or Mazurian or Bieszczadian, we're all Poles." What do you think of that, Mr. Hans?

HANS. I am happy to find myself next to so noble a personage as yourself.

MR. BLEH. My people deserve a magnificent gesture of forgiveness. Can your nation, Mr. Hans, present me something as a model?

HANS. I am glad to be of service, for my nation has a magnificent tradition of forgiveness.

MR. BLEH. Precisely. Let's dust off that tradition.

HANS. We Germans have forgiven and will forgive. Such is our lot.

MR. BLEH. It is no longer your cross to bear.

HANS. But it is beautiful to forgive.

MR. BLEH. I know it's beautiful. My heart burns to forgive.

HANS. I haven't forgiven anyone for a long time.

MR. BLEH. It could happen at any moment.

HANS. It's nice to forgive, but better to feel.

MR. BLEH. And what could you offer us as a model of forgiveness?

HANS. When you Poles lost your statehood, we Germans took you in with open arms. We allowed you to keep your religion and to speak your strange language. And how did you repay us? By kidnapping innocent German children and using their blood for black pudding. But we magnanimously forgave you.

MR. BLEH. A lovely example. What else have you forgiven us for?

HANS. For getting our diligent, but guileless peasants to drink. You Poles brought in juke joints and moonshine, got our peasants to drink, then threw them into debt. You didn't drink yourselves, you sly dogs! You know what's what. But we forgave you that, too.

MR. BLEH. Oh yes, that's in our nature, not to drink ourselves, but to pour it out for others. And what was hardest to forgive?

HANS. The hardest thing was that you crucified Our Lord Jesus. That was really hard to forgive. But we forgave.

MR. BLEH. Hans, sir, you have really given me a model of forgiveness to think about. Thank you, Hans. And now I can forgive that bastard, 99 Cent. Hear me, Nation! And you too, 99 Cent! I forgive you!

I forgive you for causing hundreds of thousands of Poles to emigrate to Honduras in search of a better life! I forgive you for causing whole villages, whole provinces, to convert en masse to Judaism and Islam! I forgive you for the fact that pensions are low and exchange rates unstable. Were it not for you, the roads in this country wouldn't be so poor, so terribly poor that you can't get where you're going. But I forgive you for all of it, for the whole cluster-fuck and bullshit we live in, for I am over-flowing with forgiveness. You hear me, my fellow country-men?! You hear me, you Kuyavian bastard? I forgive you!

23.

MR. BLEH (*to 99 Cent*). Come out of the bathroom, dog!

99 CENT. I'm no dog, but a lion who will lead Kuyavia from the desert of indignity!

MR. BLEH. Come out, you mutt!

99 CENT. I'm not coming out, you old swine!

MR. BLEH. Come out, dickless! Victoria said that you can't get it up!

99 Cent bursts out of the bathroom.

99 CENT. You'll pay for your slander! I challenge you to a duel!

MR. BLEH. That's more like it. We shall do battle. Long jump?

99 CENT (*does not trust Mr. Bleh*). No. You'll cheat for sure.

MR. BLEH. High jump?

99 CENT. Uh-uh.

MR. BLEH. 100-meter dash? Triple jump? Crunches?

99 CENT. Pistols.

MR. BLEH. Before I shoot you, I'll sing you something. I don't believe you've demonstrated your true motives for war against us.

99 CENT. Oh, really? What about the years of humiliation? The martyrdom of El-Kuyava?

MR. BLEH. I believe that your motives are rather economic.

(He sings and raps, mangling Bob Dylan)

Come you masters of war
You that build all the guns
You that build the death planes
You that build the big bombs
You that hide behind walls
You that have golden tans
I just want you to know
I'm not buying your bran.

99 CENT. Ha, ha. I've never heard of Kuyavian bran.

MR. BLEH. It was just a hypothesis.

99 CENT. And today you'll be a corpse, and I'll be getting it on with Victoria.

VICTORIA. Have you settled between yourselves that the winner gets Victoria?

MR. BLEH. I long for you, Victoria. I hope that, if 99 dies, you'll come back to me.

99 CENT. The stronger one will win, and then you'll hear the call of the wild for yourself.

VICTORIA. Like a doe?

99 Cent nods.

Like a she-moose? *(Explains)* A female moose.

99 CENT. Victoria, you're ruining it. We're gearing up for a fight to the death.

VICTORIA. Control yourselves. Hear the voice of a woman, giver of life, guardian of humanity, without whom no stone would remain on another.

99 CENT. OK. Just hurry it up.

VICTORIA. Death is the end, but at the same time it's the beginning of something new . . .

99 CENT. Fine. There are two of us, and one of you. We're not going to share.

VICTORIA. . . . Of something new. I can't fucking stand when you interrupt me.

Victoria shoots them both. They fall like dominoes.

VICTORIA (*disconcerted*). The sight of what I have done will haunt me for the rest of my life. I will never know peace. Wracked with guilt, I will expire in a barren land, trying to wash my hands of the blood I have spilled.

VOICE OF POLAND. Oh, why do you whine so over these bodies? That 99 Cent got what he deserved, and that Mr. Bleh, well, he was your husband, so you know better than anyone that you couldn't stand him.

VICTORIA. That helps a little, Poland, but what can I do? What should I do?

UNCLE ANTONI (*getting out of the bathtub*). There, go to your people.

VICTORIA. Go? How? Do you hear, Uncle? I killed them, but they're still vomiting. In my head, I mean, they're still vomiting. My husband is heaving, and my husband is spitting up. I'm drenched in their vomit. My soul, supposedly spotless but eaten away by its own stomach acid. But I can't tear out my soul, can't free it from its toxic contents. Betrayal, betrayal. Why did I allow them to puke on me, why did I degrade myself, badger myself? All this Polish-Kuyavian upchuck is eating away at me, poisoning me like the blouse of Dejinira. Uncle, what's the deal with that shirt?

UNCLE ANTONI. I know, Victoria, but many people don't. Should I say?

Uncle Antoni gets out of the bathtub and assumes the pose of an orator.

VICTORIA. There's no time, Uncle. It's no good, the boys are puking me up to high heaven.

UNCLE ANTONI (*with emphasis*). Oy, that is no good.

VICTORIA. Do you know that story, Uncle? The one about the Jew who goes up to the rabbi?

UNCLE ANTONI (*with emphasis*). Oy, it's no good, Rabbi. The count is sleeping with my wife.

VICTORIA (*with emphasis*). Oy, that's no good.

UNCLE ANTONI. But there is one good thing about it. I'm sleeping with the countess.

VICTORIA. Well, that's good.

UNCLE ANTONI (*with emphasis*). But it's really not good, Rebe. Because I'm making him counts, but he's only making me kikes.

Enter Hans.

HANS. I am listening, I am listening and not interrupting, because I see here there is a new, beautiful fire straightening Polish-Jewish relations.

VICTORIA. We're telling jokes, Herr Hans, and the fire is left over from the earlier straightening-out. Have a seat.

HANS. How's your health, Victoria?

VICTORIA. My heart aches and I have troubles, as the dead poet says.

HANS. Apropos the dead and worrying yourself to death over consequences of their deathliness, you must be worried about whether the pricks from the insurance company will pay out on Mr. Bleh's life insurance.

VICTORIA. Yes, that worries me as well.

HANS. And rightly so, because they won't pay, scheiße, it's in the fine print: "we have no intention of paying this money ever."

VICTORIA. Mr. Bleh had a premonition that they'd screw him over.

HANS. He wasn't stupid, but he couldn't spare an eye to look closely. The whole time they were cast over the country.

VICTORIA. What can I do now, Herr Hans? Beneath a coat covered in puked-up Kuyavian mushrooms and beets, my soul is fluttering. Uncle Antoni says I'm free, I should go back to my people, There. But my inconsolable, filthy soul refuses to answer, right, Uncle? Where's my uncle?

HANS. Gone. He went into the fire.

VICTORIA. Strange. What for?

HANS. He was looking for something.

VICTORIA. Did he find it?

HANS. Yes. He turned all black, only in his hand it glowed.

VICTORIA. That must have been a lovely sight.

HANS. Cute, ja.

VICTORIA. Too bad I didn't see it.

HANS. It was over fast.

VICTORIA. He left so suddenly, and I still wanted to talk to him.

HANS. He has not left. He is There and waiting.

VICTORIA. Where?

HANS. Here. And There. (*Pokes around in the fire.*) Hard to find him with so much ash.

VICTORIA. Uncle. (*She digs with Hans through the fire.*) Maybe we can dig something out. Please stop blowing, Herr Hans.

HANS. It is you who blows, Victoria. You are rather panting with nervousness.

VICTORIA. I'm not panting at all. And even if I were a little, wouldn't I have good reason? I have no husband, no lover, no insurance money, and no miraculously discovered uncle!

HANS. If you were to scream less, we might still get something out of this fire that you could pour into eine kleine scapular and take with you on your new life path. Indeed, each breath brings you closer to your uncle—is that what you meant?

POLAND. Maybe it is, and maybe it isn't. Shut up, Hans. John, Professor Safire, Théophile Gum, Zachar, 99 Cent, Mr. Bleh?! Get the fuck out here.

They all come out.

HANS/CHARLIE. Can't you manage without us, Poland?

VICTORIA. Is that really you, Poland?

POLAND. It is.

VICTORIA. Are you really speaking to us?

POLAND. So long as you live.

VICTORIA. But where's the Whore, Poland?

POLAND. She can't come out, because I am speaking in the Whore's voice.

EVERYONE AT ONCE. And why not mine? / Aren't I good enough? / I want to speak, too.

POLAND. I'm coming out.

Enter Poland.

VICTORIA. Is it you, Poland?

POLAND. It's me.

VICTORIA. I have a trumpet for you.

POLAND. A trumpet?

VICTORIA. I have a trumpet to play hymns in your honor.

POLAND. Play, then.

VICTORIA (*lays her hands on the trumpet*). Trootootoo. You're so beautiful, Poland.
Trootootoo. I love you, Poland, trootootoo.

At Victoria's direction, everyone repeats.

EVERYONE. Trootootoo. You're so beautiful, Poland.
Trootootoo. We love you, Poland

In the background, a triumphant trootootoo, trootootoo, trootootoo.

HANS. I would just add, Victoria, that you will receive no insurance money from your husband's policy, since it is not at all true that a natural death and murder-by-dolphin are one and the same.

VICTORIA. Well, then, was he right in his premonition that you'd screw him over?

HANS. Yes. He was no fool, that Mr. Bleh.

VICTORIA. And you, Herr Hans, are a pig.

HANS. My name is not Hans, but Bruner.

VICTORIA. Bruner, you pig, I'm done talking to you. Dear Poland, I killed my husband and my lover. I see no sensible path for my future. Find another husband, and kill him? Take another lover, and shoot him?

VOICE OF POLAND. There is a path, honey! That path is . . . a dolphin!

VICTORIA. A dolphin?

VOICE OF POLAND. Yes, a dolphin for a husband, cheerful, handsome, a mammal, loyal, great swimmer, doesn't need much, just a little warm sea, sun, a pool!

We hear a song:

They call him Flipper, Flipper, high on our flag,
He swims and he waves and never will sag!

VOICE OF POLAND. Go to them. You need to regroup after these terrible ordeals.

VICTORIA. But what about you, Poland?

VOICE OF POLAND. I'll breathe a sigh of relief, listen to the lark. At last, no one is looking after me.

We hear a song:

Everyone loves the king of the sea,
Ever so kind and gentle is he.
They call him Flipper, Flipper, high on our flag,
He swims and he waves and never will sag!